MARCUS ALONZO HANNA

MR. HANNA IN 1903

MARCUS ALONZO HANNA

HIS LIFE AND WORK

BY

HERBERT CROLY

New York
THE MACMILLAN COMPANY
1919

All rights reserved

COPYRIGHT, 1912,
BY THE MACMILLAN COMPANY.

Set up and electrotyped. Published April, 1912.

Norwood Press
J. S. Cushing Co. — Berwick & Smith Co.
Norwood, Mass., U.S.A.

PREFACE

THE preparation of the material upon which the following account of Marcus Alonzo Hanna's life and work is based was attended with many difficulties. No political leader of similar prominence in modern times has left such a slim public record of his characteristic achievements. He began his career as a political manager whose work consisted, not in the advocacy of legislative policies or in acts of public administration, but in political planning and negotiation, which only incidentally became a matter of public record. Throughout his career this aspect of his work remained of decisive importance. To give a full and accurate account of such plans and negotiations is almost an impossibility, and it is impossible, not merely because many of these negotiations were essentially confidential, but because subsequent accounts of them, even when given in good faith, can scarcely avoid some inaccuracy and partiality. Mr. Hanna's correspondence also throws comparatively little light upon the critical decisions and moments of his career. The really decisive negotiations were never committed to paper, and Mr. Hanna did not keep copies of many of the most important letters which he wrote and received.

In order to supplement the necessary scarcity of documentary material bearing on Mr. Hanna's life and work, all of his political and business associates were asked to contribute full and careful statements covering those phases of his career with which they were familiar. The task of taking these statements was confided to Mr. James B. Morrow, who had been for many years editor of the Cleveland *Leader*, and who brought to the work unusually high qualifications. Not only had he long been personally acquainted with Mr. Hanna and familiar with the unwritten political history of the period, but he had an unusually accurate knowledge of the complications and personalities of Ohio politics. In taking the statements of Mr. Hanna's friends and associates, he was met for the most part with a very cordial desire to coöperate. There were not more than two or three men who might have contributed anything essential to our knowledge of Mr. Hanna's life who refused or neglected to add their testimony. Besides taking these personal statements, Mr. Morrow also made an exhaustive collection of all the available documents and public records which would throw light upon any aspect of Mr. Hanna's life and work. The material so collected was placed in my hands, and has been worked over into a consecutive account of Mr. Hanna's career. Wherever it seemed necessary, I have supplemented and confirmed the material furnished by Mr. Morrow, but by far the most important part of the preparatory division of the work was done by him and done conscientiously, intelligently and impartially. Although Mr. Morrow is not responsible for a word of the text, he has, in a very real sense, collaborated in the preparation of this biography. His contribution to it has been indispensable and invaluable.

CONTENTS

CHAPTER		PAGE
I.	BIRTHPLACE, PARENTAGE AND FAMILY	1
II.	BENJAMIN HANNA, HIS FAMILY AND HIS FORTUNE	8
III.	BOYHOOD	17
IV.	THE PASSING OF NEW LISBON	28
V.	EARLY YEARS IN CLEVELAND	36
VI.	MARRIAGE AND ITS RESULTS	47
VII.	BUSINESS LIFE IN CLEVELAND	54
VIII.	MISCELLANEOUS BUSINESS INTERESTS	65
IX.	MARK HANNA AND HIS EMPLOYEES	84
X.	CHARACTERISTICS IN BUSINESS	96
XI.	BEGINNINGS IN POLITICS	110
XII.	TWO CONVENTIONS AND THEIR RESULTS	120
XIII.	POLITICAL FRIENDS AND ENEMIES	140
XIV.	THE MAKING OF A PRESIDENT	164
XV.	THE CONVENTION OF 1896	190
XVI.	THE CAMPAIGN OF 1896	209
XVII.	SENATOR BY APPOINTMENT	228
XVIII.	SENATOR BY ELECTION	242
XIX.	THREE YEARS OF TRANSITION	272
XX.	THE CONVENTION OF 1900	302
XXI.	THE CAMPAIGN OF 1900	319
XXII.	SHIP SUBSIDIES	342
XXIII.	THE DEATH OF PRESIDENT MCKINLEY	355

CONTENTS

CHAPTER		PAGE
XXIV.	THE PANAMA CANAL	369
XXV.	THE CIVIC FEDERATION AND THE LABOR PROBLEM	386
XXVI.	THE CAMPAIGN OF 1903 AND THE PRESIDENTIAL NOMINATION	411
XXVII.	THE DEATH OF MARK HANNA	447
XXVIII.	CONCLUSION	465

LIST OF ILLUSTRATIONS

Mr. Hanna in 1903	*Frontispiece*

FACING PAGE

The House in New Lisbon in which Mr. Hanna was born. It has been changed by the addition of one story	8
The New Lisbon Homestead	18
Mark and Howard Melville Hanna as Children	22
Mark Hanna as a Boy	24
The Prospect Street Homestead in Cleveland	36
Mark Hanna as a Lad of Eighteen	38
Mark Hanna in 1864	48
Mark Hanna about 1871	56
Mark Hanna about 1877	112
Mr. Hanna in the Early Nineties	150
Mr. Hanna in 1901	344
Facsimile of the Letter written by Mr. Hanna during his Final Illness to President Roosevelt	452

INTRODUCTION

BEFORE beginning the story of Mark Hanna's life and work I want to claim the unprejudiced attention, even of those readers who may be predisposed against him. His personality and his career are entitled to the fair and serious consideration of his opponents in politics and economics. They have a value apart from and beyond the controversies in which they were entangled during his own life, and in which, from the point of view of many Americans, they are still entangled. I do not underemphasize the difficulties of giving a fair account of Mr. Hanna's life or of passing a disinterested judgment on a man whose public action involved so much bitter contention and who so recently died. Grave as those difficulties may be, this book is an attempt to overcome them. It must stand or fall on the attempt.

Like all strong and capable men who fight hard for their own political purposes and opinions, Mr. Hanna made many friends and many enemies. He was loved and trusted by his friends as have been very few American political leaders. He was abused and distrusted by his enemies with no less ardor. At the outset of his public career the varying estimates of him as a man were determined chiefly by the judgments passed upon his political purposes and methods. For years he could not obtain an unprejudiced hearing, unless it were from his political allies. He was denounced as the living embodiment of a greedy, brutalized and remorseless plutocracy; and this denunciation infected the opinion of many members of his own party who had no knowledge of the man. Gradually, however, the public estimate of him improved. As his personality became better known, and as his political opinions became more fully expressed, the popular caricature of Mark Hanna began to fade from the public mind. The fair-dealing characteristic of his own attitude towards other men aroused a corresponding attitude towards him on the part of a large part of the public. The man himself began to obtain tributes of personal appreciation even from his enemies.

Since his death the favorable impression made by his personality has been partly forgotten — except, of course, by his friends and associates. But the enmities created during his career have been kept alive by the course of political controversy. Many reformers identify Mr. Hanna with everything which they most dislike in the old political and economic order; and reformers, of course, have a license to consider the men and things which they dislike as morally reprobate. The early caricature of Mark Hanna is reappearing. He is not figured in the newspapers as a dollar-mark: but he is described in the pages of books and magazine articles as the anti-Christ of the new political religion. He is ceasing to be remembered as a man, and is becoming a legendary Apotheosis of Property in its antagonism to Humanity.

I shall try in the following pages to bring the real Mark Hanna back to life. He cannot be converted into a symbol without essential distortion. Men of a drier and more rigid disposition, who have been molded by some special intellectual or practical discipline, may become sufficiently disembodied to qualify as a symbol; but Mark Hanna's clothes covered an unusually large supply of human nature, which was never forced into any special mold by an artificial discipline. He was formed under the same influences as hundreds of other men in the Middle West who combined a business with a political career. He was the same kind of a man as the rest of them; but he was more of a man. He lived the kind of life that they lived more energetically, more sincerely and more successfully. If he achieved anything more than they achieved, or represented anything more than they represented, the difference was simply a matter of personal prerogative.

The man did not impose himself on his surroundings or misrepresent them. His opinions were the reflection of his experience. His system was the outcome of his life. The system was, to be sure, largely preoccupied with the purpose of protecting property and promoting its increase — as have been all political systems since the dawn of civilization. But he did not conceive property apart from humanity. He conceived it in a certain traditional relation to humanity, and he regarded the rights of property, not as separate from human rights, but simply as one class of human rights — which they are. He deserves, consequently, to be considered primarily as a man, whose manhood conquered appreciation when it had a chance, and which should continue after death to conquer appreciation from other men whose critical judgment is not perverted by their ideas. His system deserves to be considered, not as incarnate plutocracy, but as the product of these conditions from which Mark Hanna himself derived it, — that is, from the actual, political and economic tradition and practice of the American Middle West. I trust that the reader of the following pages will approach them at least provisionally with these ideas in mind.

CHAPTER I

BIRTHPLACE, PARENTAGE AND FAMILY

MARCUS ALONZO HANNA was born on September 24, 1837, in the town of New Lisbon in Ohio. He belongs, consequently, to Ohio's second or third generation — to the generation which grew up before the end of the pioneer period, but after the edge had been rubbed off of the struggles and hardships of the early settlers, and which entered into a comparatively definite and abundant social and economic heritage. By the time Mark Hanna was of age Ohio had already become Ohio. It was no longer a wilderness. It was a settled community whose life had assumed characteristics different from those of other neighboring communities, and was offering to its citizens certain peculiar business and political opportunities. In 1858 the fact that a man hailed from Ohio did almost as much to place him as the fact that he hailed from Massachusetts or Virginia. The sons of Ohio had begun to be molded by their own state and had begun to know and to feel for their political mother.

New Lisbon is situated in a county on the eastern border of Ohio, about sixty miles from Lake Erie — a county which enjoys the peculiarly American name of Columbiana. The name was derived from mixing the Columbus of history with the ordinary Anna of domestic life. There is an anecdote that, when the adoption of the name was pending in the Legislature, a wag suggested the further addition of Maria — thus making it read Columbiana-Maria. The southeastern end of the county just touches the Ohio River, near the bend which it makes in turning east towards Pittsburgh; and this fact had an important bearing upon the fortunes of Mark Hanna and of his family.

The village of New Lisbon, which since 1895 has been called Lisbon, was founded in 1803 by Major Lewis Kinney. It grew so rapidly that it was soon selected as the county seat. Immigration poured in from Pennsylvania, Maryland and Virginia, the majority of the newcomers being either Scotch-Irish Presbyterians or German Lutherans, with now and then an adventurous Swiss mechanic. From the beginning industry went hand in hand with farming. A powder-mill and two tanneries were started almost immediately, a wagon shop followed in 1807 and a tin-shop in 1810. As early as 1808 a blast furnace was built a mile from New Lisbon by Gideon Hughes, a Quaker, who named it Rebecca in honor of his wife; and to the Rebecca furnace came in 1809 as a skilled workman one James McKinley, the grandfather of William McKinley. James McKinley had migrated from Mercer County, Pennsylvania, bringing with him a wife and son eighteen months old. The son, whose name was William McKinley, was married in New Lisbon to Nancy Campbell Allison; and their son was the subsequent President. William McKinley the second was, however, born in a neighboring county, to which his parents had removed after the extinction of the Rebecca furnace.

Some five years after James McKinley settled in New Lisbon, a Scotch-Irish Quaker named Benjamin Hanna moved into the town and opened a "general" store. Benjamin was of the third generation of Hannas established on American soil. His grandparents, Thomas and Elizabeth Hanna, had emigrated from the north of Ireland in 1763. The former is supposed to be descended from a Patrick Hannay, who in the thirteenth century built and inhabited a house called "Castle Sorby" at Galloway, in the southern part of Ayshire. At any rate, the Scots who were planted in the Irish county of Ulster during the first half of the seventeenth century came chiefly from this part of the Scotch Lowlands. Among the children accompanying Thomas Hanna was one Robert, who had been born in County Monaghan, Ireland, in 1753. The family settled at Buckingham in Bucks County, Pennsylvania, — a Quaker neighborhood, and there Thomas Hanna died within a year of his arrival in the Promised Land.

Robert Hanna was apprenticed to a farmer in the vicinity, and worked on various farms thereabouts until he became of age. In 1776 he married Catherine Jones in the adjoining county of Chester, and in 1779 he and his wife removed to Campbell County in Virginia. There in coöperation with John Lynch he laid out the city of Lynchburg. They remained in Virginia some twenty-two years. Before leaving Pennsylvania they had become Quakers, and their eight children, of whom Benjamin Hanna was the second, were brought up in that faith. In 1801 Robert Hanna, his wife and six surviving children migrated in a "Conestoga" wagon to the township of Fairfield, Columbiana County, Ohio. Later he moved into Middleton township, founded the village of Clarkson, and, it is said, built and kept a log-tavern at the crossing of two roads. Here, at any rate, Robert and Catherine Hanna lived and prospered for fourteen years, during which time their children were marrying and dispersing.

When Benjamin Hanna settled in New Lisbon he was thirty-three years old and had been nine years married. His wife was Rachel Dixon [1] — a girl of eighteen when he married her, and either of Dutch or English descent. Benjamin had passed through a good deal of rough frontier discipline. He had not shirked the hard work which was necessary to convert a wooded wilderness into a cleared, habitable and cultivated country-side. He had taken part in the two essential preliminary tasks of surveying the land, preparatory to its alienation to individuals, and of clearing it. According to the statement of his son Kersey, he began by buying for $5 an acre forty acres of forest land situated some ten miles from New Lisbon. After clearing his purchase, he sold it for enough money to buy an additional one hundred and sixty acres. The second farm was situated about half a mile east of the village of Columbiana, and like the first

[1] Joshua Dixon and Dinah Batten, his wife, moved into Fairfield township, Columbiana County, Ohio, from Fayette County, Pennsylvania, in 1802. They owned two sections of land, 1280 acres, and became sufficiently well-to-do to substitute a brick house for their first log-cabin. They brought with them to Ohio five sons and six daughters, one of each being the fruit of a former marriage of Joshua Dixon. Rachel, the wife of Benjamin Hanna, was born in 1785. The Dixons were Quakers as well as the Hannas, and the marriage was one of the first to be solemnized in Fairfield township according to the rites of the sect. Mr. Kersey Hanna, the youngest of Benjamin Hanna's sons, states that although his mother's schooling had been very limited, she was very quick at figures. During her husband's absence she attended to the store, and she was capable of waiting on ten or twelve customers in immediate succession, and keeping the bills of each accurately in her mind.

was heavily timbered. He started in to clear it, but by the time he had finished thirty or forty acres, he found the work too much for him and his health temporarily undermined. He jumped at a good chance, consequently, of adopting some less laborious occupation. The country had been so far opened up that commerce had begun. In 1812 a group of farmers organized a company for the purpose of opening a store for all kinds of merchandise at Salem, ten miles north of New Lisbon; and Benjamin Hanna was selected to take charge of it. After managing this store for about two years, he sold his interest in it and opened a store of his own in New Lisbon. There he lived until his death in 1853, and there his children and many of his children's children were brought up.

To Benjamin and Rachel Hanna were born thirteen children, all but two of whom survived to middle age.[1] One of them, Kersey Hanna, born in 1824, did not die until 1909. He has contributed many interesting reminiscences to the following account of the family's life in New Lisbon. Among other things he could recollect vividly certain journeys which he used to take as a boy of twelve with his grandfather, Robert Hanna. The old man used to travel around from the house of one of his children to that of another, and he liked to have the boy with him. It is interesting that a man living in 1909 should remember the Scotch-Irish immigrant boy who came to the colonies in 1763. These two connecting lives bound American history from the agitation for the repeal of the stamp act to the administration of William Howard Taft.

Of Benjamin and Rachel Hanna's eleven children who survived childhood, seven were boys and four were girls. They

[1] The following is a list of Benjamin and Rachel Hanna's children: (1) Joshua, Nov. 8, 1804 — died July 7, 1881; (2) Leonard, March 4, 1806 — died Dec. 15, 1862; (3) Levi, Feb. 7, 1808 — died May 5, 1898; (4) Zalinda, Feb. 23, 1810 — died Dec. 4, 1854; (5) Robert, Aug. 15, 1812 — died April 3, 1882; (6 and 7) Tryphena and Tryphosa, twins, June 12, 1814 — died May 23, 1893, and Jan. 17, 1815; (8) Rebecca, Sept. 21, 1816 — died Oct. 15, 1847; (9) Thomas B., May 22, 1818 — died Nov. 9, 1885; (10) Anna, March 3, 1821 — died Jan. 26, 1846; (11) Benjamin J., March 14, 1823 — died April 3, 1881; (12) Kersey, Oct. 6, 1824 — died 1909; (13) Elizabeth, June 12, 1827 — died Jan. 28, 1833.

were a fine, tall, vigorous family. The shortest of the brothers measured five feet and eleven inches in height. The tallest measured six feet three. The average was about six feet — so they were called "forty-two feet of Hanna." As they grew up some of the children deserted their home for one cause or another; but the majority of them remained with their father and made their lives in New Lisbon.

All the children except one were educated in the ordinary schools of New Lisbon, which at that time were private and according to all accounts most inferior. The exception was Leonard, who was trained for a professional career. After getting what preliminary schooling he could at home, he was sent to a small college in the neighboring county of Washington in Pennsylvania, and from there went to Philadelphia, where he graduated from the Rush Medical College. George B. McClellan's father was a professor in the institution at the time of Leonard Hanna's attendance. He returned to New Lisbon to practise his profession; but his career as a physician was hampered and curtailed by an accident. In mounting his horse, preparatory to a visit to one of his patients, he had barely thrown his leg over the saddle, when the animal shied and he was thrown heavily to the ground. His spine was injured and thereafter he suffered much with headaches, the attacks sometimes lasting as long as two or three weeks. The injury finally resulted in his death from the softening of the brain. Partly because of his infirmity he ceased the practice of medicine and joined his brothers Joshua and Robert in helping their father in the conduct of a continually growing business.

It must have been shortly after his accident that Dr. Leonard Hanna married; and as one of the best educated men in the town he not unnaturally married a school-teacher — Samantha Converse by name. Her parents, Porter and Rhoda Howard Converse, had migrated from Randolph, Vermont, to Ohio in 1824. Originally the Converse family[1] were Huguenots, having fled to Ireland after the massacre of St. Bartholomew; but presumably the French blood had been tolerably well diluted

[1] There is a history of the Converse family by Geo. O. Converse of Columbus, Ohio — at one time a Representative in Congress.

by the end of the eighteenth century. Porter Converse had been trained as a lawyer, but became a merchant after moving to Ohio. His wife, Rhoda Howard, derived from an old and excellent English family, and is stated to have been a woman of great energy of purpose. She lived to be eighty-seven years old. At the time of their migration they had four children — three daughters and one son. A fourth daughter, Miss Helen Converse, was born in Ohio. A son of Caroline, one of Samantha Converse's sisters, Porter Harbaugh by name, was living in 1905 in the neighborhood of New Lisbon. According to his statement his mother rode all the way from Vermont on horseback. The switch with which she accelerated the animal's pace was planted after her arrival and grew to be a large tree. She used to call it a Vermont white plum. Cuttings were given to friends and neighbors — whereby the original switch had a numerous progeny throughout the neighboring part of Ohio.

One cannot help suspecting that it is the story which has grown rather than the switch; and the suspicion is partly justified by Miss Helen Converse's positive statement that her family migrated to Ohio in a real carriage — described as a wide, old-fashioned vehicle on springs. It would accommodate three people comfortably on the back seat. The whole family rode all day in their conveyance, usually making about thirty miles and putting up every night at inns. Miss Converse had never heard of the fruitful switch — which none the less may have existed; but her account of the manner of her family's migration must be authentic. The Converses possessed means above the average of emigrants. One of Mark Hanna's sisters, Mrs. Jay C. Morse, remembers tales of her mother's about the silver tankards and plate which the Howards had brought with them from England.

Vermont has been said to be the most glorious spot on the face of the globe to be born in, provided you emigrate when you are young. Samantha Converse was eleven years old when she arrived in Ohio. Her family, coming as they did from New England, settled in Geauga County in the Western Reserve. Miss Converse became a school teacher, and went to New Lisbon for the purpose of using her knowledge to earn her living.

There she met Dr. Leonard Hanna and married him on Sept. 10, 1835, their ages being respectively twenty-nine and twenty-three. Their second child but their first son, born, as I have said, on Sept. 24, 1837, was named Marcus Alonzo Hanna.

Such was Mark Hanna's ancestry, of which any American might well be proud. It includes a compound of the best strains entering into the American racial stock. In his father's blood there was a Scotch-Irish, a Welsh and an English or Dutch strain. On his mother's side a French Huguenot, an Irish and an English infusion may be plainly traced. If a thorough mixture of many good racial ingredients constitutes, as is now usually supposed, an heredity favorable to individual energy and distinction, Mark Hanna started life with that basic advantage — an advantage which the historians of the state like to proclaim is enjoyed by an unusual proportion of the old families of Ohio. It is claimed with sufficient plausibility that a peculiarly fortunate group of conditions operated to select as the early settlers of Ohio the very best elements in the population of the older states, and that the exceptional prominence of the Ohio-born in American political and economic life since the Civil War must be attributed to this excellence of stock. Some foundation of truth may be granted to this explanation, without making Mark Hanna or the other eminent sons of Ohio any less individually responsible for their own careers. Peasantry and gentlefolk, Scotch, English, Irish, French and Dutch, New England, Pennsylvania and Virginia, Calvinism and Quakerism, — all the vague influences and forces associated with these names entered into his physical and social inheritance. He became by virtue thereof a tolerably typical American — which means a man whose past is so miscellaneous that he is obliged to seek for himself some form of effective personal definition.

CHAPTER II

BENJAMIN HANNA, HIS FAMILY AND HIS FORTUNE

THE early settlers of Columbiana County entered into a natural inheritance as rich and varied as their own blood. Its situation on the Ohio River adjoining the border of Pennsylvania was favorable. Its natural resources were abundant and diversified. The northern part of the county was undulating and excellently adapted to cultivation. Its southern half was more rugged and broken, and was on the whole better adapted for grazing than for tillage. In 1840 it stood first among the counties of Ohio in the production of wool. Along the bottom lands on the water courses, sycamore, walnut, maple and chestnut trees flourished. On the tops of the hills grew an abundance of pine and spruce. Coal, iron ore, clay and quarries were all to be found of good quality and quantity. In short, the county was a smaller copy of the whole state and afforded the best of opportunities for a combined agricultural and industrial development.

New Lisbon was located in the southern part of the county in the township of Centre. Its site consists of a stretch of level or bottom land running east and west on the middle fork of the Little Beaver Creek. To the north is a long, high hill, once crowned with a deep forest, up the side of which the village gradually spread. West and south of the village there stretches a formidable group of steep hills, the summits of which afford many picturesque views of a broken landscape. The hill to the south is particularly precipitous, and from the abundance of evergreens on its sides, used to be known as Pine Hill. Its proximity to the village, its rocks and its woods naturally made it the favorite playground of the village boys.

When Benjamin Hanna settled in New Lisbon in 1814 he leased a house in the centre of the village, which he used both as a

THE HOUSE IN NEW LISBON IN WHICH MR. HANNA WAS BORN. IT HAS BEEN CHANGED BY THE ADDITION OF ONE STORY

store and as a residence. He did not in the beginning depend for his subsistence exclusively upon the shop. He also owned a farm on the hill to the north of the town, but in all probability the shop soon came to occupy all his time. A storekeeper in a village in the interior of Ohio in the year 1815 had his difficulties. Philadelphia was the most convenient point from New Lisbon for the purchase of stock — all of which had to be hauled the length of the state of Pennsylvania over barbarous roads by means of six- and eight-horse teams. The transportation of every hundred pounds of freight in this laborious fashion cost the merchant between $5 and $10 — the average rate being about $8.50; and it was probably about as difficult for a man to finance his business as it was for him to procure his stock. During the early years there was so little currency in the country that trade was usually a matter of barter, and if currency was used, the medium of exchange was generally deerskins.

For a generation and more the economic development of Ohio and the other pioneer states was at first hampered and then determined in its form and distribution by the available means of transportation. Difficult as it was for the merchant, the situation of the farmer was worse. His bulky products could not be transported to market, and in the beginning the best that he could do was to feed his grain to stock and drive the animals across the mountains to the seaboard. The expense of this way of obtaining some purchasing power from the land was too great to endure. The roads were gradually improved. The flat steamboat made transportation by the Ohio River accessible to many counties of the state. Local markets of some value were created. Nevertheless, these improvements affected different parts of the state unevenly, and they were not sufficient to dispose of the products of the farms without occasional spells of ruinous congestion and low prices. The losses and difficulties from which so many of the pioneers of Ohio suffered must be remembered as the explanation for their subsequent craze for internal improvements and the large amount of money wasted therein. The business life of a storekeeper like Benjamin Hanna was one long fight, first against the expense and delays of transportation, and then against the relatively better means of transportation which other parts of the state had obtained.

In the end he was, as we shall see, broken by the struggle, but he had nevertheless a long preliminary period of prosperity. Steamboat navigation of the Ohio River eased some of his difficulties, and the construction of the Cumberland Road a good many more. New Lisbon itself was prosperous, and he benefited from the increased purchasing and selling powers of his neighbors. New Lisbon became, indeed, one of the busiest and most popular markets in eastern Ohio. Kersey Hanna states that his father had customers who travelled fifty or sixty miles to do business at the store. A couple of much frequented roads crossed the village, and three lines of stages gathered and distributed passengers from every direction. A newspaper had been started in German as early as 1808, but later it was transformed into the *Ohio Patriot*, and under that name still survives. There was at that time no printing establishment in Cleveland, and legal notices were for a while sent all the way to New Lisbon for publication in the *Patriot*.

Half a dozen stray bits of testimony prove both the increasing prosperity of Benjamin Hanna and his importance among his fellow-townsmen. He soon dispensed with his rented house, and built for himself on the public square a two-story brick store and residence, the living rooms being separated from the shop only by a partition. Kersey Hanna was born in this building in 1824, and so was Mark Hanna thirteen years later. It is standing to-day, and is changed only by the addition of another story. After the incorporation of the village by a special act of the Legislature in 1825 the first board of officers was organized on May 10, 1826, in Benjamin Hanna's dwelling, and he was chosen to be one of the trustees. Joshua, his first son, apparently had something to do with the business. At all events, he made a trip to Philadelphia in 1829, presumably to purchase stock, and was authorized to obtain for the village a hand fire-engine. Later, when again in Philadelphia, he bought for $485.39 a much improved machine, and on his way back remained in Pittsburgh long enough to add a dozen leather fire buckets to the equipment of the town. Finally, when the Columbiana Bank of New Lisbon was revived in 1834 or 1835, after having been dormant for a number of years, both Benjamin and Joshua Hanna were elected directors. Joshua Hanna was also director of the Columbiana Mutual Insurance Company of New Lisbon, while at a somewhat later date, another brother, Robert Hanna, became president of the association.

These sufficiently petty details are worth mentioning, because they establish the position occupied by Benjamin Hanna and his sons in New Lisbon at the time of Mark Hanna's birth and boyhood. They had become one of the leading families of the town, and local capitalists of unimpeachable standing. Benjamin Hanna himself did not continue to live back of the store. He bought and inhabited still another farm on the edge of the town. Joshua, the eldest son, built for his own occupancy a fine brick house on the brow of the hill overlooking the valley. Leonard Hanna, also, soon after the birth of Mark, moved into a house of his own, situated on High Street, which ran through a different part of the same hill. It was a spacious square building of some dignity, and betrayed a lingering allegiance to Colonial forms. It was crowned by a low pyramidal roof, broken by dormers, and its corners were emphasized by pilasters. On the front was a large entrance porch, which served as a piazza. Robert Hanna, also, had a separate establishment; and capital was supplied to Levi, wherewith to start a brewery — a business which was later abandoned because of the conversion of a large part of the family to the cause of temperance.

A business which was profitable enough to maintain about thirty feet of filial Hanna was obviously something more than a retail store. As a matter of fact, Benjamin and his sons were apparently the leading wholesale and commission merchants in what was then one of the busiest trading towns in eastern Ohio. Just how many of the sons were made partners in the business is not certain. The membership of the firm varied at different times. Accounts, due-bills and notes found among Mark Hanna's papers indicate that Benjamin Hanna, Leonard Hanna and Thomas B. Hanna were partners in business under the firm name of B., L., & T. Hanna as early as August, 1842, and as late as May, 1849.

They were less interested in politics than were the majority of the successful men of their generation. Only one out of

Benjamin Hanna's seven capable and energetic sons had any political ambition. No doubt the fact that they were Quakers, and in particular Hicksite Quakers, had something to do with this peculiarity. The sect had a tendency to keep away from political contentions and responsibilities; and no one of the Hanna family even served in the Legislature or held anything but a town office. They were nevertheless men of definite political convictions. Benjamin and all his sons were Whigs — an allegiance which followed naturally from their mercantile interests. Those who survived until the War became Republicans.

As Quakers they protested vigorously against slavery. After 1800 many Quakers had migrated from Virginia into Ohio, so that they might live in a state untainted by human bondage. In all probability Robert Hanna's final migration had been determined by the wish to escape from the neighborhood of such an institution. These Quakers later became a soil for the growth of anti-slavery feeling in Ohio; and when the underground railroad was started the majority of the stations were situated in their houses. The sympathies of the Hanna family are plainly indicated by the assistance they gave to this dangerous traffic. In the cellar of Joshua Hanna's fine brick house there had been built a secret room, which was used as a place of concealment for fugitive slaves; and presumably the rest of the family knew and approved of its existence.

As was also natural in Hicksite Quakers they had an instinctive sympathy with agitations for moral reform. The period from 1840 until 1855 was one of lively ferment of opinion, in which the preachers of all kinds of reforming creeds found many listeners and many followers. The most vital movement of this kind, abolitionism apart, was that in favor of temperance. The pioneer American [1] consumed a huge amount of raw spirits, being provoked thereto both by its cheapness and by the thirst

[1] "In May, 1832," to quote a local history, "George Graham made application for a license to retail spirituous liquors at the corner of the Public Square and Market Street. The council, being satisfied that he was a person of good moral character, granted a license for one year for the consideration of $10. Before adjournment it was decided that the next meeting of the council be held in George Graham's back room."

inevitably created by his daily consumption of bacon and salt pork. Local distilleries were among the earliest manufacturing enterprises in all pioneer communities. One had been started in New Lisbon soon after the settlement of the town, and its product was sold for only twenty-five cents a gallon. The first attempt to counteract the evils of the large amount of resulting intoxication took the mild form of temperance societies, whose members pledged themselves to confine their drinking to wine and beer.

Sterner methods and measures were, however, needed in order to check the serious evils of gross and general intoxication. In 1847 one of the famous six drunkards of Baltimore, who had been preaching total abstinence all over the country with great success, invaded New Lisbon, and held meetings every night for three weeks. No hall in the town was big enough to contain his audiences. The largest church was crowded, and outside in the street were overflow meetings. They had apparently a profound and lasting effect on the community. The Hannas had always been temperate, but some of them, at least, now became total abstainers. The brewery operated by Levi Hanna was sold, and the two youngest sons of Benjamin were among the charter members of the Total Abstinence Society.

It was, however, Leonard Hanna, Mark Hanna's father, who took the most prominent part of any of the family in the temperance movement of eastern Ohio. He was the only fraction of the forty-two feet who had an inclination towards public speaking or a gift for it. He is described as a fluent and forcible speaker, who possessed preëminently the power of interesting and dominating even an unsympathetic audience. After the visit of the eminent Baltimore drunkard, Dr. Hanna carried on the agitation for many years in the vicinity of New Lisbon. His son, H. Melville Hanna, who was two years younger than Mark, can remember the tenor of a number of his father's temperance addresses. As was natural for a physician, he emphasized rather the physiological than the moral arguments for total abstinence. Habitual whiskey drinkers, he said, were only half as likely to recover from acute ailments; and in the case of severe surgical operations their chances were even smaller.

Leonard Hanna, however, was not merely a lecturer on temperance. He was the only exception in the family to the general abstention from an active interest in politics. The extent of this interest is difficult to establish, but undoubtedly he ranked among the abler and more popular Whig stump speakers in that part of Ohio. He was compared by many to Tom Corwin, who was the leading popular orator among the Whigs. According to the custom of the day, he used to hold joint debates with prominent Democrats, the two verbal contestants travelling together from town to town in the same carriage. His opponent on one occasion was Edwin M. Stanton. On another occasion (according to Kersey Hanna) Dr. Hanna and David Todd held eleven joint discussions in different parts of the Western Reserve — one of them in Cleveland. If this is so, Leonard Hanna must have enjoyed a very considerable reputation as a political orator, for David Todd, afterwards the second of Ohio's war governors, was one of the most conspicuous Democrats in the state and a speaker of recognized ability and force.

Nevertheless Dr. Leonard Hanna was apparently not elected to any public office. His nearest approach to election occurred, according to the statement of his brother Kersey, in 1844, when he ran for Congress as a Whig and cut down the Democratic majority in his district from about 5000 to about 300 votes. A failure of this kind gives a man as much renown as would actual success; and there is every indication that Dr. Hanna stood exceptionally well among his political associates in Ohio. When H. Melville Hanna went to Washington at the beginning of the War to be examined for admission into the navy, he called on Senator Benjamin Wade at his father's request, and was warmly greeted by that rough old anti-slavery warrior. He was glad to do anything he could for Dr. Leonard Hanna's son.

His interest in politics apparently diminished very much towards the end of his life. His son, H. Melville, states that a friend once asked his father, "Why didn't you stay in politics?" "Because," the doctor replied, "I would have to get into the mud," which sounds well, but is hardly sufficient. Doubtless certain aspects of political life were repellent to his Puritan and Quaker training, but probably both his health and his business interests had much to do with his diminishing political activity. Soon after 1847 the family suffered reverses in business, which resulted in its dispersal in 1852. Dr. Hanna was forced to start his business career all over again under novel surroundings; and his new work and its heavier responsibilities could not have left him much leisure for politics.

Nevertheless, it is significant that the only one of Benjamin Hanna's sons who exhibited any active personal interest in politics was Mark Hanna's father; and this interest was apparently merely one expression of a versatile and sympathetic disposition, which was aroused to action by every serious call made upon him by his domestic and social surroundings. In addition to being a business man and a political speaker, he was an energetic temperance reformer, and he always retained a lively interest in his early profession. It was a period in which one man could easily and acceptably play many parts, and in which a man of an essential social and communicative disposition was inevitably driven to play many parts. The better men of that generation tended to spread their personal energy over a very large area.

In the case of Dr. Hanna the business interest was dominant, and the others only subordinate. He was a man who acted from personal rather than impersonal motives, from sympathies and affections rather than from strong purpose. In the absence of any special bent for professional or political life, he merged his own interest with that of the family. By the year 1840 there were not very many men in Ohio, outside of Cincinnati, who were as much like capitalists as Benjamin Hanna and his sons. The careers of the sons were determined by the opportunities which their father was able to offer to them; and in accepting this opportunity Dr. Leonard Hanna was apparently the only one who sacrificed other personal interests of any great importance. He did not travel very far either as a physician, a politician or a business man, but if his efficiency was diminished by his versatility, the same quality served only to increase the attraction of his personality.

H. Melville Hanna tells a story about his father and grandfather which is both touching and amusing, and which may fitly terminate this sketch of Mark Hanna's immediate forbears. After Dr. Leonard Hanna had moved to Cleveland in 1852, he frequently returned to New Lisbon to see Benjamin Hanna, who by that time was a very old and a very sick man. While talking over his ailments with his son, who retained in the family the authority of a physician, Benjamin said, "Dr. Speaker has stopped my smoking, Leonard. What dost thee think about it?" The other answered nothing, but going to the big mahogany sideboard, filled his father's pipe, gave it to him and lighted it. The old man took a few puffs and then said, "I was sure, Leonard, that thee knew more than Dr. Speaker."

CHAPTER III

BOYHOOD

In the house of Dr. Leonard Hanna there seems to have been less discipline and more kindliness than was usual in American homes of that period. Discipline there was, for Samantha Converse Hanna had inherited the traditions of domestic New England, and as Dr. Hanna was frequently away from home for days and weeks on end, the mother's authority was dominant and pervasive. She exercised it decisively but with fairness and good judgment. She is described as a woman of positive character, energetic mind and considerable executive ability. Her active life was centred around her home and children, but she was social by instinct, and under less primitive social conditions she would have entertained liberally. As it was, whenever any conspicuous man came to New Lisbon, she always wanted to have him at her table.

Dr. Hanna, on the other hand, was preëminently a kindly and an easy-going man. He did not believe in the practice of flogging, which at that time prevailed in many American homes; and, as we shall see, he was inclined to let his children have their own way. While his wife was bright but not witty, he had an Irishman's love of a good joke. Miss Hattie Converse, a cousin of Samantha Hanna, and for a while a school-teacher in the town, lived with the family; and she and Dr. Hanna were continually exchanging jokes and sharpening their wits at each other's expense.

The Leonard Hanna household was not only unusually genial for its time and place, but it was also unusually refined. The Converses were much more like gentlefolks than were the average pioneer settlers in the Western States. Samantha Hanna had a taste for flowers, ornaments and good furniture, and their house itself was an exceptionally good-looking building for Ohio in 1840. Whenever Leonard Hanna made one of his frequent trips to Philadelphia on business, his wife loaded him with commissions. Their furniture was all imported from the East, and what was still more unusual, the yard was planted with shrubbery, which had also to be obtained from the seaboard. The table was abundant, the food well-cooked, the linen of excellent quality, and the children well-clothed. All together very few Ohio boys of that time were brought up in such a well-equipped, well-ordered and genial home.

Of course, it remained very simple, and all hands had to share in the work. If Mark Hanna escaped the scars of that grim struggle for existence in which most Americans of the previous, and to a large extent of his own, generation were engaged, he was certainly not brought up in idleness. As soon as he was old enough, he did his share of work in the field, and he had certain regular chores assigned to him, such as driving the cows to pasture. There were no gentlemen of leisure in a Middle Western town before the War. Of course there were loafers, but they were called loafers. The possession even of considerable means did not entitle a man or his sons to abandon labor with their own hands.

In religion a mitigation of the earlier Puritanism had already taken place. Benjamin Hanna's sons did not remain strict Quakers. One of the laws of the association was that any person who was married outside the church or who was married by anybody but a Quaker minister should be disowned. The application of this rule left Leonard Hanna and all his brothers except Kersey outside the pale. It does not appear, however, that they became active in any other denomination. Their situation made them tolerant, and the process of religious emasculation which begins in toleration usually ends in indifference. Kersey Hanna stated that Leonard, in spite of certain doctrinal disagreements with the Hicksite Quakers, considered himself to be by conviction a member of that sect. Nevertheless, after leaving New Lisbon, he regularly attended the Presbyterian Church, to which his wife belonged, without becoming a Presbyterian himself. Thus in the matter of religious training the earlier rigorous standards were very much relaxed; and Mark Hanna as a boy could, as we shall see, joke with impunity about his religious convictions.

The New Lisbon Homestead

Mark was assuredly a good-looking boy. Neither he nor his brothers were as tall as the previous generation of Hannas, and Mark himself, when he grew up, looked almost short, because his broad and powerful frame seemed to need a few more inches of height. His uncle Kersey Hanna describes him as short, strong and rugged, with a full round figure. On the other hand, most of his playmates recollect him as almost slender. His complexion was fair, his hair brown and his expression frank, serious and communicative. But both as boy and man the most striking part of his personal appearance were his big, alert, shrewd, searching brown eyes, which, like his tapering fingers, he inherited from his father and which he alone of his father's sons did inherit. In this as in certain other respects Mark Hanna was another version of his father with better health, more energy and more purpose.

In describing the life led by the boys of Mark Hanna's generation in New Lisbon and certain aspects of their education, we have one very excellent authority. Shortly after Senator Hanna's death, a boyhood friend and playmate, Dr. Henry G. McCook, published a "Threnody" on Mr. Hanna, the notes to which contain an abundance of facts and stories about New Lisbon in the forties; and the reader may be referred to that volume in case he would like to know more than I shall tell him about the place, its youthful inhabitants, their occupations and sports.

He says nothing about the first school which Mark Hanna attended, which was kept by his mother's cousin, Miss Hattie Converse. Other schoolmates of Mr. Hanna have, however, furnished several authentic stories about this episode, each of which throws some light upon the school, the boy and the relations between the boy and his teacher. One lady who went to Miss Converse's school describes her fellow-pupil as pale and slender, but active and mischievous. He was accused of pushing a little boy over a bank on the hillside where a number of children were picking sorrel. Miss Converse evidently thought the offence extremely culpable, for she made him take off his coat, and switched him sharply on his bare arms — all of which frightened the little girls and made them burst into tears. On another occasion he was whipped for being late. Before going to school, he had to drive the cows to pasture, and on this particular morning they got away from him, and caused him, according to his own account, much trouble and loss of time in getting them together again. Miss Converse listened to this excuse for his tardy arrival and doubted its truth. Mark stuck to his story, said that he had never told a lie and was not then telling one. But he was none the less punished. In the end Dr. Hanna heard of the fault, its punishment, privately verified Mark's excuse and rebuked the doubting teacher.

There are other indications that Mark did not get along well with his mother's cousin. One day Miss Converse found him loitering in the street after school was over, instead of making straight for home after the manner of really virtuous lads. Here was an opening, which the excellent pedagog could not overlook; but when she took him to task, he did not tamely submit. He asserted that her authority did not extend beyond the school building and grounds. She asserted that it did. The issue was presented to his parents, and they decided in his favor, and in this decision had the support of public opinion. The episode indicates a disposition to stand up for his personal rights rare in so small a lad, and confidence in him on the part of his parents. It also indicates that even in 1845, in a small Middle Western town, the American boy was coming into his own. There were parents who could understand a boyish propensity to loiter, and there were children who were beginning to discover and insist upon the great American domestic principle of filial authority.

But I do not wonder that Miss Hattie Converse, who played the part of King George in this new struggle for independence, disliked her mischievous pupil. Like many other ladies, she had a peculiar horror of snakes. Several witnesses assert that Mark used to conceal little garter snakes in her text-books, and so cause her the utmost discomfiture. Whether he was switched for this offence, as he very well deserved, the records are silent.

They are also silent as to the length of time that Mark attended Miss Converse's school, and they conflict as to the identity of his next school-teacher. The most renowned and popular school in New Lisbon during Mark's boyhood was kept by a Scotch-Irishman named David Anderson. This man, whose rugged character was typical of many of the pioneer pedagogs of the Middle West, began to teach in Lisbon about 1835, and continued to do so until obliged to retire by failing health in 1872. He was a stern, hard Puritan, who did not scruple to use the ruler on his pupils, and apparently needed in the exercise of his calling some warlike weapon. The story is that, when he attempted to chastise some big culprit, he was assaulted by his victim, and only escaped a thrashing by virtue of the assistance rendered by the rest of his pupils. Yet his pupils, apparently, did not have any reason to be fond of him. He wore rubber shoes, and would step silently up behind his boys when they were supposed to be writing on their slates. If he found them drawing pictures or scribbling messages, he would box them soundly on the ears — first on one side and then on the other, as the head was forced over by the force of the first blow. He was also subject to violent outbursts of temper, which are attributed by one witness to the influence of a malevolent wife — a lady who in her playful moods used to threaten her husband with a butcher's knife and was popularly supposed to be a witch.

In spite, however, of his peculiarities, in spite of his sedulous laying on of two rulers, one round and one flat, in spite of his assumption of authority over the behavior of his pupils outside of the schoolroom, his memory is still reverenced in New Lisbon. Some years ago a fund was collected from his former pupils with which to erect a permanent memorial to the village teacher, but the project fell through, because of the failure of the bank in which the accumulated funds had been deposited. He was, apparently, with all his tantrums, his cuffings and his busy rulers, a kind-hearted man. The statement that he would be amiable and cheerful for the whole day whenever a new pupil happened in and paid the fee of two dollars for the first quarter, points to a hard and a fruitless fight against poverty as well as domestic unhappiness. No wonder that his temper was none of the best and his discipline harsh. The fact that in spite of all his failings the memory of "Davy" Anderson is cherished in New Lisbon sufficiently proves that when the books were balanced, his pupils could place to his credit a great deal of rough but effective elementary and moral schooling.

I have paused for a moment over the description of David Anderson and his school, because of the light which the man, his methods and circumstances throw upon the New Lisbon of the decade from 1840 to 1850; but there is some doubt whether Mark Hanna was ever cuffed and drilled by the irascible Scotch-Irishman. At the local centennial celebration in 1903 the names of Mark Hanna and "Davy" Anderson, as the two most renowned celebrities of New Lisbon, were continually being coupled. Speaking of Anderson, the Senator said to the Hon. Chas. C. Connell, who had been writing a history of the town prepared for the occasion: "I don't like to spoil your story, Connell; but I never went to school with 'Davy' Anderson." On the other hand, Dr. Henry C. McCook distinctly states that he and Mark Hanna attended "Davy" Anderson's school; and Howard Melville Hanna is equally emphatic in testifying to the same effect. There is no way now of definitely settling it; but if Mark Hanna ever did attend "Davy's" school, it could not have been for long. There is evidence that from 1850 to 1852 he was sent to another school-teacher; and authentic incidents connected with his attendance of Miss Converse's school indicate that he must have been at that time a boy of ten or twelve. Perhaps a father who objected to flogging, and who supported his son in a rebellion against the exercise of a school-teacher's authority outside of school hours, would have been loath to submit his son to "Davy" Anderson's rule and rulers.

When the "Union-School System" of graded public schools was adopted, Mark Hanna apparently went to public school. In the general re-grading and distribution of the children, Mark Hanna and Henry McCook were assigned to the high school, and were made deskmates. The school was lodged in the basement of the Presbyterian Church, and here Mark continued his education until he left New Lisbon. "As I recall him," says Dr. McCook, "in the 'roundabout' or tailless coat then worn by boys, he was a ruddy-cheeked youth, rather slightly built, certainly not stout or stocky — a pleasant, wholesome fellow, clean of tongue and with more polish of manners than many of his playmates. Nevertheless, we were in several school scrapes together, in one of which the writer saved

MARK AND HOWARD MELVILLE HANNA AS CHILDREN

his deskmate from a thrashing by resisting the teacher in what was by our schoolroom standards an unlawful mode of punishment. This diverted attention from my fellow-culprit, who in the *melée* went scot-free." Dr. McCook adds: "Several teachers had charge of the high school during the pupilage of the Senator and his deskmate, but the one who wielded the greatest and most wholesome influence upon our characters was Reuben McMillan. To him the writer owes more than any other instructor in school or college; and this affection and this gratitude were shared during his school life, at least, by Mr. Hanna."

Before leaving the subject of Mark Hanna's schooling in New Lisbon, attention must be called to an unofficial source of instruction and training which the lad shared with some of his playmates. On Jan. 12, 1850, there was instituted the "Polydelphian Society of New Lisbon," a debating club, whose constitution and behavior are so well described in a letter written by General Anson G. McCook, then Secretary of the United States Senate to Major W. W. Armstrong of Cleveland in April, 1892, that I reproduce it in part: "With what interest you read [in a book containing the constitution and minutes of the society] of the efforts to provide for every possible contingency to make our debating society a success — the elaborate way in which we provided for the duties of the officers — the limitations we placed upon debate, peremptorily shutting off long-winded orations — the amount of fines to be imposed upon disorderly members, running from '5 to 25 cents' — the power, as we expressed it in terms that very closely resemble a provision in the Constitution of the United States, to lay and collect taxes for necessary purposes — the express provision that no one shall address the chair except upon his feet and the positive prohibition 'that no member should be permitted to whistle or eat in the society'; all expressed in quaint and boyish phraseology but with unmistakable clearness and directness. From the record the first question we attempted to debate was 'Was the Mexican War justifiable?' and the minutes gravely state that 'after a good deal of arguing, the jury brought in its decision for the negative.'

"It is wonderful, too, with what splendid courage these untrained boys tackled subjects that have puzzled the best intellects of the country; and it is remarkable with what good sense and justice they decided them. In nearly every instance these boys of from 12 to 15 years of age, living in a small town in eastern Ohio, placed themselves squarely upon the side of questions that since then have been maintained by the best minds and consciences of the country. For instance, on the questions, 'Should flogging be abolished in the Navy?' 'Shall Canada be annexed to the United States?' and 'Will the conquest of New Mexico and Upper California result in more good than evil?' the society said 'Yes.' On the then comparatively new question of 'Should women be allowed to vote?' the boys also said 'Yes.' On the question, 'Have the Negroes more cause for complaint against the Whites than the Indians?' the Polydelphians even at that early day decided wisely in the affirmative; and your friend and townsman, Mark Hanna, took the side of the black man and won his cause. On the question, 'Should the United States take any part in the Hungarian struggle for liberty?' the boys stood by our traditional policy, notwithstanding the temptation to be led off by spread eagle oratory. With scarcely an exception the boys placed themselves on the side of justice, humanity, good morals and good government, and that speaks pretty well, it seems to me, for the atmosphere and influences which surrounded these boys."

Although one of the younger members, Mark Hanna was active and prominent in the Polydelphian Society. In his "Threnody" on the Senator, Dr. Henry C. McCook reproduces a copy of the minutes for one of the meetings at which Mark acted as secretary. On this occasion the portentous subject was discussed, "Which does the most good to a republican government, Virtue or Intelligence?" The secretary states that the question was decided in favor of the "negitive"; but whether the "negitive" is equivalent to Virtue or Intelligence the scribe fails to record. Mark was one of the jury. His handwriting at that time (he was just thirteen) was awkward and unformed, his spelling was far from impeccable, and his power of composition probably inferior to that of an average well-trained boy of the same age to-day. But his handwriting shows the general characteristics of his later penmanship.

MARK HANNA AS A BOY

As was natural in a community just emerging from the roughness of the frontier, the games of the New Lisbon boys sometimes took on a semblance of war, and the warring factions took their names and recruited their forces from different parts of the town. The nature and circumstances of these combats have been told in so lively a manner by Dr. Henry C. McCook, that I shall merely transcribe his account.

"The inherent tendency of men to divide into parties, factions, sects, and to contend with and for the same, often without the least apparent reasonableness, was well shown among our village boys. The town was divided into two great sections, known in the graphic rather than elegant diction of boyhood as Sheep Hill and Frog Pond. Between the two was a narrow belt called Mid-town or Middle-town, whose boundaries and subjects were determined partly by location and partly by natural and social selection. The Hanna boys, Mark and Melville, belonged to this section, and there the writer had his citizenship. For the most part the down-town boys went with the Frog-ponders, and the up-town boys with the Sheep-hillers. But there were not hard and fast lines, and the Middle-towners had recruits from both sections, determined by personal preference, special friendships and boyish fancy.

"The rivalries between these parties grew into feuds, and these were at one time so intense that individual fights and boy riots occurred, in which, as a rule, Mid-town and Frog Pond were allies. I remember one battle in which the parties met by challenge in a field and grove north of the Hanna place. The three clans marched to the rendezvous in companies, and after some preliminary skirmishing it was proposed to settle the controversy not by arbitration, but by the method of ancient chivalry, a fight between the captains of two of the factions. The Middle-town captain promptly accepted for himself and the Frog-ponders, and joined in fisticuff combat with the Sheep Hill captain, a stout and plucky lad called Loot Smith, two years older than he. Luther got the better of his opponent, and had him down, pummelling him badly, when the impatient partisans of the worsted Mid-towner broke bounds, and with a shout rushed into the fistic ring, rescued their fallen chief, and a general battle began over and around the two leaders. In this *melée* one of our side — he was a Frog-ponder — who carried a real sword, an ancestral relic of some war, badly hacked the arm of a young Sheep-hiller."

On another occasion the hostilities assumed such a serious form that a crowd of citizens, including the mothers of the combatants, gathered on the street; but in spite of weeping and imploring the boys were too excited to abandon their rough war game. It took John McCook, the father of Henry, a stalwart man, six-feet-two in height, to end this particular battle; and even he might have failed without the assistance of a "red rawhide, mighty as the sword of Gideon." Thereafter the easy-going parents of New Lisbon decided to put an end to these puerile combats. Some witnesses assert that Mark Hanna was for a while captain of the "Sheep Hill" crowd, and that the "Mid-town" gang mentioned by Mr. McCook was also called "Dutch McCook's" crowd — "Dutch McCook" being no other than Henry McCook himself. His crowd, while an independent command, usually fought with the Frog-ponders.

Boys whose mimic battles could cause such consternation to their parents came of fighting blood; and indeed in no part of the country was a more manly, vigorous and sturdy lot of people gathered together than in this particular part of Ohio. The community subsequently proved its mettle in both peace and war. One family in particular of Scotch-Irish Presbyterians, which was allied to the Hanna family by marriage, bore an extraordinary record in the war. Everybody has heard of the fighting McCooks, but everybody does not know they came from New Lisbon. George McCook and Mary, his wife, two of the early settlers of New Lisbon, had three sons. The first of these sons, Dr. George McCook, was the father of one son and seven daughters, two of whom married sons of Benjamin Hanna. It was this particular McCook who made the famous retort to a heckler, when he was urging his fellow-townsmen to enlist at the outbreak of the war. He was asked by an auditor, "Why don't you go to the War?" "Young man," Dr. McCook loudly answered, "if this war lasts six months, there will be more McCooks in the army than there are Indians in Hell."

The boys who played and fought with Mark Hanna have almost as good a civil as a military record. There have been among them "two territorial governors, a secretary of the United States Senate, who had also been a representative in Congress, several clergymen of note, college professors, authors, and editors and many physicians, lawyers and successful business men." The majority of them were picked men, — picked, that is, by the happy accident of birth and blood, a sort of a natural aristocracy.

Mark Hanna did more than hold his own among his vigorous playmates. He was one of their leaders — although not any more of a leader than were a dozen other boys. All accounts agree as to his disposition and behavior. He was active, willing, sociable, generous, friendly, mischievous, high-spirited and aggressive. He did not shirk any task which could be properly laid upon him, and he eagerly sought all sorts of games, amusements and contests of skill and strength. He learned his lessons, but he was not studious. He did his chores, but during their performance he was always planning some other and more amusing occupation. In short, he was thoroughly a boy — wise not beyond his years, but according to his years.

His behavior as a boy was not, however, entirely a matter of the natural and wholesome inconsequentiality of youth. His nature was not cast in any special mold. It was not biassed in favor of any single expression. He passed easily and freely from one occupation to another, and did not linger long over any particular task. What gave singleness and wholesomeness to his personality as a boy and later as a man was not the possession of any special faculty or interest, but an all-round adaptability and humanity. From the beginning his great gift was a gift for good-fellowship. According to the unanimous testimony of those who knew him as a boy he was expansive, good-natured and sympathetic — claiming friendship and fidelity and returning all that he received with abundant interest.

CHAPTER IV

THE PASSING OF NEW LISBON

BENJAMIN HANNA and his sons were so prosperous in New Lisbon that had the town itself continued to prosper, most of the family, including probably Mark Hanna, would have remained there indefinitely. But New Lisbon suffered one of those set-backs to which our rapidly changing economic conditions subject many American towns and cities, and from which it never fully recovered. Inasmuch as this set-back was chiefly due to the failure of an enterprise which involved the business and the capital of the Hanna firm and resulted in the dispersal of the family, its causes, incidents and consequences must be described in some detail.

The great need of the pioneer communities was cheap and adequate means of transportation. In its absence they were confined to local markets. They could do little with their corn except feed it to their hogs, and not very much with their hogs except eat them. Without transportation the very fertility of their lands and their own energy and hard work merely increased the local congestion of agricultural products. With transportation their farms doubled in value, and they could sell their superabundance of commodities for a relative abundance of cash. The consequence was that the pioneers hankered after improved means of transport very much as their forbears had hankered after salvation.

Early in the nineteenth century the cheapest and most efficient means of transport was by water. Of course road builders were active; but in the West the distances were too great to permit of the economical transportation of freight in wagons, and the country was too sparsely settled to support really good roads. The markets they wanted to reach were hundreds of miles away. Waterways were the thing; and the invention of the steamboat increased suddenly and enormously the commercial value of navigable streams. Ohio was bounded on the south by one of the greatest navigable rivers in the country; on the north by one of a string of navigable lakes; and it was cut up by a system of smaller watercourses which could be used for scows and flatboats. Those parts of the state which enjoyed immediate access to such means of transport profited enormously. The other parts of the state languished. Cincinnati was the commercial metropolis. In 1840 it possessed almost seven times as many inhabitants as Cleveland.

The only way to make up for the lack of natural navigable waterways was to build canals; and after some years of hesitation Ohio took to building canals in earnest. Between the years 1825 and 1842, when the system of state canals was completed, there were constructed in Ohio some 658 miles of canals at a total cost of nearly $15,000,000; and of these the most important was the Ohio Canal, which ran from Portsmouth on the Ohio River across the state to Cleveland at the mouth of the Cuyahoga on Lake Erie. "The effect of these improvements," says the historian of Ohio,[1] "upon the growth and prosperity of the state can hardly be exaggerated. They opened to her farmers and merchants the markets of the Ohio, the Lakes and New York. They enhanced the value of the lands and of the products. They not only united a long segregated people, but made them prosperous."

New Lisbon, however, was not properly situated to obtain any benefit from the system of state canals. It was separated from the Ohio River on the east by a dozen miles of rough country, and from the Ohio Canal on the west by several times that distance. Its inhabitants realized, as soon as the canal building began, that it would lose its standing as the busiest trading centre in the interior of eastern Ohio, unless it could obtain thoroughly good water communication with the local and remoter markets. As early as Jan. 11, 1826, the General Assembly authorized the incorporation of a company to construct the Sandy and Beaver Canal, which was to run from a point on the Ohio River through New Lisbon to a point on the Ohio Canal in Tuscawaras County. In this way the products of

[1] "Ohio," by Rufus King, p. 350.

New Lisbon and its neighborhood could be cheaply transported both to Pittsburgh and Cincinnati, and to Cleveland and Buffalo; and New Lisbon would not only hold its own, but become a populous thriving city.

Evidently, however, there were difficulties connected with the raising of capital for such a purely local enterprise. Probably it did not look as good to outlanders as it did to the people of New Lisbon. As an air line the distance between the terminal ports of the Sandy and Beaver Canal was some forty miles, but this stretch was increased to sixty by the necessity of following the watercourses and dodging hills. The engineering difficulties were serious. For eight years after the incorporation of the company the project languished, and it was not until the end of 1834 that ground was actually broken. In the meantime the Ohio Canal had been practically finished, and a large part of the state was entering upon a period of unprecedented prosperity. Wheat went up from twenty-five cents to a dollar a bushel, and corn and oats almost in proportion. Even potatoes, which previously had been too cheap to have a price, brought forty cents a bushel.

It was with high hopes, consequently, that on the 24th of November, 1834, New Lisbon celebrated the beginning of the great work. It was essentially a local enterprise. Some help had been obtained in Philadelphia, where the merchants of New Lisbon had wealthy connections; but most of the money was subscribed by business men of the town and the other small places along the line of the canal. Benjamin Hanna was president of the company. Leonard Hanna was a director. The whole family invested liberally in its stock. They realized that the future of New Lisbon depended upon the success of the undertaking.

Even after ground was broken, however, progress was far from being uninterrupted. Work had to be suspended during the panic of 1837. Reorganization was necessary; and to facilitate it Benjamin Hanna turned over half of his stock in the old corporation to the new one. After a delay of some years work was resumed, and finally in 1846 the canal was actually finished. On October 26 the first boat made the voyage from the Ohio River to New Lisbon; and the jubilation of the citizens of that

THE PASSING OF NEW LISBON

town was not apparently diminished by the fact that the boat stuck in the mud and had to be hauled to its dock, not only by horse and oxen, but by the willing arms of a large number of enthusiastic citizens. The event was properly celebrated in a spacious warehouse, which Benjamin Hanna had built on the margin of the canal, and which was filled with immense stores of grain, wool and produce for shipment to the Ohio.

The canal was a failure almost from the start. The section between New Lisbon and the Ohio River was operated with some success for a while, and large shipments of wool and pork were profitably made to Pittsburgh. But the rest of the canal was a frank fizzle. It was too difficult a problem for the local engineers. West of New Lisbon two tunnels had to be cut through the hills, one of which was three-quarters of a mile long. The number of locks made the cost of maintenance impossibly high, and scarcity of water rendered it necessary to dam several creeks and rivers and to build two large reservoirs. The work was hastily and badly done. The banks were always caving in, and the dams breaking. Water was frequently lacking. It is said that only one boat ever made the complete passage, and that boat was forced through by the contractors, so as to qualify for certain payments under their contract.

The effect of this failure upon the fortunes of New Lisbon and the Hanna family was disastrous. Not only was the country-side drained of its accumulated capital, but it was deprived of means of recovering from the loss. Two million dollars had been sunk in the ditch, of which, according to Kersey Hanna, his father and brothers had supplied no less than $200,000. All of this money was hopelessly lost. Even that section of the canal between New Lisbon and the Ohio was not operated for more than a few years. Its trade was killed by the competition of the incoming railroads — a form of transportation which the citizens of New Lisbon had resolutely and insistently diverted from their town. By 1852 the Fort Wayne and the Cleveland and the Pittsburgh roads were already being operated through Columbiana County, but at some distance from New Lisbon. The town was side-tracked. The canal of great hopes was abandoned. New Lisbon ceased to be the trading centre of the district. There was nothing for an ambitious man to do except to get out.

When overtaken by this disaster Benjamin Hanna was too old a man to move and make another start. He died in 1853, and left his children an abundance of land but very little personal property. His sons were young enough to begin again. Joshua Hanna moved to Pittsburgh and became a banker. Leonard and Robert Hanna started off in the opposite direction for Cleveland, where, in company with a fellow-townsman, Hiram Garretson, they founded a grocery and commission business. They were followed or accompanied by the other brothers. In a few years all the Hanna family had deserted New Lisbon.

Mark, then a lad of fifteen, accompanied his parents to Cleveland, but after his removal he remained tied to New Lisbon by one of the strongest of bonds. He had asserted his independence and the maturity of his years by an engagement of marriage with a young lady named Mary Ann McLain. His suit was discouraged from the start by his own family; but his parents were apparently either unable or unwilling absolutely to forbid it. Mark certainly regarded himself as regularly and definitely engaged. During many years he often revisited New Lisbon, in order to see his sweetheart, and presumably to play around with his former companions. A boy who was so much of a boy was bound to have a love-affair; and in the case of a boy who was being treated by his parents as so much of a man, the love-affair naturally threatened serious responsibilities.

It speaks well for his fidelity in his personal relations that this pseudo-engagement lasted for nine years. During that whole period he continued to go to New Lisbon whenever he could; and whenever he came, he brought with him an armful of presents — including, so it is said, dresses. Evidently after living in Cleveland he was not satisfied with the fashions of New Lisbon or Mary's ability to live up to them. His ideas about the apparel and the behavior of women were presumably changing; and his attachment to Mary, which dated probably almost from childhood, was being strained. He was always gay and sociable, and he always instinctively sought the society of people of the same temper and habit. Mary apparently was shy, awkward and not at all lively. The relation could not last.

But the way the end was reached testifies both to the good judgment of Mark Hanna's mother and to Mark's own frank courage. Mary was invited to pay a visit to the Hanna home in Cleveland. She accepted and it proved to be her undoing. Mary felt uncomfortable and out of place in the brilliant society of such a metropolis as Cleveland. She either refused to bear Mark company in his engagements among his new friends, or if she did she made an indifferent showing. It is said that when Mary returned, she realized that she and Mark could never be married; and New Lisbon firmly believed that Samantha Hanna had arranged the visit, in order that both of the young couple might have their eyes opened.

Whether the event was due to diplomacy or accident, the inevitable result soon followed. Mark made up his mind that an end must be made of it; and when his decision was once reached, he did not shirk its unpleasant consequences. He went to New Lisbon and told Mary face to face that it was all over. The poor child took her sentence hard, but she is said to have admitted its justice. As for Mark, a boy could hardly have behaved better than he did in the matter of an early and mistaken attachment to a girl. He was faithful for many years; he was both kind and generous; he evidently tried hard to make a place for his boyish attachment in the midst of a new and different life; and when he failed, he got out of his false situation as manfully as he could. Evidently his parents respected his attachment, and instead of arousing his resentment by uncompromising opposition, they had enough confidence in his good sense to allow him to extricate himself. Even at the age of eighteen or nineteen he was evidently very much his own master, and had won the right to take care of himself. His self-assertion when a schoolboy against the excessive authority of his teacher, Miss Converse, was bearing its natural fruits.

None the less the incident did not leave a pleasant impression on Mark Hanna's mind. The visit during which he broke with Mary was his last appearance in New Lisbon in almost thirty years. He did not return until 1890, and since this next visit was a sort of memorial pilgrimage of a successful man of fifty-three to the haunts of his youth, some incidents connected with it may be mentioned here. Mr. Hanna was accompanied on the trip by his wife, his mother, his daughter Ruth, his sister Miss Lillian Hanna, now Mrs. S. Prentiss Baldwin, his sister Mrs. Henry S. Hubbell and her husband, Miss Helen Converse, his mother's sister, and Howard Melville Hanna. They came in a private car, and occupied pretty much the whole of the inn kept by an Englishman named "Billy" Bradbury. They visited the old house on the hill, found that to their recollection the rooms had shrunk in size, and discovered a closet, in which Mark had been confined by his mother for some boyish misdeed until his father returned and released him. While near the house they came upon an aged man who was holding his horse while it grazed upon the grass back of the old homestead. Thinking that he looked like the man who used to drive the stage between New Lisbon and Wellsville, Mark Hanna called to him and asked, "Do you remember me?" The man looked at him indifferently and replied, "No, I don't." Not to be discouraged, Mr. Hanna continued, pointing to his brother, "This is Melville and I am Mark Hanna." "You don't say so," the old man answered without the slightest trace of interest. "And how's business your way?"

"Billy" Bradbury, the hotel-keeper, was something of a character, and he and Mr. Hanna evidently soon became great friends. "One day," says Mr. Bradbury, "Mr. Hanna was sitting in the office, and eight couples in single rigs drove up. They had come from Salem, ten miles away, to see the new railway bridge. Three of the young fellows put their horses in the barn; the other five were not so particular and contented themselves with any post they could find vacant in the street. Presently the whole eight couples walked into the hotel, and sat down upstairs in the parlor; but when supper was ready, only those who had their horses in the barn came down to eat. 'Say, landlord,' one of them asked, 'do you know why those fellows and their girls aren't eating? Because they have not got the price.' Mr. Hanna heard what was said, laughed and said to me: 'Billy, go upstairs, and bring them all down to supper. Bring the boys and the girls, and if the boys won't come, bring the girls, and feed their horses. I'll pay the bill." So he did, and no one was the wiser. When the bill was presented after a visit of three days it came to $80. The landlord received a check for $100 and was told to keep the change. Naturally he swears by Mark Hanna.

CHAPTER V

EARLY YEARS IN CLEVELAND

IN April, 1852, Leonard Hanna and his brother Robert left New Lisbon and started on their new business career in Cleveland. They were accompanied by Hiram Garretson, a fellow-townsman of Quaker parentage, and about whom we know at least that he was a man of impressive personal appearance. At one time he represented his country at an international exposition in Vienna. Before the formal opening he joined a number of minor European potentates in a special inspection of the exposition. In describing this royal procession the *London Times* is reported to have said that the most regal-looking man in the group was the American Commissioner Hiram — which was not so bad for a Cleveland grocer. He and his partners apparently had little difficulty in starting a business, which soon became sufficiently profitable to support them and their families. The family of Leonard Hanna had not accompanied him to Cleveland in the spring of 1852. They joined him in the fall of the same year, after the business had been well established, and moved into a substantial brick house on Prospect Street, between Granger and Cheshire streets.

The fact that Mark considered himself engaged to be married was not allowed to interfere with the more immediately necessary business of going to school. His education was continued during some four years and a half. One of the public schools which he attended was situated on Brownell Street, then called Clinton Street. Later he studied at the Central High School, which stood on the site now occupied by the Citizens' Savings and Trust Co. John D. and William Rockefeller were among his schoolmates, the former being about Mark's own age. Finally his education was finished by an attendance of a few months at the Western Reserve College. Nothing of any importance is remembered about his life during these years —

The Prospect Street Homestead in Cleveland

except the reason for the early termination of his career at college.

An interesting account of this incident is supplied by Mr. Hanna himself. In a speech delivered on the seventy-fifth anniversary of the founding of the college, June 13, 1901, he tells the story so well that his account deserves to be repeated in full. He said on that occasion, in the easy colloquial manner characteristic of his public speaking: "I am neither a student nor a scholar, and it is with diffidence I address this audience. My connection with the Western Reserve College reaches back as far as 1857. I had finished my education at the public schools, and I had a choice of going to work or attempting a college course. My mother persuaded me to try the latter. Western Reserve College at 'Hudson' was near at hand, and there I went. I entered what was called the scientific class, in which a kind-hearted professor made things easy for me. There were five members of the class when I entered it. Later the numbers dwindled to three, and when I left there was not any.

"My environment was largely responsible for my going. At my boarding house I fell in with a number of jolly sophomores, and they persuaded me to help them in getting out a burlesque program of the Junior oratoricals. In the division of labor it fell to my lot to distribute these mock programs. I well remember when the iron hand of Professor Young fell on my shoulder. 'Young man,' he said, 'what are you doing?' 'I am distributing literature and education,' I replied, 'at the expense of the Junior class.' Well, it was near the end of the term, anyway, and I went home. I told my mother I thought that I would go to work, and that I was sure the faculty would be glad of it. A little while after I met President Hitchcock on Superior Street. I was in jumper and overalls, for I was working. He asked me what I was doing, and I told him 'working.' He didn't say anything, but his eyes and manner said very eloquently that he thought I had struck the right level. And the moral of that story is, boys, 'Don't be ashamed of overalls.'"

The penalty of expulsion or even suspension looks unnecessarily severe for such a harmless joke. In order to account for it, the reader must understand the high importance of the

Junior "oratoricals" among the intellectual festivities of a year of the Western Reserve College. It was the great feature of the college term — more important even than the commencement exercises. Every member of the Junior class was expected to "oratorical"; and at the same time the collegiate honors, which were to be distributed among the class a year later, were indicated and practically announced.

Mr. Geo. H. Ford, classmate of Mark Hanna's, tells the story of the episode in the following words: "The 'affair' occurred April, 1859.[1] The Junior class of that year was unusually large and above the average in talent. In it were several Clevelanders. I remember W. W. Andrews, son of Judge Sherlock J. Andrews, as one of them, and John F. and Henry V. Hitchcock, sons of the president of the college. The faculty was justly proud of this class, but certain of its individual members had put on 'airs,' and the lower classmen resented it, Hanna among the rest. The coming 'exhibition' was looked forward to with great local interest. The program was prepared secretly, and to prevent accidents was sent to Cleveland to be printed. Hanna saw an opportunity of removing a little of their conceit, so he went to Cleveland, got on good terms with some one in the printing office, secured a proof of the program, and forwarded it to his fellow-conspirators in Hudson. A racy burlesque or sham program was prepared and returned to him, which he had printed in elegant style and sent back. I think, although I am not sure, he also managed to suppress, or get possession of the genuine programs, and to forward a bundle of the shams by express to the class on the morning of the exhibition, too late for a remedy. The shams were thoroughly distributed throughout the audience in the crowded chapel by boys enlisted by his co-conspirators."

Mr. Ford does not believe that Mark was expelled. He was merely reprimanded severely by the faculty, indefinitely suspended and his return made conditional on a promise of good behavior. He adds that Mark Hanna was easily a captain among the boys of his age in college — frank, fearless and ener-

[1] This is a mistake. Mr. Hanna could scarcely have been 21 years old when he entered college. He entered in 1857. The joke was played in 1858.

MARK HANNA AS A LAD OF EIGHTEEN

getic, full of fun and always ready to play harmless jokes on his companions. Once when a local fire company was making a blundering attempt to extinguish a fire near the college campus, he quickly collected thirty or forty boys, charged on the firemen, took the extinguisher away from them, seized the nozzle of the hose with his own hands, climbed to the roof of the house, and remained there until the fire was put out.

Obviously Mark Hanna's suspension was the occasion of his quitting college rather than the cause. After he had finished with the high school, his own preference was for an immediate plunge into business, and in going to college he was merely making a temporary concession to the wishes of his mother. He could make the concession out of respect for his mother, but at the first check his own will prevailed. His parents had allowed him a good deal of independence, and he was accustomed to act for himself. All his deeper instincts urged him to begin his career in business. The fact that he considered himself engaged to be married would alone have been sufficient to make the idea of a long college course irksome. Life itself was beckoning to him. Why potter over books, when there were real things to do?

From his own point of view he made the right decision. He would have gained little from a college training. He was never interested in books. He never learned much out of books. Even at high school his progress must have been slow, or he would have been ready for college before he was twenty years old. By disposition and training he was the true product of a pioneer society, in which an active life without any artificial preliminary discipline is the efficient life, and in which the action adopted is determined by the economic environment. Inasmuch as he was destined to be a business man, the sooner he began, the better. Experience was his one possible source of real education, and his experience could become edifying only as the result of actual experiment. While he had little ability to learn at second hand from books, he had or came to have a gift for learning from his own successes and failures, and so for adapting himself to the needs of his own career.

The business carried on by Hanna, Garretson & Co., into which Mark Hanna entered in the spring of 1858, afforded an excellent schooling for an energetic and intelligent young man. Nominally they were only wholesale grocers, but a wholesale grocery in Cleveland fifty years ago inevitably tended to become a general forwarding and commission business. Cleveland was at that time just beginning to reap the advantage of its situation on Lake Erie at the most convenient point for the control of the shipping and the trade, other than grain, of the Great Lakes. During the fifties both Wisconsin and Minnesota were beginning to be settled, and because of the Lakes many of the needs of the pioneer population of these states could be supplied most economically by water in the boats of the merchants of a conveniently situated city like Cleveland. Hanna, Garretson & Co. were apparently one of the first firms to anticipate the possibilities of this trade. They began early to extend their business into the Lake Superior region. In order to make their deliveries, they established a line of steamboats which carried passengers as well as freight, and for which return cargoes had to be found. And their return cargoes even at this early date were prophetic of the product, for which the upper Lake region was later to become conspicuous. The pioneers of Minnesota wanted to sell, not grain or hogs, but pig-copper, iron ore and salt fish. Hanna, Garretson & Co. used in this part of their business the *Manhattan*, one of the first steamboats regularly operated on the Lakes, and later the *City of Superior* and the *Northern Lights*.

Hiram Garretson spent much of his time in New Orleans, buying the sugar and molasses, which was sold to their customers in Ohio and along the Lakes, and which was still shipped to Cleveland by way of the Ohio River and canal. Leonard and Robert Hanna remained in Cleveland and took care of the selling end of the business. When Mark Hanna left college, his business experience began, as he himself says, in jumpers and overalls. He started as a general rustabout on the docks, and as a clerk in the warehouse on Mervin Street. His work was the same as that of any other young man in and about the store.

He was soon, however, given a more responsible job. He did not remain in the warehouse much longer than enough to obtain a speaking acquaintance with that aspect of the business. His first outside assignment was that of purser on one of the vessels for a season, whereby he obtained some knowledge of the Lake Superior country and the conditions of trade and transportation on the Great Lakes. Still later he went out as a salesman. The firm sold groceries in many towns in northern Ohio. It was not at that time customary to solicit business, but Mark was occasionally commissioned to start out and find customers. His brother, Leonard C. Hanna, believes him to have been one of the first commercial travellers in the United States — which is a distinction of a kind. He was no more afraid of the sample-case than he was of the overalls. All accounts agree that he was from the beginning an exceedingly successful salesman.

Although business interested the young Mark Hanna much more than books, he did not in the beginning apply himself to business with anything like the exclusive devotion which characterized the early career of his fellow-townsman and grocer, Mr. John D. Rockefeller. He was still wise, not beyond his years, but according to his years. He was not quite ready to settle down to serious work. He was more than anything else a young man who wanted to enjoy himself after the manner of other young men. He was by disposition gay, expansive and sociable. He eagerly sought and shared everything which Cleveland had to offer by way of sport and amusement. He joined the Ydrad Boat Club, of which he became captain. The club owned a long racing boat, and it used to row exciting races with its rival, the Ivanhoe Boat Club. He never cared particularly for horse-racing; but all his companions liked it, and he would join them because he did not want to be left behind. Although an enthusiastic card-player, he rather avoided poker. He was a conspicuous figure at dances and parties of all kinds, and he particularly enjoyed certain excursions to Rocky River for dinner, which he himself used to get up among his young friends of both sexes. He spent a great deal of time and money on these sports and diversions. In fact, he is said usually to have paid more than his share of the expenses, and certain members of his family assuredly thought that he was also spending more than a proper share of his time. He does not appear to have had any peculiarly intimate friendships as a young man, but he knew everybody, enjoyed general popularity and was one of the leaders among the young people of Cleveland.

Apparently his amusements interfered with his business career — at least in the opinion of some of his elders. His brother, H. M. Hanna, states that Uncle Robert used to complain about the number of Mark's social engagements, and of the consequent expense. But this was merely the unsympathetic criticism of a young man by an elder of different disposition. Mark was temporarily intoxicated with the wine of youth. If he had refused the cup, he might have made and saved more money, but he certainly would have been less of a man. The love of sport, combat and amusement was in his blood, and in giving free expression to them in his youth, he was behaving, as he always did, in a natural and a wholesome way. Be it added that his gayety was innocent in intention and harmless in its results. Both of his brothers testify that his youth was exemplary. As a young man he never even touched beer and whiskey, and he sowed no wild oats.

Soon, however, vicissitudes in the life both of his family and his country diminished his amusements and increased his responsibilities. Not long after Mark went to work his father's health began to fail. At about the same time Ohio and the North were in a ferment, first over a threat of civil war and finally by its outbreak. Suddenly Mark Hanna found himself confronted by the work and duties of a man.

The death of Leonard Hanna was the result of the accident which had been one cause of the abandonment of his professional career. The fall which he had received while mounting his horse had injured his spine. At the time the injury was supposed to be slight, and the only resulting inconvenience was a tendency to headaches. Later, however, these headaches became more frequent and more painful. They were localized at the very top of his spine, and he could obtain relief only by the application of very hot cloths to the back of his neck for hours at a time. As the headaches increased in number and severity, an operation was tried, and some of the nerves of the neck were cut. Thereafter the pains vanished, but his general health steadily declined. He died finally from the degeneration of the tissues of a part of the brain.

The illness which resulted in the death of Dr. Leonard Hanna on Dec. 15, 1862, had disqualified him for business throughout the two preceding years. During that interval

Mark Hanna gradually stepped into his father's place. He was the eldest son, and the one on whom the responsibility naturally fell. He represented the interests of his mother and brothers in the business, and practically became a partner. In fact, even before his father's death the firm was reorganized, and Mark Hanna entered it. A difference of opinion had arisen between Robert Hanna and Hiram Garretson about the conduct of the business. Garretson wanted to add to the trade of the firm a liquor department, because it was in liquor that the largest profits were to be made. Robert and Leonard Hanna refused on account of their temperance convictions. Late in 1862, as a result of this disagreement, Hiram Garretson withdrew from the firm; and on December 1 of that year the following notice was published in the *Cleveland Herald:*

Cleveland Herald, Dec. 1, 1862.
R. Hanna, L. Hanna, S. H. Baird, M. A. Hanna,
Robert Hanna & Co.
(Successors to Hanna, Garretson & Co.),
Wholesale Grocers, Forwarding and
Commission Merchants,
and Dealers in
Produce, Fish, Salt, etc., etc.
Central Exchange,
Nos. 169 and 171 River St., and Dock,
Cleveland, Ohio.
Agents for
Cleveland, Detroit and Lake Superior
Line of Steamers.

Notice. M. B. Clark and John D. Rockefeller, late of Clark, Gardner & Co., will continue the Produce Commission business under style and firm of Clark & Rockefeller, at warehouse recently occupied by Clark, Gardner & Co., Nos. 39, 41, 43 & 45 River Street.

This notice was published two weeks before the death of Dr. Leonard Hanna, so that Mark Hanna was soon the only representative of his immediate family in the partnership. Somewhat later his brother, Howard Melville, bought out the interest of S. H. Baird. Dr. Hanna bequeathed little to his family except his share of the business, and that, of course, went to his widow for the support of the home and the younger children. The boys received practically nothing from their father's estate.

The situation of the family before and after his brother's death determined Mark Hanna's behavior in respect to enlisting for the war. As a courageous, patriotic and combative young man, whose friends were going to the front, Mark would have inevitably enlisted, but he was prevented by his duty to his family. Some one had to remain in Cleveland, so as to manage his mother's interest in the grocery business. The choice lay between Mark and his younger brother, Howard Melville. They talked it over, and agreed that Mark's longer experience in the business designated him for service at home. His brother enlisted in the navy and served with honor and distinction.

At a later date Mark Hanna did serve for a short time, and he himself has given a brief account of the incident. Speaking at the camp-fire of the Grand Army of the Republic on the night of Sept. 12, 1901 (while President McKinley's life still hung in the balance), he said: "This is my first visit to a camp-fire. As you all know, I have been one of you but a short while. To the question why I did not exercise my right to be enrolled, I will say that I never supposed I was entitled to stand with the men who were veterans of four years' terrible war. I am but a four months' man. In 1861 I might have enlisted, but circumstances prevented me. My father was on a sick bed. I did the best I could. I sent a substitute. Four years later I had the honor to be drafted. We did have a brush with General Early, but that was all. For that reason I did not think I was entitled to become one of your comrades."

This account of his service is rather an under- than an overstatement of his participation in the war. He had joined a company of militia known as the Perry Light Infantry, which later became a company in the 29th regiment of the Ohio National Guard. In the spring of 1864, when the government was straining every resource to deal to the Confederacy a crushing blow, the 29th regiment of the National Guard together with a company of farmers from Dover in Cuyahoga County and a company of students from Oberlin College were mustered into the

Federal service as the 150th regiment of the Ohio Volunteer Infantry. The date of their entry into the service was May 5, and one week later it took train from Cleveland for Washington.

The Perry Light Infantry, composed mostly of young Cleveland business men, became Company C in the new volunteer regiment. It had been commanded by Capt. W. H. Hayward, who was elected colonel of the new organization. This left Company C without a captain. The first lieutenant of the Light Infantry was made captain of Company C; and when a further election was held to fill the position of first lieutenant, E. B. Thomas, who was serving as first sergeant, received a majority of the votes, although Mark Hanna, who had been second lieutenant of the Light Infantry, had a prior claim on the position. After a consultation E. B. Thomas refused to muster in as first lieutenant and was never commissioned as such. Mark Hanna served through the hundred days as first lieutenant, although he was commissioned only as second lieutenant.

The regiment was sent to Washington as a substitute for the troops which had been withdrawn from the defences of the city by General Grant in order to help him in the campaign in the Wilderness. Its members were marched out of the city and assigned to garrison duty in forts Lincoln, Thayer, Saratoga, Slocum, Bunker Hill, Slemmer, Totten and Stevens. The "brush with Early" mentioned in Mr. Hanna's speech occurred on July 10 and 11. General Early was threatening Washington, and all available troops were being rushed to the fortifications for its defence. But the attack never developed into anything dangerous; and such as it was, it did not fall upon that part of the Federal line at which Lieutenant Hanna's company was stationed. It was concentrated on Fort Stevens, which was separated from Fort Bunker Hill, where Company C was quartered, by Forts Slemmer, Totten and Slocum. Company C was not under fire.

Mark Hanna himself was not even with his regiment on the day when the Confederates made their feint at the defences of Washington. He had been assigned to return to Cleveland with the dead body of a comrade, and the "brush with Early" occurred during the time occupied by his return journey. In a letter written from Baltimore, where he was detained on the journey, he expressed lively chagrin at being absent from the only military "excitement" in which his regiment was involved.

Although the regiment saw no service worth the name, it was well drilled, and in every way thoroughly prepared for the field. The emergency which had called it out soon passed, and on August 13 it was returned safely to Cleveland after a disagreeable journey in a train of cattle cars. On August 23 it was mustered out, having served for one hundred and ten days. Jay C. Morse and George W. Chapin, later to become brothers-in-law of Mark Hanna, were sergeants in Company C, and Edward O. Wolcott, subsequently Senator of the United States from Colorado, and George K. Nash, subsequently governor of Ohio, were privates in other companies. The historian of the regiment, 'Major' Gleason, refers to Lieutenant Hanna as a "jolly, auburn-haired, freckle-faced youth," while his lieutenant-colonel, John N. Frazee, supplies the following description: "Lieutenant Hanna must have been six feet or over in height, weighing from 160 to 180 pounds; complexion fair, full-faced, with side whiskers; full-chested, square-shouldered; in fact a very manly man and thoroughly conscientious in the discharge of his duties."

At the time of his service in the fortifications of Washington, Mark Hanna was not so much interested in the defence of his country as he might have been. Or rather he was interested in something else very much more. He was at that moment head over heels in love, and just before starting for the front his love-affair had developed into a recognized engagement. To leave Cleveland at such a crisis was exasperating to a young man who had been obliged to overcome obstacles before he was accepted as suitor for the lady's hand; and during the whole of his enforced absence he was more preoccupied with the end of his service than with its duties and opportunities. As he was to be married soon after his return, he counted the days which he had still to wait, and was not happy until the orders were given for the journey back to Cleveland. His wedding did take place a few weeks after he was mustered out of the service; and we must now turn to the series of incidents which culminated in his marriage, and the no less important series of incidents which were its immediate consequences.

CHAPTER VI

MARRIAGE AND ITS RESULTS

THE lady to whom Mark Hanna was married in September, 1864, was Miss C. Augusta Rhodes. They had met at a bazaar in the spring of 1862, just after Miss Rhodes had returned from a finishing school in New York City. On that occasion Mark had won the favor both of mother and daughter by helping them out of an embarrassing situation. An acquaintance followed, and the two young people promptly fell in love with each other. Mark was an eligible suitor, and there was no good reason why an engagement should not have immediately followed. But when Miss Rhodes's father was approached, he met the suitor with a peremptory and probably an explosive negative.

Mrs. Hanna gives two reasons to account for the opposition. Her father, Mr. Daniel P. Rhodes, a coal and iron merchant and one of Cleveland's most successful business men, was a vigorous and self-willed man. Behind his opposition was apparently the instinctive repugnance which certain fathers have to the marriage of their children; but of course he had what appeared to be a better reason at the end of his tongue. He did not want his daughter to marry Mark Hanna because he did not like the young man's politics — which is not such a bad reason at a time when differences of political opinion were deluging the country with blood. Daniel P. Rhodes was a strong Democrat, and unlike many of his partisan associates in the Middle West, he was more of a Democrat than he was a unionist. Stephen A. Douglas was distantly related to him, and he had taken an intense interest in Douglas's political career. The defeat of his favorite in 1860 so embittered him that he could not forgive the Republicans, who brought it about. He used to say to the young suitor, "I like you very well, Mark, but you are a damned screecher for freedom."

The order was issued that the two young people should be

kept apart; but it was an order easier to issue than to execute. Mark was captain of the Ydrad Boat Club, and both conspicuous and ubiquitous in Cleveland society. The order to keep Miss Rhodes away from her lover was equivalent to an order for her to stay at home. She was forbidden to attend the dances given during the winter by the Boat Club, an enforced isolation which increased her unhappiness. Mark does not appear to have been absolutely forbidden the house, but his visits were discouraged, and he saw Miss Rhodes, if at all, only under surveillance.

For a long time the young suitor appeared to make no headway. Daniel Rhodes was really in earnest, and he was not the man to yield except under compulsion. In a country where the exercise of parental authority is sanctioned by public opinion the opposition might have proved fatal, but in the land of freedom a way is usually found to bend a stubborn parent to the will of his offspring. Mark Hanna was as obstinate a man as Daniel Rhodes, and he was armed with the swords both of Passion and of Righteousness. He persisted. Miss Rhodes was very unhappy. She pleaded and wept. Her health suffered. There was no telling what might happen. Daniel Rhodes had no peace at home or abroad. Finally he yielded. Before Mark started for Washington the engagement was recognized, and on Sept. 27, 1864, he was married to Miss Rhodes in St. John's Church — the groom being a little over twenty-seven years old and the bride twenty-one. The day of the ceremony Daniel Rhodes said to the triumphant groom, "It's all over now, Mark, but a month ago I would like to have seen you at the bottom of Lake Erie."

Daniel Rhodes may have consoled himself for the loss of a daughter by the idea that he had acquired a son. After the marriage he did his best to keep the young couple near him and under his thumb. When they returned from their wedding trip Mark Hanna and his wife lived for a while in the Rhodes mansion on Franklin Avenue, and more than a year elapsed before they set up an establishment of their own. Early in 1866 they moved into a small house on Prospect Street, in spite of the opposition of Mr. Rhodes; but their move towards independence was not a success. The young couple had one dif-

MARK HANNA IN 1864

ficulty after another, and in the end they were forced to submit to the will of the obstinate Mr. Rhodes.

In December, 1866, their first child was born and was named Daniel Rhodes Hanna, after the dominant father-in-law. A few months later Mark Hanna was seized with an acute attack of typhoid fever — the malady which was subsequently to cause his death. He was desperately sick, but being young and strong, he pulled through. While he was still struggling against the depressing after effects of his illness, he met with business reverses. Robert Hanna and Co. had built a new boat, the *Lac la Belle*, which is said to have been the best vessel on the Lakes. It appears that Mark Hanna had an individual interest in her as well as his share of the firm's interest. After only a short period of service she collided with another boat in the Detroit River, and went to the bottom — a total loss.

Nor was this all. Soon after his marriage Mark Hanna had started a petroleum refinery. It was a new industry. The buildings were small and the business uncertain. Insurance companies looked askance at the risk. According to his daughter's account Daniel Rhodes was violently opposed to his son-in-law's enterprise, not merely because he did not like the precariousness of the venture, but because he wanted Mark Hanna to join him in the coal and iron business. Every time he heard the fire bells he would say: "There! I suppose Mark's damned oil refinery is burning down." His constant repetition of this remark finally became a family joke. But one day it did burn down, and at that time Mark Hanna, while he was up and about after his attack of typhoid, was still far from well. He did not get home until two o'clock in the morning. When he came in, he said: "Well, I have got to the bottom. The boat is sunk, the refinery is burnt and worse still, my health is gone. If I were well, I would not be discouraged. As it is, I don't know what will become of us." Early the next morning Daniel Rhodes turned up at the house on Prospect Street, walked in and greeted the happy pair with the admonition: "Now, I guess you two young fools will be good and come home." They meekly acquiesced, and that very day they returned to the Rhodes house on Franklin Avenue. The father-in-law stood by, while they packed up, and consoled the young man with the

E

reiterated remark, "Your money is all gone, Mark, and I am damned glad of it." For the moment there was no fight left in Mark. It was arranged that Mr. and Mrs. Rhodes were to go abroad, Mr. and Mrs. Hanna were to keep house in Franklin Avenue, and at the same time make a home for Mrs. Hanna's brother, Robert R. Rhodes.

The new domestic arrangement involved also a new start in business for Mark Hanna. Daniel Rhodes wanted to retire. The old firm of Rhodes, Card & Co. was dissolved. Jonathan F. Card withdrew as well as Daniel Rhodes, and a wholly new firm, to be called Rhodes & Co., was to take their place. The members of this firm were George H. Warmington, M. A. Hanna and Robert R. Rhodes, the brother of Mrs. Hanna. Rhodes & Co. started business in April, 1867, and so began Mark Hanna's connection with the coal and iron industry, which was to last throughout his life.

The organization of the copartnership of Rhodes & Co. involved the withdrawal of Mark Hanna from the firm of Robert Hanna & Co., but it is improbable that Mark had many regrets on that score. The Hanna firm had been strengthened after the war by the accession of Howard Melville, Mark's brother; and apparently the younger men did not get on very well with their uncle. He is described as a large, heavy man with good business judgment, and an excellent salesman, but lacking in energy and enterprise. After his marriage Mark had begun to take business in earnest. He wanted to expand their trade rapidly, introduce a more vigorous campaign for the sale of stock, and improve their methods and machinery all along the line. His plans were continually being thwarted by his uncle, who, as the elder man, was naturally conservative. There were many disagreements. The partnership would probably not in any event have endured very long, and if Mark Hanna had continued to be a grocer, he would either have controlled the business or started a competitive firm. As it was, he withdrew at the time of the formation of Rhodes & Co., and later in the same year the business was wound up and the stock sold to a competitor.

Although Mark Hanna probably felt little reluctance in terminating his partnership with his uncle, he had not been by any means eager to enter the firm which was to take over his father-in-law's business. Not only was the coal and iron trade an unfamiliar country to him, but he was loath to abandon his petroleum refinery. He believed that large profits were to be made in oil, and as the event proved, he was right. But in addition to reasons connected with the nature of the businesses he abandoned and was asked to undertake, personal issues were involved. His father-in-law had opposed his marriage, and in the beginning had scoffed at his business ability. He would much have preferred to keep his independence and make good without his father-in-law's assistance. Had he not met with a series of reverses, he would in all probability have continued to operate the oil refinery, with the result of profoundly modifying his subsequent business career.

As it was, Mr. Rhodes seems to have offered his son-in-law very considerable inducements to enter the firm of Rhodes & Co. He had come to have much more respect for the young man's business ability, and Mark entered the firm under most advantageous conditions. The refinery, which was rebuilt, and in which Mark's mother had a substantial interest, was sold later in 1867 to his brother, Howard Melville. Mr. Hanna ran the business in partnership with his brother-in-law, Geo. W. Chapin, under the name of Hanna & Chapin. A couple of years later it was sold on advantageous terms to the Standard Oil Company.

How his subsequent business career would have been modified, in case he had become an ally of the Rockefellers, is mere speculation, but it is a kind of speculation too tempting to ignore. A man of Mr. Hanna's energy and business ability could hardly have joined the forces of the Standard Oil Company without becoming conspicuous in its management; and every man prominently identified with that company was induced by the consequent opportunities of money-making and by the nature of the business to leave his native town and go to New York. Mark Hanna might well have done the same, and if so, his subsequent political career would have become impossible. He would have made more money, but he would have broken the local ties which enabled him to develop from a business man into a political leader. The Standard Oil Company proved to be the most generous paymaster in the business history of the United States, if not of the world, but it demanded of its beneficiaries the rupture of local associations and the sacrifice of extraneous ambitions.

All unconsciously Mark Hanna escaped the danger, if danger it was, of becoming too rich, and on April 1, 1867, he made a new start on what proved to be his ultimate business career. At that time he was, according to the statement of his brother-in-law and temporary partner, Mr. Robert R. Rhodes, worth some thousands of dollars less than nothing. He had gained little from the first nine years of his business life except experience. He had ignored the rule laid down by Mr. John D. Rockefeller as constituting the sure road to business success. He had not pinched and saved, and devoted himself exclusively to his work. He was human enough to want a good time while he was young, and he had not scrupled to take it. In the meanwhile he had been seeking business success, as a young man naturally would, by the road of new enterprises, such as the oil refinery and the *Lac la Belle*. The subsequent history of the oil and the lake shipping industries prove that in making these ventures, his business judgment was sound. But his luck was not as good as his judgment, and his business strategy provided no method of retreat. When his boat and his refinery were consumed by the elements, which they were intended to exploit, he had no reserve capital with which to repair his losses. The Rockefeller rule would have insured him against such a calamity, but fortunately he had saved something better than an insurance fund. He had saved his youth, and he kept his youth with him.

In 1867, however, he was thirty years old. If he was still to be wise according to his years, he no longer had the same excuse for vagrancy. He was happily married. His children were being born. His father-in-law believed in him and had given him an interest in a well-established and prosperous business. He felt the need of making good. For the first time his energies were absorbed by his career. He began to put *himself* into his work. Notwithstanding the fact that one of his partners was his elder in years and his superior in experience and that the other was the son of the founder of the business, Mark Hanna rapidly became the leading member of the firm. The will to succeed in any enterprise which he undertook and to dominate any group of men with whom he was associated lay deep in his disposition. It now began to receive a persistent and effective expression. During the next twenty-seven years he was more than anything else a man of business. He labored unceasingly and efficiently to build up Rhodes & Co., until under the name of M. A. Hanna & Co. it became a highly individual business organization and one of the two or three largest firms in the coal and iron trade of the Ohio lake district.

CHAPTER VII

BUSINESS LIFE IN CLEVELAND

In Mr. Robert R. Rhodes's statement describing his business relations with Mark Hanna and the latter's business characteristics, Mr. Rhodes has explained in the following words the success of Rhodes & Co.: "Mark Hanna was a shrewd man. Much of the credit for the prosperity of Rhodes & Co. must attach to his individual efforts. But my idea about the success of the firm, aside from Mr. Hanna's personal contribution to it, is that we took over the business at an opportune time. Economic conditions offered us unusual opportunities for growth. We started at the right moment." It is essential, consequently, to an understanding of Mark Hanna's business career that some account be given of the economic conditions and opportunities, which confronted Cleveland business men in the decade or two immediately succeeding the war.

When Dr. Leonard Hanna moved to Cleveland in 1852, it was a small but thriving city, containing a little over 20,000 inhabitants. Its rapid growth had been due to its situation on Lake Erie at the northern terminus of the Ohio Canal. Produce of all kinds, originating not merely in Ohio, but along the Ohio and Mississippi rivers, were shipped by river and canal to Cleveland, which became an important distributing and collecting agency for the district reached by the Great Lakes. Agricultural staples were sent to the terminus of the Erie Canal at Buffalo — either for Eastern consumption or for export. The pioneer settlements in the Northwest were supplied with the few necessaries they could afford to purchase, and their products were carried to markets farther east. Its business, consequently, was commercial rather than industrial, and depended for its growth chiefly upon the increasing importance of the Great Lakes in the American system of transportation.

During the fifties the volume of lake commerce increased by leaps and bounds, chiefly because of the rapid settlement of the region in the Northwest tributary to the Great Lakes. The population of Cleveland more than doubled during the decade, and its industry and commerce not only throve, but became much more diversified. Nevertheless, even in 1860 its population was less than one-fourth that of Cincinnati, and the conditions which account for its present place in the national commercial system were barely beginning to be conspicuous. The great trade routes still lay along the navigable rivers like the Ohio and Mississippi, and the combination of lake and railroad transportation, which was to constitute the backbone of American domestic commerce, had not yet been formed.

The Civil War accelerated the predestined change in commercial routes. Navigation of the Mississippi, except for military purposes, suddenly ceased. The bond between the South and the agricultural states of the Middle and Northwest was cut. The tide of commerce began running east and west. The railroads and the Lakes took the place of the rivers and the canals. Chicago as the distributing and collecting centre for the rapidly growing states tributary to the head waters of the Mississippi and Missouri leaped into its position as the leading commercial and industrial city of its own region. Its enormous increase in population and business was due chiefly to the benefit which it obtained from the agricultural development of the West and the Northwest — a benefit dependent more upon its railroad connections than its situation on Lake Michigan, but partly on both.

Cleveland had little to gain, except indirectly, from the increase in the grain trade and the new course it was taking; and it had less to gain than had Chicago from the growing importance of railroad transportation. Its peculiar place in American domestic commerce depended upon its central and convenient location on the Lakes. It needed the railroads chiefly as supplementary to water routes. Its great opportunity came when the industrial expansion of the Middle West created a demand for crude manufacturing materials, adapted to transportation in bulk. Its merchants assembled the basic materials necessary to the industrial life of the Middle West. They brought coal from the mines in Ohio and western Pennsylvania, and sold it in the different markets on or near the Lakes. They transported the iron ore and pig copper which was already being produced in considerable quantities in the upper Lake region to the furnaces and factories south and southeast of Lake Erie. They built the vessels needed for this constantly increasing commerce. Ship building gradually became their most important single industry, but this complicated branch of manufacturing brought many subordinate industries with it. Cleveland has always been remarkable for the diversity of its manufacturing interests and the wholesome balance of its economic life.

When Mark Hanna entered the firm of Rhodes & Co. in 1867, the commercial and industrial revolution roughly sketched above was still in its infancy. The Middle West, and particularly the state of Ohio, had passed out of its period of pioneer agriculture, but it was just beginning its period of industrial pioneering. Of course many experiments had already been made, and many local industries had already been founded. But these industries had depended upon means of transportation which were now being superseded, and consequently the conditions of industrial success in the Middle West were being turned upside down. A piece of industrial and commercial patch-work had to be converted to an organic system, not only well articulated within, but properly adapted to the national economic system. It was a world of industry and commerce in the making, and offered extraordinary opportunities to an enterprising, aggressive, energetic, quick-witted, flexible and indomitable man.

The business which Rhodes & Co. took over from Rhodes, Card & Co. was well established, but its development was only embryonic. The bulk of its business consisted in the mining and selling of coal, — an industry with which Daniel P. Rhodes had been associated from the start. As early as 1845 the Brierhill mine, near Youngstown, Ohio, had been opened up by Mr. Rhodes and David Tod. Their output was some fifty tons of bituminous coal a week, which was gradually increased and which was brought to Cleveland by canal until 1856, when the completion of the Cleveland and Mahoning Railroad gave the trade a great impetus. Soon after, the opening of the Cleveland and Pittsburg Railroad made the coal-fields of Columbiana

MARK HANNA ABOUT 1871

County accessible; and in 1860 the great Massillon district, with which Mr. Hanna's firm became closely identified, was opened for production. By 1867 the railroad, steamboat and manufacturing industries in and about Cleveland were already justifying the shipment of some 600,000 or 700,000 tons of coal a year to that market.

While the mining and sale of their own coal constituted a considerable part of the initial business of Rhodes & Co. in 1867, it by no means constituted the whole of it. The firm also owned a furnace and some iron properties at Canal Dover in the Tuscawaras district; and it sold its own pig-iron and its own ore. Furthermore it carried on a considerable commission business in all these products, and it was on the whole more interested in the selling than it was in the operating aspect of its several-sided business. Under the management of Mr. Hanna and his new partners it did not change in that respect. Indeed little by little it became more than ever a commission business. Whenever either the firm or its individual members became interested in the production of coal, of iron ore or of pig-iron it was chiefly for the purpose of securing material which could be sold by Rhodes & Co.

The kind of business described above was admirably adapted to the peculiar business abilities of Mark Hanna. He was not the man to work patiently and persistently in building up stone by stone the structure of a particular industry. He liked diversity of occupation and work, constant movement and the excitement of new undertakings. The business of Rhodes & Co. developed, consequently, not along any one line, but along many lines. It became fundamentally a selling agency for a variety of products; and as a selling agency it could transact a much larger business on a certain amount of capital than it could if it were handling only the output of its iron furnaces or mines.

At the same time every possible precaution was taken to provide against the dangers to which a mere commission business was exposed — the danger of losing control of the product sold. In order to become certain of being able to handle as agent large quantities of coal, iron ore and pig-iron, Rhodes & Co., either as a firm or by the action of its individual members, extended widely its interests in mines, furnaces and later in means of transportation. It did not always own a mine or a furnace outright, but an interest in many such enterprises was purchased — always with the understanding that the product should be sold through Rhodes & Co. This method of creating business for Rhodes & Co. as a selling agency became more and more an essential part of the policy of the firm.

During the days of Robert Hanna & Co., Mark Hanna had, as we have seen, been much interested in the Lake Superior ore country. After the dissolution of the firm his brother, Howard Melville Hanna, continued to conduct a forwarding and commission business in the products and supplies of that district. It was natural, consequently, for Mark Hanna to extend the business of Rhodes & Co. into such a familiar region. He added to the connections of the firm a number of iron mines in the Northwest; and little by little he obtained control of the sale of most of the charcoal iron produced in the district. This innovation made an essential change in the scope and the balance of the firm's business. Its interests, instead of being confined almost exclusively to Ohio, were established in a strong position on the great highway of American domestic commerce.

The extension into the Lake Superior district was immediately followed by another development in the firm's business, which also naturally followed from Mark Hanna's early experience. The connection built up with the Lake Superior district soon involved the firm in the transportation as well as the sale of iron ore and coal. Rhodes & Co., or its partners individually, acquired interests in every aspect of the handling and the transport of the products, which they sold on commission.

No other extension of the business of the firm did so much as did its early interest in lake transportation to fortify its position and enable it to reap the full advantage of its opportunities. The place of Cleveland in the economic system of the Middle West was, as I have said, primarily commercial. It was excellently situated for the handling, the collection and the distribution of the basic materials of industrial production, but its situation placed it at a disadvantage in shipping finished products to the markets either in the East or the West. Its manufactures have, indeed, always been diversified and thrifty; and the Cleveland Rolling Mills Company was early one of the most progressive and prosperous manufacturers of finished steel products in the United States. But as a producer of steel the Cleveland district has never competed except in a small way with Chicago or the Pittsburgh district. Consequently in obtaining an interest so early in the sale, the transport and the handling of the basic materials necessary to the iron and steel industries, Rhodes & Co. established themselves under Mark Hanna's direction near the heart of Cleveland's growth and prosperity.

The extension of the business of Rhodes & Co. mentioned above was effected soon after Mark Hanna's entrance into the firm. Before 1870 a regular iron ore transport service was established, in which were interested, not only Rhodes & Co., but the three partners individually and Howard Melville Hanna. For many years Melville Hanna was associated with his brother in many ship-operating and ship-building enterprises, although this association did not include the other branches of Mark Hanna's business. Melville Hanna was an expert in both the technical and the commercial aspects of lake transportation and his coöperation was invaluable.

Another useful associate in his early venture in the transportation of iron ore was the Cleveland Iron Mining Company. This corporation was one of the largest shippers of ore in the Lake Superior district. A contract was made with the company for the transportation of its ore for three years, and on the strength of this contract four steamers and four tows were built and operated. Each of the several partners of Rhodes & Co., except, perhaps, Mr. Warmington, also owned and operated vessels for his individual benefit. One ship, owned by Mark Hanna and his brother, was named *Leonard Hanna* after their father. Eventually the Cleveland Transportation Company was organized to conduct this branch of the business, and later still the early association was dissolved and the Orient Transportation Company was formed, which assumed ownership, not only of all the original fleet, but of a number of new vessels.

In the meantime the other aspects of the business were not being neglected. Under modern conditions water transportation is only to a very small extent independent of transportation by rail. It was just as essential for a firm like Rhodes & Co. to have advantageous connections with railroads as it was to control mines and vessels, for almost all of the materials it produced, manufactured, sold on commission or carried by water was handled by a railroad at some point of its transfer from the mines or furnaces to the consumer. The Pennsylvania Railroad Company was inevitably the corporation with which Rhodes & Co. had most reason to be closely associated. It was the company which owns the roadway leading from the firm's mines to Lake Erie. It was the only company which at that time could convey the ore brought by boat from Lake Superior to the furnaces of western Pennsylvania. Close relations were consequently established with this railroad early in the seventies, and they have continued until the present day. The firms of Rhodes & Co.[1] and M. A. Hanna & Co. have always been known as Pennsylvania Railroad shippers. Of course, their business was not exclusively transacted with that company, but it was their first choice. The firm in which Mr. Hanna was a partner has always stood for the Pennsylvania interest on the south shore of Lake Erie. Mark Hanna himself became a director both of the Cleveland and Pittsburg Railroad, (one of the Pennsylvania's leased lines) and later of the Pittsburg, Fort Wayne and Chicago.

His firm profited very much from this connection. It leased the docks of the Pennsylvania Railroad Company at Ashtabula on the south shore of Lake Erie about sixty miles east of Cleveland, and much of the ore shipped from the Lake Superior dis-

[1] The firm continued to conduct its business under the name of Rhodes & Co. until 1885, but in the meantime Mr. Hanna's interest in it was constantly being increased. In 1875 Leonard Colton Hanna, Mark's youngest brother, entered the firm; and at about the same time it was joined by James Ford Rhodes, another son of Daniel P. Rhodes, and subsequently the historian of the United States from the Compromise of 1850. In the meantime Mr. Robert R. Rhodes and Mr. Warmington retired, and in 1885 Mr. James Ford Rhodes also withdrew. Thereafter the Rhodes interest was eliminated, and the firm name became M. A. Hanna & Co. Mr. A. C. Saunders was at one time admitted to partnership, and at a considerably later date, but during his father's life Mr. Daniel Rhodes Hanna entered the firm.

trict to western Pennsylvania was handled by these docks and carried to Pittsburgh by the Pennsylvania Railroad Company. The docks were equipped with ore-handling machinery by Rhodes & Co., and they transacted a very large business. In accordance with its usual policy of participating in the ownership as well as in the handling of the products it sold, a furnace was bought in 1879 at Sharpsville, Pennsylvania. At a later date M. A. Hanna & Co. also leased and equipped the Pennsylvania docks both at Cleveland and at Erie.

The vessels owned and operated by the Cleveland Transportation Company were, of course, built of wood, and their tonnage was comparatively small. Vessels carrying twelve or eighteen hundred tons were considered to be good-sized ships. It was Melville rather than Mark Hanna who first reached the conclusion that larger vessels should be built, and steel substituted for wood. Before acting on the conclusion he investigated the matter for two years, and employed experts to help him in testing the practicability of steel vessels from every essential point of view. When he was wholly convinced, Melville and Mark Hanna and J. F. Pankhurst bought the Globe Ship Building Company, and the keel of the first steel vessel to be navigated on the Great Lakes was soon laid. Her name was the *Cambria*, and she carried twenty-six or twenty-seven hundred gross tons. The *Corsica, Coronia* and *Coralia*, which were slightly larger, and which together with the *Cambria* were furnished for the first time with triple expansion engines, soon followed. These vessels were specially equipped for the economical transportation and handling of iron ore, and they were a success from the very start. They were, however, so much of a success that they immediately provoked extensive imitation and improvement. The Globe Company obtained orders for twelve steel vessels in one year, and the transportation methods on the Great Lakes were revolutionized.

Thus a very complicated and diversified business was gradually built up; but diversified as it was, its several parts were carefully adjusted and tied together. Its core was the copartnership of Rhodes & Co., and later of M. A. Hanna & Co., and the essential purpose of all the separate enterprises was to create an abundant business for the firm as commission merchants. To this end alliances were established covering every aspect of the production, the handling and transportation of the coal, iron ore and pig-iron. The firm itself owned coal mines in the several bituminous districts in Ohio. Its individual partners also owned mines. In other cases merely an interest had been purchased in mines operated independently. In still other cases the coal of wholly independent operators was bought outright and sold. Most of this coal was placed on the market in Cleveland, and a large part of it was carried up the Lakes in steamers owned in part by members of the firm as individuals. The same methods were repeated in the iron ore district. Iron mines were owned both by the firm, by its individual members and by outsiders to whom capital had been advanced. The firm profited from the sale of their ore, and frequently from its handling and transportation, while at the same time it transported and sold large quantities of ore for other producers.

The volume and the diversity of the business was a great help to its economic and efficient transaction. Vessels which carried iron ore down the Lakes could carry coal back. The alliance with the Pennsylvania Railroad Company was of great assistance to the selling end of the business. The large quantities of materials sold justified the development of one of the ablest sales-organizations in the country. The firm had unsurpassed opportunities of keeping in touch with every aspect of the coal and iron business and of making both its purchases and its sales to the best advantage. Finally it always consumed a certain part of the raw materials it produced or sold, and it possessed in this way a safety valve for its business. It could either sell the raw material or convert it according to the comparative opportunities of profit. A large and increasing part of the business of the firm consisted of mining its own coal and ore, transporting them in its own boats, unloading them on docks which it leases and operates, and (sometimes) smelting the ore in its own furnaces. Pig-iron, however, was its most finished product. The firm never went into the manufacture of steel, although certain of its members entered the directorate of steel-producing companies — partly in order to secure business for the copartnership.

An organization of this kind is rare, if not unique, in the history of American business. Essentially it consisted of a partnership, which constituted the nucleus of a widely ramified system of corporate and firm properties, individual properties, and personal and corporate alliances. Throughout the territory embraced by the operations of the firm, all the roads led back to the partnership itself, which gathered toll from the crossing of every bridge, the passage of every turnpike, and the safe arrival at every destination. Yet these tolls were cheerfully paid, because the firm always served its customers fairly and efficiently, and because its policy was never either grasping or disloyal. The organization has the appearance of being perilously complicated, of being dependent upon too many fluctuating conditions, and upon too many merely personal alliances. But as a matter of fact, it has stood excellently the test of long and hard wear. For over forty years, during which time the conditions of its business have been radically changed, the firm has succeeded, not merely in holding its own, but in using these very changes to make its own position stronger.

Particularly during the last thirteen years conditions in the coal and iron industry have not been favorable to commission merchants. The tendency has been to do away with the middleman, and to organize under one ownership every phase of the process of converting iron ore into finished steel products; but in spite of this tendency the organization of the firm was such that it could be adapted to the new conditions. Its alliances were strengthened by increasing the range and amount of its ownership in the products it sold; and its own business became to an even larger extent a matter of selling its own pig-iron rather than the basic materials thereof. To be sure, this development took place largely after M. A. Hanna had retired from active business; but his successors were able to meet effectively the new situation as it developed, partly because Mr. Hanna had established the business on sound foundations and made it both a tough and a flexible instrument.

The salient fact, consequently, about the organization developed by Mr. Hanna was its peculiar personal character. Although transacting a volume of business very much larger than that of many big corporations, and although it has formed many corporations for the purpose of owning particular branches of its business, it has remained essentially a copartnership. A corporate organization demands impersonality of methods and policy. It is most effective when its operations can become automatic and be reduced to rule. But the business of M. A. Hanna & Co. was the creation of sound and enterprising individual management; and it has continued to demand management of this kind. Mark Hanna made it personal; and personal it has remained. It was successful under his management, because of the excellence of his judgment, the soundness of his policy and the absolute personal confidence which he inspired among his associates. It has continued to be prosperous under his successors, because they were able to bring similar qualities to its direction. Although it is twenty-five years since Mark Hanna was actively connected with the business which bears his name, his personality still lives in it and determines the forms of its activity.

CHAPTER VIII

MISCELLANEOUS BUSINESS INTERESTS

In the account given of the business which Mr. Hanna and his partners gradually built up, no attention has been paid to other contemporaneous business interests. This particular aspect of his life has a unity of its own and can best be treated independently both of his political career and his miscellaneous business engagements. The coal and iron selling agency constituted, of course, the foundation of his business structure. Until 1894 it consumed most of his time and energy. Throughout his life it provided him with his sinews of war. It made him a wealthy man, and he needed the power which only wealth can give. But important as it was in his life, and clearly as the quality of the man was expressed in the contribution he made to the success of the firm, the actual sequence of events in his business career is for the most part irrelevant to the main current of his life.

From 1867 until 1880 he appears to have devoted practically all his time to coal and iron. The first six of these years were consumed in making himself a master of the business and in broadening its basis. The next five years constituted a period of general trade depression, during which Mr. Hanna had to struggle in order to maintain the ground which had already been won. But late in the seventies business revived, and Rhodes & Co. began to reap the reward which a period of active trade brings to a well-established and well-managed business. Mr. Hanna found himself possessed of means, which enabled him to undertake a number of other enterprises of some importance. He had become, indeed, one of the most conspicuous and prosperous of Cleveland business men, whose coöperation was usually expected in matters of local business importance.

The first of these miscellaneous ventures was nothing less than a plunge into the newspaper business; and as the incident had a certain bearing on Mr. Hanna's subsequent political career, it must be told in some detail. His interest in the matter originated in an attempt made by certain friends and associates to give renewed life to an old, well-established, but decayed local journal. At one time the Cleveland *Herald* had been the most influential organ of the Republican party in northern Ohio, and the only prosperous newspaper in the city of Cleveland. But owing to the death of one of its owners and the bad management of the remaining partner, both its circulation and its prestige fell away. In the meantime the Cleveland *Leader*, which was edited and for the most part owned by Edwin Cowles, was gradually taking its place. Later the *Herald* was bought by Richard C. Parsons and William Perry Fogg. Colonel Parsons, a former Congressional representative, a politician of considerable influence, and a cultured and able man, became its editor; and Mr. Fogg, a dealer in crockery, took charge of the business management. They put both additional capital and energy into the *Herald* and made it a good newspaper, but all to no purpose. They could not either shake the standing of the *Leader* or restore the *Herald* to its former position. The new owners could not stand the strain. Their losses threatened to ruin them, and they had to sell out.

William Perry Fogg retired, and Colonel Parsons persuaded a number of prominent men in Cleveland to come to his assistance. The new owners of the paper were a syndicate consisting of J. H. Wade, who laid the foundation of the Western Union Telegraph system; Henry Chisholm, the founder of the Cleveland Rolling Mill Company, the great local steel works; John D. Rockefeller and H. M. Flagler; Amasa Stone, the father-in-law of John Hay; S. T. Everett, Dan P. Eels, a banker, Elias Sims, one of the owners of the West Side Street Railway and Mark Hanna. An abler and more successful group of business men would have been hard to find in Cleveland or elsewhere, but they were failures as the publishers of a newspaper. The *Leader* continued to prosper and the *Herald* to lose money. Finally the weary millionnaires refused to pay any more assessments. Colonel Parsons retired for good, and the property passed into the control of Mr. Hanna and a few associates, with the former as president of the company. The new management, which took control early in 1880, immediately made an ingenious and vigorous attempt to rehabilitate the property and at the same time to crush its competitor. Every editor and reporter employed by the *Leader* who was supposed to be contributing to its success, was taken over by the *Herald* on the theory that the man behind the gun rather than the captain of the ship won its battles. The new staff are said to have boasted that they would do for the *Herald* what they thought they had already done for the *Leader*. In the meantime, certain former employees of the *Herald* went over to the *Leader*, — one of them being Mr. James B. Morrow, who subsequently became the editor of that paper.

Mr. Edwin Cowles, editor and owner of the *Leader*, bitterly resented both the way in which the new management of the *Herald* began its attack and the boasts of his former staff. He was a journalist after the manner of Horace Greeley — a blind partisan, a bitter and abusive controversialist, but a man of ability and weight. He regarded the desertion of his former staff as base treachery, and he had no scruples about allowing his personal grievances to dominate the editorial policy of his paper. The *Herald*, and Mark Hanna as its financial backer, became the object of a copious stream of vituperation and ridicule.

Throughout the next five years, Mr. Cowles used every available opportunity of making the publishing business disagreeable for Mr. Hanna. The abuse was coarse and clumsy. The editorial staff of the *Herald* was referred to as "Mark Hanna and his gang," and his management of the paper was described as "the reign of Marcus Aurelius." Neither did Mr. Cowles confine himself to editorial assaults. Mr. Hanna was becoming conspicuous in local politics, and was interested in candidates for local offices. Wherever such an interest became manifest, Mr. Hanna's candidate could always count on the opposition of the *Leader;* and when Mr. Hanna tried to get himself elected delegate to the Republican Convention of 1884, Mr. Cowles became an opposing candidate and beat him at the primaries. To a man like Edwin Cowles every fight was a personal fight, and all methods were fair in war.

To these attacks Mr. Hanna never replied in kind, and he

was probably very much surprised at the hornet's nest which he had stirred up. Of course the *Herald* announced its contempt for the *Leader* with the politeness characteristic of American journalism of that period; but its owner avoided anything like a personal squabble. The *Herald* was a side-issue with him. He never gave very much attention or time to its management, and even the brilliant bit of strategy with which he began the campaign indicated an intention of disposing of the enemy by a *grand coup* rather than by hard and patient personal work. The *grand coup* failed. Mr. Cowles was, according to the standard of the day, an able journalist; and he was an angry man, fighting with his back to the wall for all that he had in the world. At that time there was room in Cleveland for only one prosperous Republican morning newspaper. Not unnaturally the survivor proved to be the *Leader*.

In March, 1885, Mark Hanna decided to quit. His newspaper enterprise had cost him a good deal of money, and he had not even enjoyed a good time in the spending of it. The name of the *Herald*, its good-will and its subscription list were sold to the *Leader* for $80,000. Its plant and visible property found a purchaser in the *Plain-Dealer*. The *Leader* celebrated its victory in an editorial article, which described its defeated competitor as an able and a fair antagonist — a fact which no one could have suspected from a perusal of the *Leader's* pages a few weeks earlier.

Thereafter the *Leader* ceased its personal attacks on Mr. Hanna; but in the opinion of men who watched the whole affair, these attacks had something to do with the establishment of a false impression of Mr. Hanna's personality in the minds of many of his fellow-townsmen. In the succeeding years he became more and more conspicuous in local business and politics, and the kind of attack which a Republican newspaper had begun was continued, although with less persistence, by Democrats. The *Plain-Dealer* referred to him, sometimes obscurely and sometimes overtly, as a "Boss" and as an aggressive and a greedy man. The *Press*, an afternoon newspaper, which was seeking to attract popular attention by assaults on conspicuous citizens, took for a while a corresponding line of comment. He was pictured as overbearing, grasping and as indifferent to the rights of others. An attempt was made to prejudice popular opinion against him by representing him as hostile to the business prosperity of Cleveland. The lease, assumed by M. A. Hanna & Co., of the docks of the Pennsylvania Railroad Company, at Ashtabula was cited as a nefarious attempt to divert commerce from Cleveland and to snatch the bread out of the mouths of its working-men. Such misrepresentations continued for many years and contributed to establish locally a distorted popular impression of Mr. Hanna long before he became a national political leader.

Mark Hanna was as far as possible from being a callous man. His expansive and sociable disposition, and the strong ties which bound him to his own city and people, made him extremely susceptible to the injustice of this personal misrepresentation. But he had too much good sense to wince in public or to indulge in personal recriminations. He was a fighter by nature, and whenever he saw a good chance of replying to a specific case of misrepresentation, he always took it, but for the most part he bore it with silence, if not with indifference.

In assuming the management of the *Herald*, Mark Hanna had no ulterior purpose. He did not attempt to make his unprofitable newspaper pay by using it to advance his other business interests. Mr. J. H. A. Bone, who was managing-editor of the *Herald*, when it was sold to the *Leader*, stated that Mr. Hanna never meddled with the editorial department and rarely came to the office. Street railway questions were more or less discussed in the City Council, and Mark Hanna was even then the practical owner of a street railway, but he never asked the *Herald* to take one side or the other. When Mr. Bone was in doubt about the attitude which the paper should assume in reference to some political matter of importance, he sometimes consulted Mr. Hanna; but he declares emphatically that his employer never made any attempt to convert the *Herald* into a personal organ or into the covert promoter of his own private interests. He was a Republican, and the *Herald* was a Republican newspaper. Beyond that he had no personal political policy.

Mr. Hanna's connection with the Cleveland *Herald*, incidental as it was in his business life, constituted in a sense the beginning of his public career. It was the first evidence, that is, of his assumption of a certain importance in the public affairs of Cleveland. His personal force was making itself felt beyond the limits of his immediate business associations; and the very misrepresentations which were coincident with the beginning of his public life were an indirect tribute to the salience of his personality. From the outset he took a strong line of his own and by his methods in pushing along this line he both aroused enmities and conquered friends. Particularly during his early career he did not attempt to conciliate opposition. He made straight for his goal, and if any one stood in his way, the obstacle was usually and often roughly shoved aside.

The characteristic of making hard and straight for a goal could easily be confused with a domineering disposition. Such a confusion took place in Mr. Hanna's case and is responsible for the accusations of being a "Boss" which were levelled at him almost from the start. But the impulse to dominate and to succeed is very different from the impulse to domineer. He always wanted power. He always wanted to place himself at the head of his associates in the prosecution of any joint enterprise. He was sometimes intolerant of opposition, impatient with meddlers and procrastinators, brusque in manner and explosive in speech. Men who later became his friends and allies were repulsed by their first superficial acquaintance with him. But he was never a domineering man. His leadership was always founded on personal energy and efficiency, and on his ability to make other people believe in him; and as men knew better they believed in him and trusted him the more. His work and his methods were such that he was bound to create enmities; but his enemies could not accuse him of injustice any more than his friends could complain of lack of consideration. He always played fair, even if he did not always play politely; and when he sat in a game he usually won, and he usually occupied or came to occupy a seat at the head of the table.

In 1884 Mark Hanna started another outside enterprise, which was destined to be more successful than his excursion into the field of publishing. He organized the Union

National Bank, of which he became president, Sylvester T. Everett, vice-president, and Mr. E. H. Bourne, cashier. He remained its president until his death, and for a number of years he gave to it a great deal of personal attention. In fact he did more than any other one man to establish it and build up its "clientele." Mr. Bourne, who succeeded him in the presidency of the institution, testifies to the energy and ingenuity he showed in securing valuable accounts, in selecting proper assistants and in organizing the business.

After the bank had been thoroughly established, and he had gained confidence in its organization and officers, he ceased to give much time to its affairs. Nevertheless he long retained an active participation in its management. Mr. Bourne states that he continually went to Mr. Hanna for advice and that he never withdrew disappointed either in his reception or in the kind of counsel he received. His behavior as a bank president is described by Mr. Bourne in the following words: "He was earnest and decided if he thought he was right, and would persist in his opinion. But if upon argument he was convinced he was wrong, he was always willing to change his opinion. However, you always had to convert him with facts. I never saw a man who was so determined to carry out anything he thought was right and who was so willing to change his position when he found he was wrong; and he was just as firm and cordial after he changed as he was before. His judgment was usually reached very quickly, for he was an economizer of time and after that only unimpeachable facts could move him. He was one of the hardest workers I ever knew and was invariably clear, frank, honest and fearless in his conduct and conversation."

In an article on Mark Hanna published in *McClure's Magazine* in November, 1900, Mr. William Allen White inserted the following passage: "In the early eighties — apparently by way of diversion or because Satan finds some evil work for idle hands to do — when the coal, iron ore, pig-iron, steel, shipping, railway, and theatrical business became a nerve-racking monopoly, Hanna started a bank." The implication of this passage is that the bank was started, chiefly because Mark Hanna had more energy than he had outlets for it; and his energy happened to overflow into banking. It is true that his energy was inexhaustible, and that he started a bank and made it a success with an apparent ease that almost makes the job seem to be a diversion. But he had none the less a motive in starting the bank,— a motive which was not merely the instinctive expression of superabundant business energy. He wanted to help a friend — to found a business in which that friend would find a regular and a remunerative position.

Among Mark Hanna's papers was discovered the following note scrawled on a letter-heading of the Union National Bank, dated June 9, 1884 — the day on which the bank started to do business. The scrawl is itself undated, but must have been written some time in the nineties.

"Mark ! —

"In cleaning out my desk to-day I discovered this sheet and send (it to) you as a souvenir of *past events*. On the 9th of June, 1884, the struggle commenced.

For What?

To work as few men have ever worked and to accomplish what no other man in Cleveland could have accomplished in the time and

For What?

To supply a *soft snap* for an intriguing conspiring Yankee (codfish bred) who has yet to add his first account (save his own paltry one) to the business of the bank. The rewards of merit in this world are past finding, Mark, let's hope for better in the next !

(*Signed*) "Ves."

In the early eighties Mr. Hanna not only published a newspaper and started a bank, but he bought a theatre; and he came to buy it in a very characteristic way. He was walking along Euclid Avenue one day with some friends on his way to the Union Club for lunch, when one of his companions remarked that the Opera House was at that very moment being put up for sale by the sheriff. This theatre, which was at the time the largest and handsomest in Cleveland, had been built by Mr. John Ellsler, who was a citizen of Cleveland and an actor as well as a manager. The enterprise had failed, because the theatre was rather more expensive than the city of Cleveland was capable of supporting, and Mr. Ellsler was being sold up. Mr. Hanna and his friends strolled into the building in order to watch the proceedings. The bidding was under way. Somebody had made an offer of $40,000 for the property, and Mr. Hanna to his own surprise and that of his friends raised the bid a few hundred dollars. He was still more surprised, when a minute later he found himself the owner of the theatre. According to his account he did not have the remotest idea, when he entered the building, of buying the property.

The first manager placed in charge of the theatre was his cousin, L. G. Hanna, a son of Benjamin Hanna. For some time it continued to be unprofitable. Its owner did not always approve of the policy of his manager. One evening Mr. and Mrs. Hanna were driving by the building and saw a rough-looking crowd gathered about the entrance. Thinking the building was on fire, Mr. Hanna left his wife at the Union Club, hastened to the theatre and entered the box always reserved for himself. He found the theatre crowded and a wrestling match under way. The first round had just ended, and Mr. L. G. Hanna was on the stage, announcing that inasmuch as the performance was so successful, it would be repeated on the following week. But Mark Hanna did not like it. He had bought a theatre, not an arena. One account states that the irate owner stood up in his box and declared that no such performance would be repeated in the Opera House, but this version is denied by Mr. L. G. Hanna, who states that Mr. Hanna merely went behind the scenes and asked him to omit wrestling matches in the future from the list of attractions.

Augustus F. Hartz, who succeeded Mr. L. G. Hanna as lessee, had already been the manager of one theatre in Cleveland, but it burned, and he returned to his earlier occupation of prestidigitator. While he was performing in Cincinnati he received a telegram from Mr. Hanna asking him to keep an appointment [in Cleveland the next day. Fifteen minutes after their meeting the lease was signed. Mark Hanna did business without unnecessary delays. Under the new management the theatre became more successful; and Mr. Hartz continued to be its lessee from that time until Mr. Hanna's death — a period of twenty years.

Mr. Hartz states that Mr. Hanna knew all about the theatre, every part of it, and was perfectly competent to have managed it himself. He was frequently consulted about the bookings, and his judgment was rarely at fault. He had a high standard as to the character of the entertainments presented, and wanted his theatre to be known as in every respect first class. There was reserved for his use a box which he usually occupied some time during the week. Mr. Hartz states that his taste in plays and players was good.

He insisted that the Opera House should be well and thriftily managed, but he was kind and considerate to his tenant. At the end of more than one theatrical season Mr. Hartz went to him and owned up that he could not pay the whole rent. "All right," Mr. Hanna would say, "I can wait." "But," he would ask, "have you paid every one else?" As long as he knew that he was being dealt with candidly, he was willing to help and to wait; but he always insisted upon the prompt settlement of every other obligation. In the long run the theatre proved to be a good investment, paying him a return of $8000 on his investment of $40,000.

Yet when he bought the theatre he obviously had not done so merely as an investment. He preferred to keep his money in his business, and he almost never bought real estate except for his own use. Once the theatre was his, he was too good a man of business not to want to make it pay, but the impulse which prompted his successful bid did not flow merely from a quick apprehension of the cheapness of the property. It seems to have been an instinctive by-product of a lively interest in the drama and in theatrical performers. Plays and particularly players, always exercised a strong fascination upon him. He liked their animation, their gayety, their good-fellowship, and the heightening of personality which the practice of their profession bestows upon them.

Throughout the whole of his life Mr. Hanna was intensely and inveterately social. His favorite recreation consisted in companionship with other people; and even during his years of closest business preoccupation he rarely sat down to table without a certain number of guests. On Sundays and holidays he liked to have the house full. Moreover, he wanted to entertain, not merely his friends and business associates, but (as his mother did before him) prominent and interesting people who visited Cleveland; and among the visitors to Cleveland, who were necessarily prominent and usually interesting, were, of course, the constant stream of performers at the local theatres. Mr. Hanna used to entertain many of them at his house, and in this way he became more or less intimately acquainted with most of the leading American actors of his own day.

Among the actors whom he knew more or less intimately were Edwin Booth, Lawrence Barrett, John McCullough, Henry Irving, W. J. Florence, John T. Raymond, W. H. Crane and Joseph Jefferson. He met many of them at his own theatre. When he did not know them, he would go to their dressing-room to be introduced, and then take them to his home as his guests. Some of them he helped. His most intimate friend among the players was Lawrence Barrett, with whom he corresponded, and whose letters to Mr. Hanna are almost affectionate. The business man had helped the actor with a loan of $10,000 at a time when their acquaintance was still comparatively slight, and thereafter their association ripened into a warm friendship. Mr. Hanna became Mr. Barrett's business adviser and helped him both to make and keep money. Mr. Hartz states that the latter's first engagement at the Opera House promised to be a dreary failure. On Monday night the house was empty. So for Tuesday night Mr. Hanna bought all the seats in the theatre except the gallery, and distributed them among the "best" people in Cleveland. It cost him $1400, but thereafter (according to Mr. Hartz) Barrett's reputation was established in Cleveland and to a smaller extent in neighboring cities.

Mr. Hanna's excursion into the ownership of a theatre was, consequently, the result of human rather than business motives. He did not do it to make money, although once involved he managed to make the investment profitable. But his theatre brought him into closer touch with a group of people whom he found interesting and diverting, and who must have added a grateful alteration to the somewhat monotonous social life of a Middle Western city.

Mark Hanna's other and final miscellaneous business interest was a street railway company. His connection therewith began, when in 1875, after the death of his father-in-law, Mr. Daniel P. Rhodes, he took the latter's place as director of the Rocky River Railroad. This little steam road ran for five or six miles from the city westward to a point on the Lake, which was a favorite place of recreation for the young people of Cleveland. Its equipment consisted of three locomotives and twelve cars; and it successfully lost during the winter all the money it made during the summer. Its right of way was sold finally to the Nickel Plate Railroad; and as a local transit agency it was in a sense succeeded by the West Side Street Railway Company. That company had been incorporated in January, 1863, for the purpose of supplying the citizens of the West Side with a horse-car service, and in it Mr. Daniel P. Rhodes was largely interested. At his death this interest was inherited by his daughter and his sons. Its initial capital stock of $50,000 had increased by 1879 to only $80,000, which indicates that during these sixteen years its growth had not been rapid. Mrs. Hanna's interest in the road after her father's death consisted of five hundred shares. In 1879 Mark Hanna was elected a director, having qualified by the purchase of one hundred shares.

Three years later, in 1882, he purchased five hundred more shares, and in this way he and the heirs of Mr. Rhodes obtained control of the property. Up to that time Elias Sims had been president of the corporation. The management had been anything but enterprising or efficient. Its service was cheap and poor. Its passengers had the pleasure of riding in old cars which were no longer good enough to be used in New York, and these cars were drawn by horses which had been discarded as useless for any but a semi-public service. Mark Hanna did not like such management. He named a price at which he would sell his own interest or purchase the interest of Mr. Sims. That the price was liberal is indicated by the fact that in twenty-four hours Mr. Hanna had entered into control.

The West Side Street Railway Company owned about fifteen miles of track, almost all of it on the west side of the Cuyahoga River. It ran cars on Detroit, Pearl, Lorain and Bridge streets, and thence over the new viaduct to the Public

Square. Its most important line was only two miles and a half in length. In order to become a profitable road, it needed to improve its service and extend the area of its business so that it could be more economically operated. As soon as he assumed control Mr. Hanna instructed the superintendent, Mr. Geo. G. Mulhern, to buy new cars and horses, and to put the road in thoroughly good condition. "You do the work," he said, "and I'll supply the money." Little by little the lines were extended wherever possible, and every effort was made to keep the service abreast of the growth of the city.

Somewhat later a consolidation was effected with the Woodland Avenue line on the east side of the river, and then with the road on Kinsman Street. This consolidation largely increased the size of the company and the area of its operations. Its name was changed to the Woodland Avenue and West Side Street Railway Company, its capital became $2,000,000, and it obtained a long continuous route running from one end of the city to the other. Mr. Hanna was president of the new company. The Woodland Avenue line, when he assumed control, was also run down and was in need of complete rehabilitation. After a few years he converted it from a losing into a paying property.

It was about this time (that is, in the late years of the eighties) that street railroads in a city of the size of Cleveland began to be really profitable. Their traffic increased faster than the growth of population, because as the city spread, the amount of travelling became proportionately larger. Coincident with the necessary increase in travelling came the introduction of the electric trolley, which at once enormously improved the service, diminished the percentage of operating cost and made the consolidation of connecting lines necessary in the interest both of the best service and the lowest operating cost. About 1889 Mr. Hanna began the electrification of his street railways. A little later a further consolidation was effected with the Cleveland City Cable Company, which owned tracks on Payne Avenue, Superior and St. Clair streets. This new company was known as the Cleveland City Railway Company, its capital was $8,000,000, afterwards increased to $9,000,000, and the whole system was, of course, operated by electric trolleys. Mr. Hanna continued as president, and did not retire until his company, popularly known as the "Little Consolidated," was merged with the Cleveland Electric Railway Company — the "Big Consolidated."

Mark Hanna never owned a majority of the stock in any of the companies which succeeded to the old West Side Street Railway Company. His own interest and that of his immediate family amounted to about a million dollars in the stock of the "Little Consolidated." Nevertheless his control was complete. He did not interfere much in the details of operation, but he travelled on the cars a good deal and was constantly suggesting improvements in the service. On the whole, however, the operating superintendent was held responsible for the running of the road, while Mr. Hanna financed it, decided what improvements were necessary, and when and how they should be made. The directors almost always followed his recommendations; and under his energetic but thrifty management the Cleveland City Railway came to have a high reputation for the efficiency of its service.

As in the case of his other interests Mr. Hanna did not buy a street railway, because he had carefully calculated the probability of large future profits in that particular business. Indeed, in 1882 it required some imagination to anticipate that such a decrepit enterprise could ever be made remunerative. The opportunity for large profits in street railways resulted, it must be remembered, from the introduction of electrical power. He became a street railroad president as the accidental result of his wife's inherited interest in a property of that kind. Mr. Hanna saw that this interest would continue to be worth little under its existing management. Being a man accustomed to take decisive action, he made up his mind that the interest must either be sold or the business controlled. When the old management preferred to sell out, Mr. Hanna started in to build up the property.

He had another interest in the street railway besides the family interest. He lived at that time on Franklin Avenue on the West Side. One of the tracks of the company passed his door. He used the cars to take him to and from his office. His pride as a business man in being associated only with well-managed and successful enterprises was reënforced by local pride. He wanted it to be a creditable road because it served himself, his own neighbors and his own neighborhood. It always meant more to him than did an ordinary business interest. It became in fact his hobby. He used to call it his savings bank.

He called it his savings bank because he fully understood that it performed a local public function, as does a savings bank, and because he put into it for many years a portion of his surplus income. The property was built up partly with his own money, and it could not have been made profitable except by means of liberal capital expenditures. The railroad and its equipment, which he bought from Elias Sims, was, as a piece of physical property, not much better than junk. The early stockholders had all lost money. Mr. Hanna knew that he had to make a good railroad before he could have a profitable railroad, and when he took control his object was to earn a profit by excellence of service. The public responsibility which he recognized as necessarily attached to the railroad was that of giving its patrons the best possible accommodations.

That the railroad really did become profitable was due, not merely to good management, but to the growth of the city and to the substitution of electric for horse power. Mr. Hanna entered the street railway, as he did the coal and iron business, at the right time. The conditions which were to make it much more profitable than ever before were just coming into existence. The growing population of Cleveland was spreading out and was obliged to do an increasing amount of travelling in the course of a day's work. Mechanical improvements offered an opportunity of largely reducing the cost per passenger. A judicious system of consolidation and transfers could be used to stimulate traffic. Mr. Hanna took advantage of all these opportunities and managed in the end to make the railroad pay interest, not merely on the fresh capital he had obtained, but upon all the capital originally invested in the enterprise. Before the new conditions had come into existence, the most capable management could scarcely have accomplished such a result.

Mr. Hanna's personal attitude both towards his own business ventures and later towards general economic questions was that of the industrial pioneer — the man who starts enterprises, takes whatever chance they involve and builds them up with his own brains and hands. A street railway was from his point of view much like any other business enterprise. The chief difference was that the number of its customers gave it a semi-public function; but its duty to the public was simply the duty of all economic agents — that of rendering efficient service. If it rendered efficient service, the public interest no less than its own special interest demanded (from his point of view) that it should obtain the full fruits of its good management. The public had no more claim on a share of the profits of a street railway than it had on a share in the profits of the Union National Bank; and if it attempted to extort such a share, the only result would be the discouragement of private enterprise, the refusal of capital to invest and the consequent diminution of improvement and deterioration of service.

The industrial pioneer needs more than anything else a free hand. In our own country he has until recently usually enjoyed a free hand. Mr. Hanna enjoyed it everywhere except in his street railway business; and being accustomed to it, he was impatient when any unnecessary obstacles were placed in the way of his plans of improvement. His company ran its cars on many streets under grants from the municipal government. Attached to these grants were certain specific conditions. The franchises ran for a comparatively short period, because a general law in Ohio limited their term to twenty-five years. The prosperity of the company and the excellence of its service depended partly on its ability to secure other franchises, necessary to the normal development of the system, and partly upon a renewal of its existing franchises. At the time of their expiration, Mr. Hanna considered his company fairly entitled to such extensions and renewals, because they were necessary to a continuation of good service and its further improvement. He honestly believed that the interest of all concerned would be best satisfied in case he and his associates were encouraged to keep on investing their capital in the business and extending the service to the limit by means of the renewal of old franchises and the grant of new ones on liberal terms.

As a matter of fact there were always difficulties. The municipal government of Cleveland, during the years when the system of the Cleveland City Railway Company was being improved, consolidated and extended, was as corrupt as that of the average American municipality. The council, to whom was intrusted the grant of franchises, was composed of petty local politicians whose votes usually had to be secured by some kind of influence. There was no effective reform sentiment in the community. A street railway company that applied for and needed particular franchises had to purchase this influence or else go out of business. Practically every street railway in the country which was confronted by this situation (few escaped it) adopted the alternative of buying either the needed votes or the needed influence.

The West Side Street Railway Company and its successors were no exception to this rule. It was confronted by competitors who had no scruples about employing customary methods, and if it had been more scrupulous than they, its competitors would have carried off all the prizes. Mr. Hanna had, as I have said, a way of making straight for his goal. He was peculiarly intolerant of a nagging, unenlightened opposition or anything resembling a "hold up." He and his company did what was necessary to obtain the additional franchises needed for the development of the system. The railroad contributed to local campaign committees and the election expenses of particular councilmen; and it did so for the purpose of exercising an effective influence over the action of the council in street railway matters.

Mr. Hanna had in the beginning fought against the increasing corruption of municipal politics in Cleveland; but he had soon yielded and adapted himself to conditions. He was not a reformer either by disposition or by creed. He was always interested at any particular time in accomplishing some definite practical result, and in order to do so he took men and methods as he found them. What distinguished him from other American business men and politicians who used similar methods was that the results which he wished to accomplish were usually good results.

In the case of the street railway he was very anxious to give a thoroughly good service, and he was ready to perform every public duty which could in his opinion be fairly imposed upon the

G

company. He neither expected to make extortionate profits, nor had he undertaken the business for that purpose. As a matter of fact the money he made in the enterprise was small compared to the time and energy which it had cost him. The stock of the company during his management never paid over four per cent, and the amount of water it contained, compared to other street railways, was exceedingly small — amounting to only about twenty-five per cent. Before the consolidation with the cable line the property of the company never had been bonded, because Mr. Hanna was opposed to paying dividends as long as the company was in debt. His financial, like his business, methods were thoroughly sound — as sound, to use his own analogy, as those of a savings bank.

At a later date, and before Mr. Hanna died, the Cleveland surface railroads became the storm centre of municipal politics in Cleveland. They were hauled before the court of public opinion by Tom L. Johnson, and rightly or wrongly they were condemned. Whatever faults they had committed they most assuredly expiated. But the fact that the verdict went against them should not be allowed to obscure their manifest good behavior compared to the really flagrant cases of street railway mismanagement in Chicago and New York.

Mark Hanna in particular was never an ordinary street railway financier. He had no interest in any street railway system outside of Cleveland, and the local system in which he was interested was a minor one, whose cars passed his own door, and in which he took the same sort of pride that a man might take in his own stable, carriages and horses. He had bought a collection of rusty rails, worm-eaten cars and tired horses, and had converted them by virtue of hard and patient work into an efficient railroad. His mental attitude towards his railroad was always determined by his early struggles and tribulations; and the memory of them prevented him from sufficiently understanding the difference between the conditions prevailing in the street railway business of Cleveland in 1882 and 1902.

Public opinion, however, came to recognize that the street railways had passed out of the pioneer stage; and for many years the local politics in Cleveland were dominated by the clash between the old and the new conception of the proper relations between the city and the street railway companies. This clash began during Mr. Hanna's life. It was always a source of political embarrassment and weakness to him, because it involved him, as a national political leader, too much in a local political issue, and one on which public opinion was running against him. But embarrassing as it was, and much as one would like to see certain aspects of Mr. Hanna's street railway connection expunged from the record, he remained throughout the whole episode true to his own standards and characteristic personal tendencies. He had put himself into the street railway just as he had put himself into Rhodes & Co., the Union National Bank and the theatre; and he had become more of a man because of the personal expenditure. All his business enterprises were fundamentally personal investments, and returned to him something more and better than the wages of management and the current rate of interest.

CHAPTER IX

MARK HANNA AND HIS EMPLOYEES

The relation between Mr. Hanna and the men who worked for him in his various enterprises demands special treatment, not only because of its intrinsic interest, but because of the importance which it came to have during his subsequent political career. In no phase of his business life are the essential traits of the man more clearly revealed.

Mark Hanna's business career began, as we have seen, in jumpers and overalls. When he told the students of the Western Reserve College not to be ashamed of overalls, he was not posing or offering an insincere piece of advice. No doubt he had graduated quickly from overalls himself, and he never was an ordinary day-laborer, but he started with and always retained a hearty sympathy with the wearers of overalls and a real understanding of them. As his interests multiplied and as he gave more and more time to politics, he was obliged to delegate to a large extent the management of his business; but until the end Mr. Hanna was more likely to interfere in questions relating to the treatment of the employees than in any other branch of his affairs.

I have described him as fundamentally an industrial pioneer, and in no aspect of his business life is the description more correct and more instructive in its implications than in his relations with his employees. The social life of the pioneers was essentially homogeneous. It was based upon good-fellowship and a freedom and frankness of intercourse. There were inequalities of wealth and position, but they did not interfere with ease and completeness of communication and with mutual sympathy and understanding. Before the ninth decade of the nineteenth century the early pioneer society of Ohio had disappeared. A vast difference had developed between the manner of life of a prosperous business man like Mr. Hanna and that of his coal miners and freight handlers. But while the earlier homogeneity of life had vanished, no man could be true to the pioneer tradition without keeping a bond of communication with the ordinary day-laborer. The fact that Mark Hanna did do so distinguishes him sharply from the common run of very successful business men of his own generation. It is the final and best illustration of the fundamental humanity of his disposition, his practice and his point of view.

It is literally and not merely figuratively true that he kept in touch with his employees. Everybody in his employment felt free to go to him at any time. No matter whether the man was the head of a department or a common laborer on the docks, he had access to his employer. "I never knew," says Mr. Leonard C. Hanna, "my brother to turn any man away. In our business we dealt almost entirely with common, unskilled labor, and in all the interests which the firm owned and directed I suppose we had six thousand employees. We never had serious labor troubles. On our docks we occasionally had local and temporary disturbances among the ordinary employees; and whenever these occurred it was always my brother's custom to go right among the men. He would not ignore the superintendent, but would take the latter with him to the dock and hear what the men had to say. Then he would take such action as he thought to be necessary." The following despatch from Ashtabula, printed in the Cleveland *Leader* of April 28, 1876, may serve as a comment on the foregoing statement: "This morning Mr. Hanna, of Rhodes & Co., met the striking laborers on the docks at Ashtabula Harbor, and after consultation the men accepted the terms offered and resumed work."

Mr. Hanna's accessibility to his employees was not merely physical. When they reached him he always heard patiently and considered fairly what they had to say. If they had any real grievances, reparation was promptly and freely made. If they were making demands which in his opinion were neither fair nor possible, he had the gift of telling them so frankly, while at the same time not arousing any hard feeling. He could talk their language, and he could establish a common ground of good feeling which permitted full discussion of differences and which usually resulted in their adjustment.

The case of the street railway offers the best illustration of the way in which they felt towards him. The railroad was, as I have said, his hobby, and his constant use of it enabled him to know the men better than he could the workers in the mines or on the docks. When he travelled on the cars, he usually boarded the front platform and joined the motormen. They were always glad to see him, would give him a stool on which to sit, and would talk freely to him. During the eighties he knew almost every employee by name; and later, when he was less in Cleveland and there were nine hundred men on the pay-roll, he continued to remember a large part of them. From the day on which he became connected with the road there never was a strike, and never did the crew of a car refuse to take it out. The superintendent of the road, George G. Mulhern, states that at least one-third of the men who worked on the old Rocky River dummy road and who came to the West Side Street Railroad remained in Mr. Hanna's employment until he resigned as president at the final consolidation of the Cleveland City and Cleveland Electric companies — a period of over twenty-five years.

He was always ready to receive the men in his office and talk to them. The delegation or committee which went to him about grievances usually departed either convinced or satisfied. Captain O. D. Brainard, a car-despatcher on the road, states that Mr. Hanna would allow his street railroad employees to see him when he would allow no one else. "I have gone," says Mr. Brainard, "with committees to his office when there would be scores of people waiting in the reception room to see him. He would have us brought in by a side door ahead of all the rest. One day when a committee wanted to see him, he was about to take a train and had only fifteen minutes to spare. But he saw them and made his other callers wait until another time. It made no difference whether he was in his office, his house, what he was doing or whom he had as guests, he would always honor the card of an employee. He usually knew us, for if he once heard a man's name, he rarely forgot it."

Peter Cox, who was a conductor on the Detroit Street line for seventeen years, gives an interesting account of his relations with Mr. Hanna. Although working on the route used by Mr. Hanna himself, he never spoke to his employer until after an accident which had befallen Mr. Hanna during a trip on the Great Lakes. He had been going around on crutches, but on this day he walked with a cane. "When he boarded my car I said to him that I was glad to see him without crutches. He then told me the story of his accident, being as friendly and going into as many details as he would in case I were a close business associate. He said he had been to Duluth or some other northern port, that he had left the vessel at the dock, and and while returning to it he had fallen from a long ladder. I had the whole story. I never saw a man like him and I have worked for many. He always talked freely and confidentially to his men, no matter who they were."

The same conductor gives an account of an interview between Mr. Hanna and an employee with a grievance. "The barnmen wanted an increase of wages. They had gone to the company's offices and had sent in petitions for a raise of pay, but they had not received an answer. Times were good and the trackmen were all getting raises, but the barnmen were not. In those days each barnman had fourteen horses to take care of; they had to be cleaned and watered — other men did the feeding — and the harness had to be thrown on and off. One of the barnmen waited at Detroit Street and Lake Avenue, where Mr. Hanna took the car, and when he came up the man said, 'Mr. Hanna, I have appointed myself a committee of one to wait upon you and see about a raise of wages.'

"Mr. Hanna looked at him a minute and replied, 'I am hardly the one for that; you ought to see Mulhern.' [George G. Mulhern, superintendent.]

"'Well,' the man went on to say, 'we have sent petitions and got no answer. So I thought I would go to the fountainhead myself.' Then the man told how the trackmen had had their wages increased. 'But your job,' Mr. Hanna answered, 'is good for three hundred and sixty-five days a year if you want to work. The job of the trackmen is only good in summer, and in rainy weather they can't work.'

"'Yes,' the barnman replied, 'but our work can't be done by your high-priced trackmen. Put them in our places and they would fail.'

"Mark Hanna stood there and argued with that man as he

would have argued with President McKinley. After a while he said, 'I will talk with George and James and you will hear from me.' [George G. Mulhern and James B. Hanna, son of Kersey Hanna and cousin of M. A. Hanna, who was general manager of the road.] Afterwards Mr. Hanna asked the general manager, referring to the man who had talked with him, 'Who is that old fellow?' And he was told it was Frank Hunter, one of the best barnmen they had. Mr. Hanna said, 'He is a damned smart old fellow.' And the first thing the men knew they got their raise."

The management of all of Mr. Hanna's enterprises was liberal to injured employees. When one of the stage hands of the theatre fell ill, he was paid eighteen dollars a week for a year and a half. A workman who had been injured on a dock of M. A. Hanna & Co. was put on the Opera House pay-roll until he recovered — which was a mixture of kindness and prudence. The man was taken care of in this way so that his fellow-workmen should not know of it. On the street railway the men who met with accidents or fell ill drew half pay as long as they were laid off. The company had its own physician and surgeon, whose services were at the disposal of any employee, free of charge. Mr. Hanna personally loaned money to the men, with which to buy homes; and they were allowed almost to name the terms on which they paid him back. The motormen and conductors always had a lay-over of ten minutes at each end of the line — with a lounging room to spend it in, a billiard table and reading matter. No employee was allowed to drink while on duty; but whenever a man was dismissed for disobedience of this or any other rule, he was given a second chance. Mr. Hanna would frequently reinstate a man over the head of the superintendent.

The street railway employees repaid the kind and fair treatment they received by an unusual feeling of loyalty; and on one occasion this loyalty received an effective expression. In the spring of 1899 Mr. Hanna had planned to go to Europe, chiefly for his health; but at the last moment he hesitated, because of probable labor troubles in Cleveland. His own employees were content; but a strike was threatened on the lines of his larger competitor — the "Big Consolidated." He did not dare to leave without some assurance that his own men would not be drawn by sympathy into the strike, and he asked the superintendent to send a delegation of thirty men to him, so that he could reach an understanding with them. "Boys," said Mr. Hanna, when they arrived, "I have been preparing to go to Europe for a little rest. But it looks as if there would be trouble on the other road, and before I go, I want to know whether you will be drawn into it. If there is any chance of trouble on our road, I won't go. But if you are satisfied and agree to keep at work, I will go." There was not a man in the delegation who did not personally assure him that he was to go to Europe and that they would look after the railroad.

The men were as good as their word. The strike occurred on the "Big Consolidated," and it proved to be the worst of its kind in the history of Cleveland. For days together there were scenes of wild disorder. No cars could be run unless guarded by the police. The strikers did their best to establish a reign of terror, even going so far as to post observers, who were to take down the names of business men and politicians boarding the cars. Feeling ran extremely high, and the most strenuous attempts were made to induce the employees of the "Little Consolidated" to strike in sympathy. They were surrounded by men of their own class, and were told that victory would be easy if they would only leave their cars and absolutely tie up traffic in Cleveland. Every possible pressure was brought to bear upon them, but they did not waver. They continued to operate the road, and so kept their word to the man who always kept his word with them. After Mr. Hanna returned from Europe, a five-dollar gold piece was placed in the pay envelope of every employee as a small evidence of appreciation.

During the course of his business career Mr. Hanna was involved in only one serious strike. It occurred in the Massillon coal district in the spring of 1876; and it resulted in violence, bloodshed, the calling out of the militia, the shooting of at least one striker and the criminal prosecution of others. It made a deep impression on Mr. Hanna. Late in life when he became interested in a very promising attempt to diminish the number of labor disputes, and when he was delivering speeches all over the country, urging upon employers and employees a program of conference and conciliation, he referred constantly to this early experience. It had convinced him, he said, that some better method must be found to adjust the differences between capital and labor; and his own subsequent accessibility to his employees may have been partly due to his consequent determination to avoid, so far as possible, any serious misunderstandings and differences.

The first conspicuous period of American industrial expansion occurred during the few years previous to 1873. It involved among other things an enormous and sudden growth in the production of coal — a growth so sudden and enormous that very unwholesome conditions came to prevail in the industry. Many mines were opened by individuals or companies with insufficient capital, the most dangerous and wasteful methods of mining were used, and for a while extremely high prices were paid to labor. After the panic of 1873 a process of purging took place, which brought severe losses or suffering to every one interested in the production, particularly of bituminous coal. The demand for it was cut suddenly by fifty per cent. The operators were poorly organized. Cut-throat competition took place. Conservatively managed companies found the ground cut from under their feet by weak competitors, who must get the business or fail. The whole industry was disorganized.

The panic of 1873 and the prolonged business depression fell with terrible effect on the wage-earner — particularly in overexpanded industries like that of soft coal. The operators were obliged to reduce wages — in case they were to continue to produce; and the reductions were severe because the excessive rate of expansion previous to 1873 had made the wage-scale a burden on the industry. One cut succeeded another, and the miners could make no effective resistance. They were organized after a fashion, but the union was young and weak, and in any event could not have withstood the avalanche. The more disorganized a business is, the more certainly it follows that the expenses of any period of acute depression will fall largely upon the wage-earner. No employers' organization would need or dare to be as remorseless and inhuman in its bargains with labor as are a number of competitive producers, each one of whom is fighting for his life.

In the year 1873 a national association of coal miners had been organized as the result of a convention held at Youngstown, Ohio. Its officers were conservative men, and the policy of the association looked towards the strike only as a last resort. Its announced object was to secure conferences with the operators and arbitrate differences. When the crash came, the price of coal began to tumble and wages were cut. John Siney, the president of the association, knowing that the disorganized operators were helpless, counselled against strikes and advised the local organizations to make the best terms they could. In the meantime efforts were continued to increase the membership of the association, whose enrollment towards the end of 1874 amounted to 20,000 names.

The officers of the association soon felt strong enough to make overtures to the operators for the establishment of friendly relations, but they met with little success. The "History of the Coal Miners of the United States," by Andrew Roy, states that Rhodes & Co. was the only exception to a series of peremptory refusals to recognize the union which they received from the producers in Cleveland. Messrs. Siney and James (the president and secretary) saw Mr. Hanna himself, and received his assurance that if they were true to their policy, as described to him, that he would support them and do his best to get the other operators to arbitrate future differences.

About this time (that is, in the fall of 1874) the miners of Tuscarawas Valley were notified that the price of mining would be reduced from 90 to 70 cents a ton and other labor in proportion. The miners in this district had been enjoying exceptionally good wages and were unusually well organized. They determined to strike rather than accept the reduction. Both sides finally agreed, partly under the influence of President Siney of the national association, to submit the difference to arbitration. Judge Andrews of Cleveland was appointed umpire. The board met in the office of Rhodes & Co., and Mark Hanna was one of the representatives of the operators. The decision went almost wholly against the miners, the price being fixed at 71 cents a ton. The latter accepted the award reluctantly and sullenly. They continued to work, but they felt that a strike would have forced from their employers better terms. It may be added that the award reduced the price of mining in the Tuscarawas field to the level which had already come to obtain in competing fields. The miners of that district protested chiefly because they had been accustomed to wages higher than those paid elsewhere.

Shortly after, one of the coal companies in the district, which was not a member of the operators' association, made an individual advance of nine cents a ton, in order to induce its employees not to protest against the company's rejection of the usual practice of having a check-weighman at the scales. The discontent of the employees of the other mines was much increased by this advance, and they appealed to the general officers of the national association to be absolved from the decision of the umpire. After hearing their arguments the board decided to release them from the award. Immediately thereafter a formal demand was made upon the operators for eighty cents a ton; and early in April, 1875, a conference was held in Akron to discuss this demand. Mr. James Ford Rhodes, Mark Hanna's brother-in-law, presided at this meeting.

Mr. Hanna himself, as the head of the operators' association, argued the case for the employers, and his argument is worth quoting in part, because of the light it throws upon his opinions even at this early date. He admitted that the action of the Crawford Coal Company, in raising wages, had given the miners a grievance; but he argued that they would do better to stand by the award. The operators, other than the Crawford Coal Company, had refused to permit the abolition of the check-weighman, because the miners had a right to that protection; and they should not be penalized for standing by their employees in this matter by being asked or forced to raise wages. In addition he made a general argument in favor of the arbitration of industrial disputes, and of what would now be called collective bargaining between associations of employers and employees.

The men insisted on an advance, and when they began to strike the operators yielded. But not for long. On August 1 the operators succeeded in reducing the price from eighty to seventy-five cents—which prevailed in the valley until March, 1876. Then a further reduction to sixty-five cents was proposed. The officers of the union advised the miners to compromise on seventy cents, but they were ignored and a strike declared. The operators attempted to break the strike. They collected some miners in and around Cleveland, and with them manned a mine, situated a few miles south of Massillon. This mine is described as the Warmington, and belonged either to George H. Warmington, a partner of Mr. Hanna, or else to Rhodes & Co. In either event it would have been operated by the firm. About the middle of April the operators proposed to place more men at work on the mine, and on April 14 a second batch of strike-breakers was sent out under the direction of Mr. Warmington himself. Several hundred of the strikers were holding a meeting near the mine when the strangers arrived, and an orderly meeting was converted by the sight of the "scabs" into a howling mob. They made a rush for the car. Accounts vary as to precisely what occurred thereafter. According to the "History of the Coal Miners," from which I have already quoted, Mr. Warmington ordered the strikers to halt, and threatened them with a pistol. A contemporary account in the Cleveland *Leader* makes no mention of such a weapon. At any rate, the miners rushed forward, knocked Mr. Warmington down, and would have beaten him to death, had not two of their own number, Bennett Brown and William Ellwood, saved his life at the risk of their own.

Disorder prevailed throughout the district. The sheriff was helpless and petitioned the Governor, Rutherford B. Hayes, for troops. After some hesitation a company of the militia was sent to Massillon and placed in the Warmington mine. The night following their appearance the strikers captured the other mines thereabouts operated by Rhodes & Co., and set them on fire. The soldiers, however, soon suppressed the violence. Many arrests were made, and one miner was shot while attempting to escape. The disorder caused the operators to coöperate more vigorously, and in the end the strikers had to return to work with their pay diminished to sixty-five cents a ton. Within a couple of years their wages had been cut by two-sevenths.

Feeling ran high against the disorderly miners, and it was not easy to find an attorney to defend them. Finally their defence was undertaken by William McKinley, Jr., the case being tried at Canton, the county seat. His pleading was so successful that out of twenty-three indicted men only one was convicted, and he was sent to the penitentiary for three years. The trial took place just before the convention which gave to McKinley his first nomination for Congress.

Inasmuch as Mark Hanna, as the head of the operators' association, was in Canton during the trial, his first meeting with McKinley may have taken place on this occasion; but if such is the case the meeting made no impression on either of the two men. Mr. Hanna, in an article on "McKinley as I Knew Him," published after the President's death, explicitly states that he has no recollection of his first meeting with his friend. He believes it took place "early in the seventies"— as well it might, for his business interests must have frequently taken him to the region in which McKinley was a rising and popular young lawyer and politician. Judge George E. Baldwin, who was associated with McKinley as counsel of the accused miners, states that he is "sure" that the meeting at Canton during the trial was not the first meeting. He knew both men well throughout many years, and neither of them ever spoke to him about the matter — as they would be likely to do, because of his intimate connection with the case as leading counsel. In any event, even if the first meeting did occur at Canton in June, 1876, during the trial, it was merely a casual contact, which resulted in no closer association for many years.

Such is the story of the one serious disagreement with their employees in which any of Mr. Hanna's companies were entangled. If the miners were hardly treated on this occasion, that was the result of general conditions, which no individual was powerful enough to check. Mr. Hanna himself, at a time when labor-unions were regarded with even greater disfavor by employers than they are at present, was friendly to the unions. John James, the secretary of the Miners' National Association in 1875 and 1876, states that "he was the first mining operator in the bituminous fields of the United States to recognize the cardinal principle of arbitration in the settlement of wages, disputes, and the first also to recognize the 'Miners' National Association.'" During the whole of their intercourse Mr. James found him to be "one of the most intelligent, considerate and conservative" of the operators. He was always accessible to the officers of the union, and he always freely recognized the "real rights and interests of labor."

The reader must not understand that Mr. Hanna became an active advocate of labor organization and went out of his way to favor unions among his employees. His early record merely shows that he was much more liberal than the ordinary employer in recognizing the laborer's right to organize, and much more quick to perceive the advantages to both parties of collective bargaining and regular methods of industrial conciliation. But the chief fact is that he applied to his own business the method of always keeping close to his employees, always listening respectfully to their demands, of always granting the just claims of his men as a body and of always treating needy individuals with generosity. At a time when many American employers overlooked the fact that their relation to their employees was a human as well as an economic relation, Mark Hanna always treated them as far as he could as men. The subsequent interest which he took in labor problems, and the subsequent policy which he advocated as a means of avoiding industrial disputes, were both of them a result and an expression of his own practice as an employer.

CHAPTER X

CHARACTERISTICS IN BUSINESS

MARK HANNA has been described as an industrial pioneer. An analytic account of his characteristics as a business man will confirm the description. The typical pioneer of the period of rapid industrial expansion after the Civil War differed in certain respects from both the agricultural and industrial pioneers of the generation preceding the war, but the differences between the two types are insignificant compared to the fundamental similarities. Mr. Hanna was not only the sort of industrial pioneer whose methods and achievements illuminate and dignify the economic life of his generation, but he remained true to his type, even after many of his own early associates had departed from it. His political career and system, as well as his business career, cannot be properly understood except as the expression and result of his point of view and his experience as an industrial pioneer.

Mark Hanna's salient characteristic in business was initiative. He was essentially, if not exclusively, an *entrepreneur*. He broke new ground. He started and developed enterprises. The Middle West of the seventies and eighties was seething with industrial and commercial opportunities — mines to be developed, factories to be started, lines of trade to be laid out and established, mechanical improvements to be introduced and perfected, and commerce to be organized with increasing efficiency and economy. In order to take advantage of these opportunities a man needed an aggressive will, an abundant energy, and an alert, shrewd, and comprehensive mind. Such qualifications Mark Hanna conspicuously possessed, and they found full and effective expression in the policy and organization of Rhodes & Co., and M. A. Hanna & Co. Their policy aimed at the encouragement of enterprises which would produce commodities to be handled and sold by the firm; and its execution demanded business qualities, unusual in their variety, in their intensity and in the individuality of their combination. "He was choke-full of energy," says Mr. Robert R. Rhodes, his brother-in-law and early partner, "aggressive and progressive." "His very first desire was to be the head and front of every enterprise in which he was engaged," says Mr. Andrew Squire, his attorney for twenty years, "to be the leader in his own business and his own affairs." "He was always leading," says Mr. A. C. Saunders, another early associate, "and was quick to drop one thing and take up another. It is a great thing for a man to know when to let go. Mr. Hanna knew when to quit — that was one of the secrets of his apparent good fortune. He was tremendously interested in anything new. If his judgment approved of it, he was enthusiastic in pushing it and testing its value. But he quickly sensed a failure and turned to something else with equal energy and courage." This passion for leadership and this insistent but alert initiative kept pushing him forward and made him eager to seize opportunities, to stamp his own will on events, and exert effective influence and power. He was never afraid to go ahead and to take the risks and the responsibilities incidental to leadership. Under the economic conditions of his own day and region, his aggressive and dominating will resulted inevitably in a highly enterprising business policy, which he was able successfully to carry out because his initiative was sustained by an equally emphatic executive ability.

When he had anything to do, he did not spare himself in the doing of it. "He was a hard worker," says Mr. Rhodes, "and a man who applied himself very closely to his business. In industry he was unsurpassed." Another early partner adds testimony to the same effect. According to Mr. A. C. Saunders, his industry was extraordinary. "He was an inveterate worker. When I first went into his office he had to travel a good deal. He would return, write his letters and be off again. Few people realized how hard he worked. Often he used to stay until late at night, and I as his secretary stayed with him. He would tire me out." But while he worked hard he also worked well; and he could quickly change from work to play. During the years of his closest application to business he entertained freely,

H

and kept very much alive his other great interest — which was a love of companionship.

His unusual industry was directed by a mind which had mastered every detail of his business. For one thing he was during his early years an extremely successful salesman. He had the gift of persuading other people to do what he wanted them to do. Mr. Lucius F. Mellen, an early competitor, states that "Mark could beat us all in a trade and in getting customers." Mr. E. H. Bourne, who succeeded Mr. Hanna as president of the Union National Bank, but who was at one time his competitor in the coal business, tells of an occasion on which the city of Chicago was asking for bids on a large quantity of coal. Coal dealers from Pennsylvania and Ohio flocked to Chicago to try for the business, among them Mr. Hanna. Many of the salesmen stopped at the same hotel, and they were smilingly informed by Mr. Hanna one morning that the contract had been awarded to him. He beat the field, because, according to Mr. Bourne, he was remarkable in obtaining the information he needed and then in taking such action as was best adapted to get the business.

Another of his gifts which was of peculiar value to his business was an aptitude for mechanics. An understanding of machinery was natural to him, so that he was thoroughly and intelligently familiar with the mechanical details of a business, whose prosperity became in the course of years more and more a matter of the efficient use of machinery. Mr. A. B. Hough, who took many trips with him on the iron ore vessels up the Lakes, testifies to his exact knowledge, not only of the mechanism of the boats, but of every detail of its operation, including the capabilities of its officers, the details of its expense account and the like. "He used to surprise me," says Mr. Squire, "with his knowledge of the principles of mechanics. He and Mr. J. F. Pankhurst worked out a plan, by which a dynamo was directly connected to one of the engines of a power plant in which they were interested; and I think I am right in saying that this had never been done before." Partly as a result of Mr. Hanna's aptitude for mechanics, his firm was closely associated with the development of the machinery necessary for the more economical conduct of their business. We have already seen how important was the part which H. M. Hanna and his brother played in the improvement of lake shipping. The contribution made by the firm to the development of mining and coal and iron handling machinery is said to have been equally substantial.

A business which was constantly expanding, and which required the exercise of so many aptitudes on the part of its director could never become a matter of routine. Like the sea of economic conditions by which it was surrounded, it was always in a condition of unstable equilibrium. New adjustments were continually being required, and the making of these adjustments demanded the constant attention of a steady, alert, all-round man, — a man who could do many things and all of them sufficiently well. Specialism on the one hand or mere conservatism on the other would either have wrecked the business or entirely changed its character. Its director was much in the same situation as an aviator, who must sit with his hand on the lever ready for any shifting of the currents of air, and who knows that the equilibrium of his machine depends upon his ability to keep it going.

Mark Hanna in a sense made such a situation for himself. Or rather such a situation was the inevitable result of his aggressive, enterprising, dominating personality. He was always on campaign — always planning the movement of his forces so as to obtain surer and completer control of the firm's existing territory or, wherever possible, to occupy new and important strategic points. Such campaigns involve, of course, the taking of chances; but only one of his partners complains that he took dangerous and unwise chances. Mr. Rhodes states that Mr. Hanna sought to enlarge the firm's business in ways his partners did not always consider prudent. They tried to hold him down — not always with success, because he would sometimes go ahead without even consulting them. If there is any truth in this criticism, it applies to his early rather than to his later career. In the beginning he may have taken some long chances in order to accelerate the progress of the firm, but later his boldness was tempered with caution. Such is the unanimous testimony of his other partners. A man of his disposition necessarily took chances; but if he took chances, he knew how to carry them off.

Only once in his business career does he seem to have been involved in a precarious position. The Globe Ship-building Company, of which H. M. Hanna was president, and in which Mark Hanna was heavily interested, had built five ore-carrying vessels for Ferdinand Schlesinger of Milwaukee. Mr. Schlesinger was a business ally of Mr. Hanna's, in whom the latter had great personal confidence. He was the owner of some valuable iron mines in the Menominee range, including the very exceptional Chapin mine, whose product was sold through M. A. Hanna & Co. Mr. Schlesinger gave them an advantageous contract for carrying the ore in return for the vessels — thus practically pledging the mines for the payment of the boats. The brothers figured that at the end of six years the contract for transporting the ore would reimburse the company for the cost of the ships.

The arrangement looked good, because by means of the combination each of the parties to the contract was able to transact a substantially larger amount of business. Unfortunately, however, Mr. Schlesinger overreached himself and failed. He had built a railroad in order to haul his ore to the Lakes, and he had strained his resources in so doing. He was involved to the extent of several million dollars, and the brothers found their heavy investment on the strength of the contract compromised. They had what Mr. H. M. Hanna describes as a lively winter. They had to spend a large part of it in New York working out a settlement which would enable them to get back their security. Finally they succeeded. A purchaser was found for the railroad in the Northwestern Railroad Company. H. M. Hanna took back the boats, and M. A. Hanna & Co. emerged with the Chapin mine. The experience was an unpleasant one for men who, in their own business, never ventured beyond their depth; but it proved to be very profitable in its ultimate results. In 1899 the Chapin mine was sold to the National Steel Company at a large advance over its cost.

This dangerous complication was due chiefly to Mark Hanna's personal confidence in Ferdinand Schlesinger; and it should be added that his confidence was not misplaced. Partly owing to Mr. Hanna's assistance, Mr. Schlesinger later made another start, obtained possession of some iron mines of apparently doubtful value, and was justified in his judgment by their development into extremely valuable properties. Thus he completely recovered himself, and the alliance between Mr. Schlesinger and his sons and M. A. Hanna & Co. has continued until the present day.

Mark Hanna, for all his aggressive initiative, was not a man to skate on thin ice. He took certain necessary risks, but he was never a speculator in the sense of a man who merely gambled on his business judgment. He was an organizer and a manager as well as an initiator of enterprises. The different aspects of his business policy hung together, and aimed eventually at giving security as well as volume to the business of the firm. It has remained what he made it — viz. a business depending on personal direction and in some measure on personal relations; but it was none the less a carefully and intelligently wrought structure, whose stability was founded on sound economic ideas.

"In my thirty years of business experience," says Mr. Leonard C. Hanna, "I have never known a mind which had such a firm grasp on the essentials of a business proposition"; and this ability to fasten on essentials seems to have been due not merely to his knowledge of the conditions affecting any particular business affair, but to thoroughly sound general ideas and methods. He had the faculty of "getting in right" instead of wrong. The accuracy and the force of his judgment on specific business questions was assisted by a correct general estimate of the dominant values in his own business world. H. M. Hanna testifies that his brother had a definite and comprehensive conception of the channels, through which the great American domestic commerce was bound to flow and of the opportunities, which were offered to Cleveland business men of assembling the raw materials necessary to the steel and iron industries and of furnishing the means of transportation. His other brother, Mr. Leonard Hanna, states that he early acquired an equally definite idea of the dominant principle underlying the characteristic American industrial organization — the principle of keeping control of the several processes by means of which raw materials are worked up for use, and of deriving some profit from all of them. It was because the business of M. A. Hanna & Co. was based partly on this principle that it escaped the fate which might have befallen, under later conditions, an unprotected commission business.

The mixture of balance and prudence in his business policy, and of personal flexibility and impersonal stability in his business achievements, was the natural expression of two different aspects of Mark Hanna's disposition. His nature was impulsive, and his impulses frequently had an explosive expression, but at the same time he was cautious and considerate. Although his will was insistent and aggressive, it was not headstrong. He knew what he could and could not do, and he knew when and how long to wait. All the most important actions of his life were the result of unconscious instincts and intentions rather than conscious purposes; but he had no sooner acted in obedience to some deep-rooted personal instinct than his candid intelligence began with coolness and caution to search for the best means of making his will prevail. His will was strong and dominant, largely because it was not calculating; and it was effective, because once having been "set" it could call to its assistance the resources of a well-stored, ingenious and deliberate mind. Mark Hanna's experience came to him as the result for the most part of his instinctive action, but he digested and used it by virtue of a capable and considerate intelligence.

Almost all of Mr. Hanna's close associates testify to this combination of unconscious and deliberate elements in his behavior. Mr. Leonard C. Hanna remarks that while his decisions were often the result of study and reflection, they also came at times from intuition. Mr. Andrew Squire says that he seemed to know by intuition things that other men had to acquire by reading and long experience; but this shrewd witness adds that Mr. Hanna was not ordinarily a man of quick judgment. He usually canvassed a matter thoroughly before reaching a conclusion, and when once the decision was made, he was hard to move. "While Mr. Hanna was quick to reach a conclusion," says Mr. A. C. Saunders, "he was not hasty. He thought things over very carefully. He would give a matter of importance considerable time, and when his mind was made up, go into it with his whole heart. I should say that he was both a bold man and a careful one. He took risks, but he never went beyond his depth, and invariably had his enterprises safely financed before he attempted to carry them out. All of us consulted him on practically all matters, and he knew the business so well that most of his decisions would come quickly. He also consulted his partners and frequently acted on their recommendation. He was usually right, but he could be convinced of his error whenever he was wrong."

Mark Hanna's relation with other men brings out, however, his best qualities in business as in politics. His great success as an organizer was the outcome chiefly of his faculty of getting good work and loyal coöperation out of his associates; and the testimony of Mr. Saunders in the preceding paragraph affords some inkling as to the way in which such results were obtained. He organized everything with which he was concerned, and in organizing he was obliged to delegate responsibility. But his organizations never became mere machines. They were always living things, to which their director imparted his own vitality. He had the faculty of supervising without interfering, and of making his own general responsibility effective without emasculating the specific responsibilities of his subordinates and associates. His success in this respect was not, of course, due to the application of any definite rule, but to the plane of mutual confidence and understanding, on which the relationship was established.

The keystone of his business structure was absolute integrity in the fulfilment of his contracts. Mr. Leonard C. Hanna asserts that from January, 1875, when he entered the firm, until the day of Mark Hanna's death, he never knew the binding quality of any agreement, no matter how disadvantageous, to be questioned. They never considered for a moment the possibility of evading an engagement. "I have sat here," he says, "for thirty years" (his statement was made in 1905), "and during that time I have seen hundreds of thousands of dollars lost by contracts, but never was there a hint that the obligation was not to be fulfilled to the letter. If we agreed to sell pig-iron at a certain price, and an increase in the cost of the raw materials caused us to lose a very large sum of money, the man who bought the iron got it. In 1903 the price of pig-iron fell five or six dollars a ton very quickly. The firm of M. A. Hanna & Co. had a large amount of business booked ahead at the higher price; and after the fall many purchasers of our iron backed out of their contracts, and many others tried to do so. Although we could not sell the product at the price, we took all the raw materials we had agreed to buy. So it had always been during the business career of Mark Hanna." Mr. Hanna adds that his brother would never do any more business with a man who repudiated his contracts.

This scrupulous business integrity was in Mr. Hanna's case something more than ordinary honesty. It was partly an expression of the instinctive loyalty which pervaded all his personal associations. The business of M. A. Hanna & Co. was based not only on a system of contracts, but also upon a group of alliances; and the substance of many of these contracts and all of these alliances consisted of a personal tie. He had confidence in other people, and he inspired it in them. His firm, although a producer itself, could not have become and remained the sales-agent of so many independent producers unless these men knew that their agent was dealing fairly with them and was not discriminating for or against any one of its customers. The consequence was an unusual permanence in the alliances, by virtue of which M. A. Hanna & Co. procured a large part of its business. Its relations with the Pennsylvania Railroad, the Canbria Iron Co., with the Schlesingers and others, began early and endured throughout and beyond Mr. Hanna's life.

His attorney, Mr. Andrew Squire, emphasizes particularly one peculiarity of Mr. Hanna's in his method of negotiating a contract. Instead of insisting upon those aspects of an agreement which might make it look attractive to his interlocutor, his method and habit was frequently to bring out and never to disguise the dubious aspects of a proposed transaction. His motive in so doing, according to Mr. Squire, was to avoid any possible future disappointment or misunderstanding, and so, even if that particular transaction was disadvantageous, to create or maintain confidential relations with the man. Mr. Squire's partner, James H. Dempsey, testifies to the same effect. "Mr. Hanna," he says, "never made his offer so small that there was no chance of the other man taking it up. In making a large contract, he usually knew exactly what it was worth to his firm and he invariably based his proposals on a live-and-let-live rule. He never sought to get something for nothing and he never drove a hard bargain." The bargain, that is, was always subordinated to the obligation of dealing fairly with the other man.

Mr. James J. Hill cites a specific instance of Mark Hanna's candor and scrupulous fairness in business negotiations which is worth quoting in detail, and which shows why his associates had implicit confidence in him. In 1870 Mr. Hill went to Cleveland to buy a considerable quantity of gas coal. His intention was to purchase Youghiogheny coal, and he stepped into the office of Rhodes & Co., met Mr. Hanna and asked for prices on that particular stock. Mr. Hanna replied that he had Youghiogheny coal for sale, but that his firm were simply agents for it. Then going to a window and pointing across the street, he said: "There is the central office of the company that mines the sort of coal you want, and my suggestion is that you deal directly with them. I have no doubt that you can buy it as cheaply as we can, and by giving them your order you will save the commission." Mr. Hill was so much impressed by Mr. Hanna's fair dealing that the result of the incident was a series of mutually advantageous business transactions. He implies that Mr. Hanna could easily either have sold him the coal he wanted on commission or else sold him some other similar coal as a substitute.

Many of his business ties were so enduring and so personal that they were rather friendships than alliances. Indeed, almost all of Mr. Hanna's close business associates became friends, for he was never satisfied until he had made a friend out of a man whom he liked and trusted. Once the friendship was formed it was rarely shattered. Mr. Hanna would not only do anything in his power to keep his friend, but he often became blind to the man's faults. Ordinarily he was a shrewd judge of other people. His clear bright brown eyes had in them a searching quality, which made the object of his inspection feel transparent and exposed. As a matter of fact, he usually put a correct estimate upon his associates and assistants — as may be inferred from his success as an organizer. But, of course, he made his mistakes in his business as well as in his political allies, and if he had come to have any friendship for a man whom he had made a mistake in trusting, it was hard to convince him of his error. He would remain faithful to the tie — even when the man had, to the satisfaction of other people, shown himself to be unworthy, not merely of loyalty, but sometimes of respect.

Inevitably a man like Mr. Hanna made enemies in business as well as friends. He had, indeed, no gift for personal quarrels as he had a gift for personal loyalties. He did not cherish grudges. There was nothing vindictive in his nature. But he liked to have his own way, and if any other man blocked a path which he believed himself entitled to travel, the obstructor might well be somewhat roughly and ruthlessly pushed aside. When he was in a fight he fought hard, and like all strong and self-willed men he enjoyed fighting. Probably he made certain unnecessary enmities. He was at times during his business career an unpleasantly plain-dealer. Certain of his associates testify, indeed, that never in their presence was he brusque or harsh; but evidently he could be harsh, when he was rubbed or had rubbed himself the wrong way. One unfavorable witness states that during his early years he "was positively indifferent to popularity."

The witness quoted above may well be exaggerating, for he admitted some measure of prejudice. But there is sufficient corrobation for the general statement that he might at times be, or appear to be, arbitrary and self-assertive. He was a quick, impulsive man, impatient of what seemed to him unnecessary and perverse opposition, and when excited he might become peremptory in manner and explosive in speech. He might in the heat of the moment blurt out his opinions without any mincing of words, and without, perhaps, very much consideration for the feelings of others. Many men who subsequently became his friends and warm admirers were, before they came to know him, prejudiced against him by his manner and local reputation.

Judge William B. Sanders, who was for many years associated with Mr. Squire and Mr. Dempsey as attorneys for Mr. Hanna, says of him: "In Mr. Hanna's business life, before he became known as a national politician, he had not learned the art of saying 'No' without offence. He was plain and quick, and frequently hurt and offended people with whom he had a difference. However, a change came over him in this respect. I remember that I was in his room in St. Louis during the Republican Convention of 1896 when a delegation of colored men, delegates representing several Southern states, came to see him. They were after money, and he knew it. In the old days he would have kicked them out of the room; but on this occasion he politely refused them without hurting their feelings." One cannot help wishing that under the circumstances he had been less diplomatic, and had ruthlessly hurt their feelings — assuming, of course, that it was their feelings which would have been chiefly hurt by the act of kicking them out of the room.

The foregoing account of Mark Hanna will, I think, justify the description of him as a business man who carried over into the period of industrial expansion the best characteristics of the pioneer. The industrial pioneer of the seventies needed qualities and methods different in certain respects from those of the early pioneers. Mr. Hanna, for instance, was a great organizer, and he could not have made his success unless he had believed both in organization and in the delegation of power and responsibility. But like them, he was an all-round man of action, whose behavior was determined chiefly by instinctive motives and external conditions, and who used his intelligence merely for the purpose of making his will effective. Like them he was performing a necessary preliminary work of economic construction, and one in which for the most part his own interest as a maker and an organizer of enterprises was coincident with the public interest. As with them, the aggressive individualism of his private business life obtained dignity from its association with an essential task of social and economic construction. And finally, as in the case of the better pioneers, he had the feelings and the outlook of a man who has done more than accumulate a fortune. His methods in business and the way in which he gave personality and humanity to his business life all tended to the fulfilment of social as well as individual purposes.

His individual social edifice had the disadvantages as well as the advantages of being wrought at the prompting of instinctive rather than conscious motives. If it had contained a larger conscious element, it probably would not have been so effective, because it would not have squared in other respects with his essentially objective disposition. But its unconsciousness always made him callous to the fact that certain phases of his business demanded essentially unsocial action — such, for instance, as influencing elections to the Common Council in the interest of his street railway company. He was, that is, a man of wholesome and varied social instincts which had a powerful and edifying effect upon his life and the life of his associates, but he was not a man of civic and social ideals — in which again he was true to his pioneer type.

The fact, however, that his business methods were born of a deeply rooted American tradition and had a definite social value was salutary. It enabled him to draw for the success of his subsequent political career upon sources of energy outside of himself. In case he had become the kind of a business man that many rich Americans of his generation did become, any but an insignificant political success would have been impossible. A financier may buy or earn a politicial position, but he cannot accomplish much by means of it. Mark Hanna always remained a Cleveland merchant, and his business remained, as I have said, personal and local. He rarely, if ever, embarked in enterprises which he did not personally control. He never "set up" as a capitalist, and bought with his money other men to do his work. He put back his profits, either in the coal and iron business, or in some other local enterprise, over which he exercised personal supervision. All his enterprises were Cleveland enterprises or immediately related thereto. He was rooted in his native business soil, and his personality and his work depended for their value on local associations and responsibilities. He had too sound an instinct for the sources of his own personal dignity and power to let himself become a homeless financier. The consequence was that when he entered politics as a business man, he represented a vital and a genuinely popular American business tradition.

He never was essentially a money-maker. If he had been, he might have made very much more money than he actually did. His business life is inextricably entangled with his domestic and his social life. He never hesitated either to spend money or to sacrifice the making of it in the interest of something better worth while. As much as any very successful business man, and far more than the average, Mark Hanna earned by personal economic services his private fortune. He made a genuine contribution to the economic development of the Cleveland district at a time when such contributions were not disproportionately rewarded by any accession of scarcity values. When his political enemies stamped the sign of the dollar on Mark Hanna, they literally turned his relation to money upside down. What they should have done was to stamp on every dollar he made the initials "M. A. H." — the Hanna mark.

CHAPTER XI

BEGINNINGS IN POLITICS

WE have already seen that about 1880 the range of Mark Hanna's business interests began suddenly to widen. The dozen years following 1867 were spent chiefly in a laborious and enterprising effort to establish the business of Rhodes & Co. on firm and broad foundations and to expand it to the limit of its opportunities. The full fruits of this effort were not gathered until after the revival of business in 1879. Thenceforward Mark Hanna had the spare money and the leisure to undertake other enterprises. He emerges as one of a score of men who had become peculiarly prominent in Cleveland business; and almost simultaneously he began also to obtain a certain prominence in local politics. During the campaign of 1880, resulting in the election of James A. Garfield, he begins to count as a politician.

His interest in politics does not date from 1880 any more than his interest in business dates from 1867. He had always been interested in politics, although there is some conflict of testimony as to the point of departure of his earlier political activity. The statement has been made that his street railway interests first induced him to take a hand in the political game; but of all the eye-witnesses of Mr. Hanna's career only one lends any support to this explanation. Mr. Charles F. Leach, formerly Collector of Customs in Cleveland, and one of Mr. Hanna's own appointees, states that before he knew intimately his subsequent political chief, he had been prejudiced against Mr. Hanna. "I had heard of him as a local politician for what appeared to be his business interests. I had known him to stand at a corner on the West Side and peddle tickets for a candidate to the City Council who was supposed to be all right on street railroad matters or anything else that might come up." That Mr. Hanna at one time was not indifferent to the kind of men who were elected to the City Council and their attitude towards the street railway is true; but it is equally true that this was only a later and incidental phase of his political activity. The main spring thereof is to be sought in a wholly different direction.

The generation of business men to which Mr. Hanna belonged, particularly in the Middle West, took during their early lives a more earnest and innocent interest in politics than have their successors. Before the war almost all the good citizens of Ohio had been somewhat active in politics. After the war political activity became rapidly more and more professional; but the average business man still participated to a large extent in practical political work. He was likely to attend the primaries and perhaps spend the whole of election day at the polls. He did so because he was a Republican or a Democrat, not so much from inheritance, habit or interest, as from personal conviction. The memory of the war was still vivid. Republicanism was still associated with patriotic unionism, Democracy with secession. The Republican party in particular was still made up of its founders.

Mark Hanna was a primitive Republican. His family had been antislavery Whigs. His first presidential vote had been cast for Lincoln. He, his brother and most of his friends had served with the Northern forces during the war. He was a Republican up to the hilt — a Republican so black as to make him an undesirable son-in-law in the eyes of an ardent Democrat. But when a man of Mark Hanna's disposition believes in anything, he does not ruminate about it: he acts on it. Some sort of action was his essential method of personal expression. Indeed, it might be truer to put it the other way. His strong convictions were in a sense the by-products of his actions. Any conviction upon which he failed to act would have languished. He could scarcely have remained a convinced Republican unless he had actually participated in Republican party business.

That he did so from the start there is abundant proof. His wife says that ever since the beginning of their acquaintance he used to attend the primaries and perform active work at the polls on election day. As early as 1869 he was elected a member in the Cleveland Board of Education. He served for two years in this capacity, but did not attend much more than half the meetings of the board. It must be remembered that the business of Rhodes & Co. kept him travelling a great deal of the time. That he was elected for the position indicates a certain political prominence in his own ward. That he accepted an "honor" office of that kind indicates some public spirit. That he was never reëlected may mean that he could not give as much time as was necessary to the work. He was accustomed even then to dealing with large affairs in an authoritative way, and he may well have found the petty details of the work and its lack of any real opportunity for effective achievement irksome and futile.

Mr. Andrew Squire and Mr. A. C. Saunders recollect Mr. Hanna as an active party worker in the old ninth ward towards the middle of the seventies. He could always be counted on for presence at the polls and at the primaries, and for assistance in the task of getting the vote out and securing an honest count. Mr. Daniel Myers, a wholesale druggist in Cleveland, asserts that when a young man, he remembers attending a political meeting at which Mr. Hanna also was present. The date was not far from 1870. The object of the meeting was to stir up opposition to a ward boss who had been controlling the nominations for the office of city councilman. The foremost business men in the district attended the conference, and Mr. Hanna was one of the prominent speakers. He urged upon his hearers the need of an open and honest primary election, and the necessity of participation by the "better element" of the ward in active political work.

The date of another similar incident may be fixed definitely in 1873. At that time the Cleveland municipal elections were held in the spring, and were preceded by only a very short campaign. The Republicans nominated John Huntington. The nomination was unfit, and many Republicans, including Mark Hanna, decided to bolt. A meeting was called, in which Mr. Hanna was prominent, and it agreed to support Charles A. Otis, a Democrat, but not one who had been active in politics. Mr. Otis was elected, while the rest of the Democratic ticket was defeated.

MARK HANNA ABOUT 1877

These instances sufficiently indicate that Mr. Hanna's active interest in politics long antedated his connection with the street railway. Neither he nor his wife became even partial owners in the West Side Street Railway until 1876, and not until six years later did he undertake the management of that corporation. His business affairs had nothing to do with his entrance into politics, and he did not remain in politics in their interest. Quite apart from the evident fact that any benefit which his business could derive from his political connection would only be incidental, no one who understands the sort of a man Mark Hanna was can believe for an instant that his interest in politics could be derived from any source outside of itself.

He could no more help being interested in politics, and in expressing that interest in an eager effort to elect men to office, than he could help being interested in business, his family or his food. His disposition was active, sympathetic and expansive; and it was both uncritical and uncalculating. He accepted from his surroundings the prevailing ideas and modes of action. He went into business because business was the normal career for a good American. The selection of both his dominant and his subordinate business interests was influenced, as we have seen, more by personal motives than by any intention of making a large fortune. In the same way he went into politics, because politics was the other primary activity demanded of him by his local surroundings. Under prevailing conditions it was an inevitable way of asserting himself for a man who had an instinctive disposition towards an expansive all-round life — so far as such a life could be reached in action. He could no more have entered or remained in politics merely from a calculating motive, good or bad, than he could have planned to become a poet.

He went into business partly as a bread-winner and partly because it took business to keep him busy. He went into politics as a citizen. The motive, in so far as it was conscious, was undoubtedly patriotic. That he should wish to serve his country as well as himself and his family was rooted in his make-up. If he proposed to serve his country, a man of his disposition and training could do so only by active work in party politics. Patriotism meant to him Republicanism. Good government meant chiefly Republican government. Hence the extreme necessity of getting good Republicans elected, and the absolute identity in his mind and in the minds of most of his generation between public and party service.

Mark Hanna differed from the majority of successful business men of his generation in that he continued to live up to his conviction of the identity between active personal participation in party politics and public service. During the seventies and eighties successful business men were becoming so much absorbed in making money that their participation in politics was ceasing to be active and personal. The work which they formerly did in politics was being more and more taken over by professional politicians. But there was a minority of business men who never consented to any such division of labor. They continued to participate in active political work, and to proclaim by their behavior that business men had no right to shirk or shift their share of personal political responsibility. Among them was Mr. Hanna; and in remaining true to the close association between business and politics, he was loyal to a time-honored and fundamental American tradition. Once more he was proving himself to be the descendant of the pioneer who made no sharp distinction between private and public interest, and who testified to the coincidence between private and public interest by the association in their own lives between business and political activity.

A number of men familiar with the political annals of Cleveland during the seventies corroborate Mr. Myers in the assertion that a part of Mark Hanna's early political activity consisted in fighting the growing political power of the petty "bosses." He used to go to the business men of his ward individually, and try to persuade them that they ought to be more actively interested in local municipal affairs—that they, the taxpayers, and not the ward heelers, should rule the city. Little by little he organized the business men in his neighborhood, and for a while he had the local "bosses" of the West Side more or less under control. In this connection it should be remembered that the first phase of the municipal reform movement all over the country took just this form of an attempt to renew the interest of business men in local politics; and the fact that Mark Hanna himself, like most business men, may have had certain private interests mixed in with his opposition to the local "bosses" must not blind us to the meaning of his early campaign for reform. As a business man and an active politician he was fighting the fact that business and politics were being specialized and divided. He was seeking to escape from the awkward alternative of being obliged either to fight the political mercenaries or to conciliate them.

Now Mark Hanna was not by disposition a reformer. He was a man of action, whose peculiar strength was to consist in his thorough grasp of all the conditions, human as well as material, underlying immediately successful achievement. A reformer, even when he is not essentially a critic and a man of words, is obliged to subordinate action to preliminary agitation. Mark Hanna was not made to fight deeply rooted political abuses. He was not made to follow for long any path which did not lead to a visible and accessible goal. He soon abandoned his fight against the local "bosses," and eventually he came to accept their coöperation as a condition of practical political achievement. But his alliance with the professional politicians never amounted to fusion. Both his methods and purposes remained different. He always continued to be the business man in politics who was keeping alive in his own policy and behavior the traditional association between business and politics, between private and public interest, which was gradually being shattered by the actual and irresistible development of American business and political life.

In order, consequently, to understand Mark Hanna's point of departure in politics we must bear in mind (1) that he was an industrial pioneer, and instinctively took to politics as well as business; (2) that in politics as in business he wanted to accomplish results; (3) that politics meant to him active party service; (4) that successful party service meant the acceptance of prevailing political methods and abuses; and (5) finally that he was bound by the instinctive consistency of his nature to represent in politics, not merely his other dominant interest, but the essential harmony between the interests of business and those of the whole community.

In his first public appearance in national, as well as in local, politics he was inevitably cast for his one great part of a business man. It occurred during the Garfield campaign in 1880, in which he was intensely interested, because the Republican candidate was not only from Ohio, but from the vicinity of Cleveland. He is stated to have originated the idea of a Business Man's Republican Campaign Club, and of organizing out of the business men of Cleveland an effective campaign instrument. Among other services to the cause the club arranged a parade, in which Mark Hanna carried a torch among other patriotic and busy partisans. The idea had a great success. Similar clubs were organized in other cities, and aroused the interest of business men in the election. It is significant that in 1880 business men were first beginning to become conscious of their attachment to the Republican party and that Mark Hanna was associated with the first advertisement of the association.

Another incident connected with the Garfield campaign testifies both to Mr. Hanna's active participation in the work of the campaign and to his readiness to rise to an occasion and assume a risky responsibility. James A. Garfield's nomination had not been cordially greeted by the large faction in the party who had supported in the Convention the candidacy of General Grant, and who remained sulky after its defeat. This very apparent division in the party was a confession of weakness; and in order that the secrets of the confessional might remain obscure to the public, the party managers organized a mass meeting at Warren, Ohio, just to show to the public how united such a party could be. Not only was General Grant himself to attend, but also Roscoe Conkling from New York, Simon Cameron from Pennsylvania, General John A. Logan of Illinois, and other conspicuous Grant Republicans.

According to a prearranged plan the different members of the party were to meet in Cleveland and then be forwarded to Warren by the Erie Railroad. Mark Hanna was put in charge of the transportation of the harmonious Republican orchestra, and on his own initiative and without consulting anybody he decided to make the gathering useful to the party's candidate as well as to the party. He arranged that the train should return from Warren by way of Mentor, where General Garfield lived, and where he was continually receiving his loyal party associates.

What followed is described by Mr. James H. Kennedy, who was reporting the whole affair for the Cleveland *Herald*. After the meeting was over, the harmonious guests were being entertained at luncheon by Senator Harry B. Perkins in his house at Warren. Mr. Hanna called at the house and was shown into the dining room. "General," said he, addressing Grant, "it has been arranged that we return to Cleveland by way of Mentor, and if you propose to stop and see General Garfield, we shall have to start in a very short time." He made this announcement in public so as to bring the question straight to the attention of Grant. Conkling did not want to go to Mentor, and when he did not want to do anything he had a way of emphatically looking the part. His brow was like a thunder cloud. Grant saw the danger and did not dodge the issue. "We will go to Mentor," he said to Mr. Hanna, and Conkling sullenly acquiesced. Accordingly the train was stopped at General Garfield's town, and the distinguished Republicans paid their respects to the standard-bearer, whereby the country was given a still more striking proof of the wilful harmony which prevailed in the Republican party.

Mark Hanna's interest in the campaign was, of course, increased by the fact that in May, 1880, he had bought the Cleveland *Herald*. Thus he provided himself with a costly mirror in which his ardent Republicanism was reflected. And in those days Republicanism was very ardent and very innocent — particularly when the Republican candidate lived in one's native state, not far from one's home town. On the day following Garfield's election the *Herald* printed in great pica type, as an appropriate leading editorial upon that glorious event, a whole psalm of praise and thanks to the Lord: "The Lord openeth the eyes of the blind! The Lord loveth the righteous!"

During the years immediately following the election of General Garfield the range of Mark Hanna's political interests gradually broadened. He became a local political leader of importance, and evidently had some influence upon the party nominations for city and county offices. He had ceased to fight the machine and had become one of its allies and supporters. It was the period of his ownership of the *Herald* and of his management of the West Side Street Railway; and both of these interests helped to involve him more and more in politics. In the spring of 1883 George W. Gardner was nominated for mayor by the Republicans. The *Leader* charged Mr. Hanna with responsibility for the nomination, which was considered undesirable for no other reason, apparently, than the candidate's association with the owner of the *Herald;* and Mr. Gardner's election was consequently fought with bitterness, and finally with success, by Mr. Cowles. It was one among a long series of factional fights among Cleveland Republicans, the result of which frequently cut entirely away the small Republican majority in the city.

During these years, also, Mark Hanna was assuming for the first time a certain importance in state politics. His services during the Garfield campaign and his liberal contributions to campaign funds designated him for recognition at the hands of the party. Mr. George W. Gardner states that he suggested Mr. Hanna's name to the state committee as a member of the important subcommittee on finance. Mr. Hanna was named at the same time as Charles Foster, with whom he was closely and cordially associated in politics. Mr. Gardner adds that Mr. Hanna at first objected strongly to giving as much time to state politics as the position demanded, but finally allowed himself to be persuaded. He served with success, because his standing as a business man made him a good collector of campaign funds. Thereafter he remained in more or less constant association with the state committee.

The range of his political activity increased, however, very slowly, and so did his importance as a local political leader. His status in politics was merely that of a man who was giving most of his time to business, but who could be called upon for certain services to his party. He did not offer himself for public office, and apparently he had no political ambition — except his usual ambition of becoming a leader among the men associated with him in any undertaking. This period of his interest in politics may be compared to the part of his business career which antedated his entrance into the firm of Rhodes & Co. It was the experimental period, during which he had not come to realize either what he wanted in politics or what were the ways and means of attaining success in this less familiar region.

His peculiar success in business had been due largely to the formation of a group of loyal and permanent human relationships. His subsequent success in politics was to be due largely to the creation of similar ties; and the time had not yet come when the really helpful and permanent ties could be formed. In the meanwhile the enmities which he had already made in politics were perhaps even more conspicuous than the friendships. His lack of diplomacy, his indifference to popularity and his plain-dealing had more serious results in politics than they had in business. His fights with the petty "bosses," and his aggressive methods and ways had raised in his path a number of aggrieved men, who, like Mr. Cowles, were eager to oppose any candidate or measure which he advocated, and who were already describing him as a "boss" unscrupulously grasping after money and power. These personal enemies in his own bailiwick were a source of embarrassment to him throughout the whole of his political career. His political enemies were more than outweighed by his political friends, but the political friendships of these early years were, with one or two exceptions, not his permanent political friends. He had still to make a number of mistakes and failures before he knew what he could do in politics, and with whom he wanted to coöperate.

CHAPTER XII

TWO CONVENTIONS AND THEIR RESULTS

THE Republican National Convention of 1884 was the occasion of Mark Hanna's first plunge into the deeper waters of national politics. He was a delegate to that Convention, and the way in which his election was secured reveals the effect of the personal relations which he had already formed in politics. After being defeated by his enemies he was at the last moment saved by his friends. If he had not been saved by his friends and had failed to attend the Convention as delegate, his whole subsequent political career might have been different.

In the spring of 1884 Mr. Hanna offered himself to the Republicans of Cleveland as a candidate for delegate to the National Convention. There were two delegates to be elected, and there were besides himself two candidates in the field. One of them was his redoubtable opponent, Mr. Edwin Cowles of the *Leader*, who needed no other motive for coveting the honor than a desire to prevent Mr. Hanna from winning it. The other was Mr. A. C. Hord, who was put up as the particular candidate of the young Republicans of Cleveland. The young Republicans proved the quality of their youth by triumphantly naming Mr. Hord as the first delegate to the Convention. There remained a second seat to be divided between the two other candidates. The contest was bitter, because the rivalry between the two newspapers, as well as lively personal feelings, were involved. But the *Herald* and its owner were always being beaten by the *Leader* and its owner. Mr. Cowles was elected by a considerable majority.

In relation to this contest, Mr. David H. Kimberley, of whom we shall hear more later, tells the following story. Mr. Kimberley owned a flour and feed store on the West Side in Cleveland, but he was more of a politician than a merchant. For years he had been a member of the Republican County Committee, and he had such a wide circle of political acquaintanceship that he was a useful canvasser. Early in the spring of 1884 he was summoned both by Mr. Cowles and Mr. Hanna, each of whom wanted his help in getting elected delegate. As there were two delegates as well as two candidates, Mr. Kimberley saw no reason why he should not work for both men. He started out cheerfully to do so. Not long after Mr. Cowles again sent for him, and asked him if it were true that he was working for both candidates. Mr. Kimberley replied in the affirmative, and defended his action on the ground that inasmuch as two delegates were to be chosen, the interests of any two candidates were not mutually exclusive. Mr. Cowles did not agree with him. "You cannot serve two masters," he said; and added, "I understand you are a candidate for County Treasurer." Mr. Kimberley replied that he was. "Well!" he exclaimed, and his tone and manner showed Mr. Kimberley what to expect. Mr. Kimberley was placed in a difficult position. Both of the candidates controlled Republican newspapers, and he could not afford to incur the enmity of either. He went to Mr. Hanna and confided his troubles. "Go ahead and do what you can for Cowles," said Mr. Hanna, "and after he is out of the way do the best you can for me!" So Mr. Kimberley returned to the *Leader* office and assured Mr. Cowles that he would work for him and him alone until his election was secure. But Mr. Cowles was still suspicious and insisted that a reporter of the *Leader* be sent to the district convention from Mr. Kimberley's ward so that he could keep an eye on the proceedings. In Mr. Kimberley's opinion Mr. Hanna was too generous to force him to take sides in a personal quarrel and so to injure his political prospects.

The defeat which Mr. Hanna suffered in the local primaries was only the prelude to a greater victory. When the state Convention met in Cleveland his friends rallied to his support; and his services to the state organization stood him in good stead. He was assured that if he would be a candidate for delegate-at-large, he would obtain sufficient local and general support to secure his election. Apparently both Sylvester T. Everett, then a man of some political importance, and George W. Gardner had something to do with his candidacy and with his subsequent election. But he did not obtain the office without a spirited contest; and the opposition was led by his personal enemies in his own city. Something more, however, than personal motives were involved in the contest. Mark Hanna was known to favor the nomination of John Sherman as Republican candidate for the presidency. The Convention and the Ohio Republicans whom it represented were split between James G. Blaine and Sherman, so that it sent to Chicago a divided delegation. Mr. Hanna was supported by the delegates from Cincinnati and others favorable to Sherman. The delegates favorable to Blaine nearly all voted against him.

In the Convention of 1884 Mr. Hanna first came into practical political association with two men who in very different ways were to have a profound effect upon his subsequent life. Two of the delegates-at-large from Ohio were William McKinley, Jr., and James B. Foraker — both of them young men whose careers were very much in the ascendant. McKinley must have been already known to Mr. Hanna, because he was prominent in a part of the state adjacent to Cleveland, in which Mr. Hanna operated coal mines. Foraker hailed from Cincinnati and may not have been known to Mr. Hanna except by reputation. Nevertheless, when the Convention was over, it was Foraker rather than McKinley with whom Mr. Hanna had entered into more intimate relations.

A superficial reason for the intimacy which grew up between Mr. Foraker and Mr. Hanna after the Convention may be traced to their joint support of John Sherman's candidacy and McKinley's support of Blaine. But in all probability this difference of opinion did not cause any alienation between Mr. Hanna and Mr. McKinley. Sherman was the latter's second choice; and Sherman's name was presented to the Convention more as a public tribute to Ohio's greatest statesman than with any expectation of success. Sherman was much more seriously supported and made a much better showing in the Conventions of 1880 and of 1888 than in that of 1884. McKinley was rather for Blaine than against Sherman, and Foraker, as the event proved, was really about as much for Blaine as was McKinley.

The delegation from Ohio was divided almost in half. Twenty-two out of the forty-six delegates voted for General Powell Clayton, the Blaine candidate for chairman. On the first ballot twenty-one votes from Ohio went to Mr. Blaine against twenty-five for her "favorite son." Mr. Sherman's name attracted only five additional supporters from all the rest of the country. Subsequently he did even worse. The division in the delegation from his own state made the support of Sherman look Platonic. The opponents of Mr. Blaine made frantic efforts to concentrate all the "dark horse" and "favorite son" delegates on any available candidate, including Mr. Sherman, but all to no effect. Blaine was unquestionably the choice of a majority of the Republican voters and would have been nominated on the first ballot, had not President Arthur been able to concentrate all the Southern delegates on himself. As it was, the supporters of most of the "favorite sons " were merely waiting for a good chance to board the Blaine triumphal car.

Certain of the supporters of Mr. Sherman in Ohio were assuredly practising in their own minds a spectacular yielding to the magnetism of Mr. Blaine's personality. Mr. Foraker made the speech, placing John Sherman's name before the Convention; but in this very utterance one may discern verbal vistas looking toward a victorious waving plume. After the third ballot the magnetic attraction proved to be irresistible. Mr. Foraker made a sudden but apparently premature and unsuccessful attempt to carry the Convention by acclamation for Blaine. The nomination nevertheless went to Mr. Blaine on the fourth ballot — chiefly because Illinois and the entire delegation from Ohio rallied to his name.

Probably the result was not much more of a disappointment to Mr. Hanna than it was to Mr. Foraker; but he was none the less earnest in his advocacy of John Sherman's nomination. It represented on his part a genuine and a positive choice. He did not favor Sherman because he objected seriously to the nomination of Blaine. The reasons which made Mr. Blaine so obnoxious to the independents carried little weight with Mr. Hanna; and there was much about Mr. Blaine's personality and career which might well have had a strong attraction for a man of his wilful and adventurous disposition. On the other hand Mr. Sherman's personality was distinctly and notoriously deficient in warm and sympathetic qualities. If Mr. Hanna favored and continued to favor John Sherman as the Republican nominee for the presidency, he must have been and was acting in obedience to unusually strong instinctive preferences.

Mark Hanna favored John Sherman's nomination because of two reasons very different one from the other, but closely associated in his mind. In the first place Mr. Sherman lived in Ohio and at this time Mr. Hanna was not likely to be interested in any candidate who lived anywhere else. His anchorage in politics as in business was local and personal. Distant stars, like Mr. Blaine, no matter how luminous, did not fascinate him. He could not bestow his allegiance on any leader with whom he was not by way of being personally intimate; and he could not support such a leader for the presidency unless the latter's public career aroused his warm approval. For the presidency as an office he had an almost superstitious respect. For Mr. Sherman as a statesman he had an unequivocal admiration. As a business man he understood how much Mr. Sherman had contributed towards the adoption by the government and the carrying out of a sound financial policy, and how valuable the service was. No man in the country was better equipped for the presidential office by varied and prolonged legislative and administrative experience, and no man was better entitled to it on the record of his public life. That Ohio should possess a statesman eminently qualified for the presidency but denied as yet the opportunity of being a candidate was more than unfortunate; it was unjust. His national patriotism and his local pride were both aroused by the project of placing so eminent a man in so high an office. Thereafter the idea fermented in his mind.

In Mr. Hanna's life one step along a line of natural self-expression always led to another. His attendance at the Convention of 1884 sharpened his relish for politics and resulted directly in the formation of new personal political ties. He entered immediately into very close relations with Mr. James B. Foraker. In 1884 Mr. Foraker was considered to be the ablest and most promising of the younger Republicans of Ohio. He was recognized as a very effective stump speaker and as an ingenious and forcible official pleader for the nominees and policy of his party. He had no superior in the art of pursuading Republican conventions of the truth of Republican principles, the desirability of Republican policies, the impeccability of Republican administrations, and of the ability and patriotism of Republican candidates. He had been nominated for the governorship in 1883 and although beaten had made a favorable impression by the vigor of his canvass. His speech nominating John Sherman in the Convention had established his reputation as a party orator, while at the same time his eagerness to be converted to the successful candidate had been favorably noticed in Augusta, Maine. He paid a visit to the party nominee immediately after the Convention and was conspicuous on the stump during the campaign.

As a result of their association at the Convention, Mr. Hanna conceived a lively admiration and warm friendship for Mr. Foraker. Writing to him as soon as the Convention was over, Mr. Hanna said: "Among the few pleasures I found at the Convention was meeting and working with you. I hope soon to have the pleasure of renewing the acquaintance under more peaceful and comfortable circumstances. I feel that the occasion was one which will be a great benefit to you in the future, for I hear nothing but praise for you on all sides, all of which I heartily endorse and will hope to be considered among your sincere friends." A few days later he adds, "I assure you, my dear fellow, it will not be my fault if our acquaintance does not ripen, for I shall certainly *go for you* whenever you are within reach."

As a matter of fact, the acquaintance did ripen very quickly. The two men became fast personal and political associates. Foraker was renominated for governor in the summer of 1885 and elected. Mark Hanna served on the executive campaign committee and became Mr. Foraker's most effective ally in Cleveland and its neighborhood. He made a good showing on election day both for the local and the state ticket and was very much gratified at the result. Even at this time he was prominent enough in state politics to have his own name mentioned for the gubernatorial nomination, but he was not tempted by the deceptive glitter of any such prize. He was seeking political power by means of close association with popular leaders; and for the time being Mr. Foraker was the man of his choice.

Mr. Hanna evidently expected that his association with the new Governor would strengthen him as a local political leader. In all probability it did, but if so, the help which he received from this source was due rather to an increase of prestige than any control over the distribution of patronage. He was consulted about important appointments, but his advice appears to have been taken more in relation to small than to large matters. His disappointment, however, in obtaining from the Governor the recognition which he expected did not affect their intimacy or his interest in Mr. Foraker's political fortunes. The latter was renominated and reëlected in 1887; and, if one may judge from the tone of their correspondence, Mr. Hanna was as enthusiastic a supporter of Mr. Foraker in 1887 as he had been in 1885. During the second campaign he assisted Mr. Foraker with money at a time when, to judge from the warmth of the latter's thanks, such assistance was extremely necessary.

In the meantime Mr. Hanna was becoming more of a power in local politics. In March, 1885, he sold out the *Herald*, and this judicious piece of backsliding served at once to allay the enmity of Mr. Cowles. Thereafter Mr. Hanna was as amiably treated by the *Leader* as was any other good Republican, and the personal attacks on him were transferred to the *Plain-Dealer*. Mr. George W. Gardner, who had been defeated for Mayor in the spring of 1883, was elected to that office in the spring of 1885; and Mr. Gardner was a close associate of Mr. Hanna's in politics. In the fall of 1885 Mr. Hanna took a lively interest in the election of the County Treasurer. The Republican candidate for that office was the Mr. David H. Kimberley, mentioned above; and Mr. Hanna contributed liberally to his campaign expenses. The story of the contribution is so characteristic that it will be told at length in another connection. It was openly charged in the *Plain-Dealer* at the time that Mr. Kimberley was being run chiefly in the interest of the Union National Bank. Nevertheless Mr. Kimberley was elected by an unusually large majority. When he was renominated two years later charges of favoritism in the deposit of the county funds with the various banks were again made; but these charges made no particular mention of the Union National Bank. They were denied and did not prevent Mr. Kimberley's reelection.

During these years Mr. Hanna became probably as influential in local politics as any other one man in Cleveland. He was accused by the *Plain-Dealer* of being the local Republican "boss"; but the accusation was merely the natural partisan abuse of a man whose aggressive personality gave emphasis to his actual influence. He was in no sense of the word a "boss," although he may have been politically the most influential private citizen of Cleveland. Even the foregoing statement of his standing is probably an exaggeration. Whatever power he possessed in local politics was due, not to the building up of a personal machine, but to the fact that behind him were the more important business men of Cleveland. Among the professional politicians he had a few friends and many enemies. The politicians needed him, because he was personally a generous contributor and an unexcelled collector of funds; but they never recognized him as their leader.

The Republican organization in Cleveland was always unruly. The success of the party in local campaigns was continually being compromised by factional fights, revolts against regular nominations, and unexpected ebullitions of popular independence. In the spring of 1887, for instance, the Republicans nominated, apparently under Mr. Hanna's influence, William M. Bayne as their candidate for Mayor. Mr. Bayne was described to be a very honest man, but one who made his living out of politics. He proved to be a weak candidate and was decisively defeated.

Later in the same year Mr. Bayne was instrumental in altering the nominating machinery of the Cleveland Republicans in a manner which would now be considered most praiseworthy. As a means of stopping the abuse of packed caucuses a system of direct primaries was proposed and accepted by the Republican voters. The system had originated in Crawford County, Pennsylvania, and was named after its place of origin. Later many attempts were made to abolish the plan, but they were unsuccessful. Mr. Hanna himself came eventually to oppose it; but when it was first introduced he probably approved of it. Its sponsor, Mr. Bayne, was so closely associated with him that the two men presumably were agreed upon the desirability of the reform. It unquestionably served its intended purpose of doing away with packed caucuses; but it made the Republican party of Cleveland more than ever unruly.

Whatever advantage Mr. Hanna may have derived from his association with Mr. Foraker did not last very long, because in the spring of 1888, soon after Mr. Foraker's second inauguration, the association itself was broken. Mr. Foraker states that the rupture of their personal and political friendship was brought about by a disagreement over the distribution of patronage; but while there developed a disagreement of this kind, which both divided Mr. Hanna from the Governor and brought him closer to Mr. McKinley, other causes contributed substantially to the break. Before coming, however, to these other and more important causes, an account must be given of the incident to which Mr. Foraker himself attributes the dissolution of their friendship.

The most lucrative office within the gift of the Governor of Ohio at that time was the oil inspectorship — an official who was paid by the fees of the oil refineries whose product he inspected, and who had the appointment of deputies to do the work throughout the state. When Mr. Foraker was first elected both Mr. Hanna and Mr. McKinley had a candidate for the job, the former's being Mr. W. M. Bayne and the latter's a Captain Smithnight. Mr. Hanna was for a while more energetic in opposing Mr. McKinley's candidate than he was in urging the claims of his own; but later he moderated his tone. In November, 1885, he wrote to the Governor-elect: "I had a call from Major McKinley and his oil inspector candidate. The Major is never behind-hand with his claims. I tell him he 'wants the earth,' and it looks as if I were getting about where I generally do in politics — 'left' with no asset except my reputation of being a good fellow and always accommodating. However, I told McKinley I only cared for *you* in this matter." This letter was a prelude to the appointment of Captain Smithnight. It looks as if Mr. Hanna had withdrawn his claims, in order to relieve the Governor from an embarrassing situation.

The same matter came up after Mr. Foraker's second election. Mr. McKinley considered himself entitled to Smithnight's reappointment. The Governor, who had been dissatisfied with his first appointee, was resolved this time to give the office to his own part of the state. Mr. Hanna thought the patronage should remain in Cleveland, but urged the claims of his own candidate, Bayne. Finally the Governor appointed George Cox, subsequently the Cincinnati "boss," to the inspectorship, without even notifying Mr. Hanna of his intention; and when the deputy-inspectorships came to be passed around, Bayne was as usual pushed aside for the benefit of Smithnight. Mr. Hanna was so much chagrined that he ran away from Cleveland, and he wrote to the Governor that he would scarcely dare to return, in case his recommendation was ignored in the matter of another deputyship. The whole incident must have been a blow to his local political prestige.

There is no evidence, however, that this incident alone would have been sufficient to sever the friendship between the two men. At most, it indicated that Mr. Foraker was looking elsewhere for the support which the satisfaction of his political ambition required. After the incident Mr. Hanna continued to write to the Governor in a friendly, almost an affectionate, manner. The final break did not take place until after the Convention of 1888; and it was due to disagreements which occurred during the meeting of the Convention. While the complete story of this disagreement cannot be told, the substance of it, which concerns Mr. Foraker's attitude towards the campaign on behalf of John Sherman's nomination, is well known and not at all obscure.

Mark Hanna's conviction that John Sherman could and should be nominated and elected to the presidency had not been shaken by the poor showing made by his candidate in the Convention of 1884. The result of the election of that year confirmed his belief in the desirability of Mr. Sherman's nomination in the interest of party success. Immediately after the defeat of James G. Blaine he had written to Mr. Foraker: "I feel sure now in looking back over the results of the campaign that John Sherman would have been the strongest candidate; and I believe that he will be the strongest man in 1888." The narrow margin and the peculiar circumstances of Mr. Blaine's defeat made it plausible that, if Mr. Sherman had been the candidate in 1884, he would have been elected.

Throughout the next few years the project of nominating Mr. Sherman grew upon Mr. Hanna. The idea appealed to him because of its apparent practicability, because of its peculiar desirability, and because the work demanded for its realization was suited to his opportunities and abilities. At that time he had no ambition or hope of personal preferment. He was a business man with a collateral interest in politics. As a business man he could not afford the time for a slow and steady climb up the political ladder. Nevertheless he wanted to be associated with large political events and achievements. If he was going to interest himself in electing other men to office, why not the biggest man he knew and the highest office in the land? Such a job would be more interesting than electing mayors or governors; and, if successful, he would obtain by virtue of the personal association an amount of prestige and power which he could not acquire in any other way.

I do not mean by the foregoing description of Mr. Hanna's motives that his work on behalf of Mr. Sherman was merely selfish. On the contrary, his motives in this as in the other large projects of his life were primarily disinterested. It was his disposition to do things for other people. But mixed with his disinterestedness was a large amount of ambition — a keen desire for personal prestige and power. He seems at this time to have reached a fairly definite conclusion that the fulfilment of any personal political ambition must be dependent upon the contribution, which he could make to the political success of men like Foraker or Sherman. He could become a national political luminary only by attaching himself to a star of the first magnitude and shining by reflected light. In the spring of 1888 he wrote to Mr. Foraker and urged the Governor to persuade Russell A. Alger to retire in favor of Sherman. Mr. Alger's general position in politics was similar to his own: "Can you not," he said, "persuade Alger, if his strength is not encouraging, to go over to Sherman on the second ballot? Better for his future to be prominent in making a candidate than in leading a forlorn hope. Better be a power with a man like Sherman than merely a prominent citizen of Michigan." He might have added from his own point of view "or of Ohio."

He was actively working on Mr. Sherman's behalf from 1885 to 1888. Soon after the Convention of 1884 Mr. Sherman told Mr. Foraker that he would be glad to make Mr. Hanna's acquaintance. A meeting soon followed. Mr. Hanna was frequently in Washington, and he used these and other opportunities to become still better acquainted with Mr. Sherman. In 1885, probably owing to the latter's influence, Mr. Hanna was appointed by President Cleveland one of the government directors of the Union Pacific Railroad.[1] By 1887 the two men had become intimate enough to correspond freely and to exchange visits between Cleveland and Mansfield. The basis of this intimacy undoubtedly was Mr. Hanna's interest in Sherman's nomination. As the meeting of the Convention approached he gave more and more of his time to the work, and he not only contributed liberally to the expenses himself but he raised money among his business associates. Finally he was selected by the candidate as the manager of the campaign and as Mr. Sherman's personal representative at the Convention; but although almost all of Mr. Sherman's supporters approved of the selection, it was made practically by Mr. Hanna himself. He was more interested in Mr. Sherman's nomination and election than was any man in the country, Mr. Sherman alone excepted; and that interest had earned him his appointment. He had selected himself to be the leader of the Sherman forces by virtue of hard, enthusiastic and competent work.

A united delegation from Ohio was practically assured from the start. The President being a Democrat, there was no Republican candidate backed by the administration; and James G. Blaine, the only man who might have divided the allegiance of Ohio, was not allowing the use of his name. The way was

[1] This appointment was an incident of his business, rather than of his political, career — although it was of course a recognition of political service. His duties as director took a great deal of his time, and his knowledge of the coal business resulted in his being placed at the head of a committee, which took special charge of the coal interests of the railroad. Its President, Mr. Charles Francis Adams, wrote with the warmest praise of his services in this matter to the railroad.

clear, consequently, for "favorite sons" throughout the Republican states. John Sherman was the "favorite son" of Ohio, and while he had never aroused very much enthusiasm in the part, he had been cast for it so often that a very strong man would have been required to take it away from him. Moreover, the politicians of Ohio had good reason to be united on his behalf, because he had apparently a better chance for the nomination than any other one candidate.

The situation in Ohio presented only one doubtful aspect. The partisans of Mr. Sherman, and apparently Mr. Sherman himself, began to suspect the good faith of Governor Foraker. A number of small matters had served to breed suspicion. Mr. Foraker had privately opposed the indorsement of Sherman's candidacy by the State Convention of 1887, which renominated him for governor, and had yielded to the demand only on compulsion. The action of some of Mr. Foraker's friends in the district conventions in the spring of 1888 had aroused uneasiness and criticism, and stirred Mr. Hanna to remonstrate with the Governor. If we may judge, however, from the tone of Mr. Hanna's letters up to the last moment, he did not share in the suspicions of Mr. Foraker's good faith.

I know of no conclusive evidence to justify these suspicions, and for a long time their effect remained subterranean. The district and state conventions elected a united Sherman delegation, and in its proceedings there were no symptoms of any lack of harmony. William McKinley, Jr., Benjamin Butterworth, James B. Foraker and Charles Foster were named delegates-at-large. Mark Hanna was sent to the Convention from Cleveland together with Myron T. Herrick. Mr. Herrick, like Mr. Hord in 1884, was elected by the young Republicans, and Mr. Hanna escaped defeat by only a very narrow margin.

During the month of May the friction between Senator Sherman and Governor Foraker increased. It was openly hinted in the newspapers that the Governor was not acting loyally, and that consequently he would not be allowed to make the speech placing Mr. Sherman's name in nomination. The latter's friends feared, or pretended to fear, that like General Garfield in 1880, Mr. Foraker would make so eloquent a speech nominating Sherman that the Convention would bestow the honor on the advocate. The hints became so explicit that Mr. Foraker gave out several interviews stating that he was not a candidate either for first or second place on the ticket; but whether a candidate or not he was thoroughly disgruntled. On May 10 he wrote to Mr. Hanna: "I do not like the outlook for our cause. It may be it is only because no one deems it appropriate to give me any information about it. At any rate I am wholly ignorant as to Mr. Sherman's plans and wishes, hopes and prospects."

Whether or not Mr. Foraker was seriously considering the possible results to himself of the nomination of another candidate, the distrust of Senator Sherman was at least explicable. At that time the Governor was at the height of his popularity and power. He had been twice elected Chief Executive of his state. His ability and his usefulness to the party were generally recognized. No other Ohio Republican had apparently as much of a following and could look forward to a probably more brilliant future. He had, moreover, a number of extremely zealous friends, who, unlike Mr. Hanna, did not divide their allegiance between Foraker and Sherman. It was generally expected that an attempt would be made to stampede the Convention for Blaine; and if such an attempt were successful Mr. Foraker looked like the best possible choice for second place on the ticket — particularly in view of the fact that the Democrats had nominated for Vice-President Allen G. Thurman of Ohio.

With whatever justification the friction continued to increase, and affected the relations between Governor Foraker and Mr. Hanna. They were still friendly, and the latter continued to write in a cordial and confidential way to the Governor, telling about the apparent obstacles to Sherman's nomination and asking for his assistance in removing them. But Mr. Foraker could not be placated by Mr. Hanna. He felt that he was being denied the influence to which his prominence entitled him. He resented the choice of Mr. Hanna as leader of the Sherman forces and his own relegation to a subordinate position. The impression that he was being treated with scant courtesy was confirmed by the rooms assigned to him at the hotel in Chicago. As quartermaster of the delegation, Mr. Hanna had engaged accommodations at the Grand Pacific. The rooms selected for the Governor were on the floor above the Ohio headquarters instead of adjoining them; whereupon he wrote to Mr. Hanna and protested bitterly and indignantly. Mr. Hanna explained at length the reasons for the assignment, and in the end Mr. Foraker accepted the arrangement and tacitly acknowledged he had been hasty. Their final exchange of letters before the Convention was more friendly, but manifestly peace had not really been patched up. Mr. Hanna winds up his last letter with the following sentence, "Good-by, until we meet on the battlefield and my Ohio comes out victorious."

Mr. Hanna firmly believed in the probable success of the Sherman candidacy, and his anticipations were far from unreasonable. Senator Sherman was the most eminent Republican whose name was placed formally in nomination. The candidates offered by other states, such as Depew of New York, Rusk of Wisconsin, Alger of Michigan, Gresham of Illinois, and Harrison of Indiana, had no advantage over Sherman in availability, and their titles to the nomination were wholly inferior. The thundercloud of a Blaine stampede looked ominous; but if that danger could be escaped, it seemed like plain sailing. A few days before the meeting of the Convention, Mr. Hanna gave to the newspapers the following numerical estimate of Sherman's probable strength. "We hope," he said, "to have three hundred delegates. Two hundred of them will come from the South and the remainder from the West and East. Massachusetts and Pennsylvania are with us. We shall probably get the entire delegation from the latter state on the third or fourth ballot. If we get Pennsylvania and our other friends are steadfast, nothing can prevent Sherman's nomination. In the sober thought of the delegates, he better represents the wishes of the Republican party than does any of the other candidates." The phrase "sober thought" betrays the fact that the supporters of Sherman feared more than anything else a stampede for Blaine.

When the Convention assembled the outlook for Sherman continued to be favorable. The voting began on Friday, June 22, and on the first ballot Sherman received 229 votes, which was twice as many as his nearest competitor. On the second ballot the number of his supporters ran up to 249, certain accessions having been made in Pennsylvania. But his strength never equalled Mr. Hanna's estimate of 300 votes. Massachusetts only gave him 9 out of a total of 28, Pennsylvania 53 out of 60, Ohio 46, and the rest came from the South. On the subsequent ballots Mr. Sherman's strength slowly declined. He continued to lead his competitors until and including the sixth ballot, but in the meantime Benjamin Harrison had been gaining steadily. The latter was nominated on the eighth ballot, and in selecting him the Convention had nominated the next best man to Mr. Sherman.

The official proceedings of the Convention were tame enough, but behind them was a seething caldron of negotiation and intrigue. It exhibited at its worst the regular method of nominating presidential candidates, because, in the absence of a strong popular preference for any one man, free opportunity was provided for the use of dubious methods and the action of equivocal motives. During the first two days the most active subterranean intrigue was being carried on in favor of Blaine; but Mr. Blaine never gave it open and authoritative countenance. While a considerable part of the Convention was ready to be stampeded, the sentiment in Mr. Blaine's favor was not general enough to afford sufficient body to the project. Until Sunday, however, the hopes of the supporters of Mr. Blaine ran high. On Sunday they vanished, and the delegates who had been waiting for a possible Blaine stampede began really to consider whom they could gain most by nominating.

In spite of the fact that Sherman had been losing since the second ballot, he is said still to have had a fair chance on Sunday. New York was hesitating between Harrison and Sherman, and it would not have taken much to make the tide set towards Ohio. More remarkable was the sudden and unexpected strength developed by William McKinley. In spite of the fact that he was not a candidate, a few delegates persisted in voting for him, and for a while on Sunday his candidacy developed a subterranean strength which was never represented in the ballot. McKinley was, indeed, assured by the delegates of several states that Ohio might get the nomination in his person — provided Sherman would withdraw. These representations were telegraphed to Sherman, but he refused to release any of his supporters. Mr. McKinley had protested on Saturday during the session of the Convention against the unauthorized use of his name. His scrupulous loyalty to Senator Sherman was a matter of very favorable comment in Republican newspapers after the close of the Convention.

Senator Theodore E. Burton in his "Life of John Sherman" in the series of "American Statesmen" makes the following comment on the defeat of Mr. Sherman: "At this Convention (1888) the delegation from Ohio was for the first time unanimous for him. There were, however, rumors of lack of cordiality on the part of some leading members of the delegation, which did much to diminish support from other states." One of the delegates involved by these rumors was Governor Foraker. He was openly accused of treachery by the supporters of Sherman. He vehemently and indignantly denied the accusation, but he never convinced his colleagues, and his behavior had certain dubious aspects. On Sunday an interview with him appeared in the newspapers, stating that Sherman was no longer a possibility, and that on Monday he would vote for Blaine. This interview he subsequently repudiated, but if he had not given it out, why should it be fabricated? It is significant also that members of the Columbus Club had paraded the streets of Chicago waving aloft portraits of the Governor and wearing his badges on their coat. It is stated that the name of Blaine could be read on the other side of these badges.

These circumstances are mentioned, not because they afford conclusive proof that Mr. Foraker was playing a double game, but merely to explain the conviction of his colleagues that he was not loyal to John Sherman. In his statement Mr. Foraker admits the existence of bad feeling in the delegation, but attributes it to another cause. He says: "A great many colored delegates from the South, as is their custom, had tickets to the Convention which they desired to sell. They brought their tickets to our rooms at the hotel, and Mr. Hanna, in the presence of us all, bought them. I protested against such methods, saying that it would bring scandal on the entire delegation and hurt Sherman's cause. Mr. Hanna and I had a spirited discussion over the matter, and it resulted in my leaving the rooms and seeking apartments on another floor." There is some truth in the foregoing statement. Other members of the Convention state that Mr. Hanna had in his trunk more tickets to the Convention than he could have obtained in any way save by their purchase from negro delegates. Such practices were common at the time; but they were indefensible, and if they evoked a protest from Mr. Foraker, he deserves credit for the protest. The split in the delegation must, however, be traced to a wholly different cause.

Rightly or wrongly, not only Mr. Hanna, but the other leading members of the delegation believed that Mr. Foraker was secretly hostile to Senator Sherman's nomination, and that this hostility ruined Mr. Sherman's chance of success. The intimate association between the two men ended in June, 1888. After the Convention they exchanged a few acrimonious letters in respect to the distribution and settlement of the expenses incurred at Chicago. Their correspondence ceased. It was not renewed for many years, and then only on rare occasions and for purposes in which, as the two Senators from Ohio, they had a joint official interest.

The story of Mark Hanna's friendship with Mr. Foraker and its rupture has been told at some length, because the incident did much to determine the course of Mr. Hanna's subsequent political career. In case he had remained intimately associated with Mr. Foraker, he might never have become so intimately associated with Mr. McKinley. Mr. Foraker himself ventures the opinion that their break resulted indirectly in the nomination of McKinley. However that may be, the continuation of his intimacy with Mr. Foraker would probably have prevented him from attaching himself thereafter so ardently and so exclusively to Mr. McKinley's political advancement. The rupture of his first political friendship did more, however, than clear the path for the formation of the second. His more intimate association with Mr. McKinley was in a measure the immediate result of his break with Mr. Foraker.

The behavior of Mr. McKinley at the Convention made a deep impression on Mr. Hanna. The essential fabric of his own life consisted of personal relationships. He instinctively placed a higher value on loyalty than on any other moral quality. He could overlook almost any human failing, except disloyalty. Erroneously or not, he considered that Mr. Foraker had been secretly hostile to the candidacy of Senator Sherman. He knew that Mr. McKinley had been scrupulously faithful under a peculiarly severe and unexpected personal temptation. In subsequent conversations about McKinley, he often referred with the utmost admiration to Mr. McKinley's refusal to consider the possible purchase of the highest American political honor by the desertion of the candidate to whom he was pledged — even when that candidate had lost all chance of success. Thus the new political friendship was in a sense founded on the ruins of the old.

The rupture with Mr. Foraker resulted, not merely in the creation of new friendships, but also in the creation of new enmities. He and the Governor, in ceasing to be friends, became active opponents. Thereafter the Republican party of Ohio was, until Mr. Hanna's death, divided into two factions. On Mr. Hanna's side were ranged the whole group of Republicans who had been interested in Senator Sherman's nomination. It contained Mr. Sherman himself, Mr. McKinley, Benjamin Butterworth, Charles Foster and Mark Hanna. On the other side, Mr. Foraker was the only Republican of ability and prominence. He was a proud, self-contained and self-confident man, whose nature it was to play a lone hand. He himself states that he never afterwards had a political ally, with whom he was as closely associated as he had been for a while with Mr. Hanna. It speaks well for his skill in political management that he should have been able to hold his own against such a combination of popularity, effective power and political ability as Mr. McKinley and Mr. Hanna eventually constituted.

There resulted one of the most extraordinary factional fights offered by the history of American politics. Its existence was notorious. There was great bitterness of feeling. The two factions frequently came to open blows in the primaries, in the state conventions and in the legislature. Yet it was rarely, if ever, carried so far as to imperil party success. From 1888 until 1904 the Republicans of Ohio were victorious with one exception, in all the state and national elections. In spite of charges and countercharges of treachery on election day, the two factions kept their fight on the whole within the party and presented a sufficiently united front to the Democrats. Neither of them felt strong enough to push the disagreement to a finish and by risking a Democratic victory to endanger their own political plans as well as those of their adversaries. They subordinated their personal quarrels for the most part to Republican success. They spoke during the campaign from the same platforms, and they divided the offices. Nevertheless at almost every critical moment of Mr. Hanna's subsequent career he was embarrassed and at times almost defeated by the personal ill feelings consequent on his rupture with James B. Foraker.

CHAPTER XIII

POLITICAL FRIENDS AND ENEMIES

The defeat in the Convention of 1888 of the presidential candidacy of John Sherman was a severe disappointment to Mark Hanna and a source of the utmost personal exasperation. He had labored long and well for a worthy and practicable political object — only to fail at the last moment from an apparently unnecessary cause. The experience made a deep impression upon him. It constituted, as we have seen, the foundation of life-long political friendships and enmities. Thereafter his career in politics assumed, not a new direction, but a new emphasis, which proved to be salutary and edifying.

The idea of nominating and electing William McKinley to the presidency of the United States was born of those exasperating days at the Chicago Convention. There is no documentary proof of the truth of this statement, but his intimate friends date from this moment the conception of the idea, and the supposition is confirmed by a sufficient array of circumstantial corroboration. The circumstances and results of John Sherman's defeat both cleared the path for an exclusive devotion to the political advancement of William McKinley and made such an expenditure of his time and energy look eminently practicable.

Mark Hanna had made up his mind to nominate, if possible, a political leader from Ohio as the Republican candidate for the presidency. He was a man distinguished by great tenacity of purpose. The defeat of Sherman did not make him abandon the idea; but it taught him that John Sherman could never be the vehicle of its fulfilment. Thereafter that statesman had joined in Mr. Hanna's mind the majority of his fellow-countrymen in becoming a presidential impossibility. But the same series of exciting incidents which had extinguished the fires of Mr. Sherman's candidacy had unexpectedly made McKinley an obvious presidential possibility. A great name, a long and eminent career and a lot of hard work had not availed to place Sherman much nearer the nomination than McKinley had been with no work at all and a comparatively modest career and reputation. The contrast and the lesson were obvious. They became a matter of frequent contemporary comment in the newspapers, and Mark Hanna had more reason than any one else to have them stamped on his mind.

Just at the moment when Sherman's star was paling and McKinley's waxed brighter, Mr. Hanna had broken the only personal tie in politics which might have interfered with an interest in McKinley's career. James B. Foraker was transformed from a friend into an opponent under conditions which, erroneously or not, persuaded Mr. Hanna to place a higher value on McKinley's friendship than on Mr. Foraker's. McKinley took the place both of Sherman and Foraker in the hierarchy of Mr. Hanna's political and personal relationships. He became both the intimate friend with a political future of great promise and the available presidential candidate. Thereafter the determination to make Mr. McKinley President of the United States and in the meantime to promote his political advancement in every possible way became Mark Hanna's dominant interest in politics.

The friendship between the two men had grown slowly and naturally. Whatever the occasion of their first meeting, they had become intimate very gradually. During the years of Mr. Hanna's association with Mr. Foraker, he and Mr. McKinley, although coming from the same part of the state, had a different set of political associates and different candidates for important state offices. I have quoted a letter of Mr. Hanna's to the Governor, in which he complains of what he considers the exorbitance of the "Major's" demands for recognition. But Mr. Hanna's increasing activity in politics brought them into more and more frequent relations, and it may be that before the Convention the process of substituting McKinley for Foraker as the most valued of Mr. Hanna's political friends had already made headway. The Governor and the Congressman were in some measure political rivals, because they were the two rising Republican leaders of Ohio whose careers might conflict; and in any event a strong interest in the political career of one of them would have interfered with any but a subordinate interest in the career of the other. The close political and personal association which began after the convention of 1888 between Mr. Hanna and Mr. McKinley blossomed suddenly, but its roots had been slowly growing for a period of over ten years.

The startling and unforced growth of McKinley's presidential candidacy in the Convention of 1888 was due probably to his prominence as an advocate of high protection. His amiable disposition and his winning demeanor undoubtedly contributed to his popularity, and the fact that he hailed from a centrally situated state like Ohio contributed to his availability. But the chief reason why a certain number of Republicans turned almost instinctively towards him was due to his association with the policy of protecting American manufacturers to the limit. President Cleveland's message in December, 1886, and his renomination had made it certain that the campaign of 1888 would be fought and decided on the tariff issue. The Republicans were glad to accept the challenge and turned naturally towards the man who was considered to be the ablest advocate of the party's policy.

Major McKinley had been a Representative in Congress from the Mahoning Valley district since 1877, one term only excepted. He had gradually secured the confidence of his party associates by his tact, his attractive personality, his industry and his ability as a speaker. His congressional reputation had been associated almost from the start with an advocacy of high protection. When Garfield retired from the Ways and Means Committee, before his nomination to the presidency, McKinley became the member of that body from Ohio. He had a good deal to do with framing the tariff act of 1883, and increased his reputation during the debates on that measure. In the Republican Convention of 1884 he was chairman of the Committee on Resolutions and was associated with the writing of the party platform. During the succeeding years he added to his fame by his able opposition to the several proposals introduced by Democrats, looking towards tariff revision. He became in fact the leading Republican protectionist debater, and when the Republican Convention assembled in 1888 with a fight on the tariff ahead, McKinley had become the inevitable man for the chairmanship of the Committee on Resolutions. The definite establishment of the tariff issue as the dividing line between the two parties was bound to increase the political prestige of the man who had earned recognition as the most conspicuous exponent of the high protectionist idea. If Mr. Hanna had not possessed a hundred other reasons for a peculiar interest in McKinley, the latter's association with protectionism might in itself have been sufficient to create it.

A coalescence can be plainly traced at this point between Mark Hanna's dominant personal political interest and his dominant impersonal political interest. He had always represented in politics the point of view of a business man; and now for the first time a national campaign was about to be waged on an issue involving in his opinion the business prosperity of the country. The appearance of such an issue was a challenge to him to become more than ever interested in active political work — particularly in view of the fact that every victory of protection was a contribution towards the possible victorious candidacy of his personal friend, Major McKinley.

Previous to the campaign of 1888 the issue between the parties had never been definitely made on the tariff. The Democrats had shown a strong leaning towards tariff reform, but there had always been a minority of protectionist Democrats. The great majority of Republicans had been extreme protectionists, but until the secession of the independents in 1884, there had always been a minority of tariff reform Republicans. President Cleveland's message in 1886 had established the issue; and his plea for revision was based upon arguments which could not be ignored. Quite apart from any economic theory for or against protection, the existing tariff was piling up a surplus in the Treasury which for various reasons could no longer be used, as in the past, to reduce the national debt. Its accumulation was an embarrassment to the money market and an unnecessary drain on the economic resources of the country. Some revision of the tariff was necessary, and a revision in the direction of lower duties looked like the only possible way of getting rid of the surplus. The Democrats, however, advocated lower duties, not merely to reduce the income of the government, but because they proposed to destroy protectionism as the American fiscal policy. While none of the measures of revision introduced by them were framed on the basis of a tariff for revenue only, their arguments were based upon the intrinsic desirability of free trade and the iniquity of protectionism.

Business men in any way associated with protected manufacturing industries rallied with enthusiasm and determination to the fiscal policy of the Republican party. Among them Mark Hanna was not the least enthusiastic and determined. He had never known any but a protectionist fiscal system. He accepted it as the foundation, not merely of American industrial expansion, but of industrial safety. Depending as he always did upon his personal experience as his guide, he identified protectionism with the traditional American fiscal system — the system which sought to give the American producer exclusive control of the home market, and which practically allowed the beneficiaries of the tariff to draw up the schedules. The serious attack made upon the system seemed to give him as a representative in politics of the business interest a new duty to perform. Certain conditions which he considered essential to business prosperity were being threatened by political agitation. He and other business men must rally to their defence.

Thus the campaign of 1888 first brought clearly to light an underlying tendency in American political and industrial development which until then had remained somewhat obscure. Since the Civil War the national economic system had been becoming relatively more industrial and relatively less agricultural. The increasing proportion of the population dependent on industry lived, not merely in New England and in the Middle States, but throughout the Middle West. The rapid growth of industry had been partly dependent upon legislative encouragement. It had given to the people interested in the protected industries a reason for demanding helpful legislation and a reason for fearing adverse legislation. This encouragement, moreover, had not taken the form merely of protecting manufacturers against foreign competition. The large business interests of the country had been encouraged, also, by the utmost laxity in the granting of corporate privileges and the utmost freedom from state and national administrative regulation.

There had been a general disposition to grant to the business interests what they wanted, because American public opinion was substantially agreed upon the desirability in the public benefit of the utmost possible stimulation of business activity. The result had been to make business vulnerable at a hundred different points to dangerous political attacks, and thus to make business prosperity immediately dependent upon political conditions.

The first serious attack upon the traditional system made by a national party was President Cleveland's antiprotectionist campaign. The protected industries defended themselves with their natural weapons. They subscribed more liberally than ever before to the Republican electoral expenses. In 1888 more money was raised than in any previous national campaign, and it was raised more largely from business men. Its ability to obtain increased supplies from such sources was a Godsend to the machine, because the spread of the movement towards Civil Service Reform had diminished its collection from office-holders, while at the same time the constant increase of political professionalism was making electoral campaigns more than ever expensive. Large expenditures for political purposes thereafter became the rule; and the needs of professional politicians, like other parasites, soon increased up to the level of their means of subsistence.

Mark Hanna, as a representative in politics of the business interest, was necessarily connected with this increased raising and expenditure of money for political objects. The one way at that time in which he could fight the political battles of the business interests was to provide the men on the firing-line with ammunition and food; and that way he took. He became one of an auxiliary committee to the Republican National Committee whose specific duty it was to solicit campaign contributions.

Mr. Hanna was entitled to ask other Republicans for contributions because he himself set them a good example. He himself had always been a liberal contributor to the funds of his party. His own experience had taught him how far the successful conduct of a campaign under American political conditions depends upon a free expenditure of money. He knew that the expenses of speakers had to be paid, halls rented, literature distributed, impecunious candidates helped, the registration and the vote pulled out and the polls watched. He knew that much of this work had to be done by men who were accustomed to be rewarded, and that they could not all be rewarded at the public expense with offices. Some of them had to be employed. He knew that the campaign committees were always short of funds, and he knew that he could not show a more effective practical interest in politics than by helping to pay expenses. Whenever he did anything, he did it thoroughly. Probably no man in the country contributed more liberally, considering his means, to the war-chest of his party than did Mr. Hanna.

A political associate describes him as a "cheerful giver." This gentleman, who was a member of the Republican committee of Cuyahoga County for twenty-five years, states that Mr. Hanna was the only Republican in the city of Cleveland who would voluntarily draw his check for campaign purposes. Many of his business associates could be induced by personal solicitation to make contributions, but Mr. Hanna never needed to be dunned. He would say to the committee as he handed to them his first contribution: "Boys, I suppose you'll need some money. If you run short, you know where my office is." During the Garfield campaign he sent four different checks for $1000 each to the State Committee in Columbus; and this was merely one incident among a hundred. In the fall of 1887, for instance, the local campaign committee of Cuyahoga County found itself after election with a debt of $1260 on its hands. An attempt was made to collect the money from prominent Republicans, but with no success. One morning several of the committee were in their room, talking over the futile efforts. Mr. Hanna came in, and noticing the air of gloom, said: "It looks pretty blue here! What's the matter?" They told him, and much to their surprise and joy he sat down at the table and drew his own check for the whole amount. "There," he said, "pay your debts and look cheerful."

He gave as freely to individual political associates as to committees. Almost all his political friends were at one time or another in debt to him. We have already seen that he rendered to Mr. Foraker some assistance at a moment when the

Governor, at that time a poor man, was really in grave distress. He constantly helped McKinley by loans, by taking care of notes and by the financing of his friend's campaigns. General Charles Grosvenor was another local politician who was very much beholden to Mr. Hanna for financial assistance. A friend or associate who had any claim at all could depend on him for effective help; and sometimes the need of help would be anticipated and the help rendered without solicitation.

One salient instance may be specified. The David H. Kimberley whom Mr. Hanna had permitted in 1884 to work for Mr. Edwin Cowles rather than himself was nominated shortly afterwards for County Treasurer. He was poor, and his association with Mr. Hanna in politics had not been intimate. Shortly after his nomination a young man came to his store and left a package containing $500 for campaign expenses, but refused to divulge the name of the contributor. In a few weeks another $500 arrived from the same source, and just before the day of election an additional $200. The last instalment was accompanied by a note, stating that the $1200 could be returned after election, — in case Mr. Kimberley were successful, but that if he were beaten he would never be told of the name of the donor. He learned afterwards indirectly that the contributions were made by Mark Hanna. Mr. Kimberley was elected. When he was about to assume office, he found he had to supply a heavy bond and he did not know where to turn for his security. He was just coming from the court-house where he had been copying the bond with his own hands, when he met Mr. Hanna on the street. "What's the matter, Dave?" the latter asked. "You look pretty serious this morning." "I am thinking," Mr. Kimberley said, "about my bond as County Treasurer." Mr. Hanna asked for the bond and looked it over. "My gracious! a million dollars," he exclaimed; "are they ever going to stop hammering you?" Mr. Kimberley assured him that it was an exact copy of the bond of the existing Treasurer. Mr. Hanna took it, signed it himself, and persuaded five or six of his well-to-do friends also to sign it.

I have cited the case of Mr. Kimberley at some length because in this particular instance more than one motive may have prompted Mr. Hanna. Mr. Kimberley was running for the office of County Treasurer, and Mr. Hanna was building up the business of a recently organized bank. The *Plain-Dealer* asserted at the time that there might be some connection between Mr. Hanna's interest in Mr. Kimberley and his interest in his bank. If so, no action hurtful to the interests of the county resulted. Mr. Kimberley was reëlected and no irregularities were discovered, although his opponents were ready to pounce upon evidence thereof. But assuming that the help rendered by Mr. Hanna to Mr. Kimberley may have been prompted by a desire for county deposits, such a motive does not explain the way in which the loan was made. In case Mr. Kimberley had been defeated, Mr. Hanna did not want him to feel any personal obligation in the matter — an obligation which would have been onerous to a poor man. Mr. Kimberley himself attributed the loan to Mr. Hanna's wish to do a kindness to a fellow-Republican whose means were not equal to the expenses of his canvass.

However we are to regard such an incident, and however little we may like the fact that Mr. Hanna and his street railway company contributed to the expenses of electing councilmen, it is easy to over-estimate the importance of such incidents. On the whole and in the long run Mr. Hanna did not make his political gifts with any intention of buying specific services. His political gifts, both to organizations and associates, must be considered as prompted partly by the same motives as his charitable gifts, both for the encouragement of worthy causes and the success of needy persons. As I shall describe in another connection Mr. Hanna was an extraordinarily and even a somewhat indiscriminately generous man. He gave freely and without close inquiry to anybody or purpose which could fairly claim assistance. To give and to give without calculation was one of the dominant impulses of his nature. In a business transaction he was as keen as another man about getting five dollars' worth for the expenditure of five dollars; but any cause or any person which aroused his sympathies or interest would unloosen his purse strings and disarm his business scruples. His interest in political causes and friends was just as much an expression of his better nature as his interest in charitable causes and needy individuals. He spent his money liberally and innocently in every way which seemed to him worth while; and, of course, politics, and in particular Republican party politics, were from his point of view extremely well worth while.

Mr. Hanna's personal liberality and his prominence both as a business man and politician tended, however, to make the local Republican committees depend on him for a large part of their supplies. From being a generous contributor he passed by easy gradations into the position of being an able collector of campaign funds from his business associates. He had the reputation of being a man who could do really effective work in eliciting contributions from his fellow Republicans, and this reputation was responsible for his selection as financial auxiliary to the Republican National Committee of 1888. The political managers saw that the tariff issue afforded them an extraordinarily good opportunity of persuading the manufacturers to "give up." Systematic efforts were made to turn the opportunity to good account. Mr. Hanna's district was northern Ohio. He raised money in Cleveland, in Toledo, in the Mahoning Valley and in adjacent territory. His collections are said to have reached $100,000, all of which went to the National Committee. His own personal contribution to the same committee was $5000, and he also went to the assistance of the county and state committees.

Although Mr. Hanna's connection with the campaign of 1888 was confined to the work of securing contributions, it was necessary to describe at this point the complexion which the general political situation was assuming, and Mr. Hanna's own personal relation thereto. During the Convention and campaign of 1888 the political forces and tendencies which culminated in the campaign of 1896 and which gave opportunity and meaning to Mr. Hanna's subsequent career are for the first time plainly to be distinguished. The idea of nominating McKinley was born contemporaneously with the appearance of the conditions which finally resulted in his nomination, and the man who cherished the personal project became himself the political representative of a certain relation between business and politics, implied by these conditions.

The campaign resulted in the election of Benjamin Harrison, but not by any large majority. Mr. Cleveland had a plurality on the popular vote, and the change of a few thousand ballots cast in New York and Indiana would have beaten the Republicans. They succeeded none the less in keeping their majority in the Senate and in winning a small majority in the House of Representatives, which was subsequently increased by unseating Democrats wherever their elections could be plausibly contested. In the winter of 1889 and 1890, when the new Congress assembled, the Republicans for the first time in many years were in complete control of both departments of the General Government, and they were committed to the passage of some legislation looking towards the reduction of the surplus without doing any injury to the protective system.

In November, 1889, about a week before the meeting of the new Congress, Mark Hanna went to Washington. His object in making the trip was to help Mr. McKinley in his fight for the Speakership of the House, and it is significant that he took the first opportunity which offered after the Convention of 1888 to work on Mr. McKinley's behalf. He put up at the Ebbit House and took an active part in the canvass. Mr. William H. Merriam states that his part was effective as well as active, for he actually converted to Mr. McKinley some votes from Minnesota. But his efforts were unavailing. Mr. McKinley's competitor for the place, Mr. Thomas B. Reed, was selected by the caucus by a majority of one vote.

Mr. McKinley's defeat was probably beneficial rather than the reverse to his subsequent career. The Speaker appointed him to the chairmanship of the Ways and Means Committee, and as chairman he became nominally responsible for the new Republican tariff policy. The bill in which it was embodied had his name attached to it, which made him in the eyes of the country more than ever the most conspicuous exponent of the theory and practice of high protection.

Inasmuch as their victory had been won by a narrow margin, the Republicans would have done well to use it with discretion. By a few reductions in the existing schedules, they might have quieted antitariff agitation for long time without doing any injury to the protectionist system. But the beneficiaries of the tariff were in the saddle, and they pursued the opposite course. Rates were raised all along the line. The surplus was

MR. HANNA IN THE EARLY NINETIES

abolished largely by the simple device of spending it. The revenue was reduced by making duties which were almost prohibitory entirely so and by abandoning the large income derived from the duty on raw sugar, which at that time was produced only in small quantities in this country. Heavy duties were levied on many agricultural products which were not and could not be imported, except in very small quantities, and a successful attempt was made to establish new industries, such as the manufacture of tin plate and certain grades of silk. Finally, since the revenue still promised to be excessive, the appropriations for pensions and for other purposes were swollen beyond all previous records.

Such was the policy embodied in the McKinley Bill. It proved to be a dangerous policy for the Republican party. The effect of the bill was to raise prices all along the line. Every drummer became an effective campaign agent for the Democrats; and in the election in the fall of 1890, following the passage of the act, the Republicans were reduced to an almost insignificant minority in the House of Representatives. Two years later the Democrats, for the first time since the war, elected their presidential candidate, a large majority in the lower House and a small majority in the Senate. Some of the wiser Republicans, such as James G. Blaine and Benjamin Butterworth, one of Mr. Hanna's intimate friends, had predicted this result and tried to avoid it; but in truth forces had been unloosed which were beyond individual control. The policy of the Republicans in the session of 1889–1890 must be considered as a culminating expression of a method of economic legislation which had prevailed in this country at least since the Civil War. Under this method the only interests consulted in respect to a piece of economic legislation were the special interests thereby benefited; and the protective tariff was only one illustration of the practice.

In the case of the McKinley Bill and the legislation which accompanied it, the practice had been pushed to an extreme which exposed the incompatibility between the unregulated demands of a special interest and the manifest requirements of the national interest; but the error was natural, and the manufacturers were only behaving as all the other special interests had behaved. The American economic system had been conceived as a huge profit-sharing concern, the function of the government being to encourage productive enterprise in every form by lending assistance to the producers. Business of all kinds had thus become inextricably entangled with politics, and in one way or another the private income of the majority of American citizens was very much influenced by the government legislation. And whatever criticisms may be passed on this economic system or whatever the ensuing excesses, it was undoubtedly planned in good faith for the purpose of stimulating American economic expansion in all its branches and of contributing to the prosperity of all classes of American society.

The business men and politicians of the day were so accustomed to his method of promoting American economic welfare that they accepted it as a matter of course. Among others both William McKinley and Mark Hanna accepted it as so fundamental as scarcely to need any defence. Mistakes might be made in applying the policy, abuses might arise under its administration of the resulting legislation, and different special interests might fight over the distribution of the benefits, but the system itself was rooted in the American tradition of economic legislation. In spite of protests against specific excesses and abuses, public opinion overwhelmingly supported the system as a whole, and its inevitable effects were to make business prosperity depend upon the course of political agitation and the result of elections. It was precisely the interdependence between business and politics which gave to a man like Mark Hanna, who embodied the alliance, an opportunity of effective influence.

The Republican disasters in the elections of 1890 brought with them unpleasant consequences, possible and actual, for Mark Hanna and his immediate associates. In order to understand the resulting political complications, we must return to the course of political events in the state of Ohio. The prompt exhibition after the Convention of Mr. Hanna's friendship for McKinley was balanced by an even prompter exhibition of his hostility to Mr. Foraker. The latter was once again a candidate for governor. Mr. Hanna attended the State Convention held in June, 1889, at Columbus, and opposed Mr.

POLITICAL FRIENDS AND ENEMIES

Foraker's nomination. McKinley also was present and made a speech nominating another candidate, in which he had remarked that "no obligation to party can justify treachery to party associates." But Mr. Foraker was too strong for his enemies. He was nominated and stumped the state with his usual vigor. He was opposed by the Democrats, chiefly on the ground that he was seeking a third term, and he was beaten in spite of the fact that some of the Republican ticket were elected. His defeat increased the schism between himself and the McKinleyites, who were erroneously accused in the newspapers of treachery to the state ticket.

Another incident of the fall of 1889 served to intensify the ill feeling which certain of Mr. Hanna's friends bore towards the redoubtable Governor. Late in September a Cincinnati newspaper published an alleged contract which implicated the Democratic candidate for governor, James E. Campbell, in an attempt to use his official position as a congressional representative for the purpose of selling to the government a patent ballot-box. A copy of the contract had been furnished to the editor of the paper by Governor Foraker. A few days later it was divulged that John Sherman, William McKinley and Benjamin Butterworth, among others, were also signers of the alleged contract. It developed almost immediately that the paper was a forgery and that the Governor had been misled into accepting it as genuine. The fact that Mr. Foraker had given to the press a paper implicating prominent Republicans of Ohio in a dishonorable transaction without giving them any warning or allowing them any hearing was attributed by the injured gentlemen to personal malice.

In the meantime Mark Hanna was trying to procure from a Republican President certain offices for his political associates in Cleveland — thus compensating himself for the loss of his influence with the Governor. But for some reason President Harrison disliked Mr. Hanna and either ignored or forgot the efforts which the latter had used on behalf of his election. Every one of his recommendations was turned down. He did not even succeed when he requested the appointment of an old friend as lighthouse master at the end of the Cleveland Breakwater. These recommendations was usually made through

Senator Sherman and indorsed by him, but other candidates were always appointed. Senator Sherman wrote to Mr. Hanna in April, 1889, "I am weary and discouraged,—weary from pressure based upon the opinion that I can do something for my friends, and discouraged because I have not been able to do anything."

Mr. Hanna also became involved in a controversy with Congressman T. E. Burton about the appointment to the head of the Cleveland post-office. Mr. Hanna was backing our old friend William M. Bayne, — the man whom he had urged twice upon Foraker for the oil inspectorship and whom he had nominated for mayor. Mr. Burton's candidate was A. T. Anderson. In this instance the Postmaster-general, Mr. Wanamaker, was favorable to Mr. Hanna, but his influence was of no avail. President Harrison insisted that Mr. Burton, as the local congressman, was entitled to the appointment; and he received it. Mr. Burton states that his relations with Mr. Hanna remained friendly after this little passage-at-arms, but they were not quite as friendly as before. Evidently at this particular period Mr. Hanna must have felt that however interesting was this game of politics, the winnings were small in proportion to the losses.

He had, however, one compensation. He was making some very fast friends among some very fine men. At the time when his political intimacy with both Sherman and McKinley was increasing, he was also becoming extremely friendly with Benjamin Butterworth. Mr. Butterworth was not only an able man and a disinterested public servant, but he was gifted with a highly expansive and sympathetic disposition. The warmth of his feelings towards his friends obtained a very characteristic expression in his correspondence with them. His letters to Mr. Hanna are not like the letters of Mr. Hanna's other associates, that is, merely dry business scripts. They overflow with expressions of personal feeling, and are the kind of letters which only a man of lively affections and some imagination could write to a sympathetic friend. Letters of this kind are so rare in the life of a man like Mr. Hanna that they deserve to be quoted for their own and for his sake.

Under the date of June 12, 1890, Mr. Butterworth writes:

"I have your delightful scrawl before me again, and whenever I see the name of Hanna there comes before me your good-natured face and kindly bearing, the influence of which is to impel me to pack my satchel and go to Cleveland, where I can see you in the flesh, but duty rides me as if I were a flagging steed and had some devil mounted on me with whip and spur to hound me on. Never mind, the day is coming when I will have some time to devote to my friends, and the night is approaching when there will be a long rest and a delightful sleep on the bosom of our common mother. Whether all there is of us will lie down to that delightful slumber I do not know, but I know that there is in us a spark of divinity which shall vitalize a new-born man, and that together you and I will stroll along by the still waters of another world. Of course you will have a higher degree of happiness and better luck there, just as you have here, and *that* you will deserve there, even as you do here."

In February, 1891, Mr. Butterworth deals with the political situation in Ohio in the following terms: "Touching politics, you will see that the champion of forgery is still splashing in the waters and aspiring to that which only good men ought to attain to. John Sherman is as usual playing fast and loose. There is a struggle going on in regard to the postmastership in Cincinnati. Sherman is afraid of McKinley and worried about Harrison. McKinley is troubled about both Harrison and Sherman, and Sherman is as anxious to be President and continued in the Senatorial office as ever he was in his life, so that none of them exercises any influence with reference to clean and honorable politics, but simply play in the game."

A little later Mr. Butterworth, having failed of reëlection to Congress, was appointed, partly, it would appear, owing to Mr. Hanna's influence, to an official position with the Columbian Exposition Company; and on March 18, 1891, he writes from Chicago the following characteristic letter to Mr. Hanna:—

"March 18, 1891.

"My dear Hanna:—

"It is not probable that you are in a frame of mind that would enable you to enjoy a line from an old friend, who snatches a minute from an hour heavily mortgaged to other duties to tumble upon you a few rambling observations. Well! Mark, I am out of the procession. I no longer keep the lock-step prescribed by party discipline nor wear the fetters of a political bondsman. As Uncle John said (not meaning a word of it), 'I can now say just what I d—n please.' I would have added, if I had been in Uncle John's pants, 'so long as no one hears me.' I am out of it, and, my dear friend, I feel like a tired harvester at set of sun, when the cradle has been thrown aside, and he tumbles on the grass beneath some spreading tree.

"I met and lunched with our good friend Governor Merriam. He thinks you are one of the best fellows on earth, in fact, he said so; and I hadn't the heart to correct him. And to-day, so far as any remark of mine is concerned, Governor Merriam thinks his eulogy of you was approved of by me.

"It is seven o'clock P.M. I am here alone. The shadows of night have settled on this restless city. I feel less alone here communing with you, breaking your rest, than if I was in the motley throng that gathers nightly at the Palmer House."

Letters such as those of Mr. Butterworth are unique in Mr. Hanna's correspondence. He received, of course, many letters overflowing with expressions of personal feeling, but the letters which he received from political friends and associates refer merely to matters of temporary political and personal business. This is particularly true in respect to his correspondence with Mr. McKinley. Only about a score of letters and some four telegrams written by Mr. McKinley to Mr. Hanna have been preserved; and the great majority of these are trivial in character. It is, consequently, impossible to find any significant indications in their correspondence of the increasing intimacy between the two men. Mr. McKinley was in all his political relations an extremely wary man. He early adopted the practice of not committing to paper any assertions or promises which might subsequently prove to be embarrassing; and even in the case of important conversations over the telephone, he frequently took the precaution of having a witness at his end of the line. It is scarcely to be expected that any letters of his will be of much assistance, either to his own biographer or that of any political associate — in spite of, or rather because of, the fact that McKinley late in his life wrote too many of his letters with a biographer so much in mind.

All important matters were discussed between the two men in private conference. When a personal interview was impossible, a confidential intermediary was usually employed. Such methods of correspondence suited Mr. Hanna as well as Mr. McKinley, not because he was to the same extent a man of caution and precaution, but because in business he had been accustomed to settling important affairs by means of personal interviews. As in the case of almost all genuine Americans, his natural method of expression was the spoken word, not only because the spoken word was direct and frank, but because it carried with it the force of a man's will and personality. Letters were merely the forerunners and the consequences of personal interviews, or else a sort of hyphen between them.

A majority of the surviving letters written by Mr. McKinley to Mr. Hanna date, however, from this particular period. During 1889 and 1890, Mr. McKinley spent most of his time in Washington, and was, consequently, obliged to write some few notes to Mr. Hanna about patronage, and about such legislative matters as the metal schedules of the tariff bill. Later, when one of them was living in Canton and the other in Cleveland, they were connected by a special telephone service. Some of the notes of this period may be quoted, not because of their intrinsic importance, but merely as a sample of the sort of letter which Mr. McKinley was in the habit of writing to his friend.

During the fall of 1890 he was fighting hard for reëlection to Congress, and Mr. Hanna was naturally taking an active interest in his canvass. The following note was written in Cleveland, on the occasion of a short visit, unexpectedly made by Mr. McKinley during Mr. Hanna's absence.

"CLEVELAND, Oct. 6, 1890.

"DEAR MR. HANNA: —

"Awfully sorry not to see you. Came up last night and have remained until the last moment and find that you will not be home until evening. Would stay longer, but have a meeting to-night.

"Frank Osborne will *talk to you fully* and he will explain to you all. I start out to-morrow for the remainder of the campaign. The outlook is surprisingly favorable.
"Your friend,
"W. McKINLEY, JR."

A little over a month later, after he had been defeated for reelection to Congress, he wrote to Mr. Hanna as follows:—

"CHICAGO, ILL., Nov. 12, 1890.
"MY DEAR MR. HANNA:—
"I have your kind favor of Nov. 10. I am here for a little rest — sorry not to have seen you when last in Cleveland — may run up there before my return to Washington, but am not certain. At all events I will see you.
"I agree with you that defeat under the circumstances was for the best.
"With kind regards
"I am sincerely
"W. McKINLEY."

"P. S. There is no occasion for alarm. We must take no backward step."

Evidently from the foregoing note Mr. Hanna had not been at all discouraged by the Republican defeat in the fall of 1890 — at least in so far as Major McKinley's political future was concerned. He evidently argued that inasmuch as the legislation with which McKinley's name was associated had been disapproved by public opinion, it was just as well for McKinley to retire from a region of political action in which he had incurred unpopularity, and to continue his career in some other part of the political battlefield. At all events the plan rapidly took shape of nominating McKinley for governor in the summer of 1891; and this plan was successfully accomplished. The Convention was held in June, and the Major was placed at the head of the ticket, practically without opposition. He was not opposed by Foraker; that gentleman had other irons in the fire. The Legislature elected in the fall of 1891 named a Senator to succeed Mr. Sherman; and Mr. Foraker was anticipating and seeking an enlarged sphere of usefulness in Washington. The very fact which may have smoothed the way for the nomination of McKinley threatened the political future of another of Mr. Hanna's political friends — John Sherman himself.

In the campaign which followed, Mr. Hanna had, consequently, two objects to accomplish, both of which demanded unusual efforts. It was extremely necessary to elect Mr. McKinley. His political future was not necessarily compromised by the unpopularity of the McKinley Bill and his failure to be returned to the House of Representatives, because a turn of the tide might bring his policy of high protectionism back into favor. But a defeat in his candidacy for governor might well be disastrous to the presidential candidacy, which both of the friends already had in mind. It would create the impression of an insecure hold on the people of his own state, and thereafter it would be difficult to keep his figure before the public as a presidential possibility. Yet there was no certainty of McKinley's election. Republicanism was suffering a temporary eclipse all over the country. Foraker had been defeated two years before. The state of Ohio, which was always Republican on presidential years, frequently disconcerted the party machine by going Democratic on off years.

But the sentorial fight complicated the election still further, and aroused in Mr. Hanna an almost equal interest. He continued to be a close political friend of Senator Sherman, and for personal reasons ardently desired both the victory of the Senator and the defeat of Mr. Foraker. The failure to reëlect Mr. Sherman after his long service in the Senate would in Mr. Hanna's eyes have been a disgrace to his native state. Yet in order to return Mr. Sherman to the Senate, it was necessary to canvass the whole state by districts, and to see that enough candidates for the Legislature were pledged to vote for him.

In the campaign of 1891 Mr. Hanna gave even more of his time to Senator Sherman's candidacy than he did to that of Major McKinley. He undoubtedly took much more pains to secure Mr. McKinley's election than he did in the case of an ordinary Republican candidate; but his efforts for his friend were confined chiefly to raising money. He could trust the State Committee to work hard for the regular candidate for governor.

Mr. Sherman's interest, on the other hand, required personal direction, and Mr. Hanna assumed a large part of the work. His correspondence during these months is filled far more with the details of the Sherman, than with those of the McKinley, campaign.

He went, indeed, to unusual personal exertions to secure for McKinley a large campaign fund. He solicited contributions over his own personal signature, not merely in Ohio, but from manufacturers in Chicago and Pittsburgh, on the ground that the defeat of McKinley would be interpreted as a further disaster to the general cause of protection. While frequently rebuffed on the ground that Ohio ought to take care of her own protectionists, he obtained some little money from these irregular sources. He seems to have been unusually successful in collecting money in Cleveland, some of which went to the candidate himself for personal expenses. On August 30, 1891, he wrote to Mr. Hanna: "I am a thousand times obliged for your letter with enclosure. I will forward it at once to the State Committee. I beg you will give to all of my friends who participated my sincere thanks. It was most generous of you and others; and I have to thank you most of all." Two weeks later he writes: "Your favor of September 7 I find here upon my return home to-day. Please receive my sincere thanks for your goodness, and now I beg to suggest that you forward direct to the Committee any other contributions that may be placed in your hands. I have sufficient to defray my personal expenses." The payment of the personal expenses of a candidate had long been customary. Garfield received an allowance for his entertaining at Mentor during the campaign of 1880, and later in 1896 the National Committee allowed McKinley $10,000 for personal expenses.

In the case of Mr. Sherman's candidacy, Mr. Hanna's efforts were not confined to raising money. A good many thousand dollars were indeed contributed — partly by Senator Sherman himself — for the purpose of assisting legislative candidates in doubtful districts; and this money was placed in the hands of the chairman of the State Executive Committee, Mr. W. M. Hahn, who was favorable to Mr. Sherman's reëlection. But in addition special efforts had to be made to pledge legislative candidates to Sherman rather than to Foraker, and in case a pledge was refused to bring the pressure of local public opinion upon an adverse or doubtful nominee. Agents were sent all over the state to carry on this work. Not a district was neglected which offered any promise of a fruitful return.

In the beginning Senator Sherman had not taken very seriously the threatened opposition. Later, however, Captain Donaldson, a state committeeman who for years had made a specialty of looking after the legislative districts, and who was an ardent supporter of Mr. Sherman, was placed in charge of the details of the canvass. He calculated on being able to secure some fifty-three votes for Sherman in the caucus; but in order to do so he needed some $10,000 to spend in the doubtful counties. He went to Cleveland, and explained the situation to Mr. Hanna, who promised him the money. Senator Sherman himself selected the man to whom the disbursement of this fund was intrusted. They did not count upon any votes from Hamilton County, in spite of Mr. Sherman's expectations to the contrary, but a unanimous delegation from Cleveland was considered indispensable. Mr. Hanna took personal charge of his own county — the importance of which may be judged from the following extract from a letter of Senator Sherman to Mr. Hanna, dated Sept. 22, 1891. "I am assured," he writes, "from Columbus that if the nominees for the Legislature from Cuyahoga County are substantially solid for me, it will settle the senatorial contest and greatly relieve the canvass. So I feel that you are fighting the battle for the state." A week later, after the local primaries had been held, he writes: "You made a glorious fight in Cleveland, for which I am under a thousand obligations to you. The result is extremely gratifying, and I agree with you that without the active support you and others have rendered, we might have been defeated by superior organization."

On election day Mr. Hanna and his friends won a decisive victory. In a year of general Republican defeat, Mr. McKinley was elected governor by an unusually large majority. Immediately thereafter, Thomas B. Reed, the former Speaker, who had stumped Ohio during the campaign, wrote to Mr. McKinley, "I am much rejoiced over your victory, which is the only bright spot in the last elections. Your State Committee gave me a hard season, but it was wound up so delightfully at Mark Hanna's that if you ever want to coax me to do anything you had better send Hanna." The Legislature was Republican by a good majority.

Senator Sherman's friends calculated on the face of the returns that he would beat Foraker in the caucus, and they were surprised to find shortly after the election that the most confident claims were made from the Foraker headquarters of a Foraker victory. Certain members of the Legislature, including three from Cleveland, who were either pledged to Sherman or were counted upon by his managers were threatening to backslide. A week before the caucus Mr. Hanna went to Columbus and took personal charge of the Sherman campaign. The situation looked desperate; but it was saved, so Mr. Sherman himself stated to his friends, by Mr. Hanna's energy, enthusiasm and ability to bend other men to his will. Three of the Cleveland representatives, who had gone into hiding, were unearthed and forced into line. When the caucus was held, Senator Sherman received fifty-three votes to thirty-eight for Foraker.

On January 9 Senator Sherman wrote to Mr. Hanna the following letter: —

"My dear Sir: —

"Now, after the smoke of battle is cleared away, I wish first of all and above all to express to you my profound gratitude and sincere respects for the part you have taken in the recent Senatorial canvass. I feel that without you I would have been beaten. It was your foresight in securing the Cleveland delegation that gave us the strongest support and made it possible to counteract the evil influence of the Hamilton County delegation.

"You have been a true friend, liberal, earnest and sincere, without any personal selfish motive, but only guided by a sense of what is best for the people of Ohio and of the country. I wish you to know that I appreciate all this and will treasure it as long as I live and only wish the time may come when I may in some way show that I am deserving of all your kindness.

"When I was about to pay the bills, Hahn said you had assumed some or had provided means for the payment of certain expenses. It is not right that you should bear this burden, and I hope you will frankly state to me what amount you have expended and what obligations you have incurred, so that I may at least share it with you. I have so written to Hahn. It is a source of great satisfaction to me that our canvass was made without the expenditure of a single dollar for boodle, with no bitterness to our adversaries, and with no appeals for our candidate to the interested cupidity or ambition of the Senators and members.

"Please give my kindly greetings to your wife and tell her for me that she is lucky to have so good a husband, the soul of honor.

"Very sincerely yours,
"JOHN SHERMAN."

The foregoing letter speaks for itself, and calls for only one comment. In spite of Senator Sherman's professions of gratitude he never mentions Mr. Hanna's name in the lengthy account of his final election to the Senate, which appears in his "Reminiscences." Indeed, Mr. Hanna's name never appears in the entire book. The volume was published in 1895 and 1896, so that Mr. Sherman's later grievance against Mr. Hanna, if grievance it was, could have had nothing to do with the omission.

CHAPTER XIV

THE MAKING OF A PRESIDENT

THE victory in Ohio in the fall of 1891 was the first substantial triumph of Mark Hanna's political career. Theretofore the candidates in whose election he was most interested had usually been beaten; and these frequent failures must have been trying to a man who was accustomed to succeed, and whose cherished political purposes were all related to the election to office of certain friends and associates. The victories of McKinley and Sherman must, consequently, have been all the more gratifying. The first constituted an important step towards the realization of Mr. Hanna's dearest ambition. The second was a blow to the prestige of his irreconcilable opponent, and made it easier to keep control of the state organization in McKinley's interest. Thus the elections of 1891 had done much to repair the damage caused by the disaster of the previous fall. Mr. McKinley's prestige would be considerably enhanced by his selection during a year of Republican defeat to an office from which one Republican had already graduated to the presidency. McKinley had become personally more than ever a presidential possibility.

The question immediately to be considered was whether anything could or should be done to push the candidacy at the coming National Convention. The situation was difficult and complicated. The most prominent candidate for the nomination was, of course, President Benjamin Harrison. It is always a dangerous matter to oppose the renomination of a President who has done nothing to disqualify himself for a second term. A strong anti-administration sentiment is necessary to overcome the initial advantage which a President can derive from the prestige and patronage of his office; and an opponent is further handicapped because his candidacy must be based partly on a criticism of a President derived from his own party. Whenever a fight is made, it tends to become bitter and threatens a dangerous schism within the ranks of the Faithful.

Strong, however, as was the position of the President, it presented certain weaknesses, which the friends of an alternative candidate could scarcely ignore. Mr. Harrison was personally unpopular. He had made many enemies in the party, who would have been glad to see him defeated. On the surface his nomination was not by any means assured. A majority of the delegates were not pledged to vote for him. The disaffected elements in the party might be able to hold up the nomination and concentrate upon some other candidate. Among the disaffected Republicans was Mr. Hanna. He had not been well treated by Mr. Harrison and would in any event have been opposed to the President's renomination. In September, 1891, an attempt had been made to disarm his opposition. His friend, Charles Foster, who was Secretary of the Treasury, prevailed upon the President to offer to Mr. Hanna the office of Treasurer of the National Committee. It was a position which he was well qualified to fill, and which under ordinary circumstances he would have been likely to accept. But its acceptance would have tied him to the administration, and he declined. He wished to remain free to take any advantage of President Harrison's lack of strength which the situation, as it developed, permitted.

Under the circumstances the plan was adopted of keeping the McKinley candidacy above the surface but in the background. No attempt was made to secure the election of delegates pledged to McKinley. Mr. McKinley himself assumed the correct attitude of being overtly favorable to Harrison's renomination. But preparations were made to bring McKinley forward, in case Mr. Harrison's renomination proved to be difficult. Mr. Hanna's hope was that enough delegates would be kept away from the President by a revival of the Blaine candidacy to tie up the nomination and permit the introduction of McKinley into the breach. Mr. Hanna was not a delegate to the Convention, but he went to Minneapolis and opened an unofficial headquarters for McKinley at the West House. For some days he tried, not without prospects of success, to arrange combinations, which under certain possible contingencies might result in McKinley's favor.

It was, however, a useless effort. McKinley never had a chance, and he did well not to abandon his overt support of the President and his overt discouragement of his own followers. Mr. Harrison could not be beaten. Twelve of his friends, subsequently named the "Twelve Apostles," conceived the idea of collecting all the Harrison disciples together as a sort of demonstration in force, which would constrain the weaker brethren. The meeting was held in Market Hall and was attended by a sufficient number of delegates to assure the nomination. President Harrison received 535 votes on the first ballot and his selection was made unanimous. The McKinley headquarters at the West House had been closed some days before, although this fact did not prevent Mr. Hanna from continuing to work on behalf of his friend. As the event proved, it was fortunate that the President was strong enough to obtain a renomination. Probably no Republican candidate could have been elected in 1892, while at the same time the President's defeat resulted in making McKinley even more possible for 1896. He was generally admitted to be the most available man for the next nomination. No less than 182 delegates had voted for him as an unauthorized candidate, which was as many as had voted for Blaine. He had been hailed in the Convention as the candidate for '96. The symptoms could scarcely be more favorable.

The Convention was no sooner over than steps were taken in the direction of Governor McKinley's nomination in 1896. On this point the testimony of ex-Senator Charles Dick is explicit. He had been a delegate to the Minneapolis Convention; and (according to his account) Mr. Hanna and others of the Republican leaders in Ohio had talked with him about accepting the chairmanship of the State Committee in case McKinley were nominated. About two weeks later the State Committee met in Columbus, and selected Mr. Dick as chairman. As soon as he was notified, he started for Columbus to decline the honor. He had agreed to accept it only in case some Ohio man were nominated. There he had an interview with Governor McKinley, who urged him to accept and insisted that before reaching any negative decision he have an interview with Mr. Hanna. The result was that he allowed himself to be persuaded. They both of them urged the necessity of having a trustworthy McKinley man at the head of the State Committee, so that every local campaign between 1892 and 1896 could be conducted with a view to the nomination of the Governor in 1896.

No opportunity was lost to keep the candidate before the public. During the campaign of 1892 special efforts were made to make Mr. McKinley conspicuous on the stump. An unusually prolonged trip was arranged by Thomas H. Carter, chairman of the Republican National Committee, after consultation with Mr. Hanna. The Governor's route stretched as far west as Iowa and Minnesota, and as far east as Maine, and it included all the important intervening states. Wherever he went he made a favorable impression. He was not like William J. Bryan a great popular orator, but he was a persuasive and effective speaker, who could give dignity and sincerity to the commonplaces of partisan controversy. Above all, his amiability and his winning personal qualities never failed to make for him friends and well-wishers.

The defeat of Benjamin Harrison and the election of Grover Cleveland had, of course, a profound although at first a doubtful, effect upon Mr. McKinley's general standing as a presidential candidate. The campaign on his behalf would be either very much strengthened or very much weakened,— according to the success or failure of the new President's administration. Mr. Cleveland had been elected on the tariff issue. The high protectionist legislation passed in 1890 continued to be so unpopular that not only did he receive a larger majority in the electoral college than he had in 1884, but his party secured the control of both Houses of Congress. For the first time since the Civil War the Democrats were in a position to fulfil their preëlection promises. If they could pass a measure of tariff reform, which would receive the approval of the country, Mr. McKinley's chief political stock-in-trade would be very much damaged. On the other hand the failure of tariff reform as a practical economic and political policy would make him the logical candidate of his own party.

The situation, however, as it developed, brought with it an additional complication, which was to be as embarrassing to Mr. McKinley in 1896 as it was to President Cleveland in 1893. When the new administration assumed office in the March of that year, not only was the economic prosperity of the country compromised, but the security of its whole credit system had been gravely threatened. The country had enjoyed thirteen or fourteen years of practically uninterrupted agricultural and industrial expansion. The new states between the Mississippi River and the Rocky Mountains had been settled with unusual rapidity, and with an over-confident assurance that the prairie lands of the western part of Kansas and Nebraska would be as available for immediately profitable cultivation as had the better watered lands farther east. The farmers had gone heavily into debt for the sake of improving their homesteads, and were depending on a steady increase in ground value, remunerative prices for grain, and a persistently abundant supply of loanable capital in order to meet their obligations.

None of these necessities was forthcoming. The settlement of this particular region had been closely associated with an unprecedented amount of railway construction. The new mileage was built as much for the future as for the present. It had called for an enormous amount of capital, upon which sufficient returns could not be immediately earned. It stimulated the settlement of new farms to such an extent that for many years the supply of agricultural commodities tended to exceed the world's demand. This whole section of the country needed time to grow up to its improvements. Too much money had been borrowed on the strength of expectations, the realization of which would have to be postponed much longer than the borrowers anticipated.

Unfortunately, however, just at this juncture the security of the whole American financial system was threatened by the effects of the liberal purchase and coinage of silver by the government — a policy which had been favored by the West under the erroneous idea that the more money issued by the government *per capita* the more each farmer would have in his pocket. This policy eventually caused that very contraction of credit which was needed in order to compromise still more seriously the situation of the western borrowers. It had become doubtful whether the government could maintain gold payments — in the face of the persistent exportation of gold, and the steady drain on the gold reserve. At the same time the Treasury was embarrassed by a deficit resulting from a combination of industrial depression and the Republican tariff and appropriation acts of 1890.

These different causes of uncertainty and depression began to be felt in full during the early months of President Cleveland's second term. By June the country was suffering from a full-fledged panic. Mr. Cleveland, who was as much committed to the maintenance of the gold standard as he was to tariff reform, called an extra session of Congress to assemble early in August. A long and a bitter struggle took place, during which the administration had to strain all its resources, but the silver purchase act was finally repealed. Nevertheless the business of the country did not recover. The drain upon the gold reserve continued; and the government was obliged repeatedly to sell bonds in order to replenish the supply.

The business depression which accompanied and followed these events was exceptionally severe; and it was felt throughout the length and breadth of the United States. It did not have the usual effect of releasing money from active business and allowing debtors more easily to obtain loans on any sufficient security, because the whole credit system had been undermined. The borrowing farmers suffered severely, — often to the point of losing their farms. The prices of commodities fell and the cost of living was low, but business was so bad and so many men were out of employment that only a few were benefited. The suffering was acute and widespread and had an immediate effect upon the political situation. The administration was made responsible for the disasters, which it had worked heroically to avert. The tide began to set in favor of Republican candidates and policies.

These events, disastrous as they were to the country, were manifestly favorable to the candidacy of William McKinley, Jr., but just at this crisis a misfortune befell that gentleman which threatened to ruin his political career. In February,

1893, he became bankrupt, as a result of the failure of a man named Walker, of Youngstown, Ohio. He had indorsed some paper for Mr. Walker, who was a friend of long standing, and who under Mr. McKinley's encouragement had gone into the business of manufacturing tin plates. The notes he had indorsed aggregated over $100,000, which was a larger sum than the combined possessions of himself and wife. Mr. McKinley was in despair — and saw no alternative but the abandonment of politics and the devotion of the remainder of his life to the payment of his obligations.

In his distress he went to Myron T. Herrick of Cleveland, who was a close friend. Mr. Hanna was in New York at the time attending to troubles of his own, and could not immediately come to his assistance. Mr. Herrick, with the aid of H. H. Kohlsaat of Chicago and Thomas McDougal of Cincinnati, raised a fund to meet the first of the maturing obligations, but as their volume increased they found the task beyond their ability. Soon after, Mr. Hanna himself came to the rescue, took the matter in charge, and succeeded in raising in Cleveland and elsewhere a sum of money sufficient to meet all Mr. McKinley's debts. Among the contributors to this fund were H. H. Kohlsaat, Samuel Mather, John Hay, Thomas McDougal, J. H. Wade, James Pickands, A. A. Pope, William Chisholm, Charles Brush, James H. Hoyt, Charles Taft, Andrew Carnegie, H. C. Frick, Philander Knox, and many others. The list was made up as much of Mark Hanna's friends as it was of William McKinley's. The latter's personal popularity was such that a considerable sum was contributed voluntarily in small amounts by poor people.

The panic which cost Mr. McKinley, his wife and friends so much money was a blessing to his cause. It only remained for him and his co-workers to turn the opportunity to good account — which was done in the fall of 1893. He had been renominated for governor in the spring of that year, and in November was reëlected by a majority of no less than 80,000. The brilliance of this victory made a profound impression on the public mind. No such majority had been known in Ohio since the war. Hundreds of telegrams and letters of congratulation were showered on the victor, and two-thirds of them welcomed him as the next President of the United States. For the first time he began to be named, not merely as an eligible, but as the logical, candidate. Two days after the election his name was placed on the editorial page of the Cleveland *Leader* as its candidate for the nomination. More significant and interesting is the fact that on November 18 a cartoon was published in the same newspaper, in which Uncle Sam was pointing to the rising sun of McKinley in 1896 and with it the dawn of renewed prosperity.

So far as I know this was the first public advertisement of the idea that the nomination and election of McKinley would bring with it a revival of business activity. Manifestly a more popular slogan could not be found in a period of acute economic dearth; and it is significant that it apparently originated in Cleveland. Who was responsible for its origination is obscure; but as soon as it was suggested, Mr. Hanna was the man above all others to sympathize with it and understand its availability. The dominant object of political policy and action was from his business point of view the encouragement of a steady and general economic prosperity. Thereafter a systematic attempt was made to impress McKinley on the popular mind as the "advance agent of prosperity."

The "prosperity" issue was made more popular, and from the point of the Republican protectionist, more pertinent, by the course of business and politics in 1894. In that year the Democratic leaders made an attempt to revise the tariff in accordance with their campaign pledges. The attempt was bungled. The bill, as it finally passed, was so unsatisfactory to President Cleveland that he allowed it to become a law without his signature. During a period of economic dearth any legislation on the tariff was likely to make trouble. It emphasized the existing depression in several important manufacturing industries. At the same time it alienated public sympathy, because many of its schedules were just as plainly the work of selfish special interests as were those of the McKinley Bill. It was a measure of tariff reform which contained very little reform; and what was as bad it was a tariff for revenue only, which failed as a revenue law. The income tax, which was to provide the revenue needed under a tariff for revenue only, was declared unconstitutional. A heavy deficit was fastened on the Treasury at the very time when the gold reserve was being depleted by financial uncertainty. In every respect the Wilson Bill proved to be a failure, and really or apparently increased and prolonged the prevailing business depression.

The effect of the Wilson Bill in contributing to the economic privations of the American people was very much exaggerated; but the Republican leaders, and particularly the friends of Mr. McKinley, can hardly be blamed for taking what advantage they could of the Democratic failure. They had always claimed that tariff reform would injuriously affect American business; and behold! here was their prophecy fulfilled. Throughout 1894 general business continued to be prostrate. The voters attributed their privations to the party in power, and returned an enormous Republican majority to the House of Representatives in the fall of 1894.

If Messrs. McKinley and Hanna had been able to write history for the benefit of the McKinley cause, they could not have improved upon the actual course of events. The failure of the Wilson Bill clinched every argument which could be made in favor of the candidate from Ohio. Protectionism was apparently vindicated. The McKinley Bill had ceased to be odious. Its author could claim a revision of the earlier adverse popular judgment. He could more plausibly than ever assert that his nomination and election would restore prosperity, because its return was contingent upon a new application of the doctrine of high protection. Needless to say that these arguments were reiterated, emphasized and spread broadcast over the country. The Cleveland *Leader*, which was the most sedulous advocate of McKinley's nomination along the foregoing lines, was widely circulated for a period of over eighteen months at Mr. Hanna's personal expense.

Mark Hanna at that time had no inkling of the decisive effect which the increasing importance of the "prosperity" issue and its association with the McKinley candidacy would have upon his own subsequent political career. But if he had needed any further stimulus to exert all his energies in favor of the nomination of his friend, the shape which political and business issues assumed would have supplied it. He was working both on behalf of the political leader, in whom he most believed, and on behalf of the idea, embodied in his own life. For a man of his experience and outlook there could be no higher object of political leadership than the increased happiness which the American people would obtain from a revival of active business and remunerative employment. Mr. Hanna sincerely believed that the nomination and election of his friend constituted the best means of restoring to American business its normal condition of prosperous expansion and to the American people their customary amount of personal economic satisfaction.

The possibility that he might by the same act fulfil his most cherished personal ambition, make his best friend President of the United States, and contribute most effectually to the welfare of his fellow-countrymen was so alluring to Mr. Hanna that it called for some sacrifice. For fourteen years he had been a business man with incidental political interests. Now that business prosperity itself was dependent in his opinion on the political triumph of his party, and the work of nominating his friend was reaching a critical phase, Mr. Hanna decided to become a politician with incidental business interests. He decided to sacrifice his own business career and his chance of greater personal wealth to the opportunities and responsibilities of an increasing participation in politics.

In the fall of 1894 (after the Republican victory in the congressional elections) Mark Hanna went to his brother, Mr. Leonard Hanna, and declared that he proposed to withdraw from active and responsible direction of the business of M. A. Hanna & Co. He would, of course, always be ready to give his advice, and when in Cleveland to lend his coöperation; and he would retain a substantial interest in the partnership. But he did not wish to be tied down any longer to the routine of office work. He proposed to get some amusement out of what remained of his life, to go away when he wanted, and to do what he wanted. He offered to his brother as compensation for assuming the additional responsibility and work a part of his own interest in the profits of the firm; and this offer was far more liberal than Leonard Hanna himself believed to be justified by the transfer of work. In January, 1895, Mark Hanna was as good as his word. He ceased, thereafter, to do more than exercise an indirect supervision over the business whose expansion had been for almost twenty-eight years his dominant preoccupation.

Mr. Hanna never intimated in his conversation with Mr. Leonard Hanna that he was retiring for the purpose of giving his time and attention to the nomination of McKinley. But such was the fact. He had come to the parting of the ways. Politics had become more absorbing than business. He decided to make his political ambition the salient one in his life. The work of nominating McKinley was reaching its final and critical stage. It required the better part of his time and attention. Nothing else should be allowed to stand in its way.

That he realized, when he took this step, the consequences to himself of McKinley's nomination, there is no reason to believe. He was not a calculating man in respect to his own deeper interests. It was enough that the task of bringing about McKinley's nomination demanded almost undivided attention, that he saw a good chance of success and that in the distance there loomed vaguely an attractive probability of increased personal power and influence. His past life did nothing to prophecy that after McKinley's election he could occupy any political position but that of confidential adviser and political manager to the President. Not even his closest friends suspected at this time the strength of will, the flexibility of talent, the undeveloped power of personal popularity and the rare executive abilities, which enabled him subsequently to grow up to one opportunity of power after another.

Before Mr. Hanna withdrew from active business he had not pretended to keep his hands on all the details of the McKinley campaign. To a large extent the candidate had been his own general manager. No account of the promotion of his candidacy would be correct which understated the essential part played by Mr. McKinley himself. He had many friends and acquaintances among the Republican leaders in all parts of the Union, and he, himself, had established certain alliances which were of the utmost value to his personal cause. No important step was taken without consulting him, and his counsel and coöperation were indispensable to the success of the enterprise. But there are limits which a candidate cannot exceed in working on behalf of his own nomination. Above all, his own personal participation in the canvass cannot become too conspicuous. His most effective assistants, Mr. Hanna apart, were Major Charles Dick, the Chairman of the State Committee, and Mr. Joseph P. Smith, State Librarian of Ohio. These two gentlemen, and particularly the former, had been sent on missions all over the country, but chiefly in the South, preparing against the time when the work of actually electing the delegates must begin.

Mr. Hanna's first step after retiring from business was to rent a house in Thomasville, Georgia, for five years. He had never liked the northern winters, and if he were going to devote the rest of his life (as he told his brother) to the enjoyment of a good time, what better way of doing it than that of living during the cold weather in the sunshine of the South. There, somewhat later, he was joined by his friend Governor McKinley, for Mark Hanna was a sociable man, and he could not enjoy a really good time unless he were surrounded by good company. The Governor appeared to be very good company. The house party was marred by an illness of the honored guest, which blocked in part a proposed excursion to Florida; but when it was over every one agreed that the host and his guests had been benefited and entertained by the visit.

A part of the entertainment prepared by Mr. Hanna for his guest and himself consisted in inviting a great deal of company to meet the Governor. Day after day the two friends sat in the sun parlor and received these visitors. They did not come merely from the vicinity of Thomasville. Gentlemen from all over the South flocked to Mr. Hanna's house, in order to have a little chat with the Governor and his friend. As befitted good Republicans, no color line was drawn. Negroes as well as white men were introduced to the amiable Mr. McKinley; and when they departed they had all been most favorably impressed by his winning personality. The Governor showed his appreciation of the efforts which his host was making to entertain him by being unusually courteous and affable. Mr. Melville Hanna, who also had a house in Thomasville and who was present at some of these interviews, was very much impressed by the tact with which the host treated his stream of guests, the engaging candor with which he talked to them and the favorable impression made on them by Governor McKinley.

In spite of Mr. McKinley's illness the house party was a great success. The host had a particularly good time. When it was all over he could reasonably count upon having obtained for the benefit of his guest a considerable majority of the Southern delegates to the Republican Convention of 1896. The Republican politicians of the South had been converted to McKinley, and the foundation of a pro-McKinley organization laid. The work was so well done, that although frantic efforts were subsequently made by able and unscrupulous Northern politicians to stem the tide in favor of McKinley in the South, they had small success. Mr. Hanna and Mr. McKinley had put a correct estimate on the situation in that part of the country. They had nothing to offer in return for the delegates that could not be offered on behalf of another candidate — viz. the Federal offices in the event of success — but they divined that personal attention means much to Southerners; and they had used most effectively the knowledge. By making McKinley's personality familiar to Southern Republicans and popular among them, they created a species of public opinion in the South favorable to his candidacy. It was a brilliant piece of tactics, which would only have occurred to a man of sound and kindly human feelings.

During the spring of 1895, the McKinley campaign met with a discouraging set-back. At the State Convention held late in May at Zanesville, Mr Hanna and his friends lost control of the state organization. There were three candidates for governor, James H. Hoyt, Samuel K. Nash and Asa Bushnell. The pro-McKinley strength was divided between Mr. Hoyt, the Cleveland candidate, and Mr. Nash. A combination composed of Mr. Foraker, George B. Cox and A. L. Conger succeeded in nominating Asa Bushnell. Foraker was indorsed for the next senatorship — a course for which there was no precedent in Ohio. An associate of Mr. Foraker, formerly his private secretary, Charles L. Kurtz, was made chairman of the State Committee, and his predecessor, Mr. Dick, was denied a coveted nomination for State Auditor. It is true that an open breach was avoided by the indorsement of McKinley as a presidential candidate; but the McKinleyites were far from satisfied with their share of the spoils. The outcome was generally interpreted as a victory for Mr. Foraker; and Mr. McKinley's opponents in other states used it to cast a doubt upon McKinley's ability to go to the Convention with the united support of his own state. In the end the consequences of the defeat were, however, much more serious to Mr. Hanna than they were to Mr. McKinley.

Up to this time the headquarters of the McKinley organization had been situated in Columbus. After the State Convention it was moved to Mr. Hanna's own office in the Perry-Payne Building. For the first time he himself took charge of all the details, and his chief assistant, besides those already named, was the Attorney General of the state, J. K. Richards. Mr. J. P. Smith helped with the office work, while Major Dick was kept chiefly on the road. But, of course, the summer continued to be a time of preliminary preparation. The Governor made several visits to Cleveland and while there was always a guest at Mr. Hanna's house. The same tactics were employed as those which had proved to be so successful during the previous winter at Thomasville. Many prominent Republicans were invited to meet McKinley under the hospitable roof of his friend; and it was rare that the candidate failed to captivate his visitors. In the meantime general conditions continued to be favorable. There was no revival of business to diminish the value of the wares offered by the "advance agent of prosperity," and straw votes taken in many different states indicated a strong tide of popular sentiment in McKinley's favor.

Not until late in the fall of 1895 did Messrs. McKinley and Hanna learn the character and the extent of the opposition which they would be obliged finally to overcome. This opposition was not dangerous, because of the popularity of any alternative candidate. The only other candidates who had any claim on the nomination were Thomas B. Reed and ex-President Harrison. Of these Mr. Reed's strength was confined to

New England, and Mr. Harrison's, such as it was, to his own state. But although there were no popular centres of resistance, it was hardly to be expected that the McKinley bark would be allowed to sail unopposed into harbor. The Republican nominee seemed to be certain of election, and it would not do to allow him to capture the Convention without any salutation of his political masters. Certain leading "bosses" and politicians began to ask what there was in this situation for them. Before submitting to McKinley's nomination could they not make good terms for themselves?

There is not, nor could there be, any written evidence of the negotiations which followed between these "bosses" and Messrs. McKinley and Hanna. But the following account of the matter is not far from the truth. The latter were informed that the delegations from certain states could be obtained on certain terms, and late in the fall Mr. Hanna went East in order to find out what these terms were. Whatever they were they probably included one or two cabinet positions. Mr. Hanna returned, made his report, and seems to have urged the acceptance of the terms. It meant the removal of the only important obstacle to McKinley's nomination, and he could not resist the temptation. But McKinley himself absolutely refused to consent to any such bargain. He was much more alive than was Mr. Hanna to the grave objections to purchase of the presidential nomination by the payment of cabinet positions. He declared that he would rather lose the nomination than obtain it by such dubious means. Mr. Hanna at once admitted that his friend was right, and the uncompromising stand which Mr. McKinley had taken in the matter greatly increased his personal admiration of the man.

The decision was reached that in case they had to face the opposition of the local political leaders, the fight would be made upon the issue that the "bosses" were opposing the people's choice. Eventually the contest assumed precisely that shape. On January 7 there was a conference in New York between Thomas C. Platt, Senator Quay, Joseph H. Manley, Chauncey I. Filley and James S. Clarkson to devise means for preventing the nomination of McKinley. The plan was adopted of trying to keep the delegates away from McKinley by encouraging the growth of "favorite sons" in all the Northern states. At the same time the experienced politicians who attended the conference decided to put up a stiff fight for the control of the Southern local and state conventions. They did not realize how thoroughly the preliminary work among the Southern Republicans on McKinley's behalf had already been accomplished. They expected to be able to capture a much larger percentage of the delegates than they actually succeeded in doing.

At the time when it was formed, the plan of campaign looked much more promising than it subsequently proved to be. The candidacy of Thomas B. Reed would hold New England. Thomas C. Platt could deliver the delegation from New York to anybody he pleased, and he selected Levi P. Morton as an inspiring candidate. Senator Quay considered the transfer of his contingent to Reed, but finally decided that he himself was the favorite son of Pennsylvania. Iowa claimed the nomination for Senator Allison. Besides these candidates, all of whom survived until the meeting of the National Convention, there were indications that Indiana might be kept true to ex-President Harrison, Illinois to Senator Cullom and Minnesota to Senator Davis. The expectation was that in case the tide in favor of McKinley could be checked, other "favorite sons" would appear to take advantage of the vicissitudes of a divided Convention.

At this critical stage in the canvass, everything depended on the ability of Mr. McKinley and his friends to keep alive an impression of the irresistibility of his candidacy. A majority of the Republican voters favored his nomination, but their preference might be defeated — in case the local politicians came to believe that its defeat was probable or even possible. On the other hand, many of these politicians, not publicly committed to another candidate, would make haste to join the procession as soon as they realized that it was really made up of the Elect. It was a case where nothing would succeed like success.

Preparations were made immediately to establish pro-McKinley organizations in every state which was worth fighting for. In many important states confidential relations had already been established with political leaders of prominence who could be trusted to work for McKinley. In New Jersey the coöperation of Garret A. Hobart, subsequently Vice-President, was assured. In Maryland Senator Wellington could be counted upon for good work. In Michigan General Alger was a friend of both the candidate and Mr. Hanna. In Minnesota ex-Governor W. R. Merriam was an effective ally. In Wisconsin Henry C. Payne eventually helped to capture the state for McKinley. West of the Mississippi, with the exception of Iowa and one or two other states, the McKinley sentiment was everywhere dominant. In all these localities the work was comparatively easy, and did not require very much time or cause much anxiety.

In no part of the country did the contest become fiercer than south of the Mason and Dixon line. Mr. Hanna had to fight very hard to prevent the McKinley organization in several important Southern states from being broken up. The most perplexing and troublesome crises occurred in Georgia, Alabama, Louisiana and Texas. The opposition was unscrupulous and was abundantly supplied with funds. It used all the tricks known to machine politicians, such as the calling of "snap" conventions in certain congressional districts. But the net results of a fight put by four of the ablest and most experienced politicians in the Republican party was comparatively small. There were finally secured for Reed two votes in Alabama, two in Georgia, four in Louisiana, two and a half in North Carolina, one in Virginia and five in Texas. Mr. Platt picked up for Morton one delegate from Alabama and two from Florida. Quay captured two in Georgia, one in Mississippi, and divided one in Louisiana with Allison. Mr. Clarkson, who had dispensed patronage during President Harrison's administration, obtained only three votes from Texas for the Iowan candidate. These were small pickings, considering the eminence of these gentlemen as the gatherers of political fruit. They had been beaten at their own game. As Mr. Thomas C. Platt, in his "Autobiography" (p. 331) says: "He (Mr. Hanna) had the South practically solid before some of us waked up." But it was not simply a matter of organization. A genuine preference for McKinley had been created among the Southern Republicans; and, of course, he was helped in the South by his success in the North.

Different methods were used in different doubtful Northern states. Indiana was one of the first among the waverers which it was possible to line up for McKinley. On February 4 ex-President Harrison announced that he was not a candidate. Mr. McKinley had some days before received confidential information of the announcement, and an emissary, Charles Dick, was despatched to Indiana to take immediate advantage of the withdrawal. He had a long secret interview with John K. Gowdy, chairman of the State Committee, which resulted in an understanding that the latter would work for Mr. McKinley. Before Mr. Dick returned the situation all over the state was thoroughly canvassed, and many consultations were held with local leaders, whose coöperation was necessary. Owing partly to the efficiency of Mr. Gowdy's work, and partly to the pro-McKinley popular sentiment, which was unusually strong in Indiana, the delegation from that state was obtained for McKinley.

Nebraska was another state in which a special situation confronted the McKinley managers. A somewhat feeble local movement had been started in favor of General Manderson as a "favorite son," which commanded the support of most of the local politicians. A special organization had, consequently, to be formed, which succeeded in having the delegates-at-large instructed for McKinley, in spite of the opposition of Senator Thurston. In California, almost the only other Western state which required special exertions, the McKinley interest was confided to Judge James A. Waymire and Mr. J. C. Spear; and they succeeded in bringing the state into line. When the Convention was finally held Mr. McKinley was supported by the delegations of all the states west of the Mississippi, except Iowa, the three votes from Utah and those of the seceding states.

Opinions were divided among the McKinley managers whether any contest at all should be made in those Northern states, which were completely dominated by the local "bosses." But Mr. Hanna had the courage of his cause; he insisted on fighting all along the line and in capturing local delegates wherever they could. Prominent Republicans both in New York and Pennsylvania were friendly to McKinley — far more so than the votes of those states subsequently indicated. Even as it was, eight votes were secured in Pennsylvania and seventeen in New York. A great deal of very effective work was also accomplished in quietly favoring the election of delegates whose second choice would be McKinley. Mr. Hanna himself was far from objecting to the tactics pursued by their opponents. Thomas B. Reed was the only candidate he really feared, just as it was the only candidacy which was based upon genuine claims to recognition. If the opposition could have concentrated on Reed, it might have become formidable. As it was, the "favorite son" policy was a confession of weakness, which could offer no effective resistance to a candidacy like that of McKinley, which gathered volume as it rolled along.

Arrangements had been made to hold the Ohio State Convention in March, so as to place Mr. McKinley formally in nomination early in the final contest. It assembled on March 11 and was a most harmonious gathering—although the Foraker faction kept control of the state organization. James B. Foraker made the first of a long series of speeches nominating his former rival for the presidency. The delegates-at-large were divided between the two factions, and consisted of Mr. Foraker, Governor Bushnell, General Charles Grosvenor, and Mark Hanna. The platform emphasized the importance of protectionist legislation as essential to the revival of prosperity, but dodged the currency issue. It declared for sound money and the use of both metals, which were to be kept at a parity by international agreement or any other available means. In case a declaration in favor of a gold standard had been made at this time, the difficulties of the McKinley managers west of the Mississippi would have been very much increased. As it was, one State Convention after another began to instruct for McKinley. On March 19 Wisconsin was definitely placed on his list. On April 11 it was joined by Oregon. Four days later Nebraska and North Dakota fell into line, and on April 29 Vermont, under the leadership of Senator Proctor, showed that Mr. Reed could even hold all of the delegates from New England.

All this was encouraging, and together with the successes in the South it was almost convincing. But it was not entirely so. The McKinley candidacy needed the testimony of an emphatic success in an important contested state. Illinois was selected both as a good point of resistance by the opponents of McKinley, and the best point of attack by his friends. The critical contest of the campaign occurred in that state. The local politicians, particularly in and about Chicago, had been pushing the candidacy of Senator Cullom. No basing-point for a McKinley organization could be found in the regular machine, and it was necessary to secure an independent leader, who would pull together the widespread sentiment in favor of McKinley. Such a leader was found in Mr. Charles G. Dawes, the son of General R. Dawes, once a Congressman from an Ohio district. Mr. Dawes, after interviews with both Mr. McKinley and Mr. Hanna, agreed to make the fight, and he was supported vigorously by Mr. Hanna himself. It was generally understood that while McKinley might be nominated without Illinois, the capture of that state would remove any possible doubt as to his triumph. Mr. McKinley himself went to Chicago in February and delivered a speech at the Marquette Club, which helped his candidacy. Mr. Dawes proved to be a capable organizer. The results of the district conventions were favorable; but when the State Convention assembled late in April, the issue was still in doubt. A sharp struggle took place with the result dubious to the last. The margin was so narrow that an accident might tip the scales one way or the other. The fight continued for several days, on the last of which Mr. Hanna sat in his office in the Perry-Payne Building, telephone in hand, from noon until 10 P.M. He did not quit until he had learned that Senator Cullom had withdrawn and the delegates-at-large had been instructed for McKinley. He could go home assured that the project conceived eight years earlier for the nomination of his friend had been successfully accomplished.

Almost the whole cost of the campaign for Mr. McKinley's nomination was paid by Mr. Hanna. Apparently he expected in the beginning to obtain very much more assistance than that which he actually received. Early in 1896, when the demands upon him became very heavy, he cast about for some means of shifting the burden. He seriously considered the possibility of collecting a campaign fund, and had actually made preparations to do so. But further reflection convinced him that to collect a fund for the purpose of nominating a candidate was a different thing from collecting an election fund. The appeal in the former case had to be made on personal rather than party grounds. So he made up his mind to pay the expenses himself. He did receive some help from Mr. McKinley's personal friends in Ohio and elsewhere, but its amount was small compared to the total expenses. First and last Mr. Hanna contributed something over $100,000 toward the expense of the canvass.

One hundred thousand dollars and over is a good deal of money; but it is not too much for the legitimate expenses of nominating a man for President under the convention system. Such a sum would not have gone very far in case corrupt methods had been used. As a matter of fact, corrupt methods were always expressly and absolutely forbidden by Mr. Hanna. Certain of his lieutenants, particularly in the South, would have been glad enough to have plenty of money to spend, but they did not get it. He was continually checking their zeal and refusing or pairing down their applications for funds. He carefully limited the purposes for which alone the money was to be spent. It was to pay the legitimate expenses of his assistants in organizing districts for McKinley in which a sentiment favorable to the candidacy existed. He expressly warns them against any attempt to obtain merely purchasable votes.

A few quotations will illustrate the kind of letters which he wrote to assistants, who were more preoccupied with the money they wanted to spend than they were scrupulous about the methods they used in spending it. On Nov. 5, 1895, he wrote to a correspondent in California: "I am in receipt of your favor of the 28th ult., and your draft for $500, which came to hand to-day, has been paid. The Governor's friends have not been called upon to contribute any money to his campaign, because he is very much averse to that method. Of course I appreciate that it will be necessary to do something towards the actual expenses of those who are willing to give time to his service, and that I am perfectly willing to do, but the use of money to influence votes is not a method that I favor at all. This campaign must not be one in which money is used for other than necessary expenses."

His letters to his lieutenants in the South all run to the same effect. During February and March, 1896, when the combination against McKinley was using every device of the political professional to snatch the delegates away from McKinley, Mr. Hanna was overwhelmed with demands for money from his assistants in the South. He wrote to one correspondent late in January: "You are laboring under the impression that there is a liberal fund provided for distribution. Such is not the case. I am personally providing what seems to be necessary for such expenses as are legitimate. Mr. McKinley is most decidedly opposed to the expenditure of money along the line of purchasing support. Therefore I suggest that in districts where the sentiment is against us, from whatever cause, we had better avoid any fight. We will not find fault with you if you secure no districts which cannot be won on the merits of Mr. McKinley as a candidate." The difficulties under which he labored may be inferred from the following letter, written early in February: "I am in receipt of yours of the 3d and enclose a draft for $500, which is all I can possibly spare for the occasion. The fact is, my friend, I am at a point where I will have to put a stop on expenditures, until some of our friends come to our assistance, which up to date has not been done. Business is as bad as it was in '93, and I have had to borrow this money to send to you. My firm is as hard up as I am." So far from being a campaign in which money was freely disbursed, the fight for Mr. McKinley's nomination was an example of the attainment of a striking political success without any but a very economical expenditure of money.

In a speech made to his friends at the Union Club in Cleveland after the Convention was over, Mr. Hanna declared he had been forbidden by Mr. McKinley to win the nomination by means of any pledge of office or remuneration. There is no evidence either in Mr. Hanna's correspondence or in the testimony of his associates that specific pledges were made to bestow particular offices on particular men. But many promises were undoubtedly made that the local political leaders who worked for Mr. McKinley's nomination would in the event of success be "recognized" in the distribution of Federal patronage. Again and again Mr. Hanna wrote to local politicians who were known to favor Mr. McKinley that if they would organize their district or state in his favor they would be consulted after the election in respect to the appointments. In so wording the promises, Mr. Hanna freed himself and Mr. McKinley from specific obligations. They could always reject any proposed appointment in case it seemed to them unfit. The distinction between making a definite pledge and admitting a general claim for "recognition" has a validity which should not be ignored, even by those who deplore any purchase of political support by the promise of official patronage. The American Civil Service can never become efficient unless such methods are abandoned; but they are deeply rooted in our political practice, and their use was considered necessary to the nomination of Mr. McKinley. They were so essential a part of the political system, to which Mr. Hanna was accustomed, that he would have regarded their scrupulous avoidance as absurd.

In telling his friends at the Union Club that Mr. McKinley had forbidden the purchase of support by specific pledges, Mr. Hanna was probably thinking of the negotiations between himself and the Eastern "bosses." He himself came to recognize that such bargains gravely compromised the public interest; and the lesson which his friend had taught him was one which he did not forget. In the distribution of patronage after the election, most of the men who had contributed effectively to Mr. McKinley's nomination received offices, but in spite of certain mistakes an honest attempt was made to fill the higher offices with able and disinterested public servants. Both the President and his friend knew the value to the administration of good service and the danger of poor service. Under Mr. McKinley's stewardship the country was on the whole well served by its higher executive officials. The earlier mistakes were soon rectified, and the vacated offices were always filled by exceptionally strong administrators.

The promise of Federal offices, like the expenditure of money, played, however, only a subordinate part in the nomination of Mr. McKinley. Some of the other candidates had money to spend and offices to promise; but they could make slight headway by virtue of such paddles. Mr. McKinley had behind him a current of popular favor, which was skilfully and systematically exploited to the very limit. It might have prevailed, even if it had not been exploited, but neither the candidate nor his friend was taking any chances. The final success was overwhelming, because advantage had been seized of every opportunity to make it so. That the opportunities were good does not subtract from the rarity of the achievement. Mr. McKinley and Mr. Hanna succeeded because they deserved to succeed. Back of every substantial success in American politics, one may trace the influence of very personal and human forces, and the Republican nomination of 1896 was no exception.

Mr. McKinley was a man who had the faculty of making friends, not because he actually did very much for others, but because of the amiability, the tact and the good taste he showed in all his personal relationships. By virtue of his affability he usually avoided making enemies, even when he failed to make friends. The men who would not fight on his side had no special reason for fighting against him, and he sought to be as scrupulously correct in his political methods as he was scrupulously amiable in his personal relations. Added to this personal availability as a candidate was his equally decisive sectional availability. The Middle West usually furnishes the Republican presidential candidates, because by location and outlook it is more representative of the whole nation than any other part of the country. Its local interests and traditions have something in common with the interests and traditions both of the manufacturing East and the agricultural West. A candidate from an Eastern state, such as Mr. Thomas B. Reed, usually lacks this advantage, and starts for this reason under a grave handicap. The handicap is the more severe in case his state is small and by no means doubtful. Mr. McKinley represented, on the whole, a group of ideas and interests as nearly national as could any political leader of his own generation. Moreover, his personal and local merits as a candidate were raised to a higher power by the course of political and economic history from 1890 to 1895. The panic of '93, the acuteness of the resulting privations and the failure of the Wilson Bill gave real plausibility and enormous political effect to the claim that he was the "advance agent" of prosperity.

Mark Hanna seems to have been born and raised particularly for the purpose of exploiting these advantages. He loved McKinley as a man. He admired the politician. Whenever he had an enthusiasm, he could communicate it. He could make others believe in McKinley as he did. He could impart his own energy of affection and conviction to the whole movement on behalf of his friend's nomination. He himself was the kind of American citizen whom McKinley could represent only. He embodied in his own person the enterprising, homogeneous, uncritical Americanism of the Middle West which, with all its new organization and equipment, derived its vitality from the earlier economic nationalism of the pioneer. Americans of this type had always associated the American system with a generally diffused economic prosperity. Acute and widespread privation meant that the system was out of joint; and under the prevailing methods of stimulation by the government of all productive enterprise, the repair of the system became a political responsibility. The restoration of the Republican party to power and the election of McKinley assumed in his eyes the character of a patriotic mission.

His substantial successes in politics, including the nomination of William McKinley, were born of the fact that he remained an unspecialized American citizen, whose behavior awakened responsive approval among other Americans of the same kind. He expressed a phase of public opinion, which when aroused was all the more powerful, because it was only semiconscious and because it never could be completely expressed by lawyers or politicians. His ability to represent this element in the American political and economic life sharply distinguished him from the ordinary political professional. Just as in business he never became a dislocated financier, so in politics he never became the mere manipulator of a machine. He coöperated with the machine politicians. He used many of their methods. His standard of behavior in politics was not as high as his standard of behavior in business. When he supped with the Devil, he fished with a long spoon. But in these respects he was faithful to his type. The typical American has never been scrupulous about the means which he used in order to accomplish what seemed to him a worthy purpose.

Mr. Hanna became more rather than less typical, because he used the professional politicians instead of fighting them. But he never became one of them; and if he had done so, he would have been as successful in nominating McKinley as Thomas C. Platt was in nominating Mr. Levi P. Morton. There is, I believe, no close parallel in American politics for the part which Mark Hanna played in the nomination of McKinley. Of course other men have labored faithfully and efficiently to make their friends or associates a presidential candidate. A state "boss" is always calculating whether or not he cannot force some favorite candidate on the Convention. Presidents have sometimes had a good deal to do with the naming of their successors. But when Mr. Hanna began to work first for Sherman and then for McKinley, he started with no leverage not possessed by hundreds of his fellow-citizens. He was merely a well-to-do business man with some small political experience. His special qualification for the task consisted merely in the fact that he wanted to do it. The will to nominate a President aroused in its possessor the abilities necessary for its accomplishment. After he had failed with Sherman, his ambition was sweetened and sanctified by a warm and loyal personal attachment to the new candidate himself. Mr. Hanna was aroused to still greater activity and still greater sacrifices, until the accomplishment of the task absorbed all his time and energy. He proved equal to one emergency after another. He selected good subordinates. He convinced and persuaded doubters. He converted to McKinley's support a whole section of the country. He worked upon public opinion quite as much as he did upon individuals and in the most effective way. Gradually the possible candidate was made probable and then irresistible. The task was achieved. William McKinley became the Republican nominee for the presidency; and Mark Hanna was no less responsible for the triumph than was the candidate himself.

CHAPTER XV

THE CONVENTION OF 1896

By the first of May, 1896, Mark Hanna had every reason to believe that the nomination of Mr. McKinley was assured. A majority of the delegates were known to be favorable to his selection. It only remained to make assurance doubly sure by securing an organization of the Convention favorable to its prospective candidate. Such an organization was the more necessary because the fight in the South and elsewhere had resulted in the election of several contesting delegations, and it was important that those favorable to Mr. McKinley should be seated. As a matter of fact the greater victory included the less. His prospective triumph assured him the control of the National Committee. By virtue of this control definite plans were made for the organization of the Convention, the nomination for Vice-President and the several planks of the platform. A slate was prepared; and the candidate himself in coöperation with certain of his friends drew up a tentative draft of the statement of true Republican principles and policies.

The Convention assembled at St. Louis on Monday, June 15. So far as the slate was concerned, the program was carried through without a hitch. The temporary chairman was Mr. Charles W. Fairbanks of Indiana, the permanent chairman, Senator John M. Thurston of Nebraska. The Committee on Credentials paid no attention to any contesting delegations except those from Delaware and Texas, and in both cases the McKinley delegates were seated. Thus the result became more than ever a foregone conclusion, although a show of resistance continued. Thomas B. Reed, the only other serious candidate, was placed in nomination by Senator Henry Cabot Lodge of Massachusetts, but considerable as Mr. Reed's services had been to his party and his country, he remained a sectional candidate. As it was, Mr. McKinley obtained almost as many votes in New England as Mr. Reed obtained in all the rest of the country. The two wealthiest and most populous states in the Union made their better citizens blush by presenting candidates who had less than no claims for consideration. The candidate from Iowa, Senator Allison, was negligible outside of his own state. Mr. McKinley's name was placed before the Convention by Senator-elect James B. Foraker in a speech which was the more impressive because of the source from which it came. Mr. McKinley received $661\frac{1}{2}$ votes on the first ballot against $84\frac{1}{2}$ for his closest rival, Mr. Thomas B. Reed. Sixty-two of the Reed delegates came from New England, and the rest chiefly from the South. Mr. McKinley had the Middle West and the West, with the exception of Iowa, almost solidly behind him, and he had made serious inroads upon the strength of his opponents in their own particular bailiwicks. His triumph was so decisive and overwhelming that no outsider could realize how much effort and contrivance had been spent upon making it irresistible.

Inasmuch as Ohio had furnished the head of the ticket, the vice-presidential nomination, according to the prevailing practice, ought to go to some doubtful Eastern state. New York can usually claim the office under such conditions; but in the present instance sound reasons could be urged why its claims could be ignored with impunity. The bitter opposition which Mr. Thomas C. Platt had made to McKinley's nomination had created a good deal of personal ill-feeling; and as a consequence there was no candidate from New York upon whom Republicans from that state could agree. But the consideration which probably had most weight was the fact that with the word "gold" already inserted in the platform New York could hardly be called a doubtful state. On the other hand, the adjoining state of New Jersey submitted an eligible candidate in Mr. Garret A. Hobart, who had done much to strengthen the Republican party in his own neighborhood. Mr. Hobart was well known to Mr. Hanna, and in all probability his nomination had been scheduled for some time. It was practically announced early in June. He was a lawyer and a business man with an exclusively local reputation; and if he did little to strengthen the ticket he did nothing to weaken it. He proved to be a useful coadjutor both during the campaign and after the election; and he subsequently exercised more influence in the counsels of the administration than is usually the case with the occupant of the vice-presidential chair.

In all the foregoing respects the Convention proved to be a perfectly manageable body, which submitted good-naturedly to the will of its conquerors. But in one essential matter it proved to be far less manageable, and its rebellious independence in this respect made havoc of all the carefully laid plans of Mr. McKinley and Mr. Hanna. Their hands were forced in relation to the most important plank in the platform. The candidate had to accept a new definition of Republican policy in respect to the currency — and one which in its effect might well change the whole nature of the campaign. The man who had been nominated as the High Priest of Protection found his favorite policy converted into comparative insignificance and himself forced to assume a precise and vigorous attitude in relation to a question which he had always preferred to leave vague and ambiguous. Instead of running on an issue with which his whole political career was associated, he was forced to run on an issue upon which his own record was equivocal, and which in his opinion gravely compromised the success of his candidacy.

A great deal of controversy has arisen about the way in which the word "gold" was inserted in the currency plank of the Republican platform of 1896. A number of different claimants have insisted upon their individual responsibility for its insertion. Among others Mr. Thomas C. Platt asserts without blushing that the honor chiefly, if not exclusively, belongs to him. In his "Autobiography" (p. 310) he declares that "in 1896 I scored what I regard as the greatest achievement of my political career. That was the insertion of the gold plank in the St. Louis platform." In his account of the matter he admits that Senator Lodge and certain friends of Mr. McKinley, such as H. H. Kohlsaat, Myron T. Herrick, Henry C. Payne and William R. Merriam, may also have contributed to the result, but if the assertion quoted above be taken as literally true, the real hero of the incident must be Mr. Thomas C. Platt. He has admitted it himself. On the other hand, Mr. Kohlsaat declares no less emphatically that he, more than any other single individual, was responsible for the appearance of the magical word. Another equally vigorous claimant is Mr. James B. Foraker. He was the chairman of the Committee on Resolutions, and he asserts emphatically that no matter what palaver may have preceded the final decision, the Committee, of which he was chairman, was really responsible both for the general wording of the plank and for the actual insertion of "gold" before the phrase "standard of value."

Notwithstanding these conflicting claims and the more or less conflicting evidence upon which they are based, the several accounts agree upon certain fundamental facts; and a fairly complete story of what actually occurred can be pieced together, which derives nothing from controverted testimony. There will remain certain minor ambiguities and conflicts of evidence, which may be partly explained by the failure of certain witnesses to take account of events which had occurred without their knowledge on other parts of a complicated and confused field of action. In spite of these minor conflicts, some of which I shall attempt to explain, a sufficiently complete story can be told, which includes no incidents which are not intrinsically probable or which are not confirmed by more than one witness.

Undoubtedly Mr. McKinley himself wanted to subordinate the currency issue to that of protection. His own record in relation to legislation affecting the standard of value had been vacillating. He was a bimetallist, and had stood for the use of both gold and silver in the currency of the United States without inquiring too closely whether the means actually used to force silver into circulation had or had not tended to lower the standard of value. His personal political prominence had been due to his earnest and insistent advocacy of the doctrine of high protection, and he feared that if the currency issue were sharply defined, the result would necessarily be (as it was) a diminution in price of his own political and economic stock-in-trade. Considerations of party expediency reënforced his own personal predilections. His party was united on the issue of protection. It was divided on the currency issue. There were "silver Republicans," and they all came from a part of the country in which he personally was very popular. The sentiment in favor of a single gold standard was strongest in New England and the Middle States, which were more or less opposed to his nomination. If he had favored unequivocally a single gold standard, his candidacy would have been weakened among his friends, while his opponents would have merely shifted their ground of attack. Not unnaturally he proposed to evade the issue by standing for "sound money" without defining precisely what sound money really was.

Mark Hanna's personal attitude was different from that of Mr. McKinley. He was enough of a banker to realize that the business of the country was suffering far more from uncertainty about the standard of value than it was from foreign competition. Mr. William R. Merriam tells of certain interesting conversations which took place in August, 1895, on the porch of Mr. Hanna's house overlooking Lake Erie, between himself, Russell A. Alger, Mr. Hanna and Mr. McKinley, in which both the political and economic aspects of the prospective campaign issues were thoroughly discussed. In these conventions Mr. McKinley was, in Mr. Merriam's own phrase, "obsessed" with the idea of the tariff as the dominant issue of the coming campaign. Mr. Hanna, on the other hand, was, in Mr. Merriam's words, "in favor of committing the Republican party to gold, as the sole basis of currency, and he was anxious and willing to lend his aid to the furtherance of this policy."

Inasmuch as Mr. McKinley was the candidate, his views prevailed. Throughout the whole preliminary canvass the currency issue was evaded. The State Conventions, in which the candidate's personal influence prevailed, declared for sound money and the coinage of silver in so far as it could be kept on a parity with gold. Conventions such as that of Wyoming instructed their delegates for McKinley, while declaring at the same time for the free and unlimited coinage of silver. Mr. Hanna as the manager of the campaign realized how much Mr. McKinley's ambiguous attitude on the currency was helping the canvass in the Western States, and he probably desired as much as McKinley did that any more precise definition of the issue should at least be postponed until after Mr. McKinley's nomination was assured. In no event would he have insisted upon any opinion of his own in respect to an important matter of public policy in antagonism to that of his candidate and friend.

McKinley's opinion remained unchanged until the very eve of the Convention. Mr. Kohlsaat asserts that on Sunday, June 7, he spent hours trying to convince Mr. McKinley of the necessity of inserting the word "gold" in the platform. The latter argued in opposition that ninety per cent of his mail and his callers were against such decisive action, and he asserted emphatically that thirty days after the Convention was over, the currency question would drop out of sight and the tariff would become the sole issue. The currency plank, tentatively drawn by Mr. McKinley and his immediate advisers, embodied his resolution to keep the currency issue subordinate and vague. According to Mr. Foraker, Mr. J. K. Richards came to him at Cincinnati some days before the date of the meeting of the Convention, bringing with him direct from Canton some resolutions in regard to the money and the tariff questions prepared by the friends of Mr. McKinley with his approval. Mr. Foraker had been slated for the Committee on Resolutions; and the McKinley draft was placed in his hands with a view to having them incorporated in the platform. The currency plank as handed to Mr. Foraker began as follows: —

"The Republican party is unreservedly for sound money. It is unalterably opposed to every effort to debase our currency or disturb our credit. It resumed specie payments in 1879, and since then it has made and kept every dollar as good as gold. This it will continue to do, maintaining all the money of the United States, whether gold, silver or paper, at par with the best money of the world and up to the standard of the most enlightened governments.

"The Republican party favors the use of silver along with gold to the fullest extent consistent with the maintenance of the parity of the two metals. It would welcome bimetallism based upon an international ratio, but until that can be secured it is the plain duty of the United States to maintain our present standard, and we are therefore opposed under existing conditions to the free and unlimited coinage of silver at sixteen to one."

The resolutions mentioned by Mr. Foraker were placed in his hands on Monday or Tuesday, June 8 or 9. Mr. Foraker, however, did not reach St. Louis until Saturday morning; and in the meantime a good deal had been happening there and elsewhere in respect to the currency plank. Mr. Hanna had already gone to St. Louis. When he arrived he had in his possession a draft of certain resolutions, presumably the same which had been taken to Mr. Foraker by Mr. J. K. Richards. He was joined in St. Louis early in the week by a number of Mr. McKinley's friends and supporters; and in the group a lively discussion almost immediately arose as to the precise wording which should be adopted in defining the currency policy of the Republican party. This group consisted in the beginning of Senator Redfield Proctor of Vermont, Colonel Myron T. Herrick, General Osborne and Mr. Hanna himself. Mr. Hanna was so busy in rounding up his delegates and in attending to other details that he could not give much of his time to the conferences over the platform, but he was in and out and knew what was going on.

Towards the middle of the week the group of gentlemen participating in these conferences was increased by several accessions from the number of Mr. McKinley's friends in other states, among whom may be mentioned Mr. Henry C. Payne, William R. Merriam and Melville E. Stone. After his arrival Mr. Henry C. Payne became particularly active in getting the conference together and in having the platform typewritten anew, after every change, and in having copies supplied to each participant. On Wednesday morning Mr. Hanna handed to Mr. Payne the draft of the currency plank as prepared by McKinley with the request that it be revised by the conference and put into final shape. The discussion continued on Thursday. After an agreement had been reached on certain changes Mr. Payne was asked to prepare another draft for discussion on the following day, which was Friday.

On Friday morning Mr. H. H. Kohlsaat of Chicago joined the conference, having come over from Chicago in response to a telegram particularly for that purpose. Mr. Kohlsaat's relation to the whole matter was peculiar. He was a friend of long-standing both of Mr. McKinley and Mr. Hanna. He had, of course, been favorable to the former's nomination, but in the newspapers which he controlled he had combined an earnest advocacy of Mr. McKinley's selection with an even more earnest and insistent advocacy of the single gold standard. He states that he had not been allowed by Mr. McKinley and Mr. Hanna to assist in the contest for the delegation from Illinois, because they were embarrassed by his attitude on the currency question. With the addition of Mr. Kohlsaat the members of the conference consisted of Mr. Payne, Colonel Herrick, Senator Proctor, ex-Governor Merriam and Mr. Stone. Mr. Hanna was present a certain part of the time, but he had so many other matters which required his attention that he was frequently being called off.

There is some conflict of testimony as to proceedings of the conference on Friday. Colonel Herrick states that the final draft had been substantially submitted and accepted on Friday morning. Mr. Kohlsaat, on the other hand, declares that in the draft forming the basis of discussion at the beginning of the conference the word "gold" was omitted. This draft read as follows:

"The Republican party is unreservedly for sound money. It caused the enactment of the law providing for the resumption of specie payments in 1879. Since then every dollar has been as good as gold. We are unalterably opposed to every measure calculated to debase our currency or impair the credit of our country. We are therefore opposed to the free and unlimited coinage of silver except by agreement with the leading commercial nations of Europe, and until such agreement can be obtained we believe that the existing gold standard should be preserved. We favor the use of silver as currency, but to the extent only that its parity with gold can be maintained, and we favor all measures designed to maintain inviolably the money of the United States, whether coin or paper, at the present standard, the standard of the most enlightened nations of the earth."

The foregoing draft was furnished by Colonel Herrick. It differs in one or two minor respects, and in one essential respect, from the draft which, according to Mr. Kohlsaat, formed the basis for discussion at the conference of Friday. The minor differences are merely matters of order and may be ignored. The essential difference turns upon the insertion of the word "gold" before "standard." According to Mr. Herrick the draft prepared by Mr. Payne contained the word "gold." According to Mr. Kohlsaat the decision to insert that word was reached only after a protracted discussion and a sharp controversy between himself and Mr. Hanna. Not until four o'clock in the afternoon, after Mr. Hanna had withdrawn, was an agreement obtained. In view of the unanimity of his friends Mr. Hanna gave his consent and agreed to urge its acceptance on Mr. McKinley. It was Colonel Herrick who telegraphed to the candidate and obtained his approval. According to the testimony of Colonel Herrick, Mr. Kohlsaat, Mr. Merriam and Senator Proctor, the whole matter was settled, so far as Mr. McKinley and his friends were concerned, by Friday night.

In the several accounts of these conferences, the one doubtful point is whether or not the word "gold" was contained in the draft prepared by Mr. Payne. The matter is not of great importance, except in respect to Mr. Kohlsaat's claim that he, more than any single individual, was responsible for its insertion and that he was called a "d—d fool" by Mr. Hanna for his pains. The only available account from Mr. Hanna himself of his own relation to the gold plank is contained in the following letter to A. K. McClure, written on June 28, 1900.

"MY DEAR MR. MCCLURE:—

"I am in receipt of yours of the 21st inst., which has just been reached in my accumulation of letters. I do not care to have go into print all that I told you personally in regard to the gold plank of the St. Louis platform. When I went to St. Louis I took with me a memorandum on the tariff and financial questions drawn by Mr. McKinley. During all the discussions there prior to the action of the Committee on Resolutions I showed it to a few friends and had it rewritten by the Hon. J. K. Richards, the present U. S. Solicitor General. It was but slightly changed by those who considered it before it went to the Committee and as presented was passed by the Committee with little or no change. My part of the business was to harmonize all sections and prevent any discussion of the subject outside the Committee which would line up any factions against it (except the ultra silver men). In that I succeeded, and felt willing to give all the credit claimed by those who assisted. The original memorandum is in the possession of a personal friend, whom I do not care to name without his consent. The whole thing was managed in order to succeed in *getting what we got,* and that was my only interest.

"Sincerely yours,
"M. A. HANNA."

The foregoing letter, while it throws no light upon the time and occasion of the insertion of the decisive word into the draft supplies the clew which enables us to interpret Mr. Hanna's own behavior, both during these conferences and thereafter. He himself was in favor of the gold standard, and in favor of a declaration to that effect. But partly because of his loyalty to Mr. McKinley, and partly because he did not want any decisive step taken until the sentiment of the delegates had been disclosed, he preferred to have his hand forced, and he did not want to have it forced too soon. Although a decision, so far as Mr. McKinley and his friends were concerned, had been reached on Friday, public announcement of the fact was scrupulously avoided; and Mr. Hanna evidently proposed to avoid it as long as he could. It was essential, considering the divergence of opinion among Mr. McKinley's supporters, that the candidate's official representative should not assume the position of publicly and explicitly asking the Convention to adopt the gold standard. Mr. McKinley's personal popularity would suffer much less in case every superficial fact pointed to the conclusion that the gold standard was being forced on him by an irresistible party sentiment.

As a matter of fact such was the case. As the delegates gathered in St. Louis, the friends of the gold standard learned for the first time their own strength. Business men east of the Mississippi had been reaching the conclusion that the country could never emerge from the existing depression until a gold standard of value was assured. They and their representatives learned at St. Louis that this opinion had become almost unanimous among responsible and well-informed men. Mr. Hanna received shoals of telegrams from business men of all degrees of importance insisting upon such action. The substantial unanimity of this sentiment among Republican leaders, particularly in the Middle West, clinched the matter. Mr. McKinley would not have consented to any decisive utterance, had he not been convinced that the great majority of his friends and his party were unalterably in favor of it. Every one of the participants in the preliminary conferences considered it desirable, and their united recommendation constituted a constraining force which Mr. McKinley could not ignore. Such being the case, any controversy as to the precise time and occasion of the insertion of the word "gold" into the actual draft becomes of small importance. It would have been inserted anyway, not by any one man or by the representatives of any one section, but because the influential members of the party, except in the Far West, had become united on the subject. Credit, however, particularly attaches to those Middle Western politicians and business men, who had the intelligence to understand and the courage to insist that the day for equivocation in relation to this essential issue had passed, and who persuaded Mr. McKinley that he must stand on a gold platform even at some sacrifice of personal prestige and perhaps at some risk of personal success.

If Mr. McKinley had failed to consent to the insertion of the word "gold," and had prevailed upon all his intimate friends to assume the same attitude, he might possibly have prevented his own nomination. At all events, as soon as Mr. McKinley's opponents arrived, they immediately began an attack on what was manifestly the weak point in the McKinley fortifications. They knew that his nomination was assured, unless, perchance, he could be placed in opposition to the will of the Convention upon some important matter, and of course they represented a part of the country, in which public opinion in general was more united in favor of the gold standard than it was in the Ohio and Mississippi valleys. Senators Lodge and Platt reached St. Louis on Sunday. They learned of the controversy over the currency plank, but not about the decision actually reached. Senator Lodge went immediately to the McKinley headquarters. In his ensuing interview with Mr. Hanna the latter gave him no encouragement about the insertion into the plank of the word "gold." Mr. Lodge and ex-Governor Draper were shown the drafts of two resolutions, one of which was understood to have just arrived from Canton, and neither of which committed the party to the gold standard.

Senator Lodge then told Mr. Hanna that these drafts were unsatisfactory, and that Massachusetts would demand a vote upon any similar plank. After some further talk Mr. Lodge went away, but he served notice on Mr. Hanna that efforts would be made to consolidate the sentiment in the Convention opposed to any "straddle." By Monday night the advocates of the gold standard had a majority of the Convention rounded up in favor of an unequivocal declaration in its favor.

Of course, this was precisely the result which Mr. Hanna wanted. The evidence is conclusive that on Friday night both he and Mr. McKinley were prepared to accept a decisive gold plank (which he personally had always approved) but, as he says in his letter to Mr. McClure, his part of the business was "to prevent any discussion of the subject outside of the Committee on Resolutions, which would line up any factions against it." That is, he proposed to leave the action of the Convention on the plank uncertain, until the Committee on Resolutions could launch a draft which would have the great majority of the Convention behind it, and which would constrain the doubters and the trimmers. By failing to tell Senator Lodge that a draft containing the word "gold" had already been accepted by McKinley, he astutely accomplished his part of the business. He arranged for the consolidation of the sentiment in favor of the gold standard, while he prevented any consolidation of the sentiment against it, except on the part of the irreconcilables. If he had announced as early as Saturday or Sunday that a declaration in favor of the gold standard would be supported by Mr. McKinley's friends and probably adopted by the Convention, a considerable number of half-hearted and double-minded delegates might have been won over by the leaders of the silver faction. And it might have seemed like a desertion by McKinley of the pro-silver delegates, who had been prevented by the ambiguity of the candidate's previous attitude from opposing him.

The text of the plank as it came from the Committee and appeared in the platform, read as follows:—

"The Republican party is unreservedly for sound money. It caused the enactment of a law providing for the resumption of specie payments in 1879. Since then every dollar has been as good as gold. We are unalterably opposed to every measure calculated to debase our currency or impair the credit of our country. We are therefore opposed to the free coinage of silver, except by international agreement with the leading commercial nations of the earth, which agreement we pledge ourselves to promote; and until such agreement can be obtained the existing gold standard must be maintained. All of our silver and paper currency must be maintained at parity with gold, and we favor all measures designed to maintain inviolably the obligations of the United States, and all our money, whether coin or paper, at the present standard, the standard of the most enlightened nations of the earth."

A comparison of the foregoing text with the draft worked up by the preliminary conference discloses only unimportant changes. The "free and unlimited coinage of silver" gets along without the "and unlimited." The draft wants an international agreement with "the commercial nations of Europe," whereas the plank is not satisfied with an agreement with anything less than the whole earth. The plank pledges the party to promote such an agreement, and the draft does not. In the plank "we believe that" is very properly omitted before "the existing gold standard," which is to be "preserved" in the plank and "maintained" in the draft. The plank does not favor the use of silver as currency, and in this respect it is a palpable improvement over the draft. The actual wording was the result of the scrutiny and coöperation of very many minds; and on the whole the last version, the one actually presented to the Convention, is the best. But this version was, of course, the result of the closest kind of criticism applied to the original McKinley draft. It was first worked over by the conference of Mr. McKinley's friends and reduced to the form given on page 197. This form was placed in charge of William R. Merriam, the only man participating in the conference, who was also a member of the Committee on Resolutions. It was submitted by him at Mr. Hanna's request to the chairman of the Committee and presumably received his approval. Mr. Merriam is the connecting link between the preliminary conferences of Mr. McKinley's supporters and the Committee on Resolutions.

Mr. Foraker, in his pamphlet on "The Gold Plank," published

in 1899, asserts that the last draft which he received directly or indirectly from Mr. Hanna did not differ essentially from the form originally brought to him from Canton by Mr. J. K. Richards. On the other hand, Mr. Merriam states explicitly that he, at the suggestion of Mr. Hanna, submitted on Monday evening the draft containing the word "gold" to Mr. Foraker and Senators Lodge and Platt. Senator Platt in his "Autobiography" (p. 325) confirms this statement. "That night (Monday) Governor Merriam came to Mr. Platt and Mr. Kohlsaat went to Mr. Lodge with the draft of the original Hanna plank with the word 'gold' inserted, and with the statement that it would be conceded." Mr. Kohlsaat confirms the statement of an interview with Mr. Lodge on Monday. Mr. Lodge himself testifies that the gold plank was finally drafted at a meeting of the sub-Committee on Resolutions by Mr. Foraker, Governor Merriam, Edward Lauterbach of New York and himself. Senator Proctor and Colonel Herrick corroborate the assertion that the draft submitted by Mr. Merriam was identical with the draft upon which the preliminary conference had agreed three days earlier. This testimony establishes the method whereby the original draft was transmitted to the Committee on Resolutions; and it justifies the inference that in respect to this detail Mr. Foraker's recollection must be at fault.

The Committee on Resolutions is technically responsible for the plank, and to a certain extent was actually responsible. Most assuredly it improved the phrasing of the resolution; but the testimony on which the foregoing narrative is based proves that the Committee merely confirmed a decision which in substance had already been reached. Not until Monday night was Mr. Hanna ready to have the matter finally settled. In the meantime he was allowing the delegations from New York and Massachusetts to do the work for him of consolidating the sentiment of the Convention in favor of an unequivocal declaration in favor of the gold standard. Responsibility for the result was widely distributed. No one man or group of men can claim more than a minor share. The gentlemen who participated in the preliminary conferences and who secured Mr. McKinley's consent to the insertion of the word "gold," played an important part, but even if no such conferences had taken place the Eastern states could and would have forced a declaration in favor of gold. The party had become more united on the subject than its leaders realized, and there was a general and an irresistible convergence towards the goal of a single standard. That the salutary result was accomplished without a more serious bolt on the part of disaffected delegates was due chiefly to the way in which Mr. Hanna manœuvred to get the Convention to declare itself and so to give its action a higher momentum and a more authoritative force. As he says, "the whole affair was managed in order to succeed in getting *what we got*," and he might have added at the smallest possible expense.

None of the delegates to the Republican Convention of 1896 who insisted upon a declaration in favor of a single gold standard realized what the consequences of their currency plank would be. They anticipated a certain amount of disaffection, but they judged that the Democrats were so hopelessly discredited that they could afford to alienate a few silver states in the Far West. As a matter of fact, the resulting bolt of the Colorado delegates and others did not look serious, and the Republican leaders returned to their homes, satisfied that their work had been well and safely done. But their satisfaction did not last very long. The subsequent action of the Democratic National Convention did something to excuse, if not to justify, Mr. McKinley's dread of the currency issue. For a while it looked as if the very means taken to establish the gold standard might result in its disestablishment.

No wonder that the action of the Democrats at Chicago took every one by surprise, for it was without precedent in American political history. A Democratic administration was repudiated by a Convention of its own partisans. No attempt was made to defend its chief measures. On the contrary, the repeal of the Silver Purchase Act, which had been accomplished under the leadership of a Democratic President, was violently attacked. What the country needed was not less silver currency but more, and the best way to get it was to take down the bars and coin all the silver offered. The nomination was bestowed upon a young and comparatively unknown man, who had carried the Convention away by his eloquent denunciation of a currency system based on gold. Thus the Democrats refused to be placed on the defensive. They took the aggressive, brushed aside the tariff issue and placed the Republicans on the defensive by declaring that the existing gold standard must be abandoned. The final effect of their action was to set up against a rich man's cure for the business depression a poor man's cure, and thereby to convert a controversy over a technical economic question into a sectional and class conflict. This transformation of the issue between the parties had such momentous consequences, not merely on the subsequent campaign, but upon the personal career of Mark Hanna, that in the sequel it will have to be examined with some care.

On the day, however, that Mr. McKinley was nominated it looked as if the nomination was equivalent to election; and the delegates were thinking more of celebrating their performance than of casting gloomy forebodings towards the future. The celebration began not unnaturally with the offer of congratulations to the hero of the occasion, who, in the eyes of many of the delegates, was as much Mark Hanna as it was William McKinley. In the extent to which Mr. Hanna had contributed to his friend's nomination, the delegates recognized that they were confronted by a new thing under the sun of politics, and behind the new thing was a new man. The general appreciation of Mr. Hanna's performance could not be expressed with entire frankness, but during the regular process of making the nomination of Mr. McKinley unanimous, it did receive a certain outlet. The official report reads as follows: "A general call from all parts of the Hall was then heard for Mr. Hanna, who finally yielded to the entreaties of the audience and arose and said:—

"'Mr. Chairman and Gentlemen of the Convention: I am glad that there was one member of this Convention who has the intelligence at this late hour to ascertain how this nomination was made — by the people. What feeble efforts I may have contributed to the result, I am here to lay the fruits of it at the feet of my party and upon the altar of my country. [Applause.] I am ready now to take my position in the ranks alongside of my friend, General Henderson, and all other good Republicans from every state and do the duty of a soldier until next November.' [Great applause.]"

Mark Hanna was, however, not to return to the ranks as long as he lived. He was undoubtedly right in saying that McKinley had been the choice of a larger number of Republican voters than any other candidate : but no one knew better than himself that their choice might not have received effective expression, had it not been reënforced by very able and resolute assistance from Mr. McKinley himself and from Mr. McKinley's "confidential friend," Mark Hanna. The Republican leaders were also fully conscious of the ability with which the canvass had been managed, and they realized that even though Mr. McKinley were the popular choice for President as well as for Republican nominee, it would not do any harm to lend the people some effective help in making their preference good. Mr. Hanna, both by his personal relations with the candidate and his proved ability as a political organizer, was marked as the director of the campaign of 1896. He was immediately selected as chairman of the National Committee, which was, of course, absolutely in accordance with Mr. McKinley's own wishes and intentions. Instead of retiring to the ranks, he became the field general of the whole army — a position for which his peculiar training and gifts had made him extraordinarily fit. He was an expert in organization, whose success in business had been based upon his ability to communicate his personal energy to a many-headed human machine. The work on behalf of Mr. McKinley's nomination had placed him closely in touch with local political conditions in many of the most important states in the Union. Finally he had an instinctive grasp upon the human factors which at once complicate a political situation and endow it with humor and life. He never made a move in politics without feeling around for the support of a sufficient body of public opinion. He had just given an excellent illustration of his gift for the most effective kind of political management by arranging that the Convention declare for the single gold standard in a manner which caused the smallest possible friction within the party and the smallest possible loss of prestige to Mr. McKinley. The campaign was to afford him an opportunity of so managing that the claims of Mr. McKinley for election and the superiority of the Republican platform were properly placed before a bewildered and hesitating electorate.

The ovation tendered him by the Convention was the first of several which showed the popular appreciation of his contribution to Mr. McKinley's nomination. When he returned to Cleveland, he was greeted by his townsfolk as a conquering hero. A huge crowd met him at the railroad station, cheered themselves hoarse, tried to listen to a few words of thanks and escorted him through the city to his own house. On the margin of the crowd was an old friend, who had not done as well in the world as had Mark Hanna — Mr. A. B. Hough. When Mr. Hough saw the greeting which the King-maker was receiving, he began to wonder whether the big man's head would be turned, and how far he would foregather with the less conspicuous of his former friends. He soon learned. Mark Hanna spotted Mr. Hough as he rode past in the street and immediately greeted him: "Hello, Hough!" Then inflating his chest he pointed to himself with mock pride and added: "Big Injun! Me Big Injun!"

The short speech which he made on this occasion deserves to be quoted in full: —

"Mr. Chairman and Fellow-members of the Tippecanoe Club: This unexpected and almost overpowering reception robs me of what little power of speech I had left. I had little idea that anything I had done entitled me to such distinguished consideration. True, I have been for a number of months associated with a cause dear to the heart of every honest Republican in Ohio and every patriotic citizen of the United States. I entered upon that work because of my love for William McKinley. No ambition even for honors such as are being accorded to me on this occasion prompted me. I acted out of love for my friend and devotion to my country. I lay no claim to the honors you have accorded to me. I could have done nothing without the people. All I have done is to help the people in gaining a result upon which they were united — the accession to the presidency of William McKinley."

On the evening of Saturday, June 27, he was tendered a dinner at the Union Club by his lifelong friends and associates. It was attended by all the men in Cleveland among whom and with whom he had worked for forty years, and the warmth with which they congratulated him on his success must have been peculiarly gratifying to a man like Mr. Hanna, whose better life was composed so essentially of personal ties. The dinner was private, but a version of the speech with which Mr. Hanna responded to the congratulations of his friends was published the next day. All agree that in making his short reply he was almost overpowered by his feelings. "He said that to him the greatest recompense for years of hard work was to know that his friends indorsed that work. He had acted simply as an American citizen and not as a politician or 'Boss.' He was not a politician or 'Boss,' never desired to be one, never would be one. He responded to the voice of the American people, and felt that in his final success in the nomination of William McKinley his work was to a great degree accomplished. When the question of the candidacy of his friend was broached, McKinley had said in his conversation with him that he would not accept the nomination subject to a single pledge to any man of office or remuneration. Mr. Hanna told his friends that the conversation had made of him a better man and had changed the current of his thought."

CHAPTER XVI

THE CAMPAIGN OF 1896

WHEN Mr. Hanna was selected as chairman of the Republican National Committee, no one anticipated how grave and difficult his task would be. As I have said, the action of the Democratic Convention took the country by surprise and completely upset the calculations and plans of the Republican leaders. They had never suspected that the currency issue, even if made decisive, would entirely supersede the tariff issue. They never anticipated that by virtue of the currency issue the Democrats would be able to make political capital out of a period of economic privation, which had been appropriated for the political benefit of the Republicans and particularly of Mr. McKinley. A few weeks before the Republican Convention it looked like plain sailing for the Republican nominee. A week after the Democratic Convention it looked as if by sheer audacity and misguided enthusiasm the Democrats had obtained the right of way, and that the Boy Orator would be carried into the White House on a flood of popular discontent.

In July, 1896, no one could gauge accurately the actual range and force of this discontent. No one could estimate how far its ignorance could be enlightened or its impetus diverted. No one could tell with any confidence what effect Mr. Bryan's gallant and strenuous appeal to the American people would have upon the actual vote. But the extreme gravity of the situation was manifest. Many of the men most familiar with the situation believe that if the election had been held in August, or even in September, the Democratic candidate would have triumphed. Mr. Hanna himself inclined to this opinion. Mr. McKinley was gravely concerned, and chided certain of his friends for their participation in the decisive definition of the currency issue. In order to save the situation enormous exertions would be required, as well as a plan of campaign for which there was as little precedent as there was for the situation itself.

What took the Republican leaders by surprise was the peculiar effect on popular sentiment of the prevailing hard times. For some reason the business depression, coincident with Mr. Cleveland's second administration, stirred the American people more deeply and had graver political consequences than had any previous economic famine. The panics of 1837, 1873 and perhaps even of 1857 had caused as much, if not more, suffering and privation as did the panic of 1893. The effect, for instance, of the panic of 1873 upon the prevailing rate of wages was more depressing than was the effect of the panic of 1893. But in the earlier years the political consequences were not serious or dangerous. The result in 1837 was the subsequent election of a Whig in place of a Democratic administration. The result in 1873 was the subsequent capture by the opposing party of the House of Representatives and Democratic plurality of the popular vote in the presidential campaign of 1876. On each of these occasions, also, local economic heresies jumped to the surface in the Middle and Far West. But in neither case did these local economic heresies wax into a national issue and become a grave national peril. In neither case did it result in a campaign in which one of the great political parties declared that the effect of the prevailing economic system was to discriminate in favor of the possessor of loanable capital, and against the borrower, the wage-earner and the producer. The fact that so threatening an economic issue could be nationalized indicated the ebullition of unsuspected forces in American public opinion.

The public opinion of the time, confused and ill-informed as it was, saw one truth very plainly, which was that the cause of the trouble lay deeper than the administration of a Democratic President and the passage of the Wilson Bill. It turned in the beginning instinctively toward Mr. Bryan because he provided the people with an apparently better reason for their privations and a more immediately effective cure. They felt vaguely that some essential economic force was operating to deprive them of the share of economic goods to which they were accustomed; and it was both plausible and comforting to attribute that malevolent power to the men who controlled the money of the country. Thus it came to pass that Mr. Bryan's speeches inevitably assumed more and more the character of appeals to a class interest, and this was just the aspect of the matter which so puzzled and alarmed his adversaries. Not since the campaign against the National Bank, had any issue arisen which encouraged loose talk about the "Money Power" and which made the poor feel that the rich were becoming fat at their expense.

Fortunately, however, Mr. Bryan was appealing to and representing, not merely a class, but a sectional interest. For reasons already indicated, the economic dearth had caused the utmost suffering and privation among the farmers of the second tier of states west of the Mississippi. These people had gone heavily into debt upon the basis of expectations which had been frustrated by poor crops, low prices and the disturbed condition of credit. They turned willingly towards a change in the currency system which might provide them with cheaper money. But there was no reason why the desire for cheaper money should appeal either to farmers who were relatively prosperous, or to the wage-earners in the industries of the country. After the first burst of enthusiasm had been spent over a candidate and a platform which made a strong bid for popular sympathy, there was a fair chance that the more prevalent interests opposed to cheap money would assert themselves. The one thing necessary was to establish clearly and to popularize the real meaning of the demand for the free coinage of silver and the real necessity of an assured standard of value. It would be the fault of the Republicans themselves in case a purely sectional interest were allowed to obtain a national following without having its false pretensions exposed.

The manifest duty of the Republican National Committee was that of explaining fully to the voters the meaning of the Democratic platform and convincing them of its palpable error. It was confronted, that is, literally and exclusively, by a campaign of education, or better of instruction. We hear a great deal about campaigns of education, in many of which the people who need and get the education are the people who run the campaign. But in this particular case a confused and hesitating mass of public opinion merely needed elementary instruction. The prevailing popular discontent was receiving a well-intentioned but erroneous economic expression. A sectional economic interest was demanding a change in the currency system, which from the point of view of sound economics was entirely and inexcusably wrong. Unlike the controversy between free trade and protection, it was not a matter of two divergent economic policies, each of which expressed under certain conditions a valid political interest and a sound economic truth. It was a matter of undermining by thorough discussion and explanation the foundations of a dangerous and obvious mistake.

Mark Hanna and the other Republican leaders soon understood the kind of campaign work which the situation demanded. They decided to oppose Mr. Bryan's personal appeal to the American people with an exhaustive and systematic educational canvass of the country. There was no hesitation and doubt as to the kind of strategy needed. The difficulty consisted in collecting, organizing, equipping and distributing among its proper fields of action a large enough army to carry out the strategic plan. The prevalence of the heresy, the confusion of public opinion, the uncertainty as to the actual force of the Democratic candidate's personal appeal, and the general obliteration of the usual sign-posts and land-marks made it necessary to cover an enormously extended territory with operations devised to meet both the local and the general needs of the situation.

In previous campaigns the National Committee could count upon certain states as indubitably Republican and certain other states as indubitably Democratic. Only the appearance of a fight had to be made in such neighborhoods. The real work was done in half a dozen doubtful states, and the Committee could plan with some assurance the methods necessary to secure the best results within these areas. In 1896 all this was changed. Of course some states could still be placed indubitably in one column or the other, and there were a few states, ordinarily doubtful, which were sure to cast their vote either for the golden-mouthed or the silver-tongued candidate. But no one knew where certain parts of the West stood. The Middle West, the Far West and the Pacific Coast were all more or less in doubt. The result was that instead of a campaign carried on in a few dubious states, the field of action was enlarged to include half the country; and within this enlarged field of action an unprecedented amount of campaign work had to be accomplished.

The exigencies of the campaign necessitated certain departures from the customary methods of organization. For a number of reasons the work devolved to a much larger extent than usual upon the National Committee. The time was short. An enormous amount of properly correlated work had to be accomplished with the utmost possible efficiency. Since it was to be a campaign of instruction, the educational agencies had to be concentrated upon the areas in which they could do most good, and they had to be supplied with really instructive material. The State Committees could not be trusted with as much responsibility as they had been accustomed to exercise. The National Committee, instead of being a kind of central agency of the State Committees, became the general staff of the whole army. The State Committees carried out its orders. Such was the inevitable effect of a campaign which stirred public opinion as it had not been stirred since the war, and which raised an issue involving not merely the national prosperity, but the national honor and credit.

It was also a result of naming a man like Mark Hanna as the chairman of the Committee. He was not merely the nominal head of the campaign. He was the real leader of the Committee, the real architect of its plans, the real engineer of its machinery and to a certain extent the real source of its energy. In the work of the campaign no one was more intimately associated with him than the treasurer of the Committee, the late Mr. Cornelius N. Bliss, and no one testifies more cordially to his unremitting labor, his unflagging energy, his thorough grasp of the work in all its aspects, his quick insight into the different needs born of different situations and his fertility in meeting special needs with special measures.

As one necessary preliminary measure he reorganized the executive offices of the Committee. In the past its methods had not conformed to sound business standards. Mr. Hanna introduced a better system of bookkeeping and auditing, so that there would be a proper account kept of the way in which the funds of the Committee were spent. Another innovation was the establishment of two headquarters, one in New York and one in Chicago. In the beginning he anticipated that the Eastern office would be the more important, but the large amount of work which was necessitated in the West by the disaffection in that region demanded an independent organization. As the campaign developed, this double-headed organization was justified by the event. Chicago became the real centre of the educational part of the campaign, because of its proximity to the doubtful states.

Mr. Hanna had intended to divide his own attention about equally between the two headquarters, but as the campaign progressed his personal responsibility for raising money to pay the expense of the Committee kept him a large part of the time in New York. He needed, consequently, a peculiarly efficient local organization in Chicago, and he secured it by associating with him in the work unusually able men. The vice-chairman in charge of the office was Mr. Henry C. Payne of Wisconsin, who is said to be one of the most successful campaign managers of that period. With him was associated Charles G. Dawes, who had proved his abilities in the fight made by McKinley's friends for Illinois, Winfield T. Durbin of Indiana and Cyrus Leland, Jr., of Kansas. The subordinates were all men with whom Mr. Hanna had already worked and in whose abilities he had confidence. Major Charles Dick was secretary to the committee and the working head of the organization. William M. Hahn, formerly chairman of the Ohio State Committee, was in charge of the Bureau of Speakers, and Perry Heath took care of the press matter. In New York, besides Mr. Cornelius N. Bliss, the work was divided among Senator Quay, Joseph Manley of Maine, Powell Clayton of Arkansas and N. B. Scott of West Virginia.

One of the major necessities of the campaign as a whole was the adoption of some measure which would counteract the effect of Mr. Bryan's personal stumping tour, — a tour which covered a large part of the country and aroused great popular sympathy and interest. Of course the countermove was to keep Mr. McKinley's ingratiating personality as much as possible before

THE CAMPAIGN OF 1896

the public; but the Republican candidate cherished a high respect for the proprieties of political life and refused to consider a competing tour of his own. It was arranged, consequently, that inasmuch as McKinley could not go to the people, the people must come to McKinley. The latter abjured the stump, but when his supporters paid him a visit, he could address them from his own front porch. This idea was employed and developed to the very limit. Several times a week delegations of loyal Republicans came to Canton from all points of the compass to pay their respects to the candidate. The chairman of the delegation would make a short speech, telling Mr. McKinley a few little truths with which he was already familiar, and Mr. McKinley would answer at smaller or greater length, according to the importance of the delegation or the requirements of the general campaign at that particular juncture. These delegations were not mere committees. They frequently included some thousands of people and had to be carried to Canton in trains of several sections.

It is characteristic both of Mr. Hanna and Mr. McKinley that every detail of these visitations was carefully prearranged. The candidate was not taking any chance of a reference by some alliterative chairman to the party of Silver, Sacerdotalism and Sedition. In the first place, while many of the pilgrimages were the result of a genuine desire on the part of enthusiastic Republicans to gaze upon their candidate, others were deliberately planned by the Committee for the sake of their effect both upon the pilgrims and upon public opinion. But, whether instigated or spontaneous, Mr. McKinley always had to know in advance just what the chairman was going to say. The general procedure was something as follows: A letter would be sent to the National Committee or to Canton, stating that a delegation of farmers, railroad employees, cigar-makers, wholesale merchants, Presbyterians or what-not would, if convenient, call on Mr. McKinley on such a day. An answer would immediately be returned expressing pleasure at the idea, but requesting that the head of the delegation make a preliminary visit to the candidate. When he appeared, Mr. McKinley would greet him warmly and ask: "You are going to represent the delegation and make some remarks. What are you going to say?" The reply would usually be: "Oh! I don't know. Anything that occurs to me." Then Mr. McKinley would point out the inconveniences of such a course and request that a copy of the address be sent to him in advance, and he usually warned his interlocutor that he might make certain suggestions looking towards the revision of the speech.

In one instance, according to ex-Senator Charles Dick, a man took his speech to Canton, all written out, and at McKinley's request read it aloud to the candidate. After he had finished Mr. McKinley said: "My friend, that is a splendid speech, a magnificent speech. No one could have prepared a better one. There are many occasions on which it would be precisely the right thing to say; but is it quite suitable to this peculiar occasion? Sound and sober as it is from your standpoint, I must consider its effect from the party's standpoint. Now you go home and write a speech along the lines I indicate, and send me a copy of it." In this particular case, even the second version was thoroughly blue-pencilled until it satisfied the exigent candidate. Such a method was not calculated to produce bursts of personal eloquence on the part of the chairman of the delegation, but the candidate preferred himself to provide the eloquence. Knowing as he did in advance just what the chairman would say, his own answer was carefully prepared. He had secretaries to dig up any information he needed, but he always conscientiously wrote out the speech itself. If it were short, he would memorize it. If it were long, he would read it. In consequence, his addresses to the American people during the campaign, beginning with the letter of acceptance, were unusually able and raised him in the estimation of many of his earlier opponents. He made a genuine personal contribution to the discussion of the dominant issue and extorted increasing respect from general public opinion. As the campaign progressed and the strain began to count, Mr. Bryan's speeches deteriorated both in dignity and poignancy, while those of Mr. McKinley maintained an even level of sobriety, pertinence and good sense.

Mr. McKinley was only the leader of an army of speakers who were preaching the same doctrine to the American people. The Republicans had a great advantage over the Democrats in the number of speakers of ability at their disposal, who knew what they were talking about and believed in it. The National Committee took full advantage of their resources. They collected a body of 1400 campaigners, paid their expenses and sent them wherever their services were most needed. In the doubtful states the canvass was most exhaustive and more careful than ever before in the history of the country. The agents of the committee penetrated, wherever necessary, into every election district and held small local meetings. Hand in hand with these meetings went an equally thorough circulation of campaign literature. There are good reasons for believing that this work was really efficient. Early in September, for instance, a careful canvass of Iowa indicated a probable majority for Bryan in that state. During the next six weeks, speakers and campaign documents were poured into every town and village. In October the results of another canvass convinced the Committee that the state was safe for McKinley.

Even more elaborate were the provisions made for the distribution of campaign literature. This feature of the canvass increased in importance as it progressed, and finally attained a wholly unexpected volume and momentum. The greater part of the responsibility fell upon the Chicago headquarters, and this fact made the work performed at Chicago relatively more important than that performed in New York. Over 100,000,000 documents were shipped from the Chicago office, whereas not more than 20,000,000 were sent out from New York. In addition the Congressional Committee at Washington circulated a great deal of printed matter. The material was derived from many sources,—chiefly from Mr. McKinley's own speeches and from those which various congressmen had made at different times on behalf of sound money. A pamphlet of forty pages, dealing with the silver question in a conversational way, although one of the longest of the documents, proved to be one of the most popular. A majority of these pamphlets dealt with the currency issue; but towards the end of the campaign, as the effect of the early hurrah for Bryan and free silver wore off, an increasing demand was made upon the Committee for protectionist reading matter. Something like 275 different pamphlets and leaflets were circulated, and they were printed in German, French, Spanish, Italian, Swedish, Norwegian, Danish, Dutch and Hebrew, as well as English.

The National Committee had this reading matter prepared, but it was usually shipped to the State Committees for actual distribution. To a constantly increasing extent, however, the documents were sent direct to individuals from Chicago. They found by experience that the State and County Committees frequently did not coöperate with sufficient energy or sufficient intelligence in the distribution of the reading matter. Two weeks before the election, so it is said, several carloads of pamphlets had not been unloaded from the freight cars at Columbus, Ohio. The Committee also distributed material direct to the newspapers. Country journals with an aggregate circulation of 1,650,000 received three and one-half columns of specially prepared matter every week. Another list of country newspapers with an aggregate weekly circulation of about 1,000,000 were furnished with plates, while to still another class were supplied ready prints. Of course cartoons, posters, inscriptions and buttons were manufactured by the carload — the most popular poster being the five-colored, single-sheet lithograph circulated as early as the St. Louis Convention, bearing a portrait of Mr. McKinley with the inscription underneath, "The Advance Agent of Prosperity."

The most serious problem confronting the Committee was that of raising the money necessary to pay the expenses of the campaign. Its work had been organized on a scale unprecedented in the political history of the country. The cost of its organization and of its bureaus of printed matter and speakers was substantially larger than that incurred during previous campaigns. It was not only conducting an unusually exhaustive and expensive educational canvass, but it was assuming a good deal of work usually undertaken and paid for by the State Committees. Unless a proportionately large amount of money could be raised, the operations of the National Committee must be curtailed and Mr. McKinley's chances of success compromised.

The task of raising this money belonged chiefly to Mr. Hanna. He had planned this tremendous campaign, and he must find the means of paying for it. Neither was it as obvious as it is now how this was to be done. The customary method of voluntary contribution, helped out by a little dunning of the protected manufacturers, was wholly insufficient. Money in sufficient volume could not be raised locally. The dominant issue endangered the national financial system, and the money must be collected in New York, the headquarters of national finance. In 1896 Mr. Hanna was not as well known in New York as he subsequently became. He was a Middle Western business man with incidental Eastern connections. Wall Street had not favored McKinley's nomination. Its idea of a presidential candidate had been Mr. Levi P. Morton. It required some persuasion and some enlightenment before it would unloosen its purse to the required extent.

Mr. James J. Hill states that on August 15, just when the strenuous work of the campaign was beginning, he met Mr. Hanna by accident in New York and found the chairman very much discouraged. Mr. Hanna described the kind of work which was planned by the Committee and its necessarily heavy expense. He had been trying to raise the needed money, but with only small success. The financiers of New York would not contribute. It looked as if he might have to curtail his plan of campaign, and he was so disheartened that he talked about quitting. Mr. Hill immediately offered to accompany Mr. Hanna on a tour through the high places of Wall Street, and during the next five days they succeeded in collecting as much money as was immediately necessary. Thereafter Mr. Hanna did not need any further personal introduction to the leading American financiers. Once they knew him, he gained their confidence. They could contribute money to his war chest, with none of the qualms which they suffered when "giving up" to a regular political "boss." They knew that the money would be honestly and efficiently expended in order to secure the victory of Republican candidates. Never again during the campaign of 1896 or during any campaign managed by Mr. Hanna was the National Committee pinched for cash.

With the assistance of his newly established connections in the financial district, Mr. Hanna organized the business of collecting contributions as carefully as that of distributing reading matter. Inasmuch as the security of business and the credit system of the country were involved by the issues of the campaign, appeals were made to banks and business men, irrespective of party affiliations, to come to the assistance of the National Committee. Responsible men were appointed to act as local agents in all fruitful neighborhoods for the purpose both of soliciting and receiving contributions. In the case of the banks, a regular assessment was levied, calculated, I believe, at the rate of one-quarter of one per cent of their capital, and this assessment was for the most part paid. It is a matter of public record that large financial institutions such as the life insurance companies, were liberal contributors. The Standard Oil Company gave $250,000, but this particular corporation was controlled by men who knew Mr. Hanna and was unusually generous. Other corporations and many individual capitalists and bankers made substantial but smaller donations. Mr. Hanna always did his best to convert the practice from a matter of political begging on the one side and donating on the other into a matter of systematic assessment according to the means of the individual and institution.

Although the amount of money raised was, as I have said, very much larger than in any previous or in any subsequent campaign, its total has been grossly exaggerated. It has been estimated as high as $12,000,000; but such figures have been quoted only by the yellow journals and irresponsible politicians. A favorite estimate has been $6,000,000 or $7,000,000; but even this figure is almost twice as large as the money actually raised. The audited accounts of the Committee exhibited collections of a little less than $3,500,000, and some of this was not spent. Of this sum a little over $3,000,000 came from New York and its vicinity, and the rest from Chicago and its vicinity. In 1892 the campaign fund had amounted to about $1,500,000, but the Committee had finished some hundreds of thousands of dollars in debt. The money raised in New York was spent chiefly in Chicago. To the $335,000 collected in the West $1,565,000 was added from the East, thus bringing the expenditures of the Chicago headquarters up to $1,970,000.

The way in which this money was spent affords a good idea of the scope of the Committee's work. The general office cost about $13,000 in the salaries of the staff and in miscellaneous expenses. The Bureau of Printed Matter spent approximately $472,000 in printing, and $32,000 in salaries and other expenses. The cost of the Bureau of Speakers was $140,000. The shipping department needed some $80,000. About $276,000 was contributed to the assistance of local and special organizations, and no less than $903,000 to the State Committees. These figures are official and confirm what has already been stated. The distribution of pamphlets, the furnishing of speakers and the expenses of organization account for half the expenses of the Chicago headquarters. The State Committees, on whom devolved the work of special canvassing and of getting out the vote, claimed the remainder. A large appropriation to the Congressional Committee was furnished from New York. Towards the end of the campaign money came pouring in so abundantly that the Committee balanced its books with a handsome surplus. It was urged upon Mr. Hanna that out of this surplus he reimburse himself for his expenses in nominating McKinley, but, of course, he refused to consider the suggestion.

The question of political ethics involved by the collection of so much money from such doubtful sources, if it ever was a question, has been settled. American public opinion has emphatically declared that no matter what the emergency, it will not permit the expenses of elections to be met by individuals and corporations which may have some benefit to derive from the result. But in 1896 public opinion had not declared itself, and the campaign fund of that year was unprecedented only in its size. It resulted from the development of a practice of long standing, founded on a real need of money with which to pay election expenses, and shared wherever opportunity permitted by both political parties. Mr. Hanna merely systematized and developed a practice which was rooted deep in contemporary American political soil, and which was sanctioned both by custom and, as he believed, by necessity.

The unnecessary complications of the American electoral system, requiring as it does the transaction of an enormous amount of political business, resulted inevitably in the development of political professionalism and in large election expenses. In the beginning these expenses were paid chiefly by candidates for office or office-holders. When supplies from this source were diminished, while at the same time expenses were increasing, politicians naturally sought some other sources of income, and they found one of unexpected volume in the assessments which they could levy upon business men and corporations, which might be injured or benefited by legislative action. The worst form which the practice took consisted in the regular contribution by certain large corporations to the local machines of both parties for the purpose either of protection against legislative annoyance or for the purchase of favors. During the latter part of the eighties and the early nineties this practice of bipartisan contributions prevailed in all those states in which many corporations existed and in which the parties were evenly divided in strength.

We have seen that an essential and a useful part of Mark Hanna's political activity had been connected with the collection of election expenses for the Republican party in Cleveland and Ohio. Under prevailing conditions his combination of personal importance both in business and in politics was bound to result in some such connection. But he had never been associated with the least defensible phase of the practice — viz. that of contributing to both machines for exclusively business purposes. He was a Republican by conviction, and he spent his own money and collected money from others for the purpose of electing Republican candidates to office. As he became prominent in politics, however, it so happened that the business interests of the country came to rely more and more on the Republican party. It was the organization which supported the protective tariff which was more likely to control legislation in the wealthier states, and which finally declared in favor of the gold standard. The Republican party became the representative of the interests and needs of American business, and inevitably American business men came liberally to its support. Their liberality was increased because of the personal confidence of the business leaders in Mr. Hanna's efficiency and good faith, and because in 1896 these leaders, irrespective of partisan ties, knew that the free coinage of silver would be disastrous to the credit and prosperity of the country. In that year the Republicans happened to be entirely right and the Democrats entirely wrong upon a dominant economic issue. The economic inexperience and immaturity of large parts of the United States and the readiness of a section of the American people to follow untrustworthy leadership in economic matters, had given legitimate business an essential interest in the triumph of one of the political parties. Business men can scarcely be blamed for fighting the heresy in the only probably effective manner.

Mark Hanna's reputation has suffered because of his connection with this system, but closely associated as he was with it, he is not to be held responsible for its blameworthy aspects. All he did was to make it more effective by virtue of his able expenditure of the money, of his systematization of the collections, and by the confidence he inspired that the money would be well spent. The real responsibility is much more widely distributed. The system was the inevitable result of the political organization and ideas of the American democracy and the relation which had come to prevail between the American political and economic life. As soon as it began to work in favor of only one of the two political parties it was bound to be condemned by public opinion; but the methods adopted to do away with it may be compared to an attempt to obliterate the pest of flies merely by the slaughter of the insects. The question of how necessarily heavy election expenses are to be paid, particularly in exciting and closely contested campaigns, has been hitherto evaded.

Mr. Hanna's opponents have, however, made him individually and in a sense culpably responsible for a traditional relation between politics and business. The economic issue dividing the parties in 1896 was easily perverted into a class issue, and the class issue was exploited for all it was worth by the other side. The vituperation which the representatives of the poor are privileged to pour out on the representatives of the well-to-do was concentrated on Mark Hanna. He became the victim of a series of personal attacks, which for their persistence, their falsity and their malignancy have rarely been equalled in the history of political invective. Mark Hanna was quoted and pictured to his fellow-countrymen as a sinister, corrupt type of the Money-man in politics — unscrupulous, inhumanly selfish, the sweater of his own employees, the relentless enemy of organized labor, the besotted plutocrat, the incarnate dollar-mark.

The peculiar malignancy of these attacks was due partly to certain undesirable innovations which had recently appeared in American journalism. Mr. William R. Hearst was beginning his career as a political yellow journalist. He was the first newspaper publisher to divine how much of an opportunity had been offered to sensational journalism by the increasing economic and political power of American wealth; and he divined also that the best way to use the opportunity would be to attach individual responsibility to the worst aspects of a system. The system must be concentrated in a few conspicuous individual examples, and they must be ferociously abused and persistently villified. The campaign of 1896 offered a rare chance to put this discovery into practice, and inevitably Mr. McKinley and Mr. Hanna, as the most conspicuous Republican leaders, were selected as the best victims of assault.

The personal attack on Mark Hanna was begun somewhat before Mr. McKinley's nomination. Early in 1896 Alfred Henry Lewis had published in the New York *Journal* an article claiming to be an interview with Mr. Hanna and making him appear as a fool and a braggart. In a letter to the owner of the *Journal*, Mr. Hanna protested vigorously against the misrepresentation, but without effect. Later the personal attack upon him was reduced to a system. For a while Mr. Lewis appears to have been stationed in Cleveland in order to tell lies about him. He was depicted as a monster of sordid and ruthless selfishness, who fattened himself and other men on the flesh and blood of the common people. This picture of the man was stamped sharply on the popular consciousness by the powerful but brutal caricatures of Homer Davenport. Day after day he was portrayed with perverted ability and ingenuity as a Beast of Greed, until little by little a certain section of public opinion became infected by the poison. Journals of similar tendencies elsewhere in the country followed the lead with less ability and malignancy but with similar persistence.

When these attacks began Mr. Hanna was strongly tempted to bring suit for libel and to cause the arrest of Alfred Henry Lewis; but after consulting with his friends he decided that

Lewis and Hearst were aiming at precisely this result — with the expectation of profiting more from the notoriety and the appearance of persecution than they would lose in damages. So he decided to disregard the attacks, libellous as they probably were, and he continued to do so until the end. But he was very much wounded by them and suffered severely from the vindictive and grotesque misrepresentation. Like all men whose disposition was buoyant and expansive, and whose interests were active and external, he was dependent upon the approval of his associates. As the scope of his political activity increased, the approbation which he wanted and needed had to come from a widely extended public opinion. Hence, while he was by no means a thin-skinned man, and was accustomed to stand up under the blows received in the rough and tumble of political fighting, he could not but wince under a personal distortion which was at once so gross and brutal, and yet so insidious and so impossible to combat. He had been brought up in the midst of the good-fellowship characteristic of the Middle West of the last generation. He was used to a social atmosphere of mutual confidence and a general and somewhat promiscuous companionship. He was accustomed to deal fairly with other men and to be dealt fairly with by them; and this concentration upon his own person of a class hatred and suspicion wounded and staggered him, until he became accustomed to it, and was better able to estimate its real effect upon public opinion.

The practice of attaching to a few conspicuous individuals a sort of criminal responsibility for widely diffused political and economic abuses and evils has, of course, persisted; and in so large a country as the United States it has necessarily been performed by newspapers and magazines. The people who have participated in this pleasant and profitable business are recommended to ponder the following sentence from Aristotle's "Politics," which is as true of the American Democracy as it was of that of Greece. "The gravest dangers to democracy," says Aristotle, usually occur "from the intemperate conduct of the demagogs, who force the propertied classes to combine by instituting malicious prosecutions against individuals or by inciting the masses against them as a body."

Whatever one may think about the rights and wrongs of the

campaign fund of 1896, it must be admitted that it served its purpose. If the campaign of instruction had not been organized on the scale undertaken by the National Committee, the election of Mr. McKinley might never have taken place. The Committee itself had for a long time no confidence in the success of its labors. Not until early in October did they begin to feel that the tide had been turned. The decisiveness of the result must not deceive any one into the belief that it was inevitable. The momentum and enthusiasm attained toward the middle of October by the campaign on behalf of Mr. McKinley's election was the result of the vigorous, exhaustive and systematic work performed by the National Committee during the two previous months.

Mr. Hanna had a method of conducting a political campaign, not unlike that of a coach in training a foot-ball team. His attempt was gradually to wind up public opinion until it was charged with energy and confidence. The different moves in the campaign were planned in advance. All the general preparations were completed by a certain date. There followed some particularly vigorous special onslaughts on particular states; and when this work was satisfactorily accomplished, preparations were made to hold the ground while the hard work was concentrated on other less doubtful states. The execution of this general plan was carried out with the utmost care and vigor. The whole organization was inspired by the energy and confidence of its chief. Gradually a contagious enthusiasm and élan was communicated to the entire body. The different lines of work converged towards the end of the campaign. Their effect was cumulative, and their ultimate goal a condition of complete readiness on the Saturday night before election.

In the year 1896 Mr. Hanna was conducting his first National Campaign, and he was, perhaps, over-eager. At all events he pushed his preparations somewhat too hard. He was ready for the election a week before election day, and he feared that he could not hold his ground. He was afraid, that is, of overtraining; and the last week was a period for him of intense uneasiness. And he might well be uneasy, because the country had been worked up to a condition of high excitement. By skilful management and a good cause the hurrah for Bryan had been converted into a hurrah for McKinley. Enthusiasm could not be maintained at such a pitch, and if it began to subside, the recession might attain a dangerous volume. His fears proved to be unnecessary. The electorate had not only been worked up to a high state of enthusiasm, but they had been convinced. The victory on election day realized Mr. Hanna's highest hopes and expectations. No President since U. S. Grant entered office supported by so large a proportion of the American people as did William McKinley.

CHAPTER XVII

SENATOR BY APPOINTMENT

The pleasantest days in the lives of American political leaders are those which succeed some decisive victory at the polls. Public opinion takes off its hat and bows to success. It likes to crown a victor with laurels and strew his path with roses. For the time being the press and the public are far more interested in good-naturedly hailing the conqueror than they are in calling up memories of past conflicts or in anticipating future troubles. The months succeeding Mr. McKinley's election were no exception to this rule. The business of the country had been relieved of an oppressive nightmare and a really dangerous threat, and public opinion had nothing but kind wishes for the men who had accomplished its deliverance. Mark Hanna shared with Mr. McKinley this warm bath of popular approval and interest. The whole country began to recognize how unprecedented it was that a citizen occupying no official position and without any personal hold on public opinion should have been able to contribute substantially to the nomination and election of a President.

The way in which Mr. Hanna was regarded at this moment by an able and sympathetic fellow-Republican is very well expressed in the following extract from a letter written by Mr. John Hay to a friend in Paris. "What a glorious record Mark Hanna has made this year! I never knew him intimately until we went into this fight together, but my esteem and admiration for him have grown every hour. He is a born general in politics, perfectly square, honest and courageous, with a *coup d'œil* for the battle-field and a knowledge of the enemy's weak points which is very remarkable. I do not know whether he will take a share in the government, but I hope he will." Many other people besides Mr. Hay were wondering what would be the future of this man, who could decide to make a President and see his will prevail. The expectation was that he would enter the new Cabinet, and as a Cabinet officer would continue to act as his friend's political adviser and manager. It was the obvious way of recognizing his past services and securing them for the future.

So, at all events, thought the new President himself. On Nov. 12, just a week after his election was assured, he wrote to Mr. Hanna: —

"My dear Mr. Hanna: —

"We are through with the election, and before turning to the future I want to express to you my great debt of gratitude for your generous life-long and devoted services to me. Was there ever such unselfish devotion before? Your unfaltering and increasing friendship through more than twenty years has been to me an encouragement and a source of strength which I am sure you have never realized, but which I have constantly felt and for which I thank you from the bottom of my heart. The recollection of all those years of uninterrupted loyalty and affection, of mutual confidences and growing regard fill me with emotions too deep for pen to portray. I want you to know, but I cannot find the right words to tell you, how much I appreciate your friendship and faith. God bless and prosper you and yours is my constant prayer.

"Now to the future. I turn to you irresistibly. I want you as one of my chief associates in the conduct of the government. From what you have so frequently and generously said to me in the past, I know that you prefer not to accept any such position, but still I feel that you ought to consider it a patriotic duty to accept one of the Cabinet offices, which I want to fill with men of the highest character and qualifications. I want you to take this tender under the most serious consideration and to permit no previously expressed convictions to deter you from the performance of a great public duty.

"May I not expect to see you here very soon? Please give to Mrs. Hanna and the family the sincere personal regards of Mrs. McKinley and myself.

"Your friend,
"William McKinley."

The Cabinet position which Mr. McKinley had in mind when he wrote this letter was that of Postmaster-General. Mr. Hanna refused it. During the next few months the two friends were constantly consulting about the make-up of the new administration and the selections for the higher offices within the gift of the President. There is evidence that at least for a while Mr. McKinley continued to urge Mr. Hanna to accept a position in his Cabinet. On Feb. 18, 1897, when the work of Cabinet-making was coming to an end, the President-elect wrote to Mr. Hanna: "It has been my dearest wish ever since I was elected to the presidency to have you accept a place in my Cabinet. This you have known for months and are already in receipt of a letter from me, urging you to accept a position in the administration, written a few days after the election. You then stated to me that you could under no circumstances accept a Cabinet place, and have many times declined both publicly and personally to have your name considered in that connection. As from time to time I have determined upon various distinguished gentlemen for the several departments, I have hoped and so stated to you at every convenient opportunity that you would yet conclude to accept the Postmaster-Generalship. You have as often declined, and since our conversation on Tuesday last, I have reluctantly concluded that I cannot induce you to take this or any other Cabinet position. You know how deeply I regret this determination and how highly I appreciate your life-long devotion to me. You have said that if you could not enter the Senate, you would not enter public life at all. No one, I am sure, is more desirous of your success than myself, and no one appreciates more deeply how helpful and influential you could be in that position." There follows a statement of Mr. McKinley's decision to appoint James A. Gary of Baltimore to the Postmaster-Generalship.

The reasons for Mark Hanna's persistent refusal of a Cabinet position are sufficiently obvious. If he did so, he would apparently be accepting compensation for his services in contributing to his friend's nomination and election. He was willing to compensate all the other leading contributors to that result, but he refused to compromise his independence by accepting a reward for his services from the man he had served. A

Cabinet office would constitute a recognition of the past, but it would open up only a restricted vista of future accomplishment. If he was going to become anything more than a political manager, he must seek and obtain an elective office of some dignity and distinction. Only by express popular approval could his prominence in American public life become authentic.

There resulted from this sound and proper decision one interesting consequence. His peculiar abilities and his life-long training adapted him above all to an administrative position. He was one of the most capable organizers and executives in American public life. He possessed in unusual measure the gift, so rare in public officers, of infusing the energy and momentum of his own will and plans unto his subordinates. Yet he never occupied an important executive office in the American government. His peculiar gifts and training were exercised for the benefit of his friends and his party, but they were never exercised directly in the interests of efficient public administration. The reason undoubtedly was that he was not the man to take orders from anybody else. As an executive he could not be a subordinate, and probably he would never have accepted a Cabinet position even from a President, to whose election he had not himself essentially contributed.

But, as is intimated in Mr. McKinley's letter, there was an office, within the gift not of the President but of the General Assembly of his own state, which he undoubtedly wanted very much, — the position of Senator. That was the one Federal office which carried with it enough political and social prestige and gave him enough official leverage to authenticate his peculiar unofficial personal influence. Neither was his desire to be Senator the result merely of his recent success. For years a Senatorship seemed to him, as it has seemed to many of his fellow-countrymen, the prize in American politics best worth having, the Presidency of course, excepted.

There is some interesting testimony as to Mr. Hanna's attitude towards a seat in the Senate. In January, 1892, Mr. James H. Dempsey, of the firm of Squire, Sanders and Dempsey, who had long been Mr. Hanna's attorneys, chanced to be in Columbus during the thick of the fight, which Mr. Hanna was conducting for the purpose of reëlecting Mr. Sherman to the Senate. On the Sunday preceding the nominating caucus, the politicians had for the most part gone home, and the day was comparatively quiet. Mr. Dempsey spent most of it in Mr. Hanna's room at the hotel. They talked confidentially about many things, such as Sherman's lively and persistent ambition to be President and of his career in the Senate. During their conversation Mr. Hanna said, "Jim, there is one thing I should like to have, but it is the thing I can never get." When asked what it was, he replied, "I would rather be Senator in Congress than have any other office on earth." He said this with great feeling, adding that he had never betrayed his ambition to any other person. Mr. Dempsey inquired why, if he felt that way, he did not seek an election. Sherman was an old man, and could not well be a candidate again. With his position in the Republican party in Ohio, he would have as good a chance as any one else of taking Mr. Sherman's place. Mr. Hanna replied, "Jim, I could no more be elected Senator than I could fly."

Mr. Hanna's reluctance to offer himself as candidate for Senator in 1892 may be easily explained. The Senatorship was a peculiarly important and responsible office. He had done nothing to qualify himself for such a distinction. If he tried to get it, he might have been obliged to use methods, similar to those which other business men had used, to secure the necessary legislative votes.¹ His strength in politics consisted in the fact that he was working hard, not for himself, but for friends who had a valid claim upon public recognition; and he still sincerely believed that his best chance of shining in public life was by means of reflected light. Yet when President-elect McKinley offered him the job of becoming one of the official reflectors of the light radiated by the highest office in the land, he refused, and hankered after the position which, five years before, had seemed beyond his reach. A Senatorship need no longer be considered an impossibility, and he might not unreasonably believe that his services to his party and his country had given him a sufficiently valid claim even upon so important an office.

But how was he to become Senator? His old political friend and associate, Mr. Sherman, occupied one of Ohio's seats in the

Senate. His term expired on March 4, 1899. The other seat was or would be filled by his former friend, Mr. James B. Foraker, who had been elected in January, 1896, and would take office on March 4, 1897. The election of Mr. Foraker's successor was still five years away, so that the realization of his ambition had to be postponed for a long time, unless he could occupy Mr. Sherman's place.

The facts that Senator Sherman did resign his seat in order to accept the Secretaryship of State and that Mark Hanna was appointed his successor have resulted in certain ugly charges against Mr. Hanna and Mr. McKinley. They have been reproached with appointing an unfit man to the Secretaryship of State at a critical moment in the foreign relations of the country in order to make room for Mr. Hanna in the Senate, and they have also been reproached with sacrificing Mr. Sherman's personal interests for Mr. Hanna's benefit. These charges have not been made by irresponsible newspapers or political enemies, but by serious biographers and historians. Mr. Sherman himself finally came to believe that he had been ill-treated. His life, by Senator Theodore E. Burton (p. 415), contains the following passage: "It cannot be denied, however, that he left the Cabinet with a degree of bitterness towards President McKinley, more by reason of his practical supersession than for any other reason, but also with the belief that he had been transferred to the Cabinet to make room for another in the Senate."

The facts in relation to Mr. Sherman's appointment of Secretary of State, in so far as they are now accessible, do not support the claim that Mr. Sherman had any grievance on that score. It would, of course, be absurd to insist that Mr. Sherman's transferral to the State Department was made without any consideration of the desirable vacancy thereby created; but whatever Mr. Sherman's later attitude in the matter, he was glad at the time that his Secretaryship might mean Mr. Hanna's Senatorship. If he had any reluctance in resigning, it was because he feared Mr. Hanna would not succeed him. These statements are all established by Senator Sherman's own correspondence.

On Nov. 13, 1896, Mr. Sherman wrote the following letter to Mr. Hanna: —

"MY DEAR HANNA:—

"I was very much disappointed in not meeting you in New York. I went there on railroad business and remained down town so long that when I received your card at the hotel you had gone from the city. You have got the reputation of being a 'King-maker,' and I want to see you, not to help me to be a King, a President, a Senator or a Cabinet Officer, but as an old and valued friend, whom I would be glad to help and encourage, if, indeed, he is not already so well situated that offers and public honors will not tempt him to exchange his position as a private citizen of greatest influence in the United States. I know well enough that your 'head is level,' and if you wish to enter political life, I would like to be one of your backers. Whether you do or not, I would like very much to have a talk with you. Can't you, when next you visit New York, come to Washington and stay a day or two at my house? Mrs. Sherman will take good care of you.

"Very sincerely yours,
"JOHN SHERMAN."

The foregoing letter contains a plain intimation that soon after the election Mr. Sherman had some specific question to discuss with Mr. Hanna relating to the latter's embarkation on an official public career. Early in December Mr. Hanna went to Washington, immediately after a visit of several days with the President-elect, and while there he dined with Senator Sherman. As soon as he returned West he had another long conference with Mr. McKinley. We can only surmise what happened at these interviews, but one of Mr. Sherman's friends throws some light upon Mr. Sherman's own attitude both towards his transferal to the State Department and the consequences of such a transferal. Captain J. C. Donaldson was Mr. Sherman's closest political aide. He had repeatedly rendered loyal service to Mr. Sherman during the latter's Senatorial campaigns. The position he occupied for many years as Secretary of the Ohio State Committee with particular charge of the election of candidates to the Legislature made his services during a Senatorial canvass particularly valuable. His helpful participation in the close fight for Mr. Sherman's reëlection in 1892 has been described in a preceding chapter. According to a letter written by Captain Donaldson to Mr. James B. Morrow, the following is the actual sequence of events leading to Mr. Sherman's resignation.

"In 1897, Mr. Sherman expressed to me his desire to return to the Senate, should the Republicans of the state desire it, and asked me to assist him in ascertaining the drift of sentiment. A few of us sought to organize a committee in his behalf to act centrally at Columbus. Before this was accomplished General Dick, then Secretary of the National Committee, requested me to go to Cleveland, to assist in the work of the National Committee. It was then agreed by Mr. Sherman's friends in Columbus that each of us should pursue the work individually until the committee should be organized, and that I should pursue the work from Cleveland. Immediately on my arrival in Cleveland, I informed both Mr. Hanna and General Dick what I intended doing, and they both cordially assented and agreed to facilitate and did facilitate my work. I wrote a series of letters to friends in every county in the state and sent the replies without comment to Senator Sherman, so that he might be informed at first hand of the real situation in the state. Just at that time a Cabinet appointment began to be discussed, and very many of his tried and true friends urged him to round out his career in the Cabinet. I was doubtful about the wisdom of his abandoning the race for the Senate, but I never ventured a suggestion further than to assure him that I thought he could be reëlected. I could see by Mr. Sherman's letters that he was not averse to a Cabinet appointment, and finally on invitation of President McKinley did accept the Premiership without any pressure on Mr. Hanna's part."

The two letters from Senator Sherman to Captain Donaldson read as follows:—

"Jan. 10, 1897.
"CAPT J. C. DONALDSON,
  "MY DEAR SIR:—
    "Your interesting letter of the 7th inst. is received and read with attention. I am very glad to read your favorable report of the condition of opinion in Ohio. Still I feel a sense of duty

to McKinley and am strongly inclined to accept his offer. The chief impediment in the way is the fear that Governor Bushnell will not appoint Hanna to fill my unexpired term. It seems to me that I ought to be allowed to designate my successor without at all affecting the question of who should be elected Senator for the term commencing March 4, 1899. I will keep you informed of any change of condition if any should occur.

"Very truly yours,
"JOHN SHERMAN."

"Feb. 3, 1897.
"CAPT. J. DONALDSON,
"MY DEAR SIR: —
"Your letter of the 1st with inclosures is received and has been read with attention. It would seem as if Governor Bushnell is doing all he can to make it difficult to reëlect him. He ought at once to settle the question of my successor, and any other selection than Hanna would be a great mistake. I will be glad any time to get clippings, indicating the political feeling in Ohio.

"Very truly yours,
"JOHN SHERMAN."

The overture made by Senator Sherman to Captain Donaldson in respect to a canvass for his reëlection was itself probably prompted by a desire on the part of the Senator to find out whether, in case he refused a Cabinet office, he could keep his seat in the Senate. He had received a written tender of the Secretaryship of State about January 1, and had already practically decided to accept it. On January 15 he went to Canton and made his acceptance definite. He had many good reasons for being very glad of the chance to end his public career as the Premier of a Cabinet. He had been elected in 1892 only by a narrow margin and after a hard and costly fight. He could be reëlected only after another similar fight, and he had no longer the strength either to go on the stump or to manage the details of such a campaign. A position at the head of the Cabinet looked by comparison like a dignified and grateful refuge. He was glad to accept it, and he was glad that his vacant place might be filled by Mr. Hanna. If his retirement from the Senate was the result of a conspiracy, whereby he was kicked upstairs for Mr. Hanna's benefit, the victim himself was one of the chief conspirators.

The other charge — that the President-elect appointed an unfit man as his Secretary of State for the purpose of indirectly benefiting Mr. Hanna — is more serious. It has been stated in the following words by Rear Admiral F. E. Chadwick in his history of the "Relations of the United States and Spain." He charges (p. 490, Vol. 1) that "Mr. Sherman's infirm health, soon to become painfully evident, combined with his advanced age, now seventy-four years, made the appointment one to be justly criticised. Mr. Sherman's appointment, even had he been in vigorous health, and equal to the heavy duties of his office, was, in the critical condition of affairs, on account of his previous pronounced antagonistic views to Spanish procedure, a blow to peace. . . . That the appointment was a concession to certain political adjustments in his state of a decidedly personal nature, did not add to its political morality." The accusation is, consequently, that Mr. McKinley deliberately appointed as his Secretary of State a man, who was disqualified for the office both by his record and by physical infirmities, so as to supply Mr. Hanna with a seat in the Senate.

That the appointment of Mr. Sherman was a mistake, there is, of course, no doubt; but the reasons which made it a serious mistake are more obvious long after the event than they were at the time. The appointment commended itself to Mr. McKinley as one that from many points of view was extremely desirable. Mr. Sherman was, in 1897, if not the most eminent living American statesman, at least the statesman with the longest record of useful public service. His name carried more weight than that of any other political leader. He had served in the Senate, not only as chairman of the Committee on Finance, but also as chairman of the Committee on Foreign Relations. Mr. McKinley may well have been ignorant of the fact that Mr. Sherman had fulminated vigorously and ignorantly in the Senate about Spanish dominion in Cuba. He had every intention of preserving peace with Spain, and he would not, under any circumstances, have appointed a man Secretary of State who in his opinion would have made the preservation of peace more difficult. He may well have thought that he was calling to his assistance the one American statesman whose experience in relation to the foreign affairs of the country would make his services peculiarly valuable.

A political associate of Mr. McKinley's, whom the President-elect frequently consulted about the effect on public opinion of appointing different men to his Cabinet, clearly recollects a conversation with Mr. McKinley in respect to Senator Sherman's designation as Secretary of State. The consideration which seemed to be uppermost in Mr. McKinley's mind was the prestige which he hoped would accrue to the administration by the bestowal of the premier position in his Cabinet on Mr. Sherman. He had been elected on an issue involving the financial integrity of the country and the prosperity of general business. He wished above all to gain for the administration the confidence of the business interests, and in his opinion Senator Sherman's appointment would contribute effectually to that result. He recognized that Mr. Sherman was failing in health and mental vigor, but he argued that inasmuch as the country knew nothing about it, Mr. Sherman's name would lose none of its value to the administration. He expected to be able by giving Mr. Sherman a competent first assistant Secretary to obtain the benefit of the Senator's prestige and general advice, while at the same time keeping the departmental detail in capable hands.

Such arguments may well have carried much weight with Mr. McKinley. He had never been much interested in the foreign affairs of the United States, and he probably failed to understand the gravity of the approaching crisis. He did not anticipate that within a year the country would be on the verge of war, and he had every intention of preserving peace. His attention being concentrated on the domestic situation, he naturally made his appointments with the object chiefly in mind of meeting the exigencies of the country's political and business condition. He made, consequently, grave mistakes in appointing his Secretaries both of Foreign Affairs and of War, but the mistakes were natural, if not excusable. He would have been the last man in the world to have compromised the success of his administration by naming weak men to the heads of those departments — in case he had realized his subsequent need of unusually capable assistants as Secretaries of Foreign Affairs and of War.

Whether or not the arguments in favor of Mr. Sherman's transfer to the State Department would have prevailed, in case Mr. McKinley had not needed Mr. Hanna's assistance in the Senate and in case Mr. Hanna had not wanted a seat in that body, may well be doubted. But admitting that a Senatorship for Mr. Hanna constituted an important advantage of the arrangement, there was nothing reprehensible about such a redistribution of official positions among Mr. McKinley's supporters and friends. The mistake consisted, not in the arrangement itself, but in failing to understand the paramount importance at that particular juncture of the ablest possible direction of State Department. Furthermore, in estimating the probable influence of Mr. Hanna's desire for a seat in the Senate upon the tender of the Secretaryship of State to Mr. Sherman, it must be remembered that the President was running a grave risk of transferring Mr. Sherman to the State Department, while at the same time making room for an opponent rather than his most efficient friend in the Senate. As Mr. Sherman's letters indicate, they had no assurance that the new Secretary's place could and would be filled by Mark Hanna.

The Governor of Ohio at that time was Asa Bushnell. He had been nominated by the State Convention of 1895, which was controlled by the opposing faction in state politics. He was far from friendly either to the President-elect or to Mr. Hanna. He would have liked to interfere with their plans. As a matter of fact, he hesitated a long time before making the appointment, keeping Mr. Hanna in the meantime in an agony of suspense. Not until February 21, two weeks before Mr. McKinley's inauguration, and five weeks after the announcement of Senator Sherman's appointment, did he write to Mr. Hanna announcing the latter's appointment as Senator, until the Legislature should have an opportunity to act.

"COLUMBUS, February 21, 1897.

"MY DEAR MR. HANNA : —

"When Senator Sherman announced his intention of accepting the portfolio of the State Department in the Cabinet of

President McKinley, I deemed it best not to make an announcement as to my action in the matter of appointing his successor, until the vacancy actually existed. However, the interest of the people and their anxiety to know what will be done has become so evident that it now seems proper to make the definite statement of my intentions. I therefore wish to communicate to you my conclusion to appoint you as the successor of Senator Sherman, when his resignation shall have been received. This information I have understood will have been in accordance with your desire, it having been stated to me that you wish to make certain arrangements in your private affairs.

"I wish you all success in your office and many years of health and happiness. I am

"Very sincerely yours,

"Asa T. Bushnell."

The reasons stated by the Governor for his delay were disingenuous. He considered seriously the possibility of a number of alternative appointments. It is stated on good authority that he sounded several prominent Republicans in the effort to secure a man for the office, whose public services constituted a title to the distinction. But in the end he did not dare. Mr. Hanna's friends, including as they now did practically all the influential business men in the state and the majority of the important political leaders, exerted an irresistible pressure upon him. He was a candidate for a second term as Governor, and he was presumably given to understand that in case he refused Mr. Hanna the appointment, he would have no chance of renomination. Nevertheless, strong as his cards were, Mr. Hanna doubted up to the last moment whether he would get his Senatorship. Even after the announcement was published, the issue of the commission was delayed. Governor Bushnell did not actually place it into Mr. Hanna's hands until the morning after McKinley's inauguration, March 5, 1897. The delivery was made in person in the parlor of the Arlington Hotel, only a few persons being present. The commission was handed over with a great deal of formality, and, according to an eyewitness, with a total lack of cordiality on the part of the donor and of the recipient. The new Senator left immediately for the Capitol in order to be sworn in. Various reasons have been suggested for the Governor's delay in issuing the commission, of which, perhaps, the most plausible is that Mr. Hanna's colleague wished to be technically the senior Senator from Ohio.

Thus the beginning of Mr. Hanna's official career was practically coincident with the beginning of Mr. McKinley's presidential term. Mr. Hanna had obtained the particular status which he had coveted for so long, and which was the one office which offered to him a larger opportunity than ever for the exercise of his abilities as a partisan executive, as an organizer of public opinion and as a personal political force. The remainder of this book will be filled with the story of the way in which he embraced these larger opportunities and the way in which he fulfilled the responsibilities imposed upon him by his peculiar endowment of official, extra-official and personal power.

CHAPTER XVIII

SENATOR BY ELECTION

BEFORE beginning an account of Mr. Hanna's official career, it will be convenient to anticipate the actual sequence of events and tell the story of his first election to the Senate. That election did not take place until over a year after his appointment, but inasmuch as the extraordinary incidents surrounding it were the culmination of his early extra-official career in Ohio politics, they can best be related in the present sequence.

When Mr. Hanna was appointed Senator, he had made no definite decision to seek election as his own successor; but after he had once occupied a senatorial seat his political future and prestige came to depend more than ever upon his presence in the Senate. To have occupied such a position by virtue of the Governor's selection and then to have shirked a submission of his title to the people and the Legislature of his state, would have been an act of weakness and cowardice, of which he was incapable and which would have reacted injuriously upon his personal prestige. Once having been named Senator, he was compelled to seek the confirmation of an election; and once having announced his candidacy his success became a matter of keen personal feeling. For the first time in his life he threw himself ardently into a campaign whose object was the fulfilment of a specific personal ambition.

His candidacy, which was announced in the most public manner, met in the beginning with practically no open hostility within his own party. The opposing faction had been temporarily silenced by the popularity and prestige which Mr. Hanna had obtained as a result of the successful presidential campaign. The State Convention assembled in Toledo on June 23, 1897. Mr. Hanna was in complete control. The Convention of 1895 had established a precedent in Ohio politics by nominating James B. Foraker for Senator. The Convention of 1897 followed the precedent and submitted Mr. Hanna's name to the voters of Ohio as the Republican candidate both for Mr. Sherman's unexpired term and for the new term beginning March 4, 1899. No objection was made to this action. On the contrary, the utmost harmony and enthusiasm prevailed. The opposing faction was placated by the renomination of Asa Bushnell for Governor; but Charles L. Kurtz was retired as chairman of the State Committee and one of Mr. Hanna's friends, Mr. George K. Nash, was substituted for him. Mr. Kurtz resented his enforced retirement, and for this and other reasons cherished a lively personal animosity against Mr. Hanna which was later to bear fruit.

Mark Hanna, unlike so many other business men, did not attempt to enter the Senate by the back door. His candidacy was submitted to the voters of Ohio just as decisively as if the "Oregon System" of direct partisan primaries had prevailed in that state. He was, of course, nominated without a state-wide primary, but every voter in Ohio, in casting his ballot for a member of the General Assembly, knew or thought he knew or ought to have known whether he was voting for or against Mr. Hanna. The campaign was managed with his customary thorough attention to detail. The issue was deliberately and explicitly raised all over the state. The County Conventions which succeeded or followed the State Convention indorsed his candidacy. In this way the Republicans in eighty-four out of the eighty-eight counties testified to their approval of his election. The Republican nominees for the Legislature were obliged to declare publicly whether they would or would not vote for him. His candidacy dominated the campaign and either overawed or included all other issues.

The situation compelled Mr. Hanna to go upon the stump and meet the voters of his native state face to face. He was obliged to risk practically his whole political future upon the impression which his person and his words would make upon the electorate, and he was obliged to risk this attempt without any previous training or experience in public speaking. His skill as a political manager might help to decide the result. His great personal influence with the leading members of his party might rally to his aid the most effective available assistance. Nevertheless he stood before the public practically alone and in a new rôle. Heretofore he had organized the expression of public opinion and exerted his influence upon it indirectly through other men. In his new rôle he must try to shape it directly by the weight of his own words and by the contagious force of his own convictions. He must conquer popular confidence in himself as a man and as a political leader, or else he must be content to become a sort of glorified senatorial "boss" and stage manager, who, no matter how powerful and useful he were behind the scenes, never dared to make a public appearance except as a lay-figure or as a prompter.

The development that ensued constituted, perhaps, the most striking single incident in a career full of dramatic surprises. Nothing in Mr. Hanna's previous career had made his friends anticipate that he would make a success or obtain any influence as a public speaker. Mr. James H. Dempsey, indeed, states that many years before he had been surprised at the vigorous, concise and logical argument which Mr. Hanna had made before the old Board of Improvements in Cleveland on behalf of certain requests which had been submitted to the Board by the street railway company; but Mr. Hanna's experience of even this class of speaking had been slight. Such arguments were almost always turned over to counsel. Until the fall of 1897 his appearances as a public speaker had been limited to the few words he had said in response to the ovation tendered to him at the St. Louis Convention, to the little addresses which he had made to his neighbors and friends after his return from St. Louis, and to one speech of less than ten minutes delivered in Chicago during the campaign of 1896. How, then, was a man in his sixtieth year to break through the habits of a lifetime and learn the new trick of talking fluently and convincingly in public? It would not be easy to read or to memorize a carefully prepared speech, but on the stump speeches cannot or should not be prepared. Success on the stump depends far more on a man's ability to adapt himself sympathetically to a particular audience or situation than it does upon careful preparation or even upon his general ability and eloquence as a partisan orator.

It was really fortunate for Mr. Hanna that such was the case.

The lack of preparation characteristic of good stump speaking was the aspect of it which enabled him to make a success. He was a man who could think out a plan of campaign but not the ramifications of an idea or the best way of expressing it. Mrs. Hanna contributes an account of her husband's one attempt to prepare himself for his new job. It was President McKinley who first urged upon him the absolute necessity of his appearance on the platform during the fall campaign of 1897. "If I go on the stump," Mr. Hanna replied, "I'll never be elected. I can't stand up before a crowd and talk." Mr. McKinley encouraged him, advised him to think the matter over, lock himself in his library and write at least one speech, which could be changed from time to time to meet the special needs of particular crowds. "When you have written it," said Mr. McKinley, "fetch it to me, and I will look it over." The next Sunday Mr. Hanna dutifully disappeared into his library after supper and sat up until midnight, wrestling with the composition of his speech. As he finished the sheets, he put them into a drawer of his desk, and the next morning after breakfast he took them out and read them. Mrs. Hanna says that she will never forget the look of utter disgust that possessed his face during the reading. At the end he tore the sheets to pieces and threw them into the waste paper basket. "That," he said, pointing to the waste paper basket, "is the weakest and most sickening stuff I have ever read." Mark Hanna had to do things in his own way. He could not make or write a speech à la McKinley.

Thereafter he never prepared a speech or the outline of a speech. When on the stump he never carried with him notes, references, books or information and memoranda of any kind. So far as his intimate friends could judge he never even needed to turn over in his own mind the substance of what he proposed to say. His private secretary, Mr. Elmer Dover, states that he did not know definitely what he would talk about until he got upon his feet. Yet he was always ready for the three or four speeches that might comprise the day's work, and each of them would have its own special propriety and point. The only part of these speeches of which he needed some conscious preliminary control was the very beginning. He usually planned the first sentence or two. The rest of it followed of its own momentum, just as a conversation may take its own course after a subject has once been introduced. When he was in good form, he was able to talk on in this way for an hour or more, without pausing for an idea or scarcely for a word.

Naturally he did not acquire such facility immediately or without an introductory period of distress. In the beginning it required on his part a great effort to face an audience. Mrs. Hanna says that on the occasion of his first few political speeches he turned pale with discomforture. In one case his obvious distress was such that she feared he would faint. For a long time he lacked self-confidence on the platform and dreaded when the moment for his appearance arrived. During his first stumping tour in the fall of 1897 he began with little speeches which required not more than fifteen minutes to deliver. By the end of the campaign he could run on for half an hour without effort or loss of energy. The time came when he began to enjoy it and take pride in his success. After a long period of confinement in his office nothing amused or rested him so much as a week on the stump. It was exhilarating without being fatiguing. It benefited him in much the same way that a vacation accompanied by hard outdoor exercise benefited other men. It stirred him up mind and body, and he returned home refreshed and happy.

Eventually he came to be a very effective public speaker. His success was caused chiefly by the sympathetic understanding which he had the power of establishing between himself and his audience. He impressed them immediately as a large-hearted, genial and sincere man, wholly without pretence and humbug. They felt the attraction and the force of his personality. He talked to them as he might talk to a group of friends, with simple words, in a confidential manner and on occasions with bursts of explosive feeling. He did not need to prepare these speeches, because they consisted, not of ideas which he had derived from others, but of a few deep convictions based exclusively on his own life or the lives of his own people. Everything that he had to say was on the top of his mind. His public speaking was an artless revelation of his own personality and his own experience, which accounts for the ease with which he took it up and its popular success. His audiences were for the most part captivated by the man, and they were easily convinced by a group of ideas, based upon so familiar and typical an experience.

Beginning merely as a stump speaker, he finally found it as easy to talk in public about other than political topics. Several of his most successful speeches had nothing to do with politics; but whatever the subject, the substance and the method were always the same. In June, 1903, he had, for instance, been asked to make the principal address at the seventy-fifth anniversary of the foundation of Kenyon College, and he had consented to do so. His promise had, however, escaped his memory, and he went to Gambier on the appointed day merely, as he thought, in the capacity of guest. When he saw his name on the program, he was very much embarrassed; but he rose to the occasion. His speech, which was as usual composed in the face of his audience and under the stimulus of its presence, has been described by those who heard it, for the most part educated and trained men, as adequate and excellent of its kind.

Speeches such as those of Mr. Hanna do not read as well as they sound. They had a colloquial rather than a rhetorical value. They were deficient in structure, in sequence and even in the thorough expression of a single idea. They rambled about from one subject to another, with frequent retracing of paths already trod, and with abrupt chasms between one part of the journey and the next. Particularly in the beginning, the wording was sometimes clumsy, and the meaning of particular sentences obscure. The second half of a long sentence would sometimes lose any sense of filial responsibility towards the first half. But with practice Mr. Hanna gradually overcame the most obvious of these faults. He could never make a coherent speech culminating in a climax. When his feelings were very much aroused, his expression of them was forcible and explosive rather than intense and dignified. He was not, that is, an orator any more than he was a statesman; but his style of speaking suited his own audiences and message better than would any outbursts of sustained and impassioned eloquence. His own personality supplied the wire which tied all his paragraphs and sentences together, and which gave consistency if not coherence to his discourse, and force if not light to his explosions.

During the fall of 1897 Mr. Hanna spoke almost every day from September 21 until November 1. His tour covered a large part of the state and included the small towns as well as the cities. The late Senator Frye, who shared many of the platforms with him, testified that day by day Mr. Hanna gained in self-confidence and in his mastery of his hearers. The meetings were unusually large; but during the first tour the audiences were not particularly enthusiastic. They seemed to be prompted more by curiosity than a cordial and sympathetic interest. Two years later when Mr. Frye and Mr. Hanna covered substantially the same territory on another tour their audiences were, according to Mr. Frye, both larger and far more enthusiastic than they had been in 1897.

The voters of Ohio had much more reason in the fall of 1897 to be curious about Mr. Hanna than to have confidence in him. He was one of the best advertised men in the country, but the people did not know him. While they had read a great deal about him in the newspapers, their reading probably misrepresented him and predisposed them against him. He had been portrayed by his opponents as a monster of sordid greed, and as the embodiment of all that was worst in American politics and business. The ordinary man had no convincing reason for entirely rejecting these charges. Even though he discounted them heavily, he might well be prejudiced against their victim. But in any event he would be curious to see the person who was said to have made a President, and who was said to have done these and other things with such evil intentions and by virtue of such dubious methods. He would be all the more curious because Mr. Hanna had become the issue of the campaign. The candidate was being bitterly assailed by the Democrats. All the regular accusations were being revived and being spouted from every Democratic platform. Mr. William J. Bryan was pressed into service, and the campaign of the preceding year was fought over again — but with this difference: the new campaign became essentially personal. The attacks were concentrated on the man who had acted as general during the previous year; and the hope of the Democrats was that by the defeat of Mr. Hanna they could claim a reversal of the earlier verdict, weaken the administration and exclude their conqueror from public life.

I shall not quote from the speeches in which Mr. Hanna very vigorously defended himself and in his turn attacked his opponents. The course of political controversy during the next few years enabled Mr. Hanna at a later date to express very much more definitely the group of economic ideas which he believed would contribute most effectually to the welfare of the American people. The substance of his characteristic policy was, indeed, plainly foreshadowed in these earlier speeches. He was already declaring that the dominant purpose of the government's economic legislation should be the stimulation of business activity, and that as a result of such stimulation prosperity would be fairly and evenly distributed throughout the whole of the economic body. He was already claiming that the Dingley Law, which had recently been enacted, had actually begun the work of rescuing business from the depression which had prevailed since 1893. But the prosperity actually created in the fall of 1897 was neither sufficiently emphatic nor sufficiently prevalent to permit the complete and confident development of the foregoing argument. And we may postpone a completer presentation of it until Mr. Hanna could claim with more plausibility and conviction that the national economic policy of the Republican party had actually restored the American people to a condition of comparative comfort and hope. For the rest the general issues involved by Mr. Hanna's personal campaign were an echo of the discussion of the preceding fall. Mr. Bryan's participation in the discussion and the renewal of his pro-silver proselytizing were sufficient to effect this result.

In replying to the personal attacks upon himself Mr. Hanna always spoke with moderation and good judgment. He knew that the best possible answer to the grotesque misrepresentation of which he had been the victim was merely to show himself on the platform and to give his audiences the sense of his personality. So he usually began by saying that no doubt many of his hearers had come to see whether or not he had a pair of horns actually growing upon his head. Specific charges he would deny with a rough indignation that always made an impression upon his audience. The charge against him of which he most feared the effect, but which was most easy to refute, was that in his own business life he had sweated his employees and opposed their organization. Whenever he spoke in a town in which his own firm possessed interests, he challenged his opponents or his hearers to bring forward a single case in which any one or any group of his employees had been ill-treated by his firm. He could always show that he had paid the highest prevailing wages, and that his laborers were neither crushed nor had any sense of being crushed. And he could show, furthermore, that so far from being hostile to labor organization, he had been unusually friendly to those unions with which his business had brought him into contact. The record of his personal relations to his employees was in every respect thoroughly good, and his opponents in attacking him on that score were trying to storm his intrenchments at their strongest possible point. This phase of the campaign was a source of great benefit to Mr. Hanna. When the canvass was over, his associates, who had been watching closely the effect of his public appearance upon popular opinion, felt sure that he had won out.

The event justified their anticipations. On the day after the election Mr. Hanna's victory appeared certain. The Republicans were conceded a majority of fifteen on the joint ballot, which seemed to provide a margin large enough for all probable contingencies. Only a very few of the Senators and Assemblymen elected had not been specifically pledged to Mr. Hanna. The name of no other Republican candidate had even been mentioned. It looked like plain sailing. Yet the results were no sooner announced than Mr. Hanna and his friends began to anticipate trouble. On the morning of the election day the Cleveland *Leader* sounded a warning against treachery and asserted that ballots were being circulated, indicating the method whereby a voter might defeat Mr. Hanna and elect the rest of the Republican ticket. It was remarked after the returns came in that, whereas Governor Bushnell had a plurality of about 28,000, the total plurality of the Republican legislative candidates was less than one-third of that figure. A day or two later Mr. Allen O. Myers, a prominent Democratic machine politician, asserted confidently in an interview that Mr. Hanna could not hold together the Republican majority in the Legislature. He frankly confessed that the Democrats had planned to sacrifice their candidate for Governor to the capture of the Legislature.

Mr. Hanna's friends have always believed that his enemies, even before the election, deliberately conspired to defeat him by underhand means. They had submitted to his appointment as Senator because they felt sure that in the year of reaction which would probably follow upon a great Republican victory he could not be elected. When they found as a consequence of his appearance on the stump that he was becoming personally popular instead, as they had expected, unpopular, they tried to defeat him (so it was charged) by trading votes for the Governor against votes for legislative candidates. Of course these charges were never proved, but they were made plausible both by the election returns and by the alliance between the Democrats and the Republican malcontents, which was publicly announced after the election.

Among the Republicans the leaders in this conspiracy were Governor Asa T. Bushnell, Charles L. Kurtz, and Robert E. McKisson, Mayor of Cleveland. What Mr. Bushnell's grievance was, I do not know. He was a well-to-do manufacturer and a man of many excellent qualities. He had always been associated with the faction in Ohio politics inimical to Mr. Hanna; but that fact should not have been sufficient to justify an honorable man in assisting so dubious a conspiracy. He may have resented the pressure which had forced him to appoint Mr. Hanna as Senator and have resolved that his appointee should be succeeded by another man. But during the canvass he had spoken from the same platform as Mr. Hanna and had both tacitly and explicitly approved him as the regular Republican candidate for Senator. Nevertheless the day after the election he announced that a Republican would be elected Senator, but carefully eschewed the mention of Mr. Hanna's name — indicating that his line of action had already been chosen. Later he appointed to the position of Oil Inspector Charles L. Kurtz, who was the leader of the Republican malcontents. Mr. Kurtz had a personal grievance against Mr.

Hanna, which is said to have been based on a misunderstanding.

Neither the Governor nor Mr. Kurtz, however, could have done anything to endanger Mr. Hanna's election, had they not been aided by the local political situation in the two largest cities in the state. The Mayor of Cleveland at that time was Robert E. McKisson. His first election had taken place in the spring of 1895, and was the result of one of those independent movements within the local organization which so frequently disconcerted the plans of the regular Republican machine in Cleveland. McKisson had requested Mr. Hanna's support for his candidacy and had been sharply turned down, because in Mr. Hanna's opinion he had done nothing to entitle him to so responsible a position. He was nominated at the primary in spite of Mr. Hanna's opposition and had been elected. Judging from contemporary newspaper comments, he began by being a fairly good mayor, but later he sought to build up a personal machine at the expense of the city administration. He was re-elected in 1897, but in the meantime he had become very much disliked by the prominent business men of Cleveland. McKisson on his side had always retained a lively personal animosity against Mr. Hanna — although his ill-feeling had not prevented him from speaking from the same platform as Mr. Hanna and recommending the latter's election. He himself had never been mentioned as a senatorial candidate. He was still very powerful in Cuyahoga County and could control the votes of three Republican legislators.

The situation in Cincinnati and Hamilton County was different but equally dangerous. A combination had taken place between the Democrats and the independent Republicans for the purpose of beating the local Republican machine, headed by "Boss" Cox. A joint legislative ticket had been nominated, and there had been elected some few legislative candidates who were really "Silver Republicans," and who were not pledged to support Mr. Hanna. The chief interest of these men was to secure the passage of certain legislation which would help them in their fight against the local machine; but while not pledged to Mr. Hanna, they had not entered into any alliance with his enemies.

It soon became apparent that considering the probable strength of Mr. Hanna's opponents, he could not be elected without the support of certain of these independent Republicans from Hamilton County. Some weeks before the Legislature assembled, Mr. James R. Garfield, Senator from Lake County, went to Cincinnati at Mr. Hanna's request in order to interview these gentlemen and see what could be done. In that city the leaders in the Republican revolt against the machine were Edward O. Eshelby, publisher of the *Commercial Tribune,* and Judge Goebel. Through these gentlemen a meeting was arranged with Senator Voight, who was the Republican member of the senatorial delegation from Hamilton County. Mr. Garfield is not sure whether an Assemblyman named Charles F. Droste, who was a "Silver Republican" by conviction, was present or not. The net result of this interview was neither entirely discouraging nor entirely reassuring. Senator Voight stated that while his personal feelings were favorable to Mr. Hanna he did not like the latter's alliance with Cox before the election. He made it plain that his first interest was to obtain the anti-machine legislation desired by the independent Republican movement, and he would give no definite assurances of coöperation. Nevertheless Mr. Garfield returned to Cleveland with the impression that Senator Voight would join the Hanna Republicans in organizing the Senate. He was not sure about Droste, the "Silver Republican"; and as to the other doubtful member of the delegation from Hamilton County, a druggist named John C. Otis, who had been outspoken against Mr. Hanna, he never had any expectation of securing the man's support.

As the time for the meeting of the Legislature drew near, it became definitely known that two Assemblymen from Cuyahoga County, Mason and Bramley, would oppose Mr. Hanna. Both of these men had been pledged before the election to vote for him; but in one way or another they were induced by Mayor McKisson to repudiate their pledges. The Senator from Cuyahoga County, Vernon H. Burke, was non-committal, but it was feared that he also would violate a similar pledge. A week before the date of meeting Mr. Hanna himself went to Columbus and opened headquarters at the Neil House. He had with him as assistants, not merely his personal supporters in and out of the

Legislature, but prominent Republicans like George K. Nash, Charles Grosvenor and his counsel, Mr. Andrew Squire. Mr. Theodore E. Burton and many personal friends from Cleveland also went to Columbus to work in Mr. Hanna's interest. By this time they could count noses with some accuracy, and the result looked very dubious. Governor Bushnell was using the state patronage to beat Mr. Hanna, and a number of more or less prominent Republicans from different parts of the state joined the cabal. Senator Foraker did not come out openly against Mr. Hanna, but the fight was being carried on by his political associates. In the only interview with him published during the contest, he stated merely that he was doing his best to keep out of it.

During the first few days the fight went against Mr. Hanna. Vernon H. Burke, the Senator from Cuyahoga County, absented himself on the day the Senate assembled (the first Monday in January) and that body was consequently organized by the Democrats. The vote stood seventeen to eighteen. When Mr. Burke finally appeared he voted with the Democrats, thus increasing their strength to nineteen against seventeen for Mr. Hanna. Senator Voight of Hamilton voted with the Republicans, having reached an understanding with Mr. Garfield and the regular Republican Senators that the latter would support any antimachine legislation for Hamilton County, which sought to restore popular political control in that district.

In the House, also, Mr. Hanna fared ill. Ten Assemblymen did not appear at the preliminary Republican caucus. The absentees included, besides Messrs. Bramley and Mason, J. C. Otis of Hamilton, D. O. Rutan of Harrison, William A. Scott of Fulton and John P. Jones of Stark. These six men, together with Burke, were the Republicans who voted against Mr. Hanna on the official ballot. All of them, except Otis and Rutan, had been pledged to Mr. Hanna. Of the other four absentees one was sick. Assemblyman Charles F. Droste attended the caucus. Thus the "bipartisan" combination succeeded also in organizing the Assembly. Nine Republicans voted with the forty-seven Democrats and elected as Speaker, Mason, the anti-Hanna convert from Cuyahoga County. If a vote had been taken on that day, the allies could apparently have mustered on joint ballot seventy-five anti-Hanna legislators, two more than constituted the majority necessary for election.

But the allies were not ready for a vote. On Wednesday the Legislature adjourned until the following Tuesday. This adjournment proved fatal to the success of the conspiracy, but the allies were compelled to take it because they had not agreed upon a candidate. A preliminary understanding had been reached with the Democratic leaders that in order to beat Mr. Hanna, the Democrats were to vote for a Republican; but when the time came to select the particular Republican, it proved hard to force the Democratic rank and file into line. There were a few convinced Bryanites among them who would vote for none but a "Silver Republican." Charles L. Kurtz was favorably mentioned in the beginning, but his name was soon dropped. There followed some talk of electing Mayor McKisson for the short term and Governor Bushnell for the long term. The Governor was willing, but not to the point of becoming a silver-lined Republican. John R. McLean was the accepted Democratic candidate for Senator, and the course of giving him a complimentary vote before switching to a Republican was considered for a while. Finally, however, even this formal tribute to partisan consistency was abandoned. At the last moment the coalition found Mayor McKisson to be the most available candidate for both the long and the short term. The Democratic caucus was stormy, but its scruples were assuaged by the appearance of the statesmanlike candidate, who explained that while "before the people" he was a Republican, he would nevertheless stand as Senator upon the Chicago platform. That is, although always a Republican, and although he had spoken from the same platform as Mr. Hanna during the campaign, he was just as much of a Democrat as was necessary to get elected. To their credit, be it said, there were three Democratic legislators who later refused to cast their ballots for this convert to Democracy.

It was not, however, until Monday, January 10, that Mayor McKisson had been selected as the anti-Hanna candidate. During the five intervening days Columbus had been the scene of probably the most embittered and desperate fight ever developed by American party politics. The action of the Republican malcontents in combining with the Democrats to defeat Mr. Hanna had taken the state by surprise. His election had been considered secure. An extraordinary outburst of popular indignation followed. The whole state was in an uproar. Mass meetings were held in the great majority of towns and cities all over Ohio to denounce the traitors and their treachery. The meeting in Cleveland was attended by eight thousand people. Vigorous measures were taken to make these protests felt in Columbus. Delegations were sent to the capital from many parts of the state and particularly from those counties whose representatives were members of the conspiracy. The delegation from Cleveland included one hundred of the most conspicuous business men in the city.

Columbus came to resemble a mediæval city given over to an angry feud between armed partisans. Everybody was worked up to a high pitch of excitement and resentment. Blows were exchanged in the hotels and on the streets. There were threats of assassination. Timid men feared to go out after dark. Certain members of the Legislature were supplied with body-guards. Many of them never left their rooms. Detectives and spies, who were trying to track down various stories of bribery and corruption, were scattered everywhere. Much of the indignation was concentrated on the Governor. His inauguration was the ghost of a ceremony. The reception was over in twenty minutes, and out of the two hundred and fifty invitations sent to prominent people in Columbus to be present, only twenty-five were accepted. A delegation of the Governor's own fellow-townsmen and neighbors went to see him in a body and asked him to explain his behavior. Finding that he could or would return no satisfactory answer to their complaints, they insulted him to his face. They threw his lithograph portrait on the floor in front of him, and spat and wiped their feet upon it.

The excitement was caused, not merely by indignation and resentment, but by the fact that the decision one way or the other would depend on the votes of a very few men. Mr. Hanna required four additional votes, including that of Mr. Droste, who had entered the caucus, in order to be elected — assuming, of course, that he could keep all of his existing supporters. The most extraordinary efforts were made, consequently, to capture these doubtful men. For instance, among the Assemblymen who had stayed away from the Republican caucus was John E. Griffith of Union County. He had announced definitely soon after he reached Columbus that he would not vote for Mr. Hanna. Prior to the time of this declaration he had been living at the Neil House, the Hanna headquarters; but on the day of the announcement he suddenly disappeared, and Mr. Hanna's friends were unable to locate him. If they could get at him they thought they could do something with him, because his constituents had been outraged at what they regarded as his treachery, and had been passing resolutions denouncing him and calling upon him to redeem his pledge. Finally it was discovered that the man had been drugged or intoxicated, and concealed in the rooms of the McKisson men at the Southern Hotel. At the same time they learned that Griffith was weakening and was scared by the denunciations which had been showered upon him. So one night a carriage was sent to the rear of the Southern Hotel, and both Mr. Griffith and his wife were brought back rapidly and secretly to the Neil House. There they were kept under lock and key — not only for the remainder of the night, but until the day of the first ballot. It was feared that an attempt would be made to abduct them, and as a matter of fact certain partisans of McKisson did attempt to force their way to the room.

The vote of Griffith would never have been recovered, had not the fellow-townsmen of the delinquent brought home to him the consequences of his behavior. The most powerful of all forces was working on Mr. Hanna's behalf — that of an outraged public sentiment. It strengthened incalculably the hands of Mr. Hanna's friends. The most desperate tactics were used to snatch one or two votes away from Mr. Hanna; but his supporters held firm to the last man because, if for no other reason, they knew that if they deserted, they would be black-listed both by public opinion and by the Republican organization. Not only, however, were there no more converts made by the allies between the adjournment of the Legislature and the ballot, but the Hanna strength was constantly increasing. Of the ten Representatives who stayed out of the caucus of the lower House, the one who was sick recovered in time to vote for Mr. Hanna. Another was the John C. Griffith who had been drugged and almost kidnapped. Two others, Representatives Joyce of Cambridge and Manuel of Montgomery, announced before Saturday that they would return to the fold. There remained only the six Representatives and the one Senator who voted for McKisson on the first ballot and Mr. Charles F. Droste.

In the meantime the friends of Mr. Hanna were busily circulating a paper, absolutely pledging its signers to vote for him. The great majority of the signatures were readily obtained; but the pledges of the last two or three men, necessary to assure his election, came hard. A negro Representative from Cleveland, named Clifford, gave a great deal of trouble, and required constant solicitation and surveillance, although he finally signed and voted true to his signature. By one or two o'clock in the morning previous to the day of the ballot the pledges of seventy-two legislators had been secured, including that of Senator Voight of Hamilton County. Excluding the Representatives who had definitely announced that they would not vote for Mr. Hanna, the only other possible adherent was Mr. Droste. The election of Mr. Hanna on the first ballot depended on the ability of his friends to obtain Mr. Droste's consent on Tuesday morning.

Mr. James R. Garfield had from the start attended to the negotiations with the delegation from Hamilton County; and he it was who finally induced Mr. Droste to sign. The latter is described as a man who was acting in obedience to his personal convictions and pledges. He had never promised to support Mr. Hanna. He had on the contrary pledged his support to Colonel Jeptha A. Gerrard, a lawyer of Cincinnati and a bimetallist. It was hoped that Colonel Gerrard might, with Mr. Droste's vote, be elected, for he was a "Silver Republican" by conviction and had a title to consideration, in case the allies had been united on any basis of principle. He was offered the short term in return for his support of McKisson for the long term; but Colonel Gerrard refused to consent to any such bargain. If he had consented, the combination might have gone through. On the other hand, the action of the Democratic caucus in selecting McKisson for both the short and long terms, and the consequent hopelessness of Colonel Gerrard's candidacy, released Mr. Droste. He immediately promised to give his vote to Mr. Hanna, and his vote was the one which was needed in order to make up the required majority of seventy-three.

On Tuesday, January 11, the two Houses balloted separately; Mr. Hanna received seventeen votes in the Senate and fifty-six in the Assembly. On that day the total number of McKisson supporters was only sixty-eight, — one Democrat being absent and three bolting the caucus nominee. But the anxiety was not over yet. It required a joint ballot to assure the result, and one deserter could upset everything. The seventy-three Hanna legislators went to the State House under the protection of Mr. Hanna's friends. Armed guards were stationed at every important point. The State House was full of desperate and determined men. A system of signals was arranged and operated so that Mr. Hanna and his friends at the Neil House could be informed of the progress of the ballot. The seventy-three voted as they had voted the day before against seventy for McKisson. A white handkerchief waved violently by a man on the steps of the State House gave notice to Mr. Hanna, who was watching anxiously at a window, that he was elected.

One aspect of this fierce contest remains to be considered. During the days of suspense charges of bribery were freely made on both sides. An election which turned on only a few doubtful votes and which aroused such violent passions was bound to create a cloud of mutual suspicions, and no serious or impartial attempt would be made to verify the reports. Men's attitude towards them would be determined by their sympathy with or their antipathy against Mr. Hanna. One of these charges, however, became public. On Sunday, January 9, the newspapers published a specific accusation that an agent of Mr. Hanna's had attempted to bribe Mr. J. C. Otis, the "Silver Republican" Representative from Cincinnati, and that an attorney named Thomas C. Campbell was a witness to the attempt. The charge, coming as it did at a critical moment of the struggle, produced the utmost consternation among Mr. Hanna's supporters. They feared for its effect on public opinion. The charge, however, was never taken very seriously by the public. Popular opinion had decided for Mr. Hanna, and the accusation was discounted as merely a desperate attempt to stem the tide of sentiment in the Senator's favor. Mr. Hanna vigorously denied that the man accused of bribery was any agent of his, and stigmatized the whole story as a lie.

The accusation failed of the immediately beneficial effect which had been hoped for it; but even though it did not prevent his election, his enemies naturally pushed it home for his subsequent embarrassment. They controlled the state Senate. On the very morning of the day dedicated to the decisive joint ballot a resolution was passed constituting a Committee of Investigation. The membership of the Committee, however, was such as to make it appear a prosecuting rather than an investigating body. Its chairman was Vernon H. Burke, the malcontent from Cuyahoga County who was Mr. Hanna's one personal enemy in the Senate. He was assisted by three Democrats and by Senator Garfield — who declined to serve, but was not excused. An investigation conducted by such a body, which refused to permit the representation of the accused by counsel, could not be anything but extremely prejudiced. Mr. Hanna was advised by his attorneys to ignore the Committee, to refuse to recognize its jurisdiction, and neither to testify himself nor allow any of his friends and agents to testify. The consequence was that all the evidence unearthed by the Committee was dug up among Mr. Hanna's accusers. These witnesses were never sufficiently cross-examined, and their testimony was never supplemented and corrected by that of his agents said to be implicated. The report of the Committee claimed to prove (1) that an attempt was made to bribe J. C. Otis to vote for Mr. Hanna, (2) that an agent of Mr. Hanna's was the perpetrator of the attempt, and (3) that Mayor E. G. Rathbone, Charles F. Dick and H. H. Hollenbeck, Mr. Hanna's lieutenants, were implicated therein.

This report was sent to the Senate of the United States and was referred to its Committee on Privileges and Elections. The report of the United States Senate Committee declared (1) that the evidence failed wholly to prove that Mr. Hanna was elected Senator through bribery, (2) that any agent was authorized by him to use corrupt methods, (3) or that he had any personal knowledge of the facts of the Otis case. The only question upon which the Committee had any doubt was whether it should conduct an independent investigation of its own; and this it decided not to do, because Mr. Hanna's title to his seat was not impeached, and because no demand for the prosecution of any further inquiry had been received from the state of Ohio. The Democratic Senators on the Committee urged that a further investigation ought to be made, but did not claim any proof of Mr. Hanna's implication in the affair.

So the matter has rested until this day. Only on one occasion was the incident used by Mr. Hanna's political opponents. The dubious nature of the testimony which was supposed to prove Mr. Hanna's connection with the alleged attempt to bribe Otis prevented its exploitation. There is as much doubt to-day as fourteen years ago concerning what actually occurred. The true story can never be ascertained because certain essential witnesses, including the alleged agent, are dead. Our only interest in the matter relates to the attempt to make Mr. Hanna responsible for the mission which took the man to Cincinnati.

Mr. Hanna's published repudiation of any connection with the business was contained in the following words: "I deny having authorized any agent or representative of mine to make any offer to Representative Otis or any other member of the Assembly. I never sent any man to Cincinnati to see Mr. Otis. I have never known or seen this particular man in my life, and have had no transactions with him." Alongside of this comprehensive repudiation may be placed the concluding paragraphs of an affivadit of the supposed agent signed by him in Boston on March 12, 1898, and attested by Justin Whitney, Notary Public. "I did not go to Ohio by request of Senator Hanna directly or indirectly. I did not represent him, and never for a moment assumed to do so, but on the contrary I repeatedly stated that I did not act for either him or his Committee. Whatever I did there was upon my own judgment, based upon good legal advice, and for the good of the cause as I saw it. I am not now, and never have been, the agent of the agent or representative of Senator Hanna, and as I have never been introduced to him he would have no means of recognizing me if I should meet him on the street." These statements are confirmed by the testimony before the Senate Committee both of J. C. Otis and the lawyer, Thomas C. Campbell. They both state explicitly that the man denied that he knew or represented Mr. Hanna.

The Committee of the Ohio Senate attempted to prove Mr. Hanna's connection with the alleged attempt at bribery by the testimony of various detectives, amateur and professional, who shadowed the supposed agent and others and overheard telephone conversations between the man in Cincinnati and the Hanna headquarters in Columbus. The United States Senate Committee on Privileges and Elections did not dismiss this testimony as entirely unworthy of belief. "It raises suspicions," so they say, "that Mr. Hanna's representatives in Columbus knew what the alleged agent was doing." Those suspicions were justified. Major Rathbone did know of the mission to Cincinnati. The precise nature of the connection between the Hanna headquarters and the emissary remains dubious; but the following statements are corroborated by a sufficient number of witnesses to be considered as facts. The man went to Columbus at the request of Mr. C. C. Shayne, a furrier in New York, an ardent protectionist and a notorious busybody. Mr. Shayne called up the Hanna headquarters from New York and recommended him as an able talker and negotiator. Mr. Hanna probably heard about the matter, but had nothing to do with it personally. The man was turned over to Major Rathbone, and after an interview with Rathbone in Columbus he went to Cincinnati. From there he did have conversations over the telephone with Rathbone in Columbus. The testimony as to what occurred in Cincinnati is hopelessly conflicting. If there is any truth in the affidavit, the only inducements offered by him to Otis to vote for Mr. Hanna were the "cordial approval of his party and the rewards which that would naturally bring to him." He admits having offered Thomas C. Campbell, during a later interview, a "retainer," which he says Mr. Campbell demanded in return for advising Otis to vote for Mr. Hanna. After the exposure he promptly quitted the state.

It would be futile to indulge in any theories as to what actually occurred. The probability is that the emissary was the victim of the men with whom he was negotiating rather than their intentional corruptor. His connection with the Hanna headquarters is admitted both by ex-Senator Charles Dick and Major Rathbone, but both of them exonerate Mr. Hanna from any but the most superficial acquaintance with the business. Mr. Hanna's public statement does not assert that he never heard of the man, but only that he never saw him and did not authorize him directly or indirectly to make any offer to Otis. This statement is confirmed by the assertions of his own agents, by the affidavit of the emissary and by the testimony both of Otis and Campbell. Mr. Hanna's friends may very well be content to let it go at that, and his enemies should certainly give him the credit of one beneficial consideration. If Mr. Hanna had himself planned to purchase the vote of John C. Otis, it is reasonable to believe that the business would have been better managed.

Everybody most closely associated with Mr. Hanna in this fight state unequivocally that the Senator always refused even to consider the corrupt use of money. He paid the expenses of the men who were working for him. Many of his assistants and supporters were subsequently rewarded by appointment to Federal or state offices. All of the Republican malcontents were black-listed and have never since recovered any influence in Ohio politics. But he never authorized any but these usual means of rewarding his friends and punishing his enemies. Moreover, his rejection of corrupt methods was not encouraged by any lack of easy and favorable opportunities. An obvious method of preventing the election of any other candidate would have been to send a couple of Democratic representatives out of the state. Certain of them were known, not merely to be open to persuasion, but eager to be persuaded. Several conspicuous Republicans asked James B. Morrow to call Mr. Hanna's attention to one particular case. He listened good-naturedly, but answered: "I will not give a cent for any man's vote. I am not engaged in that kind of business. If I am to be defeated by the use of money, well and good; but I shall not spend a dollar illegitimately to prevent that defeat. I would not purchase a single vote — even if that were the only way to save me from being beaten." Mr. Morrow adds that during the fight he was in and out of Mr. Hanna's private room at all hours of the day and night and at the most unexpected moments, and that he never heard a suspicious word.

Mr. James R. Garfield's testimony is equally definite. He heard of two specific instances in which representations were made to Mr. Hanna that a certain vote could be purchased, but without the slightest effect. During some talk about the opportunities of aiding Democratic representatives to leave the state, Mr. Garfield said to him: "You know, of course, how I feel. If money is used I shall vote against you." The Senator replied, "Jim, I know just how you feel, and I should expect you to vote against me." No one who knows the kind of man Mr. Hanna was can doubt the sincerity of such assertions. If he had intended to purchase votes, he doubtless would not have talked about it in public, but neither would he have paraded any conscientious scruples against it. He was not a hypocrite, and he never pretended to be any better than he really was. His ambition to be elected Senator was indissolubly connected with his most vital aspirations. His own career, no less than that of McKinley's, demanded an honorable victory. Like every honest man he had conscientious scruples about buying votes for his own political benefit; and his conscience, when aroused, was dictatorial. He believed certain practices were right which may have been wrong, but if he believed a practice to be wrong, he would have none of it.

It does not follow that no money was corruptly used for Mr. Hanna's benefit. Columbus was full of rich friends less scrupulous than he. Many of these friends were Cleveland business men, who hated the idea of a possible McKisson election about as much as they did that of Mr. Hanna's defeat. They may have been willing to spend money in Mr. Hanna's interest and without his knowledge. Whether as a matter of fact any such money was spent I do not know, but under the circumstances the possibility thereof should be frankly admitted.

Some of my readers may object that in describing the opposition to Mr. Hanna's election as a conspiracy, and his Republican opponents as traitors, reprehensible methods and motives have been imputed to men who may have had conscientious reasons for their behavior. The epithets which have been used are literally correct. No blame could be attached to any Republican who, during the campaign, had either opposed Mr. Hanna or had refused to support him. But his opponents adopted other methods. During the campaign they either explicitly pledged their votes to him, or they did so indirectly by speaking from the same platform with him. If any sanctity attaches to public partisan and personal obligations, all but two or three of Mr. Hanna's Republican opponents were guilty of treachery; and they were traitors not only to their pledges and their party, but to the clearly expressed popular will. On the other hand the Democrats, in order to beat Mr. Hanna, cast their votes for a man who was a Republican "before the people" and who had not any real claim to their allegiance. The opposition was wholly without principle either in its purposes or methods. The Republicans were satisfying a personal grudge by means of a betrayal of their individual and partisan obligations. The Democrats joined them, so as to cut short then and there the political career of their most redoubtable opponent. The stock shibboleth of the conspirators was opposition to "Boss" rule; but this slogan, whatever its pertinence and weight, was sheer hypocrisy in the mouths of its authors.

If Mark Hanna had been a "Boss" in the sense that Matthew Quay or Thomas C. Platt were "Bosses," the conspiracy would have succeeded. He triumphed only because he represented the will of his party, and enjoyed the confidence of the Republican rank and file in his leadership. If he had not gone upon the stump, if he had not made a favorable impression upon his hearers, and if he had not created a genuine public opinion in his favor, his political career might well have ended in January, 1898. At this critical moment in his public life he was saved, because he had the courage and the flexibility to break away from the limitations of a political manager and to try and create a genuine popular following. Thus his political personality emerged beyond the screen which always hides the real "Boss" from public inspection. In the nice balance of political forces upon which his election depended, the scale was tipped by his ability to create among enough of the people of Ohio the same kind of confidence in himself which until then had been confined to his business and political associates.

On the day of election he made the following speech to his supporters in the Legislature: —

"Mr. President and Gentlemen of the Ohio Legislature: I thank you with a grateful heart for the distinguished honor which you have just conferred upon me. I doubly thank you, because under the circumstances it comes to me as an assurance of your confidence — the assurance, which given to me in the beginning of this term of service to you and to my state, graces me with the strongest hope that I shall be able to fulfil your expectation and do my whole part by the whole people of Ohio. Standing outside of the line of the smoke of battle, which your President has just spoken of, and viewing this situation from the standpoint of a citizen of Ohio, I come to accept this high honor, recognizing that when I assume my duties in the United States Senate that I am the Senator for the whole people of Ohio. This is my native state. I was born in Ohio. I have always loved this commonwealth, have always striven to do what might be in my power to accomplish the advancement of her development and prosperity. If my endeavor is now transplanted to a different field of duty, that duty will be none the less incumbent upon me. In accepting this honor I accept in an appreciative sense the fulness of the responsibilities which go with it, and, under God, I promise my people to be a faithful servant to their interests during the entire time of my service. I thank you."

These words are not really addressed to the Legislature. They are addressed to the people of his native state by a man who really wanted to represent his own people as a whole. He knew that he had really been elected by them; and in the moment of his triumph he recognized fully both the source of the victory and its responsibilities.

APPENDIX TO CHAPTER XVIII

During the campaign in the fall of 1897 the Democratic newspapers kept standing for days in black-faced capitals the following sentence, which was attributed to Mr. Hanna: "No man in public office owes the public anything." They obtained this little rule of official action from a letter which Mr. Hanna was supposed to have written to Mr. David K. Watson, at one time Attorney-General of Ohio, and which reproached him for having interfered with the business of the Standard Oil Company. Mr. Watson had brought suit against the Company because of the trust agreement under which its business was then conducted. Pressure of all kinds was immediately brought to bear upon him to drop it. Mr. Hanna's letter was part of this pressure. No authentic copy of the letter was published, but the New York *World*, on August 11, 1897, had printed certain alleged extracts from it, including the phrase which the Democratic papers flourished in the face of their readers.

The way in which these extracts came to be published is peculiar. When Mr. Hanna offered himself as a candidate for the Senate, a newspaper correspondent named Francis B. Gessner recollected that seven years before he had been allowed to read in Mr. Watson's office a letter from Mark Hanna about the Standard Oil suit. He went to Mr. Watson, who allowed him to read the letter, but not to copy it. On the basis of what he remembered of its text, reënforced by what other people to whom it had been shown remembered of it, he published in the *World* the extracts which contained the sentence quoted above. These extracts have been reprinted in Miss Ida Tarbell's "History of the Standard Oil Company," and do not concern us here. Mr. Watson declares that after the publication of Mr. Gessner's article he answered all inquiries by admitting the receipt of some such letter, but denying the accuracy of the alleged extracts.

Mr. Watson further declares that Mr. Hanna at their next meeting after the publication of these supposed extracts asked for the original of the letter and obtained from him a promise to surrender it. Several weeks later, when Mr. Hanna was in Columbus, Mr. Watson went to the Neil House with the letter in his pocket. He claims to have received an offer of $50,000 for the original of this document from a prominent Democratic newspaper in the state. Nevertheless he gave it to Mr. Hanna at a private interview in Mr. Hanna's room at the Neil House. After reading it, Mr. Hanna turned to Mr. Watson (according to the latter's account) and said: " Dave ! you once told me that a man who would write such a letter ought not to be a United States Senator. You were right." After some further conversation the letter was torn into small pieces and destroyed. But Mr. Watson claims that as a precaution against subsequent misrepresentation he kept a copy of it. The following is asserted to be a transcript of the original document.

"CLEVELAND, OHIO, Nov. 21, 1890.
"HON. DAVID K. WATSON, Columbus, Ohio.
    "DEAR SIR : —
        "Some months ago, when I saw the announcement through the papers that you had begun a suit against the Standard Oil Co. in the Supreme Court, I intended, if opportunity presented, to talk with you, and

failing in the personal interview, to write you a letter, but the subject passed out of my mind. Recently while in New York I learned from my friend, Mr. John D. Rockefeller, that such suit was still pending, and without any solicitation on his part or suggestion from him, I determined to write you, believing that both political and business interests justified me in doing so. While I am not personally interested in the Standard Oil Co., many of my closest friends are, and I have no doubt that many of the business associations with which I am connected are equally open to attack. The simple fact is, as you will discover, if you have not already done so, that in these modern days most commercial interests are properly and necessarily taking on the form of organization for the safety of investors, and the improvement of all conditions upon which business is done. There is no greater mistake for a man in or out of public place to make than to assume that he owes any duty to the public or can in any manner advance his own position or interests by attacking the organizations under which experience has taught business can best be done. From a party standpoint, interested in the success of the Republican party, and regarding you as in the line of political promotion, I must say that the identification of your office with litigation of this character is a great mistake. There is no public demand for a raid upon organized capital. For years the business of manufacturing oil has been done with great success at Cleveland, competition has been open and free, and the public has been greatly benefited by the manner in which the oil business has been carried on. The Standard Oil Co. is officered and managed by some of the best and strongest men in the country. They are pretty much all Republicans and have been most liberal in their contributions to the party, as I personally know, Mr. Rockefeller always quietly doing his share. I think I am in a position to know that the party in this state has been at times badly advised. We need for the struggles of the future the coöperation of our strongest business interests and not their indifference or hostility. You will probably not argue with me in this. I have been informed, though I can hardly credit the information, that Senator Sherman has encouraged or suggested this litigation. If that be correct, I would like to know it, because I shall certainly have something to say to the Senator myself. I simply say with respect to this matter, that prudence and caution require you to go very slow in this business.

"Very truly yours,
(Signed) " M. A. HANNA."

On December 13, Mr. Watson answered with the letter published by Miss Tarbell in which he disclaimed any attack on organized capital and asserted that Senator Sherman had nothing whatever to do with the suit. Two weeks later he received from Mr. Hanna an answer which is reproduced below: —

"CLEVELAND, OHIO, Dec. 27, 1890.

"HON. D. K. WATSON,
"DEAR SIR: —

"On my return from the East I find your favor of the 13th inst. and I am much obliged for your attention. I think I know a good deal about the Standard Oil and have from its beginning, as I have known the men who organized it for thirty years, and most of them are intimate friends. There has been no industry of greater benefit to our city, and there are large holdings among our enterprising business men. They are indignant at this attack, and when the time comes will make their influence felt. Therefore I have said to you in all frankness that politically it is a very sad mistake, and I am sure will not result in much personal glory for you. I am glad to know that Senator Sherman has nothing to do with it, and for the same reason I wish you might have as little to do with it as *possible* from this time.

"Truly yours,
(Signed) "M. A. HANNA."

The second of these letters is unquestionably genuine. Mr. James B. Morrow saw the original with Mr. Hanna's signature attached. The first of them is admittedly only a copy and obviously has no authenticity as a document. A man possessing a copy can make as many additional copies as he likes and add or suppress as much as suits his purpose. An alleged copy must consequently be scrutinized with care, and the copyist cannot complain, in case any part of the text is rejected which does not square with what we know about its supposed author.

There is nothing in the letter of November 21 which in my opinion Mr. Hanna might not have written in November, 1890, except two sentences. The text reads: "While I am not personally interested in the Standard Oil Co. many of my closest friends are, and I have no doubt that many of the business associations with which I am connected are equally open to attack." It is true, of course, that certain of Mr. Hanna's friends and relatives were interested in the Standard Oil Company, but, so far as I know, none of the "business associations" with which he was connected was under any suspicion of being illegal. They certainly were not organized and operated under a trust agreement, as was the Standard Oil Company, and they certainly could not have been attacked as monopolies or as combinations in restraint of trade. Of course Mr. Hanna may have written the sentence loosely and vaguely, in order to emphasize his general idea that the Standard Oil Company was merely one example of desirable organization in business, but why should he suggest to the Attorney-General of the state that part of his own business was being conducted in defiance of state laws, particularly in view of the fact that the assertion would have been untrue?

Much more serious, however, is the suspicion which must attach to the sentence: "There is no greater mistake for a man in or out of public place to make than to assume that he owes any duty to the public or can in any manner advance his own position or interests by attacking the organizations under which experience has taught business can best be done." A fair-minded man cannot read the foregoing sentences carefully without suspecting that the words "he owes any duty to the public or" have been interpolated. With those words omitted the meaning of the whole passage is consistent, whereas the phrase under suspicion adds an irrelevant idea which breaks the force of the rest of the sentence. Mr. Hanna might well have written, "There is no greater mistake for a man in or out of public place to make than to assume that he can in any manner advance his own interests by attacking the organizations," etc., but why, even had he believed it, should he be cynical and incoherent enough to throw in a remark that a public official owes no duty to the public? The supposition is incredible. One can conceive that some such remark could be passed in private among a group of the lowest professional politicians or entirely unscrupulous business men, but for a man in semi-public life, no matter how corrupt personally, to commit such an idea to paper would be to convict him of childish folly. The folly becomes more than inexplicable when it is remembered that the recommendation was addressed to a man with whom Mr. Hanna was slightly acquainted, and who would have good ground to be aggrieved by the letter. A perversion so gross, so palpable and so stupid exposes itself.

Whether or not any other passage in the letter is or is not genuine one does not like to assert with confidence. No doubt the greater part of it is authentic, but the suspicion which attaches to the whole document makes it impossible to accept absolutely any part of it and base a criticism of Mr. Hanna upon it. In general, however, there is this to be said. Much of the letter might have been written by Mr. Hanna in 1890, and, having done so, he might have wanted it destroyed in 1897. Moreover, he might have wanted to destroy it, not merely because it was troublesome, but because he was ashamed of it. A man who was to become United States Senator should not have reproached a state prosecuting attorney for bringing a plausible suit against a possibly illegal corporation, and he should not have intimated that for the attorney's own political welfare he should thereafter have as little as possible to do with such business. But Mr. Hanna had changed a good deal since the fall of 1890. He still believed that the organization of capital was a good thing and should not be discouraged by law. He still had very little curiosity whether as a matter of fact corporations like the Standard Oil Company were conducting their business illegally. He was still too complaisant about accepting money for political purposes from corporations whose legal standing was at best dubious. But he would not have reproached a state prosecuting attorney for attempting to enforce the law, nor would he have intimated that by so doing the man's political future would have been compromised.

CHAPTER XIX

THREE YEARS OF TRANSITION

An account of Mark Hanna's career in the Senate of the United States need touch only incidently upon many essential phases of the legislative and political history of his seven years of service. To associate the history of these years too intimately with Mr. Hanna's biography would be to convey a false impression of the scope of his political influence. In respect to certain problems confronting Mr. McKinley's administration, his preferences and opinions were extremely powerful. In respect to other questions, equally if not more important, his influence was negligible. He was not the man to interfere in any business with which his past training and his present position did not make him very competent to deal; and in relation to many of the most pressing questions of public policy, his opinions were no more powerful and his advice no more useful than that of a dozen other Republican Senators.

The first three years of Mr. Hanna's service in the Senate constituted a period of transition in his career. Never before had he occupied an important official position. Never before had he shouldered any personal responsibility for questions of public administration and policy. Hitherto his dominant political interest had been that of contriving the election of his friends and associates to more or less important offices. But suddenly he had become a part of the government—and an important part, by virtue both of his constitutional and his extra-constitutional powers. His extra-constitutional power as the confidential friend and adviser of the President and the chairman of the Republican National Committee was the natural product of his past achievements; and these powers were exercised with vigor and with good judgment. But his official power as Senator did not immediately attain any considerable momentum. It was allowed to grow naturally and from relatively obscure and small beginnings.

There is a certain class of Senators, usually lawyers, who immediately become conspicuous, if not powerful, in the Senate chamber by virtue of a good voice, a habit of fluent public speaking and a large amount of public self-assurance. But Mr. Hanna was still an inexperienced speaker; and he never cared to talk in public, except when he could do so with some authority. Before becoming prominent in the official proceedings of the Senate, he was bound, in obedience to his usual practice, to begin by securing the personal confidence of his colleagues. He must first establish in his new surroundings that group of personal friendships and alliances which always constituted the foundation of his leadership.

Neither could his success in becoming a Senate leader be taken for granted. That body is something of a club with strong domestic prejudices and traditions. Success, no matter how brilliant, obtained outside that body does not guarantee to a newcomer any corresponding consideration from his colleagues. He has to earn their consideration by acceptable behavior on the spot. Mr. Hanna's prominence as the friend of McKinley and as the chairman of the National Committee rather tended to make many of the older Senators suspicious. They would have been quick to resent any assumption of power or any interference with the course of legislation by virtue of Mr. Hanna's relations with the President. Moreover, Mr. Hanna was only a business man; and while many business men had managed to secure seats in the Senate, they had rarely exercised much influence therein. The typical Senator is a lawyer. The debates in that body which arouse the keenest local interest usually involve constitutional questions on which none but a lawyer can speak with authority. Thus Mr. Hanna had many barriers to break down before his leadership outside the Senate could be paralleled by any corresponding influence within that body.

By a curious fatality, moreover, the most pressing problems of the first three years of Mr. McKinley's administration were remote from those questions of domestic politics, with which Mr. Hanna's position, training and experience had made him competent to deal. As we have seen, President McKinley assumed office pledged above all to put an end to a period of economic depression and to restore prosperity. The administration was constituted with the domestic situation chiefly in mind, and a large amount of legislation was planned for the purpose of stimulating industrial activity. But all these plans were embarrassed, if not entirely frustrated, by the insurrection in Cuba. The inability of the Spanish government to suppress the rebellion, the ruthless means adopted to that end and the growing sympathy of a large part of the American people with the insurgents was gradually creating an extremely critical situation. The President and his Cabinet desired and intended to avoid war with Cuba, both because they thought it unnecessary and because they feared that war would prevent them from redeeming the pledge to restore prosperity. Yet by its attitude towards the Spanish policy in Cuba, the administration at the very outset of its career was in danger of being pushed into an unpopular position and of losing the confidence of the country.

The President had called an extra session of Congress for the purpose of restoring prosperity by means of tariff revision, and the war party in Congress used this opportunity to agitate for intervention in Cuba. A few days after the inauguration a joint resolution recognizing the belligerency of the Cuban insurgents was pressed for consideration in the Senate. The debate thereon ran along for a couple of months. Much of this time was occupied in discussing the question whether the recognition of belligerency or independence was an executive or legislative function; but behind the constitutional discussion lay two divergent opinions as to the desirability of forcing a war on Spain. Almost all the Democrats and a minority of the Republicans wanted to bring about war. The recognition either of belligerency or independence was a means to that end. A resolution recognizing the belligerency of the Cuban insurgents passed the Senate on May 20, 1897. Senator Hanna, opposed as he was to war and committed as he was to the support of the President, voted uniformly with the minority. A very small minority it was. Only thirteen Senators voted with him, while forty-one favored the resolution. The resolution itself was never even considered in the House of Representatives.

Not, however, until the following spring was the Cuban situation to become really critical; and the interval gave Congress an opportunity to undertake the legislation which the President and Mr. Hanna believed to be essential to the cure of the economic depression. As it happened, the complexion of the two Houses enabled the Republicans to pass a tariff bill, but prevented them from taking any action on the currency. They had a large majority in the House, but in the Senate the balance of power was held by a body of pro-silver protectionists chiefly from the Far West. In a little over two weeks after the meeting of Congress, the Dingley Bill had been reported and passed in the House, only twenty-two out of its one hundred and sixty-three pages being discussed in detail. The Senate was more deliberate, and its contribution to the final form in which the bill was enacted was correspondingly substantial. The bill was not reported until the eighth of May, and it was not signed by the President until July 24.

The Republican leaders in both Houses desired to pass a bill which, while raising the rates, would not run any danger of incurring the unpopularity of the McKinley Bill. But they were obliged ultimately to accept a series of schedules which ranged higher than they intended. The wool schedule was the heart of the matter. By a combination between Senators representing woollen manufacturing states and those representing wool growing states, who were none other than the pro-silver protectionists, the duties on wool and the compensating plus the protective duties on woollen goods were restored to about the level of the McKinley Bill. On cotton goods the general tendency was to impose slightly lower duties than those of 1890. On silks and linens, on the other hand, the changes were radical, and the duties higher than ever before in the history of the country. On chinaware the rates of 1890 were restored, whereas most of the metal duties were left very much as they had been in 1894.

Whatever opinion one may form either of the political or economic desirability of the Dingley Bill, it apparently served the purpose of its progenitors. Increasing business activity followed upon its enactment; and the high protectionists sincerely believed that without such a stimulus President McKinley would never have proved to be the advance agent of prosperity. Senator Hanna, of course, warmly approved the changes proposed by the bill, but just how much influence he had upon its details cannot be traced by any public indications. He was not a member of the Finance Committee, and not once did he open his mouth during the public discussion of the schedules. His colleague, Senator Foraker, in a speech made on the stump during the fall of 1897, gave the following description of Mr. Hanna's contribution to the making of the Dingley Bill. "No man not on the Committee did more than Senator Hanna to win the success that was achieved. I doubt if any other man did as much. He devoted himself with assiduity to the study of the various schedules. He listened with patience to the claims and appeals of all, and with rare good judgment aided the Committee and the Senate in reaching just conclusions." Only slight changes were made in those schedules in which his own firm was financially interested. The rates on iron ore remained at forty cents a ton, and that on pig-iron at four dollars. The duty on coal was increased from forty to sixty-five cents a ton, but it was not restored to the level of 1890, which had been seventy-five cents a ton.

Senator Hanna's only appearance in public during this first session of the fifty-fifth Congress was for the purpose of calling up a bill, introduced by himself and providing for a new public building in Cleveland. It was passed without opposition. Of course, he also introduced a number of private pension bills. The committees to which he was assigned included that on Enrolled Bills, Mines and Mining, Naval Affairs, Pensions, Railroads and the Select Committee on Transportation and Sale of Meat Products. During the second session of the same Congress Mr. Hanna remained in the background. Not once did he address the Senate. His behavior was doubtless dictated by his wise preference for silence when he could not speak with authority and effect.

If he did not speak during the second session of the fifty-fifth Congress, it was not because the course of events failed to interest him. It was during this session that the stubborn purpose of President McKinley and his Cabinet to avoid war proved abortive. The intention of the Republican leaders had been to transact only necessary business, and then to adjourn early, if possible by May 1. They wanted to avoid any further agitation until the slowly rising wind of business activity had scattered the fruits of "prosperity" over the whole country;

and above all, they sought to leave the administration free to deal with the Cuban situation without interference from Congress. These plans were frustrated by the increasing fury of the demand for intervention in Cuba; and after February 15, the date on which the *Maine* was blown up in the harbor of Havana, it became extremely doubtful whether a war with Spain could be avoided. Indeed, war became certain, in case the investigation indicated that the explosion which wrecked the vessel and killed the crew could be traced to a source outside of its hull.

Before, however, the critical phase of the Cuban situation was reached, the Senate was occupied with certain routine business. The way in which Mr. Hanna voted upon several of these matters must be recorded as indicating his attitude upon public questions. In the first place he voted in favor of Senator Lodge's bill, imposing an educational qualification on immigrants; and in casting the vote he had with him, not only his regular Republican associates, but a majority of the Senate. In the second place he voted in favor of seating in the Senate one Henry W. Corbett, who had been appointed Senator from the state of Oregon by a Republican governor, after the failure of a Democratic Legislature, because of Republican abstentions, to elect a Democrat. This was a matter on which there was some division of opinion among the abler constitutional lawyers in the Senate, Mr. Spooner being in favor of seating Mr. Corbett and Mr. Platt of Connecticut being against it. Mr. Hanna's vote is interesting, chiefly because of his subsequent vote in relation to a similar question affecting the title of Senator Quay of Pennsylvania to his seat. Finally on January 28 Mr. Hanna was one of a minority of twenty-four who during a discussion of a currency resolution, raised for political purposes, voted in favor of the payment of all bonds of the United States in gold coin or its equivalent.

In the meantime the administration was unable to stem the tide which both in Congress and the country was making for war. Up to the last moment the President sought to find some middle ground. He sought to placate American public opinion by acting energetically on behalf of American citizens in Cuba, and by pressing Spain to improve its conduct of the war and to redress the grievances of its Cuban subjects. If the *Maine* had not been blown up, he might have succeeded, for Spain was willing to make almost any concession which did not actually terminate its possession of Cuba. As it was, the President risked his popularity and the confidence of the country by his reluctance to abandon a peaceful solution. He has been severely criticised for not holding out until the end; but had he done so, he might well have ruined his administration and split his party without actually preserving peace. Congress wanted war and had the power to declare it. The people were willing. If war had been declared, in spite of his opposition, neither Congress nor the country would have had sufficient confidence in him as the commander-in-chief of its army and navy.

In the end the President consented to a reversal of policy, which squared badly with the spirit and purpose of his earlier negotiations with Spain. Such was the price which Mr. McKinley and the country had to pay for his erroneous estimate of the general situation. Public opinion had come to believe that the independence of Cuba was the only satisfactory cure for the maladies of Cuba; and it was willing, if necessary, to fight for that conviction. The President had made the kind of a mistake which, in case he had been an English Prime Minister, would have forced him to resign and to pass on his executive responsibility; but as an American President, faced by a question of war or peace, he had no such alternative. He was obliged to turn warrior and keep the country's confidence as the commander-in-chief of its army and navy.

Senator Hanna's attitude absolutely coincided with that of the President. The outbreak of war seemed to imperil the whole policy of domestic economic amelioration which he placed before every other object of political action. He expected that it would check and perhaps extinguish the tendency towards business recovery which had really gathered some headway during the early months of 1898. His fears were groundless. The Spanish War in its immediate effect helped and strengthened the conscious and unconscious forces in American life, upon which the realization of his favorite economic policy happened at that juncture to depend. The uncertainties of the war and the resulting increase in taxation no doubt checked the returning tide of prosperity, but only for a short time. On the other hand, a foreign enemy served to distract attention from the deep-lying domestic dissensions which had been exposed by the campaign of 1896. The pulse of the country was quickened by its little adventure. The sense of common national feeling and interest, which becomes weak and dull after a generation of economic sectional and class conflicts, was reawakened, and the new vitality imparted to the national consciousness was bound to work in favor of a party and an administration which represented the traditional national economic policy.

In spite of the inefficient management of the war, the administration pulled through this troubled period credited with an increase in public confidence. By virtue of this access of popularity it obtained a freer hand in dealing with questions of domestic policy. In the absence of a war with Spain, it is at least doubtful whether such would have been the case. If the Dingley Bill failed to have the same effect upon the political fortunes of its creators as the McKinley, Wilson and Payne-Aldrich bills, the war rather than the provisions of that measure may be considered partly responsible. The congressional and state elections of the fall of 1898 were favorable to the Republicans. They retained their control of the lower House and gained the control of the Senate. The still more decisive victory which followed in the presidential campaign of 1900 was as much the effect of the war as it was of the revival of prosperity.

The foregoing remarks are true, not only of the war, but of the immediate political consequences of the war. Both Mr. McKinley and Mr. Hanna would have been glad to avoid the risks and the complications involved by the acquisition of the Philippines and Puerto Rico. The policy of extra-territorial expansion did not harmonize with the President's inherited phrases. But he was enough of a realist in politics to know a Solemn Fact when it was forced upon his attention. Under the influence of men like Senator Orville Platt, he finally consented to accept responsibility for an American Colonial policy. In the end both he and Mr. Hanna became convinced Imperialists; and their Imperialism may have been due to a final understanding of the close relation between the traditions of the Republican party and a policy of national expansion. A party which originated in the deliberate assumption of a neglected national responsibility cannot well avoid the assumption of new responsibilities, whenever such a course is dictated by a legitimate national interest.

In the meantime Mr. Hanna was very slowly and tentatively developing his own legislative preferences and was finding, as it were, his senatorial legs. During the third and final session of the fifty-fifth Congress he began to appear in more conspicuous parts than that of a silent voter. On Dec. 19, 1898, he introduced a bill "to promote the commerce and increase the foreign trade of the United States and to provide auxiliary cruisers, transports and seamen for government use, when necessary." This measure which came finally to be known as the Hanna-Frye Subsidy Bill, and which was very much amended before it emerged from the Committee on Commerce, never came to a discussion, much less a vote, during the fifty-fifth Congress. It embodied a policy in which Senator Hanna became more and more interested and which must be considered his legislative hobby. He had already been preaching on the stump the desirability of some governmental subsidy for the American merchant marine, and he continued to do so until the end. The reasons for its peculiar importance in Senator Hanna's eyes will be explained in a later chapter.

It must not go unrecorded, also, that during this final session of the fifty-fifth Congress Senator Hanna first appeared as a speaker on the floor of the Senate. The occasion of his appearance is characteristic of the man. Its object was to perform a service for an insignificant but deserving person who, as he believed, was not being fairly treated. A German-American named Louis Gathmann had invented a so-called aërial torpedo which he had submitted to the Bureau of Ordinance of the Navy Department. Making no impression on its chief, Mr. Gathmann took his story to the Naval Committee of the Senate, of which Senator Hanna was a member, and aroused the Senator's interest. By means of Mr. Hanna's influence with Assistant Secretary Roosevelt, the inventor obtained a chance to test his shell at the proving grounds of the navy at Indian Head, Maryland. Several other tests followed which convinced Senator Hanna that the "Gathmann Torpedo" was a good thing. He submitted an amendment to the naval appropriation bill, authorizing the Secretary of the Navy to spend $250,000 in equipping two coast defence monitors with the shells. The amendment was not mandatory, but placed the spending of the money at the discretion of the Secretary of the Navy. Mr. Hanna's associates on the Naval Committee agreed to this recommendation. There were some objections to it in the Senate, and Mr. Hanna on several occasions spoke briefly in its favor. The appropriation was adopted in the Senate, rejected by the House and failed in conference. Mr. Hanna's only interest in the matter was derived from his confidence in the inventor and his belief that a prejudice against the inventor by the navy and army chiefs had prevented the "Gathmann Torpedo" from obtaining a fair trial.

As soon as Congress adjourned, Senator Hanna, accompanied by his family, went for over a month to Thomasville, Georgia, where President McKinley and others were entertained as his guests. His health at this time was not as good as it had been, and he was taking what opportunity he could of rest and recreation. By May he was in Cleveland again, but not for long. He was planning a trip abroad, — the first which he had ever taken, — for the purpose of seeking some alleviation for his increasingly frequent rheumatic attacks. When he was about to start, it looked as if the trip would have to be abandoned, because a serious strike was threatened on the Cleveland street railway, which competed with the one of which he was President. But the employees of his own company proved loyal to the management, and Senator Hanna was able to get away. He returned in the fall, not particularly pleased and benefited by the trip, and resolute never to go to Europe again.

When the fifty-sixth Congress assembled in December, 1899, the Republicans were in a position to exercise much more complete control and to adopt a more vigorous policy than they had during the fifty-fifth Congress. Their majority in the House had been maintained; and they had gained in the meantime a majority in the Senate sufficient for all party purposes. The session was one of the utmost importance, less because of the large amount of legislation accomplished, than because the policy of the government in dealing with Puerto Rico and the insular dependencies was established — not, to be sure, in its details, but in its general outlines. A bill was passed organizing a territorial government for the Hawaiian Islands and defining temporarily the fiscal relations between Puerto Rico and the United States. It was this bill which provoked the most prolonged and virulent debate. It raised both a legal question as to the extent of congressional authority in the insular dependencies and how far it was subject to constitutional restrictions, and the economic question whether as a matter of policy Congress should impose any tariff on imports from Puerto Rico into the United States.

From the point of view of Senator Hanna's life these questions do not have to be discussed on their merits, because, as has already been pointed out, he was in relation to them a follower rather than a leader. Throughout all these long debates, extending over so many months, during which the legal abilities of Senator Spooner and others were conspicuously expressed, and during which the senior Senator from Ohio, Mr. Foraker, also displayed talents of a high order, Senator Hanna did not break his silence. He voted, of course, throughout for the orthodox Republican policy; and the aspect of the matter with which he was most concerned was its effect upon the coming presidential campaign.

Another question which the fifty-sixth Congress at its first session effectually disposed of was that of the standard of value. Inasmuch as the Republicans were for the first time in absolute control of both Houses, they were in a position to redeem their pledges and to establish gold as the statutory standard of value of the United States. This they did not hesitate to do, in spite of the fact that an election was coming on. They felt that they had the country behind them. They had weathered the squalls of the Spanish War. The business prosperity of the country had really been restored, and there was every evidence that a still further business expansion would follow. Prices had increased, but so had wages. A general air of satisfaction was overspreading the country. It was just the time to redeem the pledge of 1896, and to establish the gold standard, not merely as a matter of policy, but with a definite legal sanction.

In the debates on the currency bill Senator Hanna did not break the silence, which with but one insignificant exception had characterized his behavior in the Senate. The occasion had not yet come for his appearance in public as a senatorial leader, although it was fast approaching. His public attitude and behavior is of importance in relation to only three incidents of the session; and these incidents differ widely one from another in their relative importance and in their subject-matter.

The first of these questions concerned the title of Mr. Matthew S. Quay of Pennsylvania to a seat in the Senate. Mr. Quay's term as Senator had expired on March 3, 1899. The Legislature began to ballot upon his successor on January 17. Daily ballots were taken from that date until April 20, the day of adjournment, no candidate having in the meantime received a majority of the votes. Mr. Quay was the caucus nominee of his party, but a sufficiently strong minority of "insurgents," who objected to his political methods and record, had persisted in supporting another candidate. The day after the Legislature adjourned Governor Stone appointed Mr. Quay Senator until the next meeting of the Legislature. A question was immediately raised as to the legality of the appointment; and on Jan. 23, 1900, the Committee on Privileges and Elections of the Senate reported a resolution to the effect that Mr. Quay was not legally entitled to the seat. The question was exhaustively debated during the following three months and did not reach a final vote until April 24. On that day the report of the Committee was adopted by a vote of 33 to 32, so that Mr. Quay's claim to the seat was denied. Mr. Hanna was paired with Senator Depew on this roll-call, and although not present, his vote counted against Mr. Quay. Had he voted the other way, the latter would have been seated.

The incident is of interest because it raised important political as well as legal issues. A grave and ambiguous Constitutional question was involved. State Governors have the power, in case vacancies occur during a recess of the Legislature, to "make temporary appointments until the next meeting of the Legislature, which shall then fill such vacancies"; but in this instance the vacancy had occurred during a session of the Legislature and the Legislature had failed to fill it. Does the Governor's power of appointment extend to cases in which a Legislature has had the opportunity of electing a Senator and has failed to take advantage of it? While there were precedents on both sides, the weight of authority tended against any such interpretation of the Governor's power. In the same way the abler Constitutional lawyers in the Senate were for the most part opposed to the seating of Mr. Quay. Nevertheless they were far from unanimous in their opinion. Senators Hoar and Spooner, for instance, believed that Mr. Quay was entitled to his seat. In casting their votes, individual Senators were evidently influenced by great diversity of motives. The majority of the Republicans voted for Mr. Quay and the majority of the Democrats against him, but among the pro-Quay Democratic minority were some of the better lawyers and more public-spirited Senators in the party, while among the anti-Quay Republican minority were Senators as different as Hale, Gallinger, Hawley, Orville Platt, Proctor and McMillan.

The question was one on which party lines were not decisively drawn, and on which a Senator might have voted either way in good company. A vote, actually determined by considerations of political or party expediency, could be defended by plausible legal arguments. A man in Senator Hanna's personal position would naturally allow his vote in reference to an ambiguous legal question to be determined chiefly by a group of political considerations, which might well have dictated the indorsement of Mr. Quay's claim. Mr. Hanna believed in party organization and party loyalty. Quay was the caucus nominee. His opponents were insurgent reformers, who had bolted a regular nomination, and who were making trouble within the party just previous to a National Convention to be held in Philadelphia and a presidential campaign. The question was being judged all over the country, not on legal but on political grounds. The bolters were being praised, because they had dared to defy the caucus, in order to defeat for Senator a political "boss" of doubtful integrity. Mr. Hanna's own election had been opposed by analogous methods and on ostensibly similar grounds. Two years earlier Mr. Hanna had supported the claim of a Senator from Oregon whose legal title to the seat was of the same general character as that of Mr. Quay. Nevertheless he voted against Mr. Quay and thereby incurred the embarrassing hostility of a man who continued to be powerful in an important

Republican state. When Mr. Quay's name was read aloud in the Philadelphia Convention as the member of the National Committee from Pennsylvania, the applause consumed several minutes.

His vote cannot be explained on the ground of any former antagonism between the two men. Mr. Hanna was the last person in the world to allow a personal quarrel to interfere with desirable action in the interest of Republican harmony. Neither was his vote likely to be dictated merely by technical Constitutional reasons, although these may have had some weight. He must have believed that a Governor has no right to fill a vacancy in the Senate with a man whom the Legislature might have elected, but instead deliberately took the opportunity of rejecting. Such a belief would have squared with the dependence, characteristic of his political methods upon the support of public opinion.

Mr. Hanna never left any public record of the reason for his anti-Quay vote, but soon thereafter a question did come up, which aroused him to participate in a somewhat important Senate debate. This question was connected with the administration of the Navy Department. It will be recollected that his one previous utterance in the Senate chamber concerned a small detail in the business of the same department. Ever since his appointment as Senator, he had been a member of the Committee on Naval Affairs. He had devoted a good deal of time to the work of the Committee; and as a large portion of it involved the sort of business questions with which he was peculiarly competent to deal, he became very influential in the Committee and finally took part in the public discussion of naval affairs.

The immediate cause of his first important intervention in the public debates was a disagreement that had arisen over the price which the government was to pay for armor-plate. The occasion of this interference, its purpose and its spirit are all characteristic of the man. The House had differed from the Senate, not only as to the price which the government ought to pay for armor-plate, but also as to the source from which it should be procured. There were only two plants in the United States equipped for its manufacture — those of the Carnegie and Bethlehem companies; and they did not compete with each other. They had both been insisting on charging $545 a ton on all contracts for plate. The Senate believed that this charge was extortionate. It had, consequently, amended the House Bill, which made the price discretionary with the Secretary of the Navy, in a very radical way. It had insisted that in case the Secretary could not obtain armor-plate for $445 a ton, he should proceed with the construction of a government factory. When the bill went into conference, the conferrees could not reach any agreement in reference to this difference, and they returned to their respective Houses for further instructions.

While the Senate was discussing the question whether it should insist upon its own provisions or make certain concessions, Mr. Hanna took part in the debate. He was evidently provoked because certain Senators, who had no technical knowledge of steel manufacturing, had jumped without sufficient inquiry to the conclusion that the price was extortionate. The purpose of his speech was to insist that the price of $445 a ton, under the conditions then prevailing, was a low rather than a high price, that a government factory could not be built inside of five years, that, if constructed, government plate would cost more than plate manufactured by the Carnegie or the Bethlehem companies, and that the whole question was one which should be left, as the House of Representatives proposed, to the discretion of the Secretary of the Navy. His argument was made with force and with effect. He was constantly interrupted by Senator Tillman and others, and at one juncture he protested against these interruptions because he was a "tyro" in debating and wanted "half a chance." Nevertheless he held his own very well. He was particularly tenacious in sticking to the main thread of his discourse, in spite of many attempts to raise irrelevant issues. The only action immediately taken by the Senate was to send the bill back to conference.

Again the attempt to reach an agreement in conference failed, whereupon Senator Penrose proposed that the question of a "reasonable and equitable" price be left to the Secretary of the Navy, but he was required, in the event of failure to purchase on reasonable terms, to build a factory. Mr. Hanna spoke in favor of this amendment, which corresponded much more closely with his views than did the previous action of the Senate. After an acrid discussion in which the Democrats freely accused their opponents of favoring the armor-plate companies in return for campaign contributions, the Penrose amendment was adopted by a vote of 39 to 35. A number of Republican Senators, including Beveridge, Foraker, Perkins, Chandler and Spooner, voted with the Democrats. To all appearances Mr. Hanna's interference on this occasion served to determine the Senate's final action. Until he spoke the tendency both of the discussion of the subject and of the several votes had been to preclude any agreement with the armor-plate companies. A proposal to build a government factory, in case they would not accept a price of $400 a ton, had been defeated by a majority of only two. Mr. Hanna was the first Senator to come out vigorously and unequivocally for a policy of making a compromise with the companies. The Penrose amendment virtually repudiated the attitude which for some years the Senate had assumed on the matter. It was intended to bring about the actual purchase of the armor-plate imperatively needed by the government. This policy prevailed; and it prevailed chiefly by virtue of Mr. Hanna's arguments and influence.

The policy openly and successfully advocated by Mr. Hanna in this matter was the natural result of his political and economic creed. As a man trained in business he knew that the question of what was or was not a reasonable price for armor-plate was one which should be left to a responsible administrative official. He believed that the Senate had been acting on erroneous information in placing such a low limit upon a reasonable price for armor-plate. What he knew of the steel and iron business convinced him that the manufacturers had not been extortionate in their demands; and, of course, he instinctively sympathized with the point of view of a business man. But it required some courage to announce these opinions. The armor-plate companies were unpopular. He could and would be charged with favoring for partisan benefit a manufacturing interest which was seeking to bleed the Treasury; and in answering these charges he was at a disadvantage, because he could not appeal to any authentic figures in support of his opinion. He was obliged to rely upon personal estimates which differed from those of Republican colleagues on the Naval Committee. Moreover, he went too far in his defence of the armor-plate companies when he asserted that the government was not entitled to accurate information from the companies' books as to the cost of the plate. When pressed on this point during the debate, he tended to back down. But he was sincere in his conviction that the interests of the navy demanded an agreement with the companies; and the history of the subsequent relations between the government and the plate-makers indicates that he was right.

With a national campaign impending, the Democrats immediately took advantage of the opening to charge that the action of the Senator was dictated by the necessities of the chairman of the National Committee. He accepted the challenge without flinching. He never sought to disguise the fact that he represented business interests in politics or to shirk responsibility for his opinions. On this particular occasion there resulted an acrimonious and disagreeable personal quarrel. During the debate Senator Pettigrew of South Dakota had stated that in 1892 a manufacturer of war-ships had contributed $400,000 to the Republican campaign fund upon the assurance that he would be reimbursed from the contracts for naval construction. The assertion aroused no immediate protest, and it was later repeated by Senator Bacon in a debate upon an anti-trust bill. This time the attack provoked a denial from Senator Carter, the chairman of the Republican National Committee in 1892, and a general disclaimer of any relation between campaign contributions and government contracts from Senator Hanna. Senator Pettigrew immediately returned to the charge, and after reiterating that his information was derived from Mr. Cramp himself, went on to make a personal attack upon Mr. Hanna. He brought up the report of the Committee on Privileges and Elections in reference to the validity of Mr. Hanna's own seat in the Senate. He quoted at length from the minority report of that Committee, which had urged the desirability of further investigation. The Senate Committee, it will be remembered, had refused to make any investigation of its own, but had dismissed the whole matter on the ground that the testimony taken by the Committee of the Ohio State Senate, headed by Vernon

Burke, was entirely inconclusive. Mr. Hanna immediately claimed the floor as a matter of personal privilege and made the following statement: —

"Mr. President: I feel like offering an apology to the Senate for pursuing this subject any farther. The fact that the Senator from South Dakota had the document on his desk, and the readiness with which he seemed to be prepared to take up these questions, show that it is all a prearranged plan. So his statement that he has been forced into this discussion by any remarks of mine goes for nothing.

"I wish to say a few words with reference to the personal aspects of this matter. Of course it is well known to the country that there was a pretty lively personal fight in Columbus, and it is also known, because it was given the widest publicity, that there was a conspiracy (to defeat me) on the part of the Democratic party and a few traitors in the Republican party of the same nature and kind as the gentlemen from South Dakota.

"This is the first time I have heard that report,[1] and I was interested very much in the cunning devices that were concocted, as I believe, out of whole cloth. The first knowledge I had that anything of this kind was going on came to me in a publication of a Democratic evening paper in Columbus on the evening of the day when the conversation so reported was said to have taken place. I immediately sent for a reporter of the Associated Press and dictated a few lines to the public, denying *in toto* the truth of any statement made that I had any connection with it or knew anything about it. That was my case and there it has rested from that day to this.

"As far as the instigators of this conspiracy are concerned I have never seen or heard of them from that day to this, and as to the perpetrator of the deed, it was the Democratic party in the state of Ohio through its agents in the State Senate at Columbus, and its allies and traitors, prominent among whom was this man Burke, from my native city, who upon every stump in that campaign pledged himself that if elected to the State Senate, it would be his first privilege and duty, to vote for me for the United States Senate. He got to the Senate through these promises.

"Mr. President, with reference to the investigation in the Legislature, Mr. Burke's vote was the balance of power in the Ohio Senate. He

[1] Mr. Pettigrew had quoted from the testimony of the Burke Committee as to a telephone conversation between the alleged agent and a "Major" (Dick or Rathbone), in which the "Major" answered after an apparent consultation with Mr. Hanna.

was a traitor; and he lent himself to this conspiracy. When the investigation was ordered there was one Republican in the Senate, Mr. James R. Garfield, who was conceded the privilege of being one of the investigating Committee. The others composing the Committee were three Democrats and this traitor Burke. When Mr. Garfield made the request, or the demand rather, that I should be represented by counsel, it was denied. Every particle of testimony produced before that Committee was arranged beforehand, and everything that looked to defence was stricken out or driven out."

I have quoted the foregoing statement because it is the only one which Mr. Hanna ever made in reference to the bribery charge. The incident practically terminated therewith, although Mr. Foraker took the floor for a while with a short defence of his colleague, based entirely upon Mr. Garfield's minority report. The only public echo of the proceedings was the publication in the Congressional Record of the testimony taken by the Senate Committee and its report; and that doubtless was the chief object of the Senator from South Dakota. The matter was never pursued any farther either in or out of Congress. As a consequence of the attack, Mr. Hanna conceived a lively resentment against Senator Pettigrew; and this personal feeling influenced, as we shall see, his behavior during the approaching Presidential election. The whole fracas, which took place on June 5, 1900, was merely a preliminary skirmish in the National campaign, which on that date had already been practically started.

By the spring of 1900 the peculiar combination of personal and political vicissitudes, which for some years had kept Mr. Hanna somewhat in the background of politics, had passed. The Spanish War had come and gone. The country was prepared to return with quickened interest to the consideration of its domestic problems. The issue between the Imperialists and their opponents had still to be fought; but its discussion tended more and more to bring out the relation between the adoption of a Colonial policy and the expansion of the foreign trade of the country. The American people were becoming aroused to the fact that the promised restoration of prosperity had taken place, and also that prosperity, like economic famine, has its dangers and its victims. Mr. Hanna's dominant interest in politics was centred on the relation between politics and business, which the renewal of interest in national economic problems had again brought to the front. He was prepared to become more conspicuous than ever in the discussion of these problems. He was no longer merely the political manager and friend of a Presidential candidate or a President. During the three intervening years he had slowly and quietly been establishing on firm grounds his own personal power and influence in the new fields of action, which had been opened for him by Mr. McKinley's election to the Presidency.

He had made a place for himself in the Senate. Little by little he had gained the confidence of the leading members of that body, so that when a proper occasion was offered he assumed a share of leadership. Such an occasion was presented by the debate over the policy of the Government in respect to the purchase of armor-plate. He had seized it, and had suddenly disclosed the amount of personal influence which he had acquired among his colleagues. Never after the first session of the fifty-sixth Congress was he merely an apparently obscure voting member of that body. Not being a wordy man he did not speak frequently, but he spoke whenever the occasion demanded speech and always with effect. But whether he spoke or not he had become one of the half-dozen men who had become practically responsible for the successful despatch of the business of the Senate.

He had, since the winter of 1898, been established in his leadership of his own state, as well as of the Senate. The outburst of popular indignation which had helped him to overcome the conspiracy to prevent his election left him in effective political control of the state of Ohio; and that control he retained until his death. Open opposition to him within the party practically disappeared. He did not attend the Convention held in Columbus on June 21, 1898, because so soon after the outbreak of the war, Congressional duties kept him in Washington; but his absence did not diminish his influence. He sent to that body a letter which is a good illustration of partisan phrase-making, and which is quoted as an example of his increasing ability to work up his fellow-Republicans with "ringing" words: —

WASHINGTON, D.C., June 20.

"H. M. DAUGHERTY, ESQ., Chairman.

"MY DEAR SIR:—

"I sincerely regret that my duties here will prevent my acceptance of the honor to preside at the State Convention on the 21st instant. It is a great disappointment to me and I am only reconciled by the consciousness that I am better serving my party by remaining at my post in Washington. I am with you in spirit and offer as my keynote — 'Republicanism in its *broadest, truest* sense — devotion to principle and loyalty to party organization — the administration of President William McKinley as a fulfilment of our pledges to the American people, and as a guarantee of the future prosperity of the country.'

"In offering my rights to the Convention please convey to the representatives of the Republicans of Ohio my high appreciation of the compliment and honor they have paid me and the desire I have to always merit their confidence and respect.

"Believing that wisdom and good judgment will control their deliberations and with best wishes, I remain

"Sincerely yours,
"M. A. HANNA."

He had, of course, the best of reasons for believing that wisdom and good judgment would control their deliberations.

During the fall of 1898 no local officials of any importance were elected in Ohio, and Mr. Hanna was under no necessity of bestowing much attention on his own state. His great preoccupation was with the outcome of the Congressional elections. In case the Republicans lost control of the Lower House, as so frequently happened on an "off year," and particularly on an "off year" succeeding the passage of a tariff bill and a decisive victory, both the prestige and the plans of the administration would be very seriously damaged. As a matter of fact, there was serious danger of such a loss. The popularity of the administration had suffered because of the conduct of the war. The Republican Congressional Committee scarcely expected to elect a majority of Republican Representatives. In looking the situation over, it was decided that the best place to make the fight was in the West. The war was popular in that part of the country, and there appeared to be a fair chance of winning back some of the ground which had been lost by the party on the silver issue.

Ordinarily the Chairman of the National Committee does not have much to do with a Congressional campaign; but in the fall of 1898 Mr. Hanna rendered the Congressional Committee effective and indispensable assistance. On October 14 he wrote to Mr. Thomas H. Carter, who had preceded him as Chairman of the National Committee: —

"MY DEAR SENATOR: —

"I have just returned after three weeks' absence in the East, where I have been working harder than I ever did in my life to secure funds for the Congressional Committee, without which they would have been obliged to shut up shop. I milked the country and turned over all the funds to Chairman Babcock. I don't know whether I can get any more; but I can try and I assure you it will give me pleasure to serve you in any way I can.

"Sincerely yours,
"M. A. HANNA."

He did succeed in raising more money, which was spent chiefly in the states of Kansas, Nebraska, Montana, Idaho and Wyoming with the object, not only of obtaining additional Republican representation in the Lower House, but of the electing Legislatures which would return Republican Senators.

The outcome may be described in Mr. Hanna's own words. After the election a meeting of mutual congratulation was called by the Tippecanoe Club of Cleveland. On this occasion Mr. Hanna said: "It is a matter of great congratulation to us of Cleveland that the election resulted in a vote of confidence in the administration and its policy. When I went East in September I was met with the statement that we would lose the House. Chairman Babcock of the Congressional Committee told me that we would surely lose the House east of the Mississippi River, which proved to be true. But there is great gratification in noting that the House was saved by the states west of the Missouri River — the very states where the free silver craze had its strongest hold on the people. The Republicans of those states, who had wandered after strange Gods, returned to worship at the shrine of prosperity." The evidence indicates that it was the war rather than prosperity which had brought these Republicans back to the fold. In the East a certain reaction in public opinion against the administration was noticeable. Mr. Theodore Roosevelt, who in the eyes of the country was the chief military hero of the war, was elected by only a small majority to the Governorship of New York. But the West, which had wanted the war more unanimously than had the East, which had an instinctive relish for the excitements and the hazards of war, and which was Imperialist in feeling and conviction, rallied to the administration, which, however unwillingly, had responded to the call of military patriotism. The war, rather than the timid beginnings of an era of prosperity, was uppermost in the voters' minds during the fall of 1898. The truth of this explanation of the facts is confirmed by the irresistible demand, which a year and a half later proceeded from the Republicans of the West, for the nomination of Theodore Roosevelt as Vice-President.

During the following year Mr. Hanna's leadership of the Republican party in Ohio received still more emphatic confirmation. Mayor McKisson was, indeed, renominated by the Cleveland Republicans after a bitter fight at the primaries, but failed of reëlection. Not for ten years did a Republican again become Mayor of Cleveland. Nevertheless, although Mr. Hanna exercised less control over the political destiny of his own city than he had a decade earlier, he continued supreme in the state. The Convention held in Columbus on June 1, 1899, nominated for Governor Mr. George K. Nash, one of Mr. Hanna's close associates. The nomination was the outcome of an understanding between Mr. Hanna and Mr. George B. Cox, the "Boss" of Cincinnati. A letter from Mr. Hanna to Mr. Cox, written about a week before the date of the Convention, gives some idea of the relations existing at that time between the two men.

"MY DEAR SIR: —

"I am in receipt of yours of the 19th inst., the contents of which were carefully noted. I fully sympathize with your position that we should be guided by whatever is for the best interests of the party in our action at the State Convention. I will be glad to coöperate with you to that end. Of course, no one can tell about the choice of candidates. I will tell you frankly that I am not pledged to any one, but I am opposed to Mr. Daugherty from a party standpoint, and I understand that we agree in that position. You are right in your judgment that we should not meet before going to Columbus; but I will see you some time during the night before the first day of the Convention.

"I admire your good sense and good management and have faith that we can work together.

"Sincerely yours,
"M. A. HANNA."

The campaign that followed in the fall of 1899 was very lively. Mr. Hanna's personal prominence and his relations with the administration made it of national importance, while the fact that John R. McLean was the Democratic nominee gave the people of Ohio a chance to vote on an echo of the senatorial fight of January, 1898. The speakers on both sides discussed national issues exclusively. Mr. Hanna put in a large part of October on the stump, and was greeted everywhere with favor and enthusiasm by large crowds. He spoke incidentally on the issue of Imperialism; but in the great majority of his speeches he claimed support for the Republican party, because of the fulfilment of its pledges. By the fall of 1899 prosperity had been undoubtedly restored, and equally without doubt the revival of business enterprise was in part due to the increasing confidence of business men in the political situation. A political party can very rarely claim any responsibility for the course of business during one of its periods of domination; but in this case the Republicans were justified in crediting themselves and their leaders with the business improvement. The Bryan Democracy and the "Populistic" agitation in the West associated therewith had threatened the business of the country with real dangers; and their successful opponents had contributed both to the exorcism of the free silver ghost and to the renewal of general confidence.

The speeches of Mr. Hanna delivered in the fall of 1899 give the first clear and well-rounded expression of his answer to the general American economic problem. The situation had changed essentially since 1897. Not only had prosperity really come, but it had brought with it unexpected developments. The latter part of 1898 and 1899 had constituted a period of unprecedented industrial reorganization. Almost every morning newspaper was filled with accounts of the formation of new railroad and industrial combinations. The relation between this process of business consolidation and the existing Republican political supremacy was unmistakable. It became the subject of Democratic attack during the fall of 1899, and Mr. Hanna did not hesitate or fear to come out frankly in favor of these combinations. He approved of them as a natural business growth, due to the excesses of desperate competition which had prevailed during the business depression. He regarded them, furthermore, as necessary instruments for the development of the export trade of the country, which at that juncture was becoming unprecedentedly large in manufactured products. He urged upon his listeners the desirability of his own bill subsidizing American shipping as a necessary help to the proper development of this export trade. He wanted the government to take this further step in promoting industry, in order that American manufacturers might have the advantage of adequate means of transportation in making their assault on the markets of the world.

The result was an emphatic indorsement of the administration. Mr. George K. Nash was elected by a plurality of about 50,000 votes over McLean. The tide had evidently turned in the East as well as in the West. Similar testimonials were obtained in other states, and undoubtedly the increasing prosperity of business and the effect thereof upon the earnings of labor contributed decisively to the Republican success. The renomination of the President, who had fought the war and under whose administration prosperity had returned was assured, while at the same time there was every indication that Mr. Bryan would again be the candidate of the Democratic party.

Seldom has any administration after three years in office commanded such united support from its party as in the beginning of 1900 did the administration of Mr. McKinley. Much of the credit of this result belongs to the diplomacy with which the President handled the Republican leaders in and out of Congress.

He had the gift of refusing requests without incurring enmity, of smoothing over disagreements, of conciliating his opponents, of retaining his friends without necessarily doing too much for them, of overlooking his own personal grievances and of steering the virtuous middle path between the extremes and eccentricities of party opinion. But decisive as was the President's contribution to the popularity of his administration, Mr. Hanna also deserves a certain share of the credit. More than any other single man, with the exception of the President himself, Mr. Hanna was responsible for the operation of that most vital of party functions, the distribution of patronage. Under his direction and that of the President the appointments to office became, as it rarely had been in the past, a source of strength to the McKinley administration.

During these years Mr. Hanna accomplished in an exceptionally able manner the work of reënforcing and consolidating the existing leadership of the Republicans. The distribution of patronage necessarily occasions many personal disappointments and grievances, which weaken the President with certain individuals and factions in his party. Any disposition on the part of the President or his responsible advisers to play favorites or to cherish grudges, any tendency to misjudge men and to be deceived by plausible misrepresentation, any failure to distinguish properly between the more influential and the less influential factions, has a damaging effect upon party harmony and its power of effective coöperation. To name only recent examples Mr. Cleveland, Mr. Harrison and Mr. Taft have all weakened their administrations by mistakes in selections to office. No doubt President McKinley and Mr. Hanna made similar mistakes both from the point of view of administrative efficiency and of good feeling within the party, but on the whole they certainly exercised the President's power of appointment with unusual success. They not only selected for the higher offices efficient public servants, but by virtue of an unusually clear understanding of individuals and local political conditions, they made leading Republicans feel, in spite of certain individual grievances, that the offices were being distributed for the best interests of the whole party.

So far as Mr. Hanna was concerned, this success was due to

his usual ability in partially systematizing and organizing the distribution of offices, while at the same time giving life to the system by tact and good judgment in dealing with individuals and with exceptional cases. In all those Northern states in which the Republicans exercised effective power, the system was already established and required merely good judgment in its application. It was in the South that he introduced a new and what he believed to be a definite system of making Federal appointments. The local offices were usually filled on the recommendation of the defeated congressional candidate, and Mr. Hanna expected by the recognition of these leaders of forlorn hopes to induce a better quality of men to run for the office. For the higher Federal offices, such as the United States Judges and Attorneys, the recommendations were usually accepted of a Board of Referees — consisting of the defeated candidate for Governor, the chairman of the State Committee, and the member of the National Committee from that state. To a large extent the system worked automatically all over the Union, but of course any such method goes to pieces, in so far as conflicting individual or factional claims are intruded. It was in dealing with these exceptional cases that Mr. McKinley's tact was useful as well as Mr. Hanna's gift of understanding other men, of getting their confidence and of bending or persuading them to his will.

In all these matters Mr. Hanna's disposition to live and let live, his instinct for dealing candidly and fairly with the other man, was as much of a help to him in politics as it had been in business. When he could not do what was asked of him, he did not hesitate or equivocate. He told plainly why he must refuse, and as his reasons were usually convincing, the applicant rarely departed with a grievance. Moreover, his decisions and recommendations were really dictated by the welfare of the party and not by personal interest or favoritism. He did, indeed, pursue relentlessly the Ohio Republicans, who had entered the conspiracy against his election to the Senate, and he rewarded almost all of his prominent supporters. But the testimony is unanimous that in other respects his recommendations for office were both disinterested and wise. He never presumed upon his own power either with the President, the heads of departments or with his colleagues. His influence was based largely upon his instinctive sense of its own necessary limits. If he had really been or tried to be an autocrat beyond the limits within which autocratic management was permissible under the official and unofficial rules, his influence would soon have withered away.

Certain of Mr. Hanna's political methods have frequently been misinterpreted. The facts that he was indifferent to the Civil Service law and believed in rewarding party workers with government offices, have created an impression that he was also indifferent to efficiency in public departmental work. Such was far from being the case. He wanted to put good men in all important offices. Once they were installed, he was careful to leave them alone. Many different officials, who directly or indirectly owed their appointment to Mr. Hanna, have asserted emphatically that he never bothered them with recommendations about their assistants or about the conduct of their offices. Pressure was continually being brought to bear upon him to obtain favors for various people from the heads of executive departments in Washington. He would sometimes write letters, stating the request and adding that he would be glad to see it granted. But in such cases he would almost always add a postscript in his own handwriting, advising his correspondent that if his request was in any way injurious to departmental discipline or efficiency, it should be ignored — as indeed they often were. As another illustration to the same effect I have before me a copy of a letter to Mr. Frank M. Chandler in which he was advising the latter about the nomination of certain judges for the Court of Common Pleas in Cuyahoga County: "Pick good men above all other considerations," he wrote, and emphasized the sentence with an underline. "I would rather take our chances with good candidates, and if defeated, be defeated with good men." Many other letters to similar effect could be quoted.

He objected to Civil Service reform as much from the point of view of a business man as from that of a politician. He knew that any private business would be ruined which tended to make subordinates independent of their chiefs. When he named a man for a responsible office, he always allowed the appointee to select his own assistants. After Mr. Charles F. Leach had been made Collector of Customs in Cleveland, he went to Mr. Hanna's office and showed the Senator a long list of good Republicans who had applied for places. Mr. Hanna refused to interfere. He mentioned certain names and said that he would be glad to have them considered, but he told Mr. Leach to use his own judgment. "You will be responsible for the conduct of your office and must select your own subordinates." When Mr. Frank M. Chandler was appointed United States marshal in Cleveland he was advised by the Department of Justice to be very careful in his selection of deputies, and what followed can best be told in his own words: "I talked matters over with Mr. Hanna, who was in Washington, and he told me to be careful about my selections, but he mentioned certain men whom he would have liked taken care of, if possible. I did as he suggested, and found that the men named did not meet the standard which I wished to maintain. I laid the result of my investigations before Mr. Hanna, and he said: 'That doesn't look as if you wanted my men. You must be responsible for the conduct of your office. Go ahead and select whom you want. Get good men on whom you can rely.'" Mr. Charles C. Dewstoe, who had been appointed Postmaster of Cleveland on the recommendation of Congressman Burton, but who consulted Mr. Hanna about his subordinates, supplies testimony to a similar effect.

It would be of course absurd to claim that Mr. Hanna did not frequently have incompetent party workers appointed to office. He was a practical politician, who worked with the machine. He looked askance at any attempt to reform prevailing political methods, which might temporarily interfere with partisan harmony and efficiency. He coöperated with some of the worst elements in his party as well as with the best. He conceived it as his business above all to keep the Republicans united, so that they could march to victory under his leadership. They could be kept united only in case the existing local organizations were accepted and possible corruption overlooked. Reformers who were opposed to the local machines, and were thereby endangering local Republican ascendency, obtained no sympathy from him. But although he worked exclusively with the machine and used government offices to pay personal and partisan political debts, he was far from indifferent to the desirability of appointing to office able and upright men. The dislike which Civil Service reformers entertain for the business of distributing the spoils of office for the purpose of rewarding party politicians have tended to make them class all spoilsmen together and to visit on them all a joint condemnation. But the task of distributing patronage has a very human side to it and involves rules and values of its own. Mark Hanna accepted the system; he believed in it under existing political conditions; he even developed it. He and Mr. McKinley between them actually made it a source of strength rather than a source of weakness to the administration and to the party. But if they did so that was because in some measure they dignified it. They put a large measure of fair play and an honest demand for efficient service into a system of public appointment that offers strong temptations and opportunities for mere favoritism, for prejudice, for misjudgment and for abuses and perversions of all kinds.

CHAPTER XX

THE CONVENTION OF 1900

No National Convention of either party ever assembled under fairer auspices than the Republican Convention of 1900. There was little disagreement or misgiving within the party as to the candidate who was to head the ticket or as to the platform on which he was to stand. The unanimity with which President McKinley was renominated was a fair expression of a substantially unanimous sentiment in his favor among Republicans of all classes and all sections. The only suggestion of discontent against the official leadership came from the Republican machine of Pennsylvania, headed by Matthew Quay; and everybody knew that the causes of this discontent were personal. Even personal grievances were, however, the rare exception. Few Presidents at the end of their first term have ever received a more general and hearty indorsement from his partisan associates than did William McKinley.

The indorsement of Mr. McKinley included the indorsement of his political prime minister — Mark Hanna. The party, as a whole, was as well satisfied with his share of the leadership as they were with the President's. In some parts of the country he was, of course, more popular than in others. Certain of the states of New England, for instance, were no more than lukewarm. Their leaders would not have been sorry to embarrass the administration and Mr. Hanna, but they were powerless. Mr. Hanna had the Middle West solidly behind, and he had the organization, almost all over the country, enthusiastically in his favor. The personal leadership which he had been quietly reënforcing and consolidating during the intervening years was, when the Convention met, suddenly made conspicuous and manifest. He did not control the Convention. In one important respect, it proved, like the Convention of 1896, to have a will of its own. But he was by far the most influential Republican among those who gathered in Philadelphia and in all but one matter his will was dominant. Immediately after the Convention he disclosed to a friend in a confidential moment that he would not exchange the personal power which he was able to exert with that of the President.

Throughout the fall of 1899 and the winter of 1900 he labored hard and successfully to establish the dominant issue for the coming election. He wanted above all the campaign of 1900 to be the continuation and consummation of the campaign of 1896. The fundamental fact was that the Republicans had been placed in power in order to accomplish certain results; and they had been as good as their promises. They had established the gold standard; they had restored the confidence of business men in the American financial system; they had disproved the claims of Mr. Bryan that the single gold standard meant economic privation and disaster; and they had bestowed comparative prosperity on the business man and on the wage-earner. Although the party in power, they could afford to take high ground. They were not on the defensive. If any administration and party ever had a right to claim a continuation of public confidence, because of a sequence between promise and performance, the first McKinley administration and the President's party were most assuredly in that position.

Mr. Hanna in his speech before the Ohio State Convention on April 24, 1900, attempted to strike the proper keynote of the campaign. "I say the spirit of the hour should be one of absolute fearlessness on the part of the Republicans. We are conscious, as your chairman has said, of having fulfilled every promise made. We took this country into our hands and under our care after four years of unprecedented vicissitudes in business. At our Convention in St. Louis we proclaimed the doctrine and policy of the Republican party, upon which for twenty years had been built the material interests of the country. We promised such reforms and such economic legislation as would produce a return of these benefits. We even said that we would go beyond the ideas of our fathers in the benefits which would flow from the perpetuation of our policy. We now stand on what we have achieved and accomplished in respect to the material interests of this country. Looking in the face of such results, I repeat your chairman's words: 'Do we want a change?'" Such was the stock Republican campaign argument, which was repeated during the next six months from every platform, and which was finally summed up by Mr. Hanna in the phrase "Let well enough alone."

The wicked Democrats, however, repudiated the statement that any such simple and definite issue divided the parties. They proposed to divert the minds of the voters from the success of Republican policy and from the substantial benefits of Republican control by raising various additional questions. As Mr. Hanna said in the speech from which I have already quoted: "The Republicans of the United States are confronted to-day with many new propositions and issues thrown around us like tangled grass in our pathway by the Democratic party": and it was difficult to judge in advance whether any of these issues would actually serve to distract public attention from the smoking factory chimneys and the full dinner-pail.

When the Republican Convention assembled in June, the Democratic Convention was two weeks away, but its candidate and doctrine could be accurately predicted. William J. Bryan was to be the candidate and he was to be supported by a combination of the old Democracy and trans-Mississippi Populism. The platform was to reaffirm the silver heresy of 1896, because Mr. Bryan would not repudiate a doctrine which he had urged upon the American people with so much eloquence and confidence; but not very much homage was to be paid to it during the campaign. The Republicans were to be denounced, partly because they had committed the country to a perilous and undemocratic Imperialistic adventure in the Philippines, and because they had been recreant to the "plain duty" of the national government towards Puerto Rico. But most of all they were held up to execration because during their four years of office the process of industrial combination had made enormous strides, and because the Republicans had delivered the American people bound hand and foot into the power of the big corporations.

The administration did not and could not avoid the issue raised by the acquisition of the Philippines and the bloody suppression of the Philippine rebellion; but Mr. McKinley did not want too much emphasis placed upon it. Both the Cuban War and its consequences had been forced upon him. He had finally insisted upon the cession of the Philippines by Spain, not because he welcomed the assumption by the national government of such responsibilities, but because the alternative looked still more dubious. By a refusal he would have alienated that part of the country which contributed most of his personal following, while at the same time he would not have avoided a certain responsibility towards the Philippines, created by the military situation in those islands. He would have liked to keep the country and his administration free from any such entanglements, both because they squared ill with his inherited phrases and because they prevented the country from concentrating its attention on the great drama of prosperity, of which he was the advance agent. Consequently, while ably and vigorously defended a policy of expansion, it was more or less a source of embarrassment to him. There was a real danger that public opinion might be shocked and alienated by the necessarily bloody suppression of Philippine insurrection. In all these respects Mr. Hanna agreed with his chief. He was enough of a realist in politics not to have any scruples against a policy of extraterritorial expansion, but was not interested in it, and he regarded its intrusion into the campaign as a mere befogging of the essential issue.

The "trust" issue, on the other hand, Mr. Hanna welcomed rather than feared. More than any other American political leader of equal prominence, he was not afraid to identify himself openly with the cause of corporate aggrandizement. His public attitude towards the matter was modified somewhat by Mr. McKinley's consistent desire to keep in the middle of the road. He always declared his opposition to the "trusts," in so far as they endeavored to create a monoply and absolutely control prices. But his sympathies were on the side of organized capital. He knew that the enormous impulse, which the process of railroad and industrial consolidation had received since 1898, had been caused by a desire to escape from certain critical evils resulting from unrestrained competition; and he knew that the organization of larger corporate units resulted in many real and desirable economies in the transaction of business. Any forcible

x

interference with the process might have injurious effects on industrial and economical activity. The revival of prosperity was associated with the reorganization of business methods, and Mr. Hanna believed so devoutly in the former that he was not disposed to question the latter.

In holding this belief Mr. Hanna was fairly representative of the dominant trend of public opinion. There were, indeed, plain indications that certain elements in public opinion, not ordinarily inclined to sectionalism or radicalism, were becoming uneasy at the spectacle of unchecked corporate aggrandizement. But their uneasiness had not become lively and aggressive. Radical opposition to the large corporations was still confined chiefly to Western Democrats and Populists, and their opposition alienated public opinion, because it was associated with so many economic and financial heresies, and because it was so plainly biassed by sectional interests and objects. In spite of certain misgivings the ordinary patriotic American was inclined to accept the process of consolidation as inevitable and desirable and to associate the enemies of the "trusts" with the enemies of prosperity. At that particular juncture the majority of American voters, whether farmers, business men or wage-earners, were, after their many years of famine, prosperity-mad.

The "trust" issue, consequently, did not cause very much alarm at the headquarters of the Republican national committee. Mr. Hanna knew that it would be flourished valiantly all over the country, but he felt that the criticism would be discounted, because of the source from which it came. The "trust" plank in the platform of 1900 was written by Mr. Hanna himself after consultation with the President. A draft of it exists in Mr. Hanna's own handwriting, and it is reproduced in facsimile, in order both to give an example of Mr. Hanna's handwriting and to call attention to the emendations in the draft. The word "honest" is added before "aggregations of capital," possibly at the suggestion of the prudent President, and as originally written the plank declared such "aggregations" to be necessary only to the development of foreign trade. The change is of importance chiefly as indicating the way in which Mr. Hanna instinctively regarded the relation of the "trusts" to American business. In 1900 exports of manufactures were increasing by leaps and bounds, particularly in the highly organized industries. The large industrial unit was considered to be a more effective agent in the difficult work of creating foreign markets than the smaller one. This aspect of the matter always bulked large in his mind and was closely associated, as we shall see, with his determined advocacy of ship subsidies. It need only be added that the plank, as reproduced herewith, was accepted by the Committee on Resolutions of the Convention practically intact. The word "legitimacy" became "propriety," and the first sentence was made coördinate with the second instead of dependent upon it.

Facsimile of the "Trust" Blank in the Republican Platform of 1900 in Mr. Hanna's Handwriting.

With its leading candidates and its platform practically dictated, the Convention of 1900 might have been expected to be too harmonious for anything but words. The only task which circumstances had left to the discretion of the delegates was the nomination for Vice-President; and American parties and partisan conventions have usually refused to get interested in the candidate for that contingently important office. After the question of the Presidential candidate is settled, the delegates are so anxious to go home that they allow a Vice-Presidential candidate to be imposed upon them by the head of the ticket. The more conspicuous and able party leaders do not want the office, which has a way of ending the political career of the man who wins it. The successful candidate is usually some subordinate leader who is supposed to be able to carry an important state, remote from the residence of the Presidential candidate.

In 1900, however, this ordinarily neglected task was the only aspect of the Convention's work in which the delegates had a chance to get interested. They seized it with avidity, and soon became almost as much excited over their choice for the minor as they usually were for the major office. The influence of the administration was not being exerted in favor of any candidate. Both Mr. McKinley and Mr. Hanna had their preferences, but their favorite candidates spurned the office. Mr. McKinley's choice, Senator Allison, was satisfied with his seat and his position in the Senate. Mr. Hanna's choice, Mr. Cornelius N. Bliss, to which the President would have cordially assented, refused to permit the use of his name. Mr. Bliss had been for about a year and a half Secretary of Interior in Mr. McKinley's Cabinet. During the period of their joint official service in Washington, the warm friendship between him and Mr. Hanna, which had started during the campaign of '96, became still more affectionately intimate. They lived together for a while during the summer of '98, and both used subsequently to refer to these months as peculiarly pleasant — in spite of the trying nature of their official duties. It was natural, consequently, that after Mr. Hobart's death, Mr. Hanna should have wished to put Mr. Bliss in his place.

If Mr. Bliss had consented to allow the use of his name, Mr. Hanna would have planned his nomination months in advance, and might well have succeeded. The latter never had any doubt about his ability to bring about the nomination of any really available candidate. But Mr. Bliss refused. Even after the Convention had assembled, Mr. Hanna continued to urge Mr. Bliss, who was a delegate from New York, to consent. For a moment there was some hesitation. Mr. Bliss was so far persuaded that he even yielded — provided Mr. Hanna would disarm the opposition of Mrs. Bliss. But Mr. Hanna threw up his hands at the proviso. He had already incurred Mrs. Bliss's disfavor by persuading her husband to accept a Cabinet office, and he declined to travel any farther along that road.

With Senator Allison and Mr. Bliss eliminated there was no candidate whom either the President or Mr. Hanna very much preferred. The other men frequently mentioned for the place were Governor Roosevelt, Jonathan Dolliver, then a Congressman from Iowa, ex-Secretary of the Navy, John D. Long, Charles M. Fairbanks of Indiana and Timothy Woodruff, a New York politician. Mr. Roosevelt, who was much the most prominent of these candidates, was being proposed for the office very much against his own will, while at the other end of the scale was Mr. Woodruff, who was enthusiastically in favor of his own selection.

Mr. Roosevelt's candidacy was being assiduously promoted by Senator Thomas C. Platt, the "Boss" of New York. The Governor during his term of office had exhibited a good deal of undesirable independence in respect both to the legislation which he favored and to his appointments. He had come into sharp collision with Senator Platt and the New York Republican machine over several matters, particularly the question of the handling of the insurance department and the Franchise Tax Bill. He achieved his object in having the bill passed in proper shape, but only at the cost of serious trouble with the organization. After its passage Mr. Roosevelt soon found that the regular leaders were more or less covertly hostile to him and were anxious to prevent his renomination. They feared he might succeed, in spite of their opposition, and they hit upon the plan of getting rid of him by bringing about his nomination for Vice-President. Before the Convention assembled, Mr. Roosevelt had no idea that the Vice-Presidential candidacy was anything but a device contrived by Senator Platt and the machine to end his career as Governor, and announced that he would not accept the nomination. He went to the Convention primarily for the purpose of preventing it.

Both Mr. McKinley and Mr. Hanna were as much opposed to Mr. Roosevelt's candidacy as was the candidate himself. When the latter arrived in Philadelphia, he had no definite plans, except to nominate Mr. Bliss (if possible), and to prevent the nomination of Mr. Roosevelt. The Colonel of Rough Riders, after his return from Cuba, had been free in his private criticism of the conduct of the war, and his whole attitude towards the war had been different from that of the administration. Although he had always behaved as a loyal Republican, he was regarded as erratic and "unsafe,"— as, indeed, he undoubtedly was from the point of view of an administration of the affairs of the country chiefly in the interest of business. The Vice-Presidency might have seemed to be one of the safest offices in the government in which to confine an unsafe political leader; but Mr. Hanna had gone to Philadelphia with the intention of engineering the nomination of a Vice-Presidential candidate who would make from his point of view a thoroughly good President. It was characteristic of him to provide, if possible, in advance against the inconvenient contingency of having his Harrison succeeded by a Tyler.

There is a story to the effect that when Mr. Timothy Woodruff was urging upon Mr. Hanna his personal advantages as a Vice-Presidential candidate, the latter asked him:—

"Do you think that the Convention would nominate you for the Presidency?" Mr. Woodruff allowed that the Convention would not. "Then," said Mr. Hanna, "don't you know that there is only one life between the Presidency and the Vice-Presidency and that it would be foolhardy to nominate a man for Vice-President who would not be big enough to be President?" What Mr. Woodruff replied, the chronicle sayeth not; but he might have retorted that the nomination of politicians for the Vice-Presidency who were not fit to be President was one of the most ancient and best established of American political traditions, and that from any such point of view his qualifications were unimpeachable. He might have urged, also, that his own removal to Washington, unlike that of Mr. Roosevelt, would have been a benefit to the cause of good government in New York.

Although Mr. Hanna was emphatically opposed to Mr. Roosevelt's nomination, neither he nor, of course, the President had given any public expression to his opposition. Nor had he taken any precautions to prevent it. He did not think such precautions necessary. Inasmuch as Mr. Roosevelt himself did not want it, and as the New York delegation was divided between Mr. Woodruff and the Governor, the prospects of such a nomination did not look serious. Mr. Roosevelt arrived in Philadelphia on Saturday, June 16, and in an interview shortly thereafter with Mr. Hanna, he repudiated so decisively the idea of becoming a candidate that Mr. Hanna gave out a statement in reference to the matter. He declared himself opposed to Mr. Roosevelt's nomination on the ground that the candidacy should not be forced on any man. He undoubtedly expected that this declaration would settle this matter. The Convention had shown no disposition to question his leadership, and preferences for Vice-Presidential candidates never had much vitality. With Mr. Roosevelt out of the way the nomination seemed to lie between Jonathan Dolliver and John D. Long, with the chances in the former's favor.

What followed can best be narrated in Mr. Roosevelt's own words: —

"Immediately on reaching Philadelphia, I was made aware that there was a very strong movement outside of the State of New York in favor of my nomination, the motive of these men outside of New York being the exact reverse of the motives of the politicians from New York; for the men outside New York wished me nominated because they believed in me and wished me to continue in public life. However, it was some little time before I attached full weight to this outside movement, my attention being absorbed by the effort within the New York delegation to force me as a candidate. Senator Platt had come on, and personally and through his lieutenants was assuming control of the delegation, and they were insisting that I would have to be nominated, and that New York would insist upon presenting my name. I insisted that I would not be nominated, and that I would not permit New York to present my name.

Finally a caucus of the New York delegates was called, and it was while this caucus was being held that I had my interview with Senator Platt. As soon as the caucus came together it became evident that a concerted effort would be made to force me into the acceptance of the nomination, without regard to my wishes. I taxed the leaders of the movement with desiring merely to get me out of the Governorship — for my term as Governor would end the following January, and the Convention to nominate a Governor would be held some three months after the Presidential Convention which we were then attending. Some of those I thus taxed with wishing to eliminate me from the Governorship acknowledged the fact with a laugh; others denied it. I told them that I would not permit them to nominate me for Vice-President, that I would not only make the fight in the caucus, but also if necessary in the Convention, and explain fully what I believed their purpose was; and that most assuredly after such public explanation by me, it would be impossible for them to nominate me.

"This caused a good deal of commotion, and in a short while one of Mr. Platt's lieutenants came to me and stated that the Senator wished to see me in his room, to which he was confined because of an accident with which he had met. I accordingly went upstairs and saw him. He told me that it had been decided that I was to be nominated for Vice-President, and that they could not accept any refusal, and that I would have to yield. I answered that I was sorry to be disagreeable, but that I regarded the movement as one to get me out of the Governorship for reasons which were not of a personal but of a public character; that is, for reasons connected with the principles in which I so heartily believed, and that I would not and could not consent to go back on those principles, and so I would refuse to accept the nomination for Vice-President. Senator Platt again said that I would have to accept. I again told him that I would not. He then said to me that if I did not accept, I would be beaten for the nomination for Governor, and some one else nominated for Governor in my place. I answered in effect that this was a threat, which simply rendered it impossible for me to accept, that if there was to be war there would be war, and that that was all there was to it; and I bowed and left the room.

"As I went downstairs to the room in which the New York delegates were gathered, I made up my mind that the wise course was to take the aggressive at once, and with all possible force. Accordingly as soon as I entered the room, I announced to half a dozen men that I had just had a conversation with Senator Platt; that Senator Platt had informed me that I must take the nomination for the Vice-Presidency and that if I did not I would not be nominated for Governor; that this threat rendered it impossible for me to consider accepting the Vice-Presidency; that I intended to announce immediately that I was a candidate for Governor and would fight for the nomination, and that every man who voted for my nomination for Vice-President must do so with the understanding that I would see that the people in their turn understood that he was thus voting at the direction of Mr. Platt, in order to remove me from the Governorship; that I should make this statement instantly in the full meeting, that I would make it to the newspapers afterwards, and that I would fight for the nomination on this issue. The minute that I took this position the whole effort to bring pressure upon me collapsed. There was great confusion, and one of Senator Platt's lieutenants came to me and begged me not to say anything for a minute or two until he could communicate with the Senator, whom he was certain must have been misunderstood by me. I laughed and said that I had very clearly understood him, but that of course I would wait for a few minutes until he could be communicated with. In three or four minutes this gentleman came downstairs, saying that the Senator wished to see me again, that he was very sorry he had spoken in a way that caused me to misunderstand him, that he was under the influence of opiate to reduce the pain caused by the injuries he had received, and that he supposed he had expressed himself badly in consequence. Accordingly I went upstairs, and Mr. Platt substantially repeated this explanation to me, saying that he was sorry if he had shown temper or expressed himself badly, and that of course in view of my feeling the effort to nominate me for Vice-President would be abandoned, and that he wished me to be assured that he and all his friends would favor my renomination as Governor. I thanked him, bowed, and went downstairs. The delegates took their cue at once. No further effort was made to nominate me for the Vice-Presidency at this New York caucus and they voted to present the name of Mr. Woodruff."

The caucus of the New Yorkers had been held on Tuesday night, June 19. In the papers on Wednesday morning, every attempt was again made to create the impression that the Roosevelt candidacy was dead. An account of the decision of the New York delegation was telegraphed all over the country. The fact was flourished that Mr. Roosevelt was advising his friends to vote for ex-Secretary John D. Long; and the persistent efforts to nominate the Governor against his will were ascribed to the desire of the "Bosses" of New York and Pennsylvania to "run" the Convention and embarrass the administration. Mr. Hanna himself was at the bottom of these renewed efforts to get Mr. Roosevelt out of the way; but this time they had the appearance of being forced. The correspondents pointed out that the matter could not be considered settled, until Mr. Roosevelt had declared definitely that he would refuse absolutely to accept the nomination. No such declaration had been made. In a statement published in the press on Tuesday morning, he had said merely that in his opinion he could help the national ticket most in case he were renominated for Governor; and he begged his friends to respect his wishes.

If the only forces working in favor of Mr. Roosevelt's nomination had been Senator Platt's wish to transplant such an "erratic" but thrifty political plant out of the green valley of New York state politics and the purpose of the Quay machine, which had formally indorsed the Roosevelt candidacy, to embarrass the administration, Mr. Roosevelt would never have received the nomination, and the administration, represented by Mr. Hanna, would not have been in the least embarrassed. But the difficulty was that the Roosevelt candidacy had developed a spontaneous strength which astounded the candidate himself and really did embarrass Mr. Hanna. Before the meeting of the Convention no one had suspected either the extent or vigor of the demand for Mr. Roosevelt's nomination. A large proportion of the Republican voters had willed that his name should be on the ticket; and no amount of discouragement either from the candidate or from the National Committee could break their will. The delegations from certain Western states insisted that they would nominate him in spite of any opposition from any quarter. They would not listen even to an absolute refusal on the part of the candidate himself to accept the nomination.

No political leader in a democracy can trifle with a plain popular mandate — no matter how inconvenient its consequences may be. Mr. Roosevelt was sincere in his wish to avoid the nomination. He had every apparent personal interest in desiring to continue his career as Governor in New York. But he was staggered by the insistence of the sentiment among the delegates. For that reason he left the door slightly ajar, and the majority of the Convention pushed him through the opening. He and Mr. Hanna, either alone or together, could have beaten "Boss" Platt; but they could not and did not dare to disobey their common master. Such an unequivocal and enthusiastic expression of a popular preference both deserved and commanded acquiescence, and in acquiescing Mr. Roosevelt had this consolation. If from one point of view his transfer to the Vice-Presidency looked like the incarceration of a very promising political career in a cold storage box, from another point of view such a flattering evidence of the Sovereign's favor looked like the finger of Destiny.

Mr. Hanna, on the other hand, had no such consolation. Again and again he had thought and announced that the Roosevelt candidacy was dead. But on Wednesday morning, after its technical murder at the hands of the New York state delegation the night before, it proved to be more alive than ever. Mr. Hanna was taken by surprise, but he was not discouraged. He had come to the Convention with the intention of securing a Vice-Presidential candidate who in his opinion could be depended upon to continue Mr. McKinley's work, and he would not yield his purpose. He continued for some time further to use his own influence and the credit of the administration in an effort to stem the tide. He was prepared, if necessary, to carry the fight to the floor of the Convention. By so doing he was taking a grave risk, for, even had he succeeded, his success would have awakened deep resentment. Already there was a growing undertone of discontent and criticism, because the general preference for Mr. Roosevelt was meeting with organized opposition — emanating from the representative of the administration at the Convention.

According to the veracious Mr. Platt, it was he who persuaded Mr. Hanna to abandon his opposition. He tells of a conference between the two on Tuesday night, while the caucus of the New York delegation was in session, which ended in Mr. Hanna's conversion and the latter's promise *"that night"* to issue a statement approving Mr. Roosevelt as nominee. This account runs on about the same level of accuracy with Mr. Platt's other contributions to history. Mr. Hanna's statement was not given out on Tuesday night. On Wednesday he was systematically collecting all his own forces and those of the administration for the purpose of preventing the Governor's nomination. What the result would have been, had he been allowed to continue the fight, is doubtful; but his own friends and those of Mr. McKinley feared the outcome. They were as much afraid of the resentment, which would have been caused by an administration victory, as they were by the loss of prestige, which would have resulted from defeat.

A friend of both the President and Mr. Hanna's, Mr. Charles G. Dawes of Illinois, who understood the risk of further opposition, expostulated with Mr. Hanna. He was told that Mr. Hanna was only carrying out the President's wishes. Thereupon he called up Mr. McKinley on the long distance telephone, explained the situation to the President at length and the risk of committing the administration to any uncompromising opposition to the general sentiment of the Convention. He was instructed by Mr. McKinley to ask Mr. Hanna to discontinue all opposition. As soon as Mr. Hanna was informed of the President's wishes he immediately yielded — not without some chagrin and bitterness of spirit, but with the loyalty which he always exhibited and upon which the President confidently counted.

It was on Wednesday evening that Mr. Hanna learned of the President's wishes, and about the same time he was informed that the unwilling candidate had also signified his consent. Late that night, after many consultations with leaders from all over the country, Mr. Hanna gave out the following statement:

"The administration has had no candidate for Vice-President. It has not been for or against any candidate. It has desired that the Convention should make the candidate and that has been my position throughout. It has been a free field for all. Under these circumstances several eminent Republicans have been proposed, all of them distinguished men with many friends. I may now say on behalf of all of these candidates, and I except no one, I have within the last twelve hours been asked to give my advice. After consulting with as many delegates as possible in the time at my disposal I have concluded to accept the responsibility involved in this request. In the present situation, with the strong and earnest sentiment of the delegates from all parts of the country for Governor Roosevelt, and since President McKinley is to be nominated without a dissenting voice, it is my judgment that Governor Roosevelt should be nominated with the same unanimity." This proclamation, which was very ingenious, but not wholly candid, did of course settle the matter. Mr. Hanna's "advice" was accepted. No other name was presented to the Convention for Vice-Presidential candidate; but curiously enough it was not presented by the candidate's own state. The effective demand for Mr. Roosevelt's nomination had come from the West, and to Iowa, as the only Western state which had favored a serious local candidate, was accorded the honor of placing Mr. Roosevelt's name before the Convention. Colonel Lafayette Young made the speech accompanying the nomination, and Mr. Roosevelt received 925 votes out of 926 — one delegate from New York, presumably the candidate himself, having failed to vote.

The dislike which President McKinley and Mr. Hanna felt towards Mr. Roosevelt as Vice-Presidential nominee was natural, but the immediate effect of the nomination was as fortunate for them as its ultimate effects were for Mr. Roosevelt. The Republican ticket was decidedly strengthened by the presence on it of one who at that time was, more than any other single man, the hero of the Cuban war. The facts that both the President and Mr. Hanna had been opposed to the war, that they had been reluctant to accept its consequences, and that in their political system the most important object of political policy was the encouragement of business, — all these facts made them underestimate the effect of the war on public opinion. It was the popularity of the war in the West which had saved them in the Congressional election of the fall of 1898; and it was the same element in public opinion which at the Philadelphia Convention had demanded the nomination of the Colonel of Rough Riders. Thus Mr. Roosevelt added a kind of strength to the ticket which it could not have obtained from the success of any alternative candidate.

That the promised revival of business had taken place during Mr. McKinley's administration constituted unquestionably the President's best claim for reëlection. If the country had not become relatively prosperous, the Republicans would surely have been defeated. But just in proportion as prosperity returned, it lost some of its value as a political issue. A hungry man can think of nothing but food, but when the hunger is satisfied he needs other interests. The war had aroused national feeling and had made the people more alive to their joint national interest. It had given to the American people a new sense of the meaning of American nationality and of the scope of American national purposes. All these vague emotions and ideas demanded some medium of expression. If the Republican ticket had not provided them with a candidate who appealed, as Mr. Roosevelt did, to their patriotic imagination and aspirations, it would have failed wholly to satisfy a widespread and vital element in public opinion. Against their own will Mr. McKinley and Mr. Hanna had called to their support the one man who could most effectively supplement their own strength with the American people — the one man who could make the ticket represent the nationalism of the future as well as that of the past and of the present.

CHAPTER XXI

THE CAMPAIGN OF 1900

IN spite of the threatened conflict over the nomination for Vice-President, the Convention of 1900 was, from the point of view of party harmony and efficiency, one of the most successful ever held by the Republicans. It named a ticket which was as capable of vigorous aggression as it was impregnable on the defence. The whole party was confident of success and eager to contribute to it. Never had the Republicans been more efficiently organized and more competently led. The leaders had the confidence of the army. The army was not divided against itself. They felt that they represented the better part of the nation and that in their persons the nation was marching on to new industrial conquests and towards new political horizons.

Mr. McKinley was apparently as much pleased with the final result and the means whereby it had been reached as was the average Republican. As soon as the Convention was over, he wrote from Washington to Mr. Hanna, who had gone to Cleveland, the following letter: —

"DEAR SENATOR: —

"I am greatly pleased with the work of the Convention. You have added another claim to leadership and public confidence. All comers from the Convention commend you and all accord you the courage and sagacity of true leadership.

"I am delighted that you have accepted the Chairmanship of the National Committee. It is a great task and will be to you a great sacrifice. Before you arrange for the Director of the Speaking Bureau, I will be glad to talk with you.

"Hoping you will get some much needed rest and find your family well, believe me,

"Your true friend,
"WILLIAM McKINLEY."

It had already been announced that Mr. Hanna would again head the National Committee. Everybody had assumed, as a matter of course, that he would do so. His selection for the place was only a proper recognition of his service to the administration and the party and his proved ability as a campaign manager. Yet there was a period of some weeks previous to the meeting of the Convention, during which Mr. Hanna himself began to suspect and fear that he would not be selected. The naming of the Chairman was the practical prerogative of the head of the ticket; and Mr. McKinley's behavior was at least suspicious.

Early in the spring of 1900 Mr. Hanna began complaining to certain of his intimate associates that Mr. McKinley had said nothing to him about managing the coming campaign. Time passed and still nothing was said. Mr. Hanna became very much worried. The moment arrived when preparations ought to be made and when it was natural that the matter should be settled. The worry seems to have had a damaging effect on his health. Late in April he had an attack of heart failure, while writing a note in his office, and fainted away. He recovered almost immediately and even went that same night to the theatre; but his intimates, who knew his physical habits and realized how distressed he was, attributed the attack to the anxiety caused by the President's persistent silence. If at that particular juncture Mr. Hanna had been superseded as Chairman of the National Committee, one of the most essential supports of his personal prestige and power would have been removed. It would have meant that he no longer retained the friendship and confidence of the President. Fortunately, however, his suspense was not further prolonged. A little later Mr. Hanna appeared at his office one morning with every trace of anxiety vanished from his face and in the highest spirits. Mr. McKinley had the night before asked him to accept the office and its work, and had insisted upon his immediate and unqualified consent.

Considering the relations between the two men, one's natural suspicion would be that Mr. Hanna's anxiety was due to over-sensitiveness, and that Mr. McKinley had never even considered the selection of another Chairman. But from remarks which Mr. McKinley made to other people, it is probable that the President really was hesitating. How serious the hesitation was, and upon precisely what grounds it was based, remains obscure; but unquestionably at this period a certain alteration was taking place in the relationship between the two men. The President's delay in asking Mr. Hanna to serve as Chairman, and Mr. Hanna's consequent anxiety, was only the first of a series of incidents which indicated such a change. The incidents will all be told frankly, because they are part of the true story of Mr. Hanna's life. They indicate not any estrangement, but simply the stress under which an old and fast friendship was adapting itself to new conditions. The new condition was Mr. Hanna's increasing personal power as a Congressional and as a popular leader. This power was assuming such formidable dimensions that the President might well begin to wonder how his own prestige was beginning to look by comparison. But in spite of the strain, the testimony is unanimous that at the end of the campaign the friendship of the two men remained substantially unimpaired.

Whatever the grounds of the President's hesitation, he really did not have a practicable alternative. No other man had a tithe of the qualifications possessed by Mr. Hanna for the office of Chairman. He could have claimed it, merely because of his ability as a campaign manager, even though as a political leader he was less popular than was actually the case. Mr. Hanna alone had in his mind a complete and accurate map of the political landscape. He knew just what the situation was in the different parts of the country, and just what states needed and would repay the most arduous efforts for their retention or conquest. During the four years that had elapsed since the previous campaign he had been studying the conditions and opportunities which would be presented in 1900. Responsibility for the work could not have been shifted without confusion, cross purposes and loss of efficiency.

Mr. Hanna's personal relation to the work in 1900 was very much the same as it had been four years earlier. He was the real supervisor and director of the whole campaign. Its management was absolutely his. Of course, he constantly consulted the President and other leaders; but, as in the case of any other efficient general, he acted often on his own initiative and his own personal responsibility. His private secretary, Mr. Elmer Dover, states that he laid out the actual work of a campaign without taking any one into his confidence. His plan was, as in 1896, based on what he believed to be the general condition of public opinion throughout the Union, from which he inferred how much work needed to be done, where it should be placed and what its character ought to be. As in 1896, also, the work was planned to be cumulative in its effect, culminating a few days before the election in an outburst of common conviction and enthusiasm. Early in the campaign even his intimate associates were puzzled as to his reasons for making certain moves, but their relation to the general plan was gradually unfolded. Every part of the work was well organized, and every part of the organization was thoroughly energized.

Of course his task was much less onerous than it had been in 1896. He did not have an uphill fight on his hands, or an almost country-wide campaign of popular instruction. He did not employ as many speakers, nor did he need to distribute as much literature. It is true that with his usual habit of making a sure thing doubly sure, he canvassed the country much more thoroughly than it ever had been canvassed before 1896. But with every intention in the world of leaving nothing undone which could possibly contribute to Republican success, there was very much less to do. In 1900, as in the campaigns previous to 1896, certain results in many parts of the country could be taken for granted. The hard canvassing could be concentrated on a smaller area of peculiar strategic importance. To continue the military analogy, he was operating in a familiar and a friendly country, instead of in a country which was hostile and comparatively unexplored.

He needed, consequently, much less money, and what money he needed he had much less difficulty in raising. In 1900 the total collections were approximately $2,500,000, and not all of this sum was used. By this time Mr. Hanna enjoyed the complete confidence of the big business men of the country. They would have placed at the disposal of the Committee just as much money as he demanded. If he did not raise any more than $2,500,000, it was because the expenditure of a larger sum would have contributed nothing to the chances of Republican success.

A significant change had taken place since 1896 in the nature and reasons of the support which business men were affording to the Republican party. Four years before the responsible business interests of the country, small as well as large, had united in condemning the free coinage of silver. A certain amount of the same feeling was carried over into the campaign of 1900. The fact that Mr. Bryan was again running on a free-silver platform, and the fact that even though elected on the issue of anti-Imperialism, he might be able and willing to disestablish the gold standard, took the heart out of business during the summer of 1900. The issue, however, between financial aberration and financial sanity could not be as sharply drawn as it had been in 1896, and there was a tendency among smaller business men to return to their traditional partisan allegiance. The Republicans could not demand the support of business just because it was business. They could not assess the National Banks all over the country for a certain percentage of their capital, because Democratic success would certainly cause acute financial disaster.

During the years between the two campaigns certain classes of American business had been radically reorganized. The process of combination had made enormous strides. It had infected more or less every important department of industry. It had, indeed, become the dominant characteristic of American industrial practice. But in proportion as this process of combination increased in volume, it became subject to political attack. The large corporations had a doubtful standing under state and federal anti-trust acts. They were not overscrupulous about conducting their business according to fair and legal methods. Even those whose standing under existing laws was unimpeachable were liable to severe injury from adverse state and national legislation. Agitation against them and against the millionnaires interested in them was becoming both violent and widespread. The large business interests could no more disregard the sort of denunciation which was more than ever hurled at them than the Southern slaveholders could ignore the denunciation of the abolitionists; and its effect in the two cases was very much the same. Big business men became "class conscious." They needed political power more than ever for the protection of business interests, and the power which may have been acquired in self-protection would inevitably be used for aggressive purposes.

In 1900, consequently, it was as much big business as general business which began to depend upon the Republican party for political protection. The Democratic platform and candidate denounced the process of business organization, while the Republican candidate and platform recognized that it had a certain validity. The whole corporation interest rallied more enthusiastically than ever to the Republicans and opened its purse more liberally than ever. To be sure, the distinction between big business and general business was not sharply drawn. The "prosperity" of which the Republicans boasted and which they promised to continue was necessary to both, and the waving of the "prosperity" banner was intended to appeal to both. Nevertheless, the distinction had become plainer than it was in 1896, and it had a profound bearing upon the campaign and its results. When Mr. McKinley was reëlected, big business undoubtedly considered that it had received a license from the people to do very much as it pleased.

Mr. Hanna himself never distinguished sharply between the interests of general business and big business. His own business life, except in relation to the street railway company, had never become entangled either with the methods or the interests characteristic of the larger corporations. He intended to represent in politics the essential interest of business itself — irrespective of size, location, organization or character. The "prosperity" which he wished to promote was necessary to all sorts of business, and the policy of his opponents was dangerous to all sorts of business. Farther than that he did not go. Nevertheless, the necessities of practical politics brought him closer and closer to the representatives of large corporate interests. It was much more convenient to get the money needed for an effective campaign from them than from a larger number of smaller subscribers; and such was particularly the case because the smaller business men were much less conscious of their political interests and responsibilities than were their more opulent associates. Mr. Hanna wanted, as usual, to accomplish the largest and surest results with the utmost economy of time. So in 1900 he solicited and obtained support from Wall Street more explicitly and more exclusively than he had in 1896.

The explicit recognition on the part of the contributors that they were paying for a definite service enabled Mr. Hanna still further to systematize the work of collection. The size of a contribution from any particular corporation was not left wholly to the liberality or discretion of its officers. An attempt was made with some measure of success to make every corporation pay according to its stake in the general prosperity of the country and according to its special interest in a region in which a large amount of expensive canvassing had to be done. In case an exceptionally opulent corporation or business firm contributed decidedly less than was considered its fair proportion, the checque might be returned. There are a number of such cases on record. On the other hand, an excessively liberal subscription might also be sent back in part — assuming, of course, that the Committee had collected as much money as it needed, or more.

The Standard Oil Company contributed $250,000 in 1900, as it had done in 1896; and there was, I believe, only one other contribution received by the Committee of the same size. When the election was over the officials of the Company were astounded to receive a letter from the Committee containing a check for $50,000. They had contributed more than their share, and the surplus over and above the necessities of the campaign permitted the Committee to reimburse them to that extent. Incidents of this kind naturally increased the confidence of business men in the new management of the Republican party. Money was not being extorted from them on political pretexts for the benefit of political professionals. They were paying a definite sum in return for protection against political attacks. Imagine the feelings of an ordinary political "Boss" upon learning that good sound dollars, which had been received as a political contribution, were actually being returned to their donors.

Instances of this kind indicate that Mr. Hanna had introduced some semblance of business method into a system of campaign contributions, which at its worst had fluctuated somewhere between the extremes of blackmail and bribery. If it had been allowed to develop farther, the system might have become a sort of unofficial taxation which a certain class of business was obliged to pay, because in one way or another its prosperity and even its safety had become dependent upon the political management of the country. Even in the extreme form which it assumed in 1900, the system itself remained the natural outcome of a relation between business and politics, which the politico-economic history of the country had conspired to produce and for which in a very real sense the mass of the American people were just as much responsible as were its beneficiaries and perpetrators. Mr. Hanna merely developed it, and removed from it, so far as possible, the taint of ordinary corruption. Just as the work performed by individuals on behalf of McKinley's first nomination was never paid for by the promise of particular offices, so these contributions were not accepted in return for the promise of particular favors. In one instance a cheque for $10,000 was returned to a firm of bankers in Wall Street because a definite service was by implication demanded in return for the contribution. The men whose hands went deepest into their pockets understood in general that, if the Republicans won, the politics of the country would be managed in the interest of business — a consequence which was acknowledged by all the Republican speakers and by none so frankly as by Mark Hanna.

But the more the practice of assessing corporate interests for the benefit of one party was reduced to a system, the more impossible it became. The very means which were taken by business to protect itself against hostile political agitation was bound in the long run to inflame the irritation; and the more the irritation became inflamed, the greater the injury which business would suffer when it eventually lost control. The intimate association of business prosperity with illegal and unfair business practices was bound to make general business, whether innocent or guilty, pay the final costs. It is extraordinary that the hard-headed men who throughout so many years spent so much money for political protection, did not realize that business could not permanently succeed in having its own way in politics by the use of merely business means and methods — without corrupting the country. The prevailing tendency of politics to ignore business in the treatment of business questions is merely the inevitable consequence of the tendency of business, when it had political power, to exercise it in a manner which ignored the fundamental political well-being of a democratic state.

In making use of his abundant resources in 1900 Mr. Hanna was not trying, as he had been in 1896, merely to win the election. He was planning a victory so decisive and so comprehensive that the Republicans would be unquestionably marked as the dominant party. He was planning above all as a matter of practical politics to increase the narrow Republican majority in the Senate, and thus to obtain a more effective and responsible control over legislation than the party had hitherto possessed. Where he expected to make the necessary gains was west of the Mississippi River. He counted on being able to keep all the Eastern States which went Republican in 1896. He was just as confident that the Middle West would stick to its allegiance. A very general impression existed that Indiana would go Democratic, but Mr. Hanna insisted that he could win it. He devoted a great deal of time to that state, and he succeeded. But the part of the country in which he was most interested was the territory west of the Mississippi River, which had formerly been Republican, but which since the rise of "Populism" had fallen away from the true faith. The results of the Congressional elections of 1898 encouraged him to believe that possibly the great majority of these states could be carried. In spite of the popularity of Bryan in the region and the enthusiastic indorsement of the Democratic ticket by all the "Populistic" organizations, he proposed to concentrate his biggest guns on the Far West. He himself spent two-thirds of his time in Chicago and only one-third in New York.

Mr. McKinley, as President, could not play as important a part in the campaign as he had in 1896; but in his Vice-Presidential candidate Mr. Hanna had a most effective substitute for the vacancy. Mr. Roosevelt was as indefatigable a speaker and traveller as Mr. Bryan himself, and the National Committee used him to the limit of his endurance. Mr. Hanna was not slow to perceive how much assistance Mr. Roosevelt might be to him in carrying the Northwestern States. It was the Republicans of this region who had been most stirred by the war and most clamorous for Mr. Roosevelt's nomination.

Hence, while the Vice-Presidential candidate stumped the whole country, the emphasis of his canvass was given to the West. He was by far the most prominent Republican speaker during the campaign, and made a substantial contribution to the decisive nature of the Republican triumph. More so than any other Vice-President who became President, his services gave him a certain subordinate claim on the major office.

In spite of Mr. Hanna's confidence he had some bad moments during the campaign. In the beginning there was too much of a disposition among the Republicans to take victory for granted; and the manager had to exert himself unnecessarily in order to put enough energy into his associates. He was continually complaining that not he, but General Apathy, was running the campaign. The earlier period of overconfidence was succeeded by a slump, particularly among business men. Many of them could not dismiss the idea of the dire consequences of Mr. Bryan's election, and until the threat was removed the process of business expansion ceased. Trade was slack during the summer and fall. Many laborers were out of employment and many dinner-pails were empty. Certain Republicans became alarmed at the outlook. They wrote to Mr. Hanna, anxiously telling about the number of former McKinley votes which were being transferred to Bryan, and recommending the most strenuous efforts. But Mr. Hanna was never really alarmed. His confidence was based on the results of the most careful canvasses made in doubtful states. But, of course, he continued to take every precaution. He used all his influence among the manufacturers to get them to keep as many men as possible on their pay-rolls, until business revived after the election. He personally interfered to put an end to an embarrassing strike in the anthracite coal regions of Pennsylvania. In these and other ways his personal power over business was used for the benefit of the ticket. Until the end he never fully betrayed how confident he felt. His own tour through the Northwest late in October was proof positive that he was convinced of Republican victory in the East and the Middle West.

Two of the most important incidents of the campaign from Mr. Hanna's personal point of view involved his relations with the President, and they must be told in some detail. The first concerns a matter of campaign methods. In it Mr. McKinley's action was irreproachable, but his manner was such that one can hardly blame Mr. Hanna for being annoyed. On August 3, he wrote the following letter to the President: —

"MY DEAR MR. PRESIDENT: —

"Chairman Odell has been talking with me with reference to two matters which seem to be of very great importance to this state.

"The first is the discrimination against the Brooklyn Navy Yard with the consequent laying off of men. This means, in addition to the voters themselves, that the tradesmen and others over there are inclined to believe that Brooklyn is not getting its share of the work. Mr. Odell informs me that the work is being sent to the Boston Navy Yard, where there is a lack of men to work, while here men are being discharged. He also tells me that he has wired you concerning it, and he believes it to be very important, as it means the loss of several hundred votes in that particular direction.

"Another matter in which he is interested is the employment of men at Iowa Island on the Hudson River, where a man by the name of Dugan, Sergeant Dugan, is in charge. He has employed Democrats, and in one instance has contemptuously thrown aside a letter of recommendation from the member of Congress from that district.

"Very truly yours,
"M. A. HANNA."

Some days later Mr. Hanna received the following answer to his complaints: —

PERSONAL
"DEAR SENATOR HANNA: —

"Mr. Dawes has just called here and presented to me your letter of August 3d addressed to me and one of the same date addressed to him.

"I am sure when you know the facts you will have no reason for criticism or complaint. Mr. Odell telegraphed me with reference to the Brooklyn Navy Yard. I at once communicated with Secretary Long and received a most satisfactory reply, a copy of which I enclose. It would not be right, and I am sure you would not have the Department employ men at the Navy Yard who are not needed, nor would you have work done there which could be best done at some other Navy Yard in the country.

"With reference to the letter of Mr. Litchman which you forward, addressed to you, complaining that an order had been issued by the Secretary of the Treasury forbidding travel on the part of any of the employees of that Department, unless the order for travel is given by the Secretary or Assistant Secretary and signed by the same, it would seem to me that this is a wise safeguard. Surely there should be no travel expense paid by the Government which is not for the public service, and I am absolutely and totally opposed to any use of the public money for travel or any other expense for party interests; and in this sentiment I know you share.

"As to the conduct of Sergeant Dugan at Iona Island on the Hudson, referred to, I know nothing about it, but will at once make an investigation. If he is using his office for the appointment of Democrats for party purposes, he shall be called to account. This is a time when every effort will be made to have the administration do questionable things. It is a period of great temptation, just the sort that will require the highest courage to meet and resist. If elected I have to live with the administration for four years. I do not want to feel that any improper or questionable methods have been employed to reach the place, and you must continue, as you have always done, to stand against unreasonable exactions, which are so common at a time like the present.

" Very sincerely yours,
(Signed) "WILLIAM McKINLEY."

After Mr. Hanna had read the foregoing letter he threw it on the floor in great irritation; and since apparently the President's position was unassailable, the cause of his irritation needs some explanation. In requesting that during a campaign employees of the government should not be discharged and the distribution of departmental work arranged so as to hurt the canvass of the party in power, Mr. Hanna was only doing what previous Chairmen of the National Committee had done. Local campaign managers were continually making demands of that kind on the Committee, and the Committee had been accustomed to pay too much attention to them. In the same way it had been customary for certain employees of the Treasury department to "travel" in the interest of the party in power, although when they travelled their expenses, so I am informed, were paid not by the government but by the National Committee. Neither of these practices can be defended, and Mr. McKinley in repudiating them was contributing, as he did in so many other instances, towards the establishment of higher administrative standards. Usually the President and Mr. Hanna agreed in not allowing political considerations any more weight than could be helped in the conduct of government business; but pursued as he was by the demands of local committees and leaders, and responsible as he was for Republican success, Mr. Hanna was inclined to yield more frequently than was the President himself. When such cases arose, Mr. McKinley's action in refusing indefensible demands was often admitted by Mr. Hanna to be as much for his own protection as for the President's.

What aroused his irritation in this particular instance was not so much the fact of Mr. McKinley's refusal as its form. The President's letter had been written with more than usual care and had been copied for the White House file, thus becoming a matter of public record. Mr. Hanna apparently believed that the form of the letter and the necessary publicity attached to it was prompted in the President by a desire to secure full public credit for his action — even if such credit were obtained somewhat at his friend's expense. As Mr. Hanna put it, the letter had been written as much for the President's biography as for the immediate occasion. No doubt it is true that Mr. McKinley throughout his official career kept his biographer a good deal in mind; but it is no less true that he had in the present instance a valid reason for giving his refusal official publicity. He thereby established an authentic precedent, which might help to emancipate both himself and his successors from similar demands.

Later in the campaign another incident occurred which also provoked in Mr. Hanna a temporary resentment. Throughout the whole canvass there had been lively demands on the part of various state committees for Mr. Hanna's services as a stump speaker. He had in the past made very few speeches outside of Ohio, while at the same time the gradually increasing effect of his public personality had stimulated popular curiosity about him. Republican audiences wanted to hear him. For a long time he refused on the ground that he had too much to do at Committee headquarters, but towards the fall he began to yield. He spoke once in Chicago about the middle of September, once in New York ten days later, and he made an excursion to Indiana for the benefit of a Congressional candidate, Mr. C. B. Landis. After he had once yielded it became more difficult to refuse other requests. The Committees of South Dakota and Nebraska were particularly clamorous for a short stumping tour which should include their states. After careful consideration Mr. Hanna consented to go.

He had several reasons for consenting to make this particular trip. The general situation was well in hand; in his opinion Republican success assured. When in fair health he enjoyed stumping, and he looked forward to the tour as an exhilarating vacation from the pressure of office detail. His great object throughout the campaign had been to make, as we have seen, conquests in the strong Bryan states west of the Mississippi; and out of all of this district Nebraska and South Dakota were the two states in which he was working hardest to make a good showing. Inasmuch as Nebraska was Mr. Bryan's own state, its conquest would add a peculiar relish to the approaching victory. South Dakota was represented in the Senate by Richard F. Pettigrew — who had been elected as a Republican but had bolted on the silver issue. Mr. Hanna had a special reason for wishing to defeat him, because of the personal attack which he had made upon Mr. Hanna in the Senate. The local committee assured Mr. Hanna that, if only he would go to South Dakota, he would do more to defeat Pettigrew than a cohort of ordinary speakers. So the tour was arranged. While the project was under consideration, most of Mr. Hanna's friends and associates advised against it. Several members of the National Committee opposed it warmly, and a number of the closest friends outside of the Committee warned him that he was making a mistake. They urged that he was not a professional campaigner, that his selection of South Dakota would look like the persecution of Mr. Pettigrew by the most powerful man in the Republican party and would react in that gentleman's favor, and that he had better keep out of the hot and critical fight which was being made in those particular states.

After the decision was made the President himself decided to interfere. One day the Postmaster-General, Mr. Charles Emory Smith, turned up in Chicago, and sought an interview with Mr. Hanna. He began in a somewhat indirect way to develop the reasons against the proposed Northwestern tour, dwelling particularly on the danger of personal violence. In pressing these arguments he claimed to be expressing the opinion of several other members of the Cabinet. But his manner implied that there was something behind the protest; and finally Mr. Hanna became impatient and asked him point blank, "The President sent you, didn't he?" When Mr. Smith acknowledged that he was an emissary of the President, Mr. Hanna answered (according to an account given immediately after the incident to an intimate friend), "Return to Washington and tell the President that God hates a coward," — a sentence which has a familiar ring, but which the reader may feel confident was not uttered for the benefit of Mr. Hanna's biography.

Mr. Hanna was exasperated at this interference with his personal plans and his management of the campaign. He was a quick-tempered man, and under the influence of high feeling contemplated courses of action which his sober judgment could not approve. In his anger he even considered for a moment the sending in of his resignation; but his head was too cool not to prevent the commission of such a mistake. The course on which he decided was to justify his own judgment by making his stumping tour a success.

His lively resentment is to be explained partly on other than obvious grounds. Of course he did not like to have his judgment impeached in relation to a very important piece of campaign business. He had decided upon the trip only after considering fully and patiently adverse opinions. The decision for or against was a matter which lay absolutely within his discretion as campaign manager. But this formal protest from Washington indicated, not merely distrust of his judgment, but a fear of the impression which Mr. Hanna would make on his audiences. It indicated a wish to keep his personality out of the campaign and away from the people; and in considering its meaning Mr. Hanna could not help connecting it with Mr. McKinley's hesitation in asking him to remain at the head of the National Committee. He and the President expected opposite results from his appearance on the stump. Nowhere in the country had Mr. Hanna been more abused than by the "Populist" orators of the Northwest. He proposed by means of the trip to counteract the effect of this abuse, whereas the President apparently feared that his public appearance would confirm rather than confound the diatribes of his enemies. Manifestly Mr. Hanna could not submit to such a limitation of the range of his political action without implicitly circumscribing his own subsequent political career. The question fundamentally was whether his appearance so conspicuously on the stump would weaken the ticket or contribute to its election. He believed that he could both set himself right with the people of the Northwest and make votes. It hurt and angered him that so many leading Republicans, including his old friend the President, held to the opposite opinion. He determined to vindicate by the results his own judgment, and thereby to increase his own personal political prestige.

The tour was carefully planned. Instead of aiming directly for South Dakota and Nebraska, he made dates also in Wisconsin, Minnesota and Iowa, so that his excursions into the states on which he particularly desired to exert influence would not look like a special attack on any individual. It was to occupy a week all together, of which two days were spent in South Dakota. He was accompanied by a considerable suite. His own car contained the two speakers who were to assist him on the stump, his old campaign comrade, Senator William P. Frye, Mr. Victor Dolliver, brother of the late Senator Dolliver of Iowa and his private secretary, Mr. Elmer Dover. In the newspaper car there were representatives of the Associated Press, the Scripps-McRae League, the Minneapolis *Journal*, the Chicago *Tribune*, *Times-Herald*, *Record*, *Inter-Ocean*, and an official stenographer. The rest of the train consisted of a diner, a reception car for the Committees and a baggage car. An immense territory was covered in a short time because the train was given the right of way over all other trains.

Senator Frye had prepared two speeches, one of which took over an hour to deliver and the other about forty-five minutes. Mr. Dolliver also had brought two speeches in his grip, one of which was very short for breathless stops and the other an elastic harangue which could be stretched from fifteen to thirty minutes. Wherever they spoke they made one of their two speeches, and after the first day the correspondents ceased to report them. Mr. Hanna made seventy-two speeches, varying between five minutes and an hour in length, and no two of them were alike.

Throughout the tour Mr. Hanna was extraordinarily and continuously successful in exciting popular interest. Two years before President McKinley had visited South Dakota, in order to welcome some soldiers returning from the Philippines. He had drawn the biggest crowds in the history of the state. Mr. Hanna's crowds were anywhere from about one and one-half times to twice as large as Mr. McKinley's. They were larger also than those which had greeted Mr. Roosevelt in the same district a few weeks earlier. At seven o'clock in the morning the train would stop at a station where one could see no more than half a dozen houses, yet there would be a congregation of three hundred people to hear Mr. Hanna speak. Farmers in the neighborhood had started at midnight and had driven many miles, in order to be at the station when the train arrived. At Sioux Falls, as well as at the larger places, a crowd three times as large as the population of the town gathered at the meeting.

They were all practically out-of-door meetings, except those held during the evenings in the big towns. In South Dakota the Populist Legislature had passed a law a few years before prohibiting political gatherings which were addressed from the tail-end of railway cars. Nor could such assemblies be held within two hundred feet of the railway track. The object of this discriminating use of the police power was to enable the Populist party to campaign on even terms with the Democrats and Republicans. The Populists could not afford the political luxury of special trains. The consequence was that the wayside meetings in South Dakota were all held at some distance from the tracks. The Committee would have a carriage at the station and would drive the Senator to a platform, situated at a strictly legal distance from the tracks, where a local spellbinder would be holding the crowd together. Mr. Hanna would speak for a few moments, the whistle would blow, cutting short his eloquence, and he would be hurried back to the train.

The crowds were not only large, they were almost always respectful and attentive, and they were often enthusiastic. Of course he was interrupted and heckled, but such interruptions usually helped him with the audience. A public speaker with a bold, familiar and winning personality like Mr. Hanna's can always get the better of a heckler — provided he is not irritated and disconcerted by the interruption and can make a ready and plausible retort. Mr. Hanna always gave his annoyers a fair chance, and he was never disconcerted, because he was never making a set speech. He had at his disposal a fund of rough pleasantry which, while it often reads clumsy and even coarse, was received with gusto by his boisterous audiences.

A few instances may be given of the way he met these emergencies. In one small town he was introduced by an abject chairman as a "Joshua, who, if he wanted to, could command the sun to stand still." To allow such a silly adulation to stand unnoticed might be dangerous. Mr. Hanna in opening his speech said that the only suns he would like to command would be the sons of guns of Populists and honest Democrats to vote for McKinley. Its author is not to be congratulated on the deftness of this sally. It is given not because it was happy, but because it was clumsy yet effective. It at once set him right before the audience as, not a strange or remote animal, but as one of themselves. All the correspondents agree that he thereby captured the crowd and kept it with him. He was in a little better form at another place, when in beginning his speech, he said that he was not a politician. "Mark Hanna not a politician!" shouted a scornful voice in the audience. "No, I am not a politician, because I don't know how to tell you what is not so"—a retort which also proved to be a success and enabled him to go ahead with the sympathy of his audience.

At Auburn in Nebraska, about 2500 people had assembled

around a platform, from which Mr. Hanna was speaking. The platform was a flimsy structure, and it broke down under the weight of the men and boys who were trying to clamber on it. It looked like a serious business, for some fifty people had fallen about six feet and were struggling to free themselves from one another and from the débris. "Is Hanna hurt?" "How is Hanna?" shouted the spectators; and there was danger of a panic. Just then his body emerged from the confused mass; there was a twinkle in his eye and his smile was broader than usual. Holding up his hand to command silence, he cried: "It's all right. No one is hurt. We were just giving you a demonstration of what is going to happen to the Democratic party. This must have been a Democratic platform"—at which the crowd cheered vociferously.

Another incident which proved to be popular in the newspapers also occurred in Nebraska. Just outside Weeping Water a stop was made by the engineer for the purpose of permitting Mr. Hanna to shave before his night meeting in Omaha. The photographer of the Omaha *Bee* took advantage of the opportunity to secure a picture of Senator Hanna and his party. Just as the Senator was about to be photographed alone, the engineer, grimy with coal and grease, sauntered up to see what was going on. "Here, you are just the man I want," said Mr. Hanna, grasping the engineer by the arm and drawing him into the field of the lens. "We are both engineers, I run the Republican party and you run me." "Well! I guess I've got you faded then, Senator," said the engineer, with a grin, as the camera clicked. The picture of the "two engineers" was reproduced extensively at the time and certainly enabled a good many people to understand one of them somewhat better.

Throughout the whole of the tour he never once mentioned Senator Pettigrew's name in public. But although he was discreet enough to avoid a personal attack on the man against whom he had a personal grudge, he was far from avoiding all personalities. He could not do so, because his own personality was being made an issue, and because the object of the trip was to convert precisely that personal issue into a source of strength to the ticket. That he succeeded is indicated by the following curious fact. One of the peculiarities of the tour was the large number of school children who turned out to see and hear him. At Winside in Nebraska this was especially the case, in spite of an immense placard nailed to a telegraph pole, which screamed an awful warning : —

POPULIST FARMERS,
BEWARE ! ! !
CHAIN YOUR CHILDREN TO YOURSELVES
OR
PUT THEM UNDER THE BED.

MARK HANNA IS IN TOWN

In his speech at Lincoln, Nebraska, he turned on Mr. Bryan. The Democratic candidate had recently declared that the Republicans were raising an enormous corruption fund, with which they were going to intimidate laboring men, bribe election judges and purchase votes. This is the way in which Mr. Hanna dealt with the charge. He said: —

"In regard to that statement, which I have just read, I want to hurl it back in his teeth and tell him it is as false as hell. [Applause.] When it comes to personalities I am willing to stand before the American people on my record as a business man. I have been in business forty years. I employ 6000 men, pay the highest wages, treat the men like men and they all respect me. [Great applause.] When Bryan or any other man charges me in that way — and I am willing to appropriate it all as Chairman of the board of managers of the Republican campaign — I promise as I said to hurl it back and denounce him as a demagog in his own town. [Great applause.] [Continued cheering.] [Voice: 'Hit him again.']"

He went on to say: —

"In 1897, when I had a little singing school down in Ohio, Bryan came down there to help Johnnie McLean defeat me for the Senate. He went across the state, back and forth from one end to the other and through the mining districts, and he told the people of Ohio what a bad man I was. He told the men working in the mines that Hanna was a labor crusher. He forgot that they knew that I was born and always lived in that state, and that my record with organized labor was better than any other man's in that state [applause], because I was the first employer that I know of in the state of Ohio that ever recognized and treated with organized labor. I have done it from that day to this. [Applause.]

"Now I am entitled to tell another story of justification in Mr. Bryan's town. [Voice: 'Tell it to them.'] At the close of that campaign I was at Cincinnati. The meeting was in the great music hall as full as this theatre from top to bottom,— a very intelligent and appreciative audience, I thought, right under the shadow of the Cincinnati *Inquirer*, who had lied like a thief about me every day in the week and kept that Davenport cartoon on the front page of its paper. I was pictured as a bogie man. That was intended to frighten the workingmen away from supporting the members of the legislature that they knew would vote to send me back to the Senate. Bryan had done his work and left the state, and that was the last night in the campaign, and I thought I would make a little statement there for the benefit of those fellows. So I said: 'Now, gentlemen, this campaign is over. As far as my appearance before the public is concerned it is closed, but I want to make one proposition not only to the people of Ohio, but to the people of the United States. Mr. Bryan, who once aspired to be President of the United States, came to Ohio this fall to tell the people in my own state, who had known me since I was a boy, that I was a bad, wicked man, and that I was a labor crusher, which was worse than all. Now I want to make this proposition. If any man who ever worked for me in any capacity can truthfully say that I have ever knowingly done him a wrong or an injustice; that I have failed to pay the highest rate of wages; that I have ever refused to receive in my presence either individually or by committee any man in my employ, whether members of the union or not; that I have ever questioned a man when employing him whether he belonged to a union or not, or discharged him because he belonged to an organization or union; if that can be brought to me and proved, I will resign as Senator tomorrow.' [Applause.]"

The speeches made by Mr. Hanna during this Northwestern trip constituted a serious and an honest contribution to a discussion of the issues of the campaign. Taken as a whole they contain the best and most comprehensive statement which he ever made of his own personal attitude towards the political and economic problems of the day. He addressed his audiences in a tone of earnest conviction, and he argued his case before them candidly and instructively. He had none of the tricks of the ordinary stump speaker, and none of the insincerity and obliquity of the ordinary partisan advocate. He reasoned with his hearers and tried to persuade them to vote the Republican ticket on what seemed to him absolutely sufficient grounds. When he told one audience that he was not a politician, because he did not know how to tell them what was not so, he was speaking the truth. His hearers went away with the impression that he was speaking the truth; and this fact, taken together with his big, imposing, yet engaging personality, accounts for his success.

That the tour was a success from every point of view, all accounts are agreed. The results vindicated his judgment. The campaign in the Northwest obtained as a consequence a greatly increased momentum, which did much to excite contagious confidence and enthusiasm among the Republicans in the neighboring states. By his personal appearance on the stump he had really helped the ticket, and he had placed his own personality in a much more favorable light among an important section of the American people. Indeed, this trip, more than any other single cause, helped to make Mr. Hanna personally popular throughout the West, just as his first stumping tour in Ohio had made him personally popular in his own state. As soon as he became known, the virulence and malignity with which he had been abused reacted in his favor. When he appeared on the platform, the crowd, instead of seeing a monster, found him to be just the kind of a man whom Americans best understand and most heartily like. He was not separated from them by differences of standards and tastes or by any intellectual or professional sophistication. The roughness of much of his public speaking, and its lack of form, which makes it comparatively poor reading, was an essential part of its actual success. He stamped himself on his speeches just as he had stamped himself on his business. His audiences had to pass judgment on the man more than on the message, and the man could not but look good to them.

When he returned to Chicago the campaign was virtually over. Only a little over a week remained, and during that time there was nothing to be done but to gather the fruits of four months of preparation. During the final weeks the different lines of work came to a head precisely as planned. There were no misgivings at Republican headquarters, and the rank and file of the party were made to feel equally confident. The enthusiasm was not as great as it had been during the final week of the previous campaign, but it did not need to be as great. They had been able to conduct an aggressive campaign from a defensive position, not only because their defences were strong, and their resources in men and money were large, but because the attack upon them never developed much impetus. The American people were expansionist in their general attitude, and they were willing to incur the risks and pay the expenses of a policy of national expansion. They were also satisfied with the prospects of continued prosperity, which the reëlection of Mr. McKinley guaranteed; and they were willing to believe that prosperity with the trusts was better than famine without them. So the Republicans won their most overwhelming victory since 1872. McKinley and Roosevelt obtained a plurality of 832,000 over Bryan and a clear majority of 443,000 in a total popular vote of almost 14,000,000. In the North Bryan carried only the mining states of Colorado, Idaho, Montana and Nevada. In South Dakota Richard F. Pettigrew lost his seat in the Senate and was replaced by a Republican. Bryan was beaten in his own state. The Populist agitation, which had so long dominated the agricultural states west of the Mississippi River, was done to death. The Democrats were so weakened and discredited that they ceased for the time being to constitute even an effective opposition. The Republicans had received a clear mandate to govern the country in the interest of business expansion.

CHAPTER XXII

SHIP SUBSIDIES

THE triumphant reëlection of President McKinley consolidated the work with which the political leadership of Mark Hanna was peculiarly, if not exclusively, associated. For the first time since Mr. Cleveland made a serious attack upon the protective tariff in 1887, the business of the country was in all its branches guaranteed at least for a time against the disconcerting effects of inimical political agitation. The election of 1896 had not completely restored confidence, because his previous misfortunes had unstrung the nerves of the average business man, and because, after the Spanish War was over and business began to revive, there loomed up in the near future another disconcerting election. Not until that contest was favorably decided could confidence be entirely restored. So much hinged upon the result that as the first of November approached, business men became more rather than less hesitant and apprehensive. Their relief was correspondingly great when the Republican victory proved to be comprehensive and decisive. All hesitation at once vanished, and there began a period of unprecedented business expansion.

Mark Hanna had labored to bring about this result; and his own personal prestige was substantially enhanced by its appearance. After the election he began to exercise an amount and a kind of political power which has no parallel in American history. The group of causes which, after his appointment to the Senate, had limited his activity and made his influence at Washington somewhat subterranean, had lost their force. The Spanish War was over. The attention of the country was to be fastened for some time on his own favorite subject of political economics. He had passed through his apprenticeship as Senator. He had won the confidence of almost all his colleagues in the Senate and the warm affection of many of them. He was thoroughly established as one of the steering committee of the Upper House. His successful stumping tour during the campaign had increased the area of his personal popularity with the American people. At the same time none of the former ingredients of his effective power had suffered any diminution. In spite of his disagreements with Mr. McKinley before and during the campaign, their relations were never more close and confidential than they were during the early months of 1901. And, of course, the reëlection of Mr. McKinley decidedly increased his influence both with the leading business men of the country and with the local leaders of the Republican party.

Mr. Hanna exercised his power so discreetly that it rarely became a matter of public comment or protest; but occasionally some evidence or expression of it slipped out. One such incident occurred during the short session preceding Mr. McKinley's second inauguration. Certain Democratic Senators were pressing the passage of a bill providing for the immediate construction of a canal from the Atlantic to the Pacific by the Nicaraguan route, but they could accomplish nothing, because the Republican leaders were not ready to act on the matter, until pending negotiations with Great Britain for the abrogation of the Clayton-Bulwer Treaty were concluded. In the midst of the discussion, Senator Clay of Georgia made the following appeal to Mr. Hanna, which reads curiously in the light of the latter's subsequent activity in relation to an interoceanic canal.

"I appeal," said Senator Clay, "to the National Chairman of the party in power to come to the support of the bill providing for the construction of this waterway. Does the distinguished Senator from Ohio recognize that this great waterway is of more importance to the people of the United States and to American commerce than his ship-subsidy scheme? I appeal to the Senator from Ohio because I know the influence which he exerts among his party associates. I realize that a word from him would mean success to this great enterprise. We all know that he largely shapes and molds the policy of his party. We know the influence he has exerted in keeping before the Senate this ship-subsidy scheme, which has consumed so much of the time of the Senate."

It is scarcely necessary to add that this somewhat naïve supplication failed to move the hard heart of Mr. Hanna; but the Senator from Georgia was a true prophet in asserting that a word—albeit a long word—from Mr. Hanna would eventually have much to do with the success of an interoceanic canal.

If Mr. Hanna made no response to the appeal of the Senator from Georgia, it was not because he repudiated some measure of responsibility for the passage of a legislative program. His position, indeed, demanded that he should do what he could to carry out the promises of his party in the matter of legislation, and the position of the party itself made the redemption of such promises more than ever important. Never since the reconstructed Southern States renewed their representation in Congress had the Republican control over all the departments of government been so complete and so secure. Never, apparently, had the party been so thoroughly united on all questions of public policy. Never had it possessed such general confidence in the ability and good faith of its leadership. If partisan responsibility amounted to anything at all, an energetic effort must be made to pass the legislation to which the party was pledged. Mr. Hanna's complex position as the Congressional representative of the President, as Chairman of the National Committee and as one of the most prominent Senators made it inevitable that he should play a leading part in redeeming such pledges.

The only kind of legislation in which Mr. Hanna could take any lively personal interest would necessarily have for its object the promotion of business activity. That was the cause with which his personal political career was identified, and on behalf of which the Republicans had assumed and retained power. For the most part all that business needed in order to become more prosperous was to be let alone. Existing legislation both national and state was encouraging it in almost every possible way. But there was one branch of American industry and commerce, which was far from prosperous, and which assuredly needed some additional protection on the part of such a solicitous government. The American merchant marine engaged in foreign trade was notoriously decrepit. Over nine-tenths of the imports and exports of the country were carried in vessels which were not built in American shipyards, which did not

MR. HANNA IN 1901

employ American labor, and the foreign owners of which collected their tolls from American merchants. In the absence of some additional legislation this condition was likely to become worse rather than better, because the American either as shipbuilder or operator could not compete on equal terms with foreigners, and particularly with Englishmen and Germans. Unless the government gave to him the same kind of assistance that it gave to the other branches of American industry, the American merchant marine would continue to stagnate.

As early as 1888 the problem of re-creating an American merchant marine had been considered by the Republican leaders. The subsequent platforms of the party had declared in favor of some effective means of restoring the American flag to the high seas. But throughout the whole of this period legislation in regard to the matter was not seriously pressed, because other issues had forced themselves to the front. Now, however, that the Republicans were in full control, and were free to deal with domestic economic problems, it was inevitable that the matter should come up for insistent consideration. They could not have avoided the attempt to pass some kind of a bill, even if Mr. Hanna had not been on hand to urge them on; and Mr. Hanna's personal influence made the attempt the more unavoidable and the more energetic.

Ever since Mr. Hanna had entered public life he had been interested in the revival of the American merchant marine as he had been in no other economic policy. His own business career had been continuously connected with the building and operation of ships, so that he brought to the subject a prolonged and instructive personal experience. When he entered the Senate he was appointed to the Committee on Commerce, partly because he wanted to have a hand in the work of framing the legislation the passage of which had already been approved by the party leaders. The one important measure which he personally introduced was the original Hanna-Frye Subsidy Bill of 1898. It could not be pressed at that time, but he frequently discussed the necessity of such legislation in his speeches on the stump. He was doing his best to create a more vigorous public opinion in its favor throughout the Middle West. That part of the country had never been much interested in the restoration of the American flag to the high seas, and it was not easy to make its audiences listen to arguments in favor of the desired legislation. But the fact that he was risking his popularity in keeping the subject before his constituents did not deter him. His private secretary, Mr. Elmer Dover, states that ship subsidies were the one subject which he persisted in preaching, even when he was boring his audiences and knew that he was boring them.

His lively and insistent interest in ship-subsidy legislation was not, however, due merely to his own personal participation in the upbuilding of American fresh-water shipping. The subject made a strong appeal to him as a matter of national policy. Mr. Hanna had a sound and comprehensive understanding of the principles underlying American economic legislation. He saw that every branch of American industry, agriculture and domestic commerce rested more or less on encouragement by the government, and that such encouragement was granted on the assumption that the public economic interest was most effectually promoted by the stimulation of private enterprise. On this basis a national economic system had been created, the several parts of which were closely connected, and which with one exception included every essential economic activity. The one exception was that of American shipping engaged in foreign trade. He never could understand either why this exception had been allowed to occur or why it was not immediately remedied. It was to him incomprehensible that such an opportunity of employing American capital and labor should be neglected, and that the builders and possible operators of ocean-going ships should not be granted the same encouragement as that which every other essential American economic activity had obtained in one form or another.

In the winter of 1900 and 1901 certain recent developments in the character of American exports gave peculiar pertinence to legislation in aid of American shipping. It was just at this moment that American manufacturers, particularly of metal products, had begun a very successful invasion of the foreign markets. The exports of manufactured articles had increased suddenly and enormously. The prevailing opinion was that certain of them had outgrown the home market, that their productive capacity was far in excess of domestic consumption and that better arrangements must be made to introduce American products abroad. The grouping of many manufacturing plants under one ownership and management was explained and defended as a necessary step in the development of American export trade. It was claimed that the government could contribute substantially to the better organization of the export trade by subsidizing American marine carriers. From this point of view, ship-subsidy legislation became an essential part of a really efficient national economic organization. A government which had encouraged American manufacturers, when they were occupied in selling almost exclusively to the home market, should be all the more ready to supply them with an economic agency which would help them to make their profits out of foreigners.

The decision was reached, consequently, to tackle seriously the question of subsidy legislation during the short session which began on Dec. 1, 1900, and this decision was attributed chiefly to Mr. Hanna. For the first time his leadership became a conspicuous fact in the conduct of the Senate's business. He was not in actual charge of the measure on the floor of the Senate. That duty devolved upon Senator Frye, who was Chairman of the Committee on Commerce. But he was none the less more responsible for the legislative career of the bill than was its floor manager. In Senator's Frye absence he assumed charge of the measure. He frequently intervened in the debate, which occupied a large part of the Senate's time from Dec. 4, 1900, to Feb. 18, 1901. On December 13 he made on behalf of the bill the first long speech of his career as Senator — a speech which was generally acknowledged to be a credit to its author and a very able presentation of his side of the case. At the same time he was actively canvassing among his colleagues, in order to find out how they would vote; and he was using his influence all over the country to create a more widespread public opinion in favor of the proposed legislation.

Notwithstanding the apparently vigorous attempt made to pass a subsidy bill during the short session, it is improbable that its advocates really intended to do more than concentrate public attention on their legislative enterprise. Even if they could have brought the bill to a vote in the Senate, there was no time to force it through the House in the last weeks of a Congressional session. As a matter of fact they were powerless even to secure a vote on it in the Senate. The opposition of the Democrats was furious and determined. They had decided that it should not be voted upon at that session, and the rules of the Senate permitted them to discuss the measure at sufficient length to kill it. The Republican leaders must have realized their powerlessness. In pressing the bill they must have been making a demonstration in force, preparatory to a better sustained movement under the more favorable conditions of the ensuing long session.

Just as soon as the fifty-seventh Congress assembled on Dec. 1, 1901, a renewed attempt was made in the Senate to pass a subsidy bill differing in certain essential respects from the former measure. Its discussion was begun on March 3, 1902, and it occupied the entire time of the Senate until March 17, when a vote was obtained. During this second debate Mr. Hanna played, if anything, an even more important part than he had the year before. He did not, indeed, make any long set speech on behalf of the bill, but he made a number of extemporaneous statements in reference to particular phases of the discussion; and superficially he was more interested in the measure and more responsible for it than was the Chairman of the Committee.

The vote taken on March 17 was favorable to the bill. There were forty-two Senators recorded in its favor and only thirty-two in opposition — its opponents including four such good Republicans as Senators Spooner, Allison, Dolliver and Proctor. It was then sent to the House, but although the session was still young, it was never voted on by that body. The attempt to stimulate the building and operation of American ships in foreign trade consequently failed; and its failure under the circumstances must have been due to the influence of very powerful opposing currents of public opinion. At a period when the Republican party was in full control of the government and was powerfully organized for united action, its most prominent leaders were unable to secure the acceptance of a measure which, whatever its faults, was an honest and carefully considered attempt to meet an apparent public need and redeem a party pledge. The failure was, moreover, not due to the Democratic minority, which had far less power under the rules of the House than it had under the rules of the Senate. It was due chiefly to the impossibility of creating much interest in the object of the bill among Middle Western Republicans. They failed to see how the interests of their constituents would be helped by subsidy legislation; and in the absence of any local benefit they did not want to incur the unpopularity which might result from the actual appropriation of national funds for the benefit of a particular industry.

If the attempt to pass the bill had been successful, I should have been obliged to consider in detail its provisions, its merits and its consequences. But the ultimate failure of the attempt makes it unnecessary to discuss the measure, except in relation to the motives and ideas which induced Mr. Hanna so enthusiastically and tenaciously to favor it. Why he attached so much importance to it has already been indicated in a general way; but it is desirable to explain somewhat more in detail and partly in his own words his personal attitude towards the matter. Its importance in his eyes will seem either blind or sinister to people who object on principle to any attempt at the promotion of a public interest by the subsidizing and encouragement of private interests. But Mr. Hanna never addressed his arguments to people of such opinions. The system to which he had been accustomed all his life, and which determined all his own economic ideas was one which had identified the public interest with the encouragement of every phase of private productive enterprise. It had deliberately sought to bestow upon the farmers, the manufacturers, the miners, the cattlemen, the timbermen, the railroads and corporations of all kinds direct or indirect subsidies. Such had been the national economic policy since the Civil War. It was the system actually in existence, and it seemed to him really national in its scope, in its meaning and in the distribution of its benefits.

He is continually arguing that the adoption of some measure which would restore American shipping to the high seas is a necessary part of this national economic policy. Considering the protection which the government extended to other industries, it was unjust as well as unwise that similar encouragement should be denied to American shipping engaged in foreign trade; and there were many ways in which the national economic interests were really endangered thereby. A war between Germany and England might work upon the large percentage of our foreign commerce carried under the flags of those powers, a serious injury which the government of the United States would be powerless to avert. The efficiency of the American navy and its supplies of men and auxiliary ships depended on the existence of a flourishing merchant marine. In these and other similar respects the encouragement of American shipping was merely a political precaution demanded by the necessities of general national policy; but it was equally demanded by the prevailing conditions of international commercial warfare. All the other great trading nations had built up a merchant marine partly for the sake of stimulating their export trade. American merchants and manufacturers were hampered by the lack of such an engine, and the benefit of supplying the need would be out of all proportion to its actual cost.

"The whole question," he wrote in an article in the *National Magazine* for January, 1901, "resolves itself into this: If the American people can be brought to understand the need and value of an American mercantile marine to the nation, they will support a bill which makes provisions for just such an accomplishment. The benefit aimed at is for the nation. To secure that benefit for the nation, incidentally certain individuals — those willing to risk their capital in American-built ships in our foreign trade — will be safeguarded against loss in competition with foreign ships. This result, it cannot be said too emphatically, will utterly fail of accomplishment unless a very substantial reduction is brought about in the rates of freight charged for the carriage of our exports and imports, because only by reducing rates can American ships expect to wrest any of the business from their foreign competitors. The reduction in rates will, it is believed, several times repay the American people for whatever expenditure the government may make directly to the beneficiaries of the bill." Again in his speech in favor of the bill, delivered on Dec. 13, 1900, he said:

"This question is broader than can be written in the lines of the bill. It will be widespread in its benefits. It is not aimed at any class or any particular industry. It is one of those measures whose influence will permeate every industry and every class in the length and breadth of the United States. When I am told that the people of the interior of this country are not interested in the shipping question, I say it is not true in fact. Every man, no matter what his vocation in life, is interested and will be benefited directly or indirectly, because you cannot create an industry like this, requiring first the development of our raw materials and then the construction of ships which open up the markets of the world and give greater opportunities to our merchants and manufacturers, without benefiting every industry and every line of business."

These words of Senator Hanna's were uttered in absolute good faith. He sincerely believed that in promoting legislation which in his opinion would restore the American flag to the high seas, he was making an essential contribution to a constructive national business policy. He could not understand why so many Republicans who were willing to subsidize manufacturers with high protective rates should shrink from granting to the shipping industry similar encouragement. He himself knew that there was no essential difference between paying the money directly out of the Treasury and collecting it indirectly from the consumers — except perhaps that the second method was more costly. Yet certain Republicans and protectionist Democrats talked as if the two cases were different, and as if the only object of the ship-subsidy bill was to make a gift of the people's money to a group of wealthy men interested in ocean transportation. An accusation of this kind was continually being flung at his head by the Democrats. These charges of bad faith and equivocal motives aroused in Mr. Hanna an honest indignation, and on one occasion, Feb. 15, 1901, he answered the taunts with dignity and self-restraint. I quote his short speech on that occasion almost in full : —

"Mr. President, I have listened patiently for days to this discussion, and have listened with astonishment to many of the reckless statements which have been made by the opponents of this bill, statements which cannot be borne out by facts and which are intended to place before the country a misconception of the merits of this measure. I have known perfectly well of the intended opposition to defeat the measure. I have heard insinuations with reference to men who have been connected with the measure in this body and out of it which made me blush, and I resent them. I have heard the scolding from our friend from Colorado [Mr. Teller]. But, Mr. President, we are not children. We believe when we present a measure on the floor of this Senate and advocate it, whether as a Republican measure or simply as a public measure, that we are entitled at least to be considered as honest in our purpose. From the time that this bill was introduced until this hour the effort I have made to secure its enactment into law has been for the purpose of accomplishing what it has been stated it would accomplish — to upbuild the merchant marine of the United States and to better the conditions of the people.

"I do not claim to have any greater technical or general knowledge than the average of men, but I claim to have some knowledge, as the result of experience, that leads me to make certain deductions as to economic measures; and when I advocate this measure from my seat in this Senate I think I should have the same right and the same consideration at the hands of this body that I am willing to grant to any other Senator; that I am sincere and honest in my convictions, and that I am advocating the measure, not for the purpose, as is claimed here, of looting the Treasury of the United States, but for advancing the material interests of the people of the United States.

"Mr. President, as far as I am concerned as one of the advocates of this shipping bill, after having made this statement I propose to occupy the same position from now until the 4th of March that I have occupied from the beginning — to demand at the hands of this body fair treatment for an honest measure with an honest intent; and I do not propose to be side-tracked by any Senator from the other side of the Chamber. I myself will decide when I will go on the side-track.

"For my part I have tried to be fair, and even liberal, to the other side; and I am met with the taunt, almost descending to personality, that the purposes of those who are advocating this measure is to pay back subscriptions to political campaign funds, to pay political debts, and that the Republican party is the only party that descends to such political measures — an insinuation that, by virtue of my position as Chairman of the National Republican Committee, I am responsible for this legislation here in order to make recompense to those who, you say, have contributed to the campaign fund of the Republican party. Is that a part of an economic question to be discussed in this body? Is that what you call fair treatment in legislation?

"Mr. President, as I have said in the beginning, my interest in this measure is because I believe it to be for the interests of the people of this country. I believe that it means the upbuilding of a new industry, a kindred industry to those industries which have made this country great and prosperous. It means another step in the direction of development, not confined to section or to party, but for the good of the whole country."

In conclusion Mr. Hanna turned upon his critics, and accused them of passing without a murmur a river and harbor bill containing provisions which made the ship-subsidy bill by comparison look white and innocent. Whether any particular measure for the encouragement of trade was called a looting of the Treasury or a piece of constructive economic legislation depended upon the number of Congressional districts which it happened to benefit. I have read a great deal of Mr. Hanna's private correspondence with the ship-builders and operators who would have benefited from the operation of the subsidy bill, and I failed to discover any intimation that the bill was not framed in good faith to accomplish its ostensible object. Whether, as a matter of fact, it would have done so without any benefit to private interests, beyond the amount absolutely necessary to accomplish the desired object, is a question upon which none but an expert can pass. In the course of the debate Senator Spooner made some shrewd criticisms of the details of both the bills, which might well have caused doubts in the minds of his hearers. Such doubts are bound to arise whenever the people actually benefited by any attempt to encourage a private industry have a great deal to say about the terms of its encouragement. Economic legislation which seeks to accomplish a constructive business purpose by the direct or indirect subsidizing of private interests should be framed, as it is in Germany, by experts whose opinions cannot be biassed by any prospect of personal advantage. Our American practice had, however, been entirely different. With some few exceptions all American economic legislation before 1900 was practically dictated by its beneficiaries. In allowing its beneficiaries to have a good deal to say about the ship-subsidy bill

Mr. Hanna and his associates were following a long-established precedent. But the precedent was based upon the idea that the public and private interests involved were substantially identical. Mr. Hanna himself believed them to be substantially identical; and when the subsidy legislation failed it was his honest opinion that a wise and necessary measure for promoting the expansion of American commerce had been killed by cowardice and sectional prejudice.

CHAPTER XXIII

THE DEATH OF PRESIDENT MCKINLEY

IN the preceding chapter the fate of the attempt to revive American shipping engaged in foreign trade has been followed to the end, although the end did not take place until after the occurrence of many other extremely important incidents in Mr. Hanna's life. In the meantime Mr. McKinley's second inauguration had taken place amid much jubilation and personal and party congratulations. Mr. Hanna had charge of the ceremony, and during its progress was, according to the newspapers, almost as much its hero as was the President himself. But the man who, according to his Western flatterer, could make the sun stand still could not prevent the rain from falling. The combined ceremony and festivity was marred by the usual foul weather of early March.

Local politics in Cleveland occupied much of his time during the spring of 1901. At the municipal election held in April Tom Johnson was elected Mayor of Cleveland for the first time by a substantial majority over the Republican candidate. Mr. Johnson continued to be both Mayor of Cleveland and a thorn in the flesh to Mr. Hanna for the next three years. With all his talent for political management he never succeeded in keeping the Republicans in control of his own city—and that in spite of the fact that the city usually went Republican at national elections. His street railroad interests were undoubtedly a serious embarrassment to him in his handling of the local political situation, and prevented him from acting or from appearing to act as disinterestedly as he did in state and national politics.

Senator Hanna himself was inclined to attribute the ill success of the local Republican organization chiefly to one cause. Since 1886, as we have seen, the Republicans of Cuyahoga County had been nominating their candidates for office under the so-called Crawford County system of direct primaries. The system in its operation had undoubtedly handicapped the local machine, when it attempted to dictate the party nominees, but it had also encouraged factional quarrels, weakened the organization's fighting power, and produced a lot of second-rate candidates. Mr. Hanna's own opinion of its effects and defects is expressed in a speech made by him to the Tippecanoe and other Republican clubs on May 11, 1901. He said:—

"I have watched very closely the workings of these two plans. As to the Crawford County plan, I have found that its application in the rural districts has resulted very successfully, but in the large cities we must judge theory by practice. The arguments in favor of the convention plan are conclusive. In the cities it is impossible to nominate the best candidates by the direct vote plan. The Crawford County plan does defeat the will of the majority. It has done so time and time again.

"The primaries in the city of Cleveland last spring, and in fact for several years, have not been representative of the Republican vote. An enrollment of Republican voters is advocated, but even then we are liable to be imposed upon. There are two things of the utmost importance, which cannot be accomplished under the Crawford County plan—the distribution of candidates, geographically; also the proper recognition of nationalities. Both are very important. The good men of all nationalities should have an opportunity, and they do not have it under the Crawford County plan. Only in a deliberative body, such as a convention, are they given consideration. These impressions come from close observation. Change the plan now, and we will change the trend of things in Cuyahoga County." Not even Senator Hanna's influence, however, sufficed to make Cleveland Republicans go back to the convention system of nominations. In a democracy nothing is more difficult than to withdraw from the people any power which they have once exercised.

While Mr. Hanna was meeting with stumbling blocks in Cleveland, the Republicans in the state accepted his leadership without question. The State Convention assembled in Columbus on June 25, and in it Mr. Hanna was the dominating influence. It is a rule in the politics of Ohio that one good term as Governor deserves another. Mr. George K. Nash had served satisfactorily for two years, and there was no question about his renomination. Senator Foraker was as usual the orator of the occasion, and not even Mr. McKinley's warmest friend could have extolled the administration in more glowing terms. Mr. Hanna may have chafed at times, because he was obliged to coöperate in public politics with a man with whom he was on such bad terms in private, but if so, he may have been consoled, because of the part which Mr. Foraker was obliged to play on formal occasions as official praise-monger for the administration. Mr. Hanna followed Senator Foraker, and in his speech brought the gospel of prosperity down to date. Now that it had really come, how was it to be continued? Manifestly by continuing to support the party who had brought it about. Only in this way could the newly-made confidence be retained.

"The foundation of prosperity is confidence—confidence in the future. The business man, the large operator, if he does business but for to-day and to-morrow only considers to-day and to-morrow. If he is limited to that space of action he governs his actions accordingly, and he only operates for a few hours in advance because he knows not what the future may bring forth. Now, I made it as a statement as infallible as the laws of nature that, in order to sustain present conditions in this country he must have absolute confidence as to what is in store for the future. Therefore, resting upon that foundation of security in our finances, upon the policy which has built us up as a nation, upon the policy which has carried us forward as a progressive nation, the great mass of people will continue to trust those men and that party and adopt it as evidence of security in future operations. It is the operation of that future that makes business. It is the confidence in the future which induces capital to expand and develop and that brings to all classes of labor more work."

As there was no disposition in Ohio to displace the ruling powers, the campaign was not very strenuous. Mr. Hanna himself went on the stump for about ten days just before the election, but he could have spared himself the trouble. The result was a foregone conclusion, if only because of Mr. McKinley's assassination, which had occurred in September. Mr. Nash was reëlected by a plurality of 60,000. The whole Republican state ticket was also elected as well as a safe majority in both Houses of the Legislature—thus assuring Mr. Foraker a second term in the Senate.

During the summer a very good-looking and gay little exposition was being held in Buffalo for the sake ostensibly of celebrating the great fact or cause of Pan-Americanism. President McKinley had been scheduled to pay Buffalo a visit early in September, and he decided to take the opportunity of making a speech which would outline the future policy of the administration. The recent increase in the American exports of manufactured goods had convinced him that the country should enter upon a more liberal commercial policy—one which would promote exports from this country by allowing other countries increasing opportunities of trading in the markets of the United States. According to his usual habit he carefully prepared a speech along the foregoing lines; and just before going to Buffalo he met Mr. Hanna by appointment and they discussed fully the text of the proposed address. The speech was delivered on September 5, and was received with an outburst of approval from practically the entire country.

About four o'clock on the afternoon of the following day, during a popular reception held in one of the Exposition buildings, President McKinley was shot by a demented anarchist. The wound was serious, and all of Mr. McKinley's friends and official family hurried to Buffalo. Among them was Mr. Hanna. There was, of course, nothing to do but wait; and it looked, in the beginning, as if the waiting would not be in vain. The wounded man appeared to be recovering. After several days of apparently uninterrupted progress on the part of the patient, the group of secretaries and friends assembled in Buffalo began to disperse. Mr. Hanna finally decided that he himself could risk a brief absence. The national encampment of the Grand Army of the Republic was being held in Cleveland during the coming week. His attendance had been promised. He wanted to keep his engagement, because he had just been elected a member of the organization, and a political leader always desires to stand well with the Grand Army.

After making up his mind to risk a short absence, he went to the doctors in attendance on the President, and told them that he was going over to Cleveland to keep an engagement with the Grand Army. He asked them for their very best judgment as to Mr. McKinley's condition so that he could give to his audience absolutely authentic news about their President's and comrade's chances of life. The doctors authorized him to say that Mr. McKinley had passed the critical point of his illness and would live. So he went to Cleveland with a light heart and made his speech, part of which has already been quoted in another connection. Before going on the platform he received by telegraph from the President's secretary, Mr. Cortelyou, a final confirmation of the news—which was announced to the audience and which was received with the liveliest expressions of relief and joy. Few Presidents of the United States have been more sincerely and generally liked than was Mr. McKinley. A committee of Cleveland citizens was formed, which organized and held a meeting of thanksgiving for the President's promised recovery.

That same night, however, Mr. Hanna, who had been exhausted by the strain and fatigues of the last week, was awakened at 2 A. M. by a message from Buffalo that Mr. McKinley's condition had suddenly taken a turn for the worse. By four o'clock he was on his way back to Buffalo in a special train, and when he reached there he found the President's condition actually critical. On the evening of that same day, when the doctors realized that death was a matter only of a few hours, a number of relatives and friends, who were waiting in Mr. John G. Milburn's house, were allowed to have a last look at the dying man. First Mrs. McKinley was shown in, then Abner McKinley, Justice Day and Mr. Hanna. The President was unconscious and barely alive. On no other occasion during the illness was Mr. Hanna allowed to see him. Some days before, the President had inquired: "Is Mark there?" and had been told of his friend's attendance but of the impossibility of any interview. Mr. Hanna was very much touched by this evidence of the sufferer's interest. Although a self-contained man, he utterly broke down after his visit to the sick room and cried like a child.

With almost a dozen other relatives and friends, Mr. Hanna waited in the Milburn library from seven o'clock in the evening until the President's death was announced, almost seven hours later. Early in the night he called to him his secretary, Mr. Dover, Colonel Myron T. Herrick and one or two others, and discussed with them the necessary arrangements for the care and transportation of the body and the funeral. The different parts of the work were divided up among the different members of the party, the necessary coöperation of the railroad officials secured, and all the other details planned. Under such circumstances any action was a relief, and even such painful preparations diminished the distress of the dreadful suspense. About 2 A.M. Mr. Cortelyou announced to the group that death had finally come. Not a word was spoken. They all left the room silently and soon afterwards the house.

The next morning Mr. Hanna arose early, and drove down to the business section of the city. There he interviewed the railroad company's officers, and attended to his share of the necessary arrangements. While returning from the undertaker's he passed the house of Mr. Ansley Wilcox, and noticed in its immediate vicinity an unusual commotion. A number of soldiers, policemen, attendants and by-standers were gathered around the entrance. Suddenly he realized that Mr. Roosevelt had been staying in the house, and that the new President must have been taking the oath of office. Mr. Hanna decided to call. As soon as his presence was announced Mr. Roosevelt invited him in and repeated to him the promise of future policy and behavior which had just been made to the members of the Cabinet. The new President, realizing that he had been elected under the shadow of the dead man, had declared that he proposed to continue unbroken his predecessor's policy and Cabinet. What followed can best be narrated in Mr. Roosevelt's own words.

"In the evening Senator Hanna by arrangement came to call. The dead man had been his closest friend as well as the political leader whom he idolized and whose right hand he himself was. He had been occupying a position of power and influence, because of his joint relationship to the President and Senate, such as no other man in our history whom I can recall ever occupied.

"He had never been very close to me, although of course we had worked heartily together when I was a candidate for Vice-President and he was managing the campaign. But we had never been closely associated, and I do not think that he had at that time felt particularly drawn to me.

"The situation was one in which any small man, any man to whom petty motives appealed, would have been sure to do something which would tend to bring about just such a rift as had always divided from the party leaders in Congress any man coming to the Presidency as I came to it. But Senator Hanna had not a single small trait in his nature. As soon as he called on me, without any beating about the bush, he told me that he had come to say that he would do all in his power to make my administration a success, and that, subject, of course, to my acting as my past career and my words that afternoon gave him the right to expect, he would in all ways endeavor to strengthen and uphold my hands. There was not in his speech a particle of subserviency, no worship of the rising sun. On the contrary, he stated that he wished me to understand that he was in no sense committing himself to favor my nomination when the next Presidential election came on; for that was something the future must decide; but that he would do all he could to make my administration a success and that his own counsel and support within and without the Senate should be mine in the effort to carry out the policies which had been so well begun. I, of course, thanked him and told him that I understood his position perfectly and was grateful for what he had said.

"He made his words good. There were points on which we afterwards differed; but he never permitted himself, as many men even of great strength and high character do permit themselves, to allow his personal disapproval of some one point of the President's policy to lead him into trying to avenge himself by seeking to bring the whole policy to naught. Any one who has had experience in politics knows what a common failing this is. The fact that Senator Hanna never showed the slightest trace of it, and never treated his disagreement with me on some difficult point as any reason for withholding his hearty support on other points, is something which I shall not soon forget.

"Throughout my term as President, until the time of his death, I was in very close relations with him. He was continually at the White House and I frequently went over to breakfast and dinner at his house; while there was no important feature of any of my policies which I did not carefully discuss with him. In the great majority of instances we were able to come to an agreement. I always found that together with his ruggedness, his fearlessness and efficiency he combined entire straightforwardness of character. I never needed to be in doubt as to whether he would carry through a fight or in any way go back on his word. He was emphatically a big man of strong aggressive generous nature."

Because of Mr. Roosevelt's fine pledge to continue the policy of his predecessor, the death of Mr. McKinley and the accession of a new President made at the moment a smaller alteration in the political situation than might have been anticipated. But there remained the terrible wound dealt to Mr. Hanna's personal feelings by the loss of his friend. The strength of his attachment to Mr. McKinley received a striking testimonial, when after his visit to the dying man, he broke down and burst into tears. He was a man of intense feelings, which were rarely, if ever, betrayed in public. Indeed, it seemed almost like a point of honor with him, as with so many men of strong will, not to permit any outward expression of his personal affections. After long separation from relatives, to whom he was and had shown himself to be devotedly attached, he would after their return greet them in a very casual way or not greet them at all. He shrank instinctively from revealing his affections in the ordinary way, not because he was callous or indifferent, but because, perhaps, they were so lively that he could not risk their expression in words. He allowed his actions to speak for him.

His attachment to Mr. McKinley was peculiarly deep and strong, because it was compounded, as Mr. Roosevelt has suggested above, of two elements — each of which was fundamental in his disposition. He had in the first place a veritable gift for friendship. His personal relations with other men constituted the very core and substance of his life. He had served Mr. McKinley, as he had served so many others, because of disinterested personal devotion; but in the case of Mr. McKinley the personal devotion was heightened by feelings derived from another source. This particular friendship had awakened his aspirations. His general disposition was such that an ideal could make a peculiarly strong appeal to him only when it was embodied in a human being. Mr. McKinley's finer qualities aroused in him the utmost admiration. He was profoundly impressed by the unfailing patience, consideration and devotion which his friend had lavished on an ailing and difficult wife. He was, perhaps, even more impressed by Mr. McKinley's repeated refusals to obtain any political advantage by compromises with conscience. As he himself has said, Mr. McKinley's declaration that there were some things which a Presidential candidate must not do even to be President had made a better man of him. And undoubtedly his friend's influence upon his life and career was really elevating. His own personal standards of behavior in politics steadily improved, partly because he was fully capable of rising to a responsibility, as well as to an opportunity, but also partly because of the leavening effect of his association with his friend. This association had meant to Mr. Hanna more than his fame, his career and his public achievements. It had meant as well the increase of public usefulness and personal self-respect which a man can obtain only by remaining true to a certain standard of public behavior.

Towards the end of his life Mr. Hanna became increasingly aware of a difference between himself and Mr. McKinley in their respective attitudes towards personal ties and responsibilities. He never gave explicit expression to this difference, but he was glancing at it in the following passage in the *National Magazine* on "McKinley as I knew Him." "We were both," he says, "of Scotch-Irish descent, but opposite in disposition. He was of more direct descent than I, but it was thought from our dispositions that he had the Scotch and I had the Irish of the combination." What he means by this is probably that personal relationships were not so vital to Mr. McKinley as they were to himself. Mr. McKinley acted less than he did on the prompting of instinct and affection. The mere fact that the President was the more conscientious man of the two tended also to make him more conscious and less consistent in his feelings. Mr. McKinley was solicitous of the appearance which he was making to the world and posterity, and this quality might sometimes give his behavior at least the appearance of selfishness. I am not implying that he was not a loyal and in his way a sincere man; but loyalty was not to him as fundamental a virtue as it was to Mr. Hanna. He might have considered the possibility of breaking with his friend under conditions which would in Mr. Hanna's eyes have wholly failed to justify the rupture. In point of fact the latent and actual differences between the two men never gathered to a head. I have told the story of their few important disagreements; but the wonder is, not that they were there to tell, but that they were not more frequent and more serious. They do not in any way invalidate the popular impression that the association between the two men was, perhaps, the most loyal friendship which has become a part of American political history.

An honest friendship endures, not because it does not have any differences to overcome, but because it is strong enough to overcome such differences as inevitably occur. The association of Mr. Hanna and Mr. McKinley was punctuated with many trivial disputes which never became serious, partly because of the President's tact. The two men had to reach a mutually acceptable decision about thousands of bits of official business or policy in the course of a year. Their decisions were at times bound to diverge, and when such divergence arose they might for a moment wear the appearance of being serious. Mr. Hanna was a plain-dealer, honest and fearless to a fault, brusque sometimes in manner, quick in feeling and explosive in speech. When he disagreed with another man he might say so with both heat and energy. Under such circumstances Mr. McKinley was at his best. He was too tactful and prudent to make matters worse by any contradiction or disputation. He knew that in a few minutes or hours the storm would blow over, and that Mr. Hanna would then be willing to resume the discussion with a cool head and the utmost good temper.

These, however, were small things. What really tested the friendship was the change which gradually took place in their respective public positions. Mr. McKinley was, as I have said, extremely solicitous of his reputation. From the day he was first elected President he was represented as being under Mr. Hanna's control far more than was actually the case and to an extent which must have been galling. In matters of public policy he was always his own master — at least so far as Mr. Hanna was concerned; and even in the latter's own special field of political management he by no means merely submitted to Mr. Hanna's dictation. Mr. George B. Cortelyou, who had the best opportunities for judging, considered that Mr. McKinley was an abler politician than Mr. Hanna — and this in spite of the fact that he ranks Mr. Hanna's ability very high. Mr. McKinley did not get the credit for being either as independent, as courageous or as self-dependent as he really was. Furthermore, as time went on, Mr. Hanna increased rather than diminished in public stature; and as he increased the President became not absolutely but relatively smaller. Comic papers like *Life* published cartoons, in one of which Mr. Hanna was represented as a tall robust English gentleman with Mr. McKinley at his side dressed in a short coat and knee breeches. It was entitled "Buttons." Such a portrayal of their relationship would have been exasperating even had it been true; but it was not true.

If there had been any truth in it, the friendship between the two men could not have lasted. Mr. McKinley was bound to overlook the occasional public perversion of their relation one to another, because as a matter of fact Mr. Hanna had always recognized in his behavior towards his friend the essential difference in their positions. Mr. McKinley was the master, Mr. Hanna was only the able and trusted Prime Minister. The latter never presumed upon his friendship with the President, upon the contribution he had made towards Mr. McKinley's nomination or election or upon the increasing independence and stability of his own public position. Everybody most familiar with their private relations testifies that Mr. Hanna asked for nothing in the way of patronage to which he was not fully entitled. The extent of his ability or his willingness to obtain favors on merely personal grounds was very much overestimated. He was erroneously credited, for instance, with many of Mr. McKinley's own appointments to offices in Ohio. Of course he was more assertive in urging upon the President appointments which were in his opinion necessary for the welfare of the party, and his judgment about such matters frequently differed from that of the President. But even in this respect their peculiar relationship was mutually helpful, because each could in some measure protect the other against excessive demands on the part of Republican politicians.

At bottom the central fact in the relationship was the disinterestedness of Mr. Hanna. He was able to maintain his friendship with the President under very trying conditions because his recommendations were made, not in his own interest but in that of the President, the party or the country. He never sought to use his existing power, from whatever source it came, for the sake merely of increasing it. His waxing personal influence was always the by-product of his actual services to some individual, organization or cause. The late Bishop Potter said of his management of the Civic Federation that he had grown up to the job; and the comment supplies the clew to all the success of his career. He had grown up to one job after another. He had grown up to the job of nominating his friend as Presidential candidate, to the job of managing a critical and strenuous national campaign, to the job of securing the personal confidence of the American business interest, to the job of making himself personally popular with the people of Ohio, to the job of becoming one of the steering committee of the Senate, and finally, as we shall see, to the job of obtaining effective influence over organized labor as well as organized capital. But in his assumption and exercise of these activities he had never planned his own personal aggrandizement. He was loyal, that is, to the proper limitations of his various official and unofficial duties; and this just estimate of the limits of his power was merely another aspect of his personal loyalty — of his disposition to allow other people a freedom of movement analogous to his own. He did not pervert his opportunities, because he would not bring pressure to bear upon his friends or demand of them excessive and unnecessary sacrifices.

In the case of President McKinley he was the more bound to scrupulous loyalty because of his affection for the friend, because of his reverence for the office and because of his admiration for the man. He spoke and wrote of Mr. McKinley, particularly after the latter's death, in terms that may seem extravagant, but which are undoubtedly sincere and which really revealed his feelings at the time. "It is difficult," he says, "for me to express the extent of the love and respect which I, in common with many others, felt for him personally. The feeling was the outgrowth of an appreciation of his noble self-sacrificing nature. My affection for him and faith and confidence in him always seemed to be reciprocated, to the extent that there was never an unpleasant word passed between us, and the history of his administration, his Cabinet and his associations with public men was entirely free from intrigue and base selfishness. I had the closest revelations of William McKinley's character, I think, in our quiet hours of smoking and chatting when all the rest had retired. For past midnight we have sat many times talking over those matters which friends always discuss — and the closer I came to the man, the more lovable his character appeared. There was revealed the gentle growing greatness of the man who knew men, respected them and loved them. These pleasant episodes of a purely personal nature are emphasized more and more as I think of him, and it is these that I most cherish in the memory of the man. His greatness as a statesman was but the reflection of his greatness as a man." And in an address delivered at Toledo in September, 1903, on the occasion of the unveiling of a memorial statue to Mr. McKinley, Mr. Hanna said: "The truest monument of the life of William McKinley was built and erected stone by stone as he lived his noble useful life until it touched the sky and was finished by the hands of the angels. It is the monument of a good man's great love for his country and will forever and forever remain as an example to us all."

The preceding quotations must not, of course, be considered as a critical judgment on Mr. McKinley's character and career, but as the tribute of a friend, the warmth of whose admiration had been increased by the President's tragic death. In Mark Hanna's life Mr. McKinley had been the personal embodiment of those qualities of unselfishness, kindness and patriotism which in the preceding quotations the Senator celebrates with so much emotion. There was just enough difference between the ideas and standards of the two men to enable one to have a profound and edifying effect on the other. Neither of them was a political idealist or reformer. Neither of them had travelled very far ahead of the current standards of political morality and the current ideas of political and economic policy. Both of them combined in a typically American way a thoroughly realistic attitude towards practical political questions with a large infusion of traditional American patriotic aspiration. These agreements in their general attitude towards public affairs made the chief difference between them all the more influential in Mr. Hanna's life and behavior. While not a reformer, Mr. McKinley was more sensitive to the pressure and the value of a reforming public opinion; and he was more scrupulous in considering whether the end justified the means. He had no call to eradicate American political and economic abuses, but he did not want his own success to be qualified by practices which might look dubious to posterity. He succeeded in making Mr. Hanna realize the necessity and the value of these better standards, and by so doing stimulated in the latter a higher realism, which increased with age. Each of the two friends, consequently, owed much to the other, and each of them paid his debt. Their friendship was worthy of the respect and of the renown which it inspired in their contemporaries.

CHAPTER XXIV

THE PANAMA CANAL

In view of the intimate association between the political careers of William McKinley and Mark Hanna, the former's death might have been expected to injure the political power and prestige of his friend. Nothing of the kind occurred. If anything the assassination of President McKinley strengthened the position of Mr. Hanna and made the sources of his power flow more abundantly. The interval of two years and some months between Mr. McKinley's assassination and Mr. Hanna's death constituted the culminating period of the latter's political career — the period in which his influence was most effective, his activities most varied and wholesome, his personal merits most widely understood and appreciated and his prospects most flattering.

The mere fact of Mr. McKinley's assassination reacted in Mr. Hanna's favor. There was a general feeling that the rancorous abuse of which the dead President had been the victim had at least indirectly contributed to the tragedy. The public knew that Mr. Hanna had been even more malignantly and systematically abused than had his friend, and they knew better than ever how little he had deserved it. His hold on popular confidence was increased by the grief and indignation caused by Mr. McKinley's assassination and by the belief that the martyred President's mantle had descended on his shoulders. The conservative public opinion of the country came more than ever to consider Mr. Hanna as its leader and representative, and to have faith that his leadership would be both politically and economically successful.

One of the clearest expressions of the change in public sentiment towards Mr. Hanna which had been gradually taking place, was given in an address made at a dinner which Mr. Hanna offered to the Gridiron Club of Washington in March,

1902. The Gridiron Club is composed of the Washington correspondents of newspapers, scattered all over the country, and their usual attitude toward the public men who dine with them is far from being reverent or even respectful. Mr. Hanna had, however, made himself popular with the newspaper correspondents, as he did with every one else who came into actual contact with him, and they were glad to bear witness to his increasing personal prestige. The following address was made by Mr. Raymond Patterson:—

"SENATOR HANNA:

"It is generally understood that the man who gives a dinner is safe from the assaults of his guests. Even an Indian or an Ohio Democrat would refrain from tomahawking his host, at least until they had finished the pie. But as you know, the Gridiron Club is not bound by ordinary rules, and we claim the right to kill our mountain lions wherever we find them. It becomes my painful duty, therefore, as the representative of this club, to impeach you of high crimes and misdemeanors. You, sir, have proven yourself the most despicable hypocrite of the century. You have betrayed our confidence most shamefully and you have failed to live up to your reputation in a way which should cause the blush of shame to crimson your brazen cheeks.

"We cherished in our bosoms a most precious scoundrel and here you have developed into a most tawdry saint. You arrived in our midst indorsed by popular clamor and by Homer Davenport as a plutocrat and a dollar-mark, the vicious tool of wicked trusts, and the embodiment of financial arrogance. How have you lived up to this reputation? Dare you deny that you have failed to justify the confidence reposed in you? You have outraged all decency, let me tell you, by your shameless backslidings toward virtue. Instead of an illiterate parvenu we have been forced to associate with a polished gentleman, and the ignorant politician has degenerated into the shrewd statesman.

"Where is our brutal political leader, our grasping money grabber, our stock-jobbing boodler? What have you done with him? Are you prepared either to produce the body or confess the crime? How comes it that the mere buyer of legislatures, who was supposed to be as voiceless in public as the tomb, made his début before this club with a ready wit and a merry humor which have become historic? How comes it that the enemy of the working man is now the chosen instrument for the settlement of disputes between capital and labor? Which is Jekyll and which is Hyde?

"I was delegated to present to the real Mark Hanna a souvenir of the feelings of the Gridiron Club, but I scarcely know whether to make a presentation to the memory of the reprobate the people were told you were or to the real Hanna of to-day, the statesman, the broad-gauged man of affairs, the good fellow and our friend. There are in this club sixty men, and as slight testimonial of the fact that all of them join in this expression of sentiment, the face of every one of them has been photographed indelibly on the indestructible copper of this sacred gridiron. It is unique, as you will see, but the sentiment behind it is far from singular.

"These sixty faces may recall to you the fact that you have achieved a triumph such as comes to but few men. You have destroyed a popular myth, and now to-day across the length and breadth of the country, Mark Hanna the boodler, Mark Hanna the bullying political boss, Mark Hanna the trickster and the parvenu, has absolutely disappeared from the public press. The purity of your life, the exquisite good-fellowship which we learned so rapidly to recognize, the steadfastness of your purposes, the honesty of your methods and above all the fidelity to the dead McKinley more tender even than to the living President, all these qualities have dissipated the black clouds of envy, of malice and of partisan venom, and have won for you a peculiar place in the hearts of the people.

"So, sir, it becomes my duty to present to you this emblazoned gridiron, bearing on its polished bars the individual portraits of our membership, which shall be at once a monument to the dead and gone Hanna the people tried so hard to hate, and also it shall be the final testimonial of the living Uncle Mark we have so learned to love."

Another cause contributed to the enhancement of Mr. Hanna's political prestige. The death of Mr. McKinley had not apparently done anything to diminish his influence at the White House. He entered at once into very intimate and confidential relations with the new President. When two men occupying responsible positions and forced by those positions into constant association work together smoothly and efficiently, the result looks so natural and inevitable that few people stop to consider how much easier and more natural a disagreement might have been. In the case of Mr. Roosevelt and Mr. Hanna a disagreement might have been plausibly predicted. In the past they had never been closely associated, and each was aware that he had been more or less criticised by the other. Each was aware of certain fundamental differences of opinion and political outlook.

But both were also aware how necessary it was for Republican success that the new President and the old organization should not fall into a suspicious and hostile attitude one to the other.

When the new President, the day after his predecessor's death, gave his wise and reassuring pledge that he would not depart from the policy of the McKinley administration, the way was open for a working agreement. Mr. Hanna immediately entered the opening. He was always willing to meet another man more than halfway, and after Mr. Roosevelt's pledge he was not only ready but eager to offer his services to the new President. They both had the good sense and the good feeling to recognize what the situation demanded and both proved capable of acting up to its needs. Each of them came to understand that he was dealing with a man who was dealing fairly and considerately with him. They became, consequently, not only efficient co-workers, but good friends. As they knew each other better, they liked each other the more. The President was loyal to his promise that during the remainder of the term he would consider himself as in a sense his predecessor's deputy. Mr. Hanna was equally true to his promise that the administration should have his loyal support and his best advice. With Mr. Roosevelt, as with Mr. McKinley, his influence, whatever it amounted to, was not due to friendship or favor. He was powerful with both men, because he was disinterested and because he was really useful, and apparently he was almost as frequently consulted by one as by the other. The private secretary of both the old President and the new states that Mr. Hanna's counsel was as influential in the White House in 1902 as it had been early in 1901.

Furthermore, during the long session of 1901–1902 Senator Hanna looms up, at least for the public eye, as a much bigger figure than ever in the legislative counsels of his country. I have already traced the gradual transition from his earlier silence in the public debates of the Senate to an active participation in the discussions of at least certain economic questions. The ship-subsidy bill first brought him prominently into notice as a legislator and debater; but during the long session of 1901–1902 his Senatorial activity was far from being confined to that one subject. He was throughout that session emphatically the most energetic and conspicuous member of the Senate. The business man, who not long before had asked the indulgence of his colleagues as a tyro in debating, had become, not of course the best debater in the Senate, but the speaker to whom all listened most attentively and whose words actually carried most weight.

He spoke during the session of 1901–1902 upon a much wider range of public business. It happened to be a very active legislative year, in which many important measures were enacted, and in which a still larger number received more or less consideration. Among the acts passed was one providing for the construction of an Isthmian Canal, one continuing in force the policy of excluding immigrants from China, one providing for civil government in the Philippines, one instituting a national system of irrigation, and one founding a Department of Commerce and Labor. In addition the ship-subsidy bill was, as we have seen, exhaustively debated and passed in the Senate, and the question of Cuban reciprocity received some preliminary consideration. Mr. Hanna took no part in the debate upon the Instrument of government for the Philippines nor in that upon the Irrigation Act; but in the discussion of all the other subjects of legislation his participation was in all cases important and in two cases absolutely decisive.

This enlargement of the scope of his legislative action is of peculiar significance in relation to the development of Mr. Hanna's public personality. He entered political life as a successful political manager and as a business man — the representative in politics of a business interest. He brought to his new task no special equipment for public life. He had never held an administrative office. He had never made any special study of the political and economic history of his own and other countries. He had never been trained to express himself with precision and with cumulative effect. He was entirely without that legal discipline which, in the majority of American political leaders, is substituted for a sound political and economic education. For a long time, consequently, he was dumb, except as the spokesman of his original interest in business; and he was dumb, because he was conscious of his own deficiencies and would not speak, except whereof he knew. But he had an alert and open mind. If he could not learn from books, he could learn even more from other men and from the increasing personal activities and responsibilities. He was gradually growing up to the job of being in a way the representative in the Senate of a responsible administration. Little by little experience of large affairs took the place of preliminary training. He began to participate in the discussion of other than business questions, because he had gradually come to know his own mind, and, still better, to formulate a group of general ideas in respect to public policy.

His increasing participation in the debates is not to be confused with a growing loquacity or fluency. If on the one hand he had no intellectual imagination or interest in ideas for their own sake, so, on the other, he had no more facility either with words or ideas. He was enterprising and experimental in action, but not in thought and in expression. Whatever he said was always the result of an actual experience. His ideas were his actions, and what he took to be his responsibilities turned inside out. When he spoke upon a wider range of public questions, it meant that he had become in a way an authority on those questions—an authority, not in the sense that he knew all about them and could discuss them exhaustively and luminously, but in the sense that he felt himself authorized to speak as a matter of personal experience and conviction and of public duty.

His attitude towards public questions was usually determined by a sense of national administrative responsibility. Thus during the session of 1901–1902 he argued at some length on behalf of a Department of Commerce and Labor, in order that the government might be equipped to serve the industry of the country as well as its agriculture. Again he argued in favor of the traditional policy of excluding Chinese immigration, but against certain proposed amendments to the Exclusion Act, which would have violated American treaty obligations and unnecessarily have injured Chinese susceptibilities. He spoke in favor of a proposed agreement with the Pennsylvania Railroad Co. providing for the erection of a Union station in Washington, whose location and design would be worthy of the capital of the United States. Finally he earnestly urged the adoption of a treaty of commercial reciprocity with Cuba on the ground chiefly of moral obligation. This final instance is particularly illuminating, because important business interests were opposed to the adoption and pressed him not to come out in its favor. He denied that any injury would result to American business, but he urged that the national moral obligation to promote the welfare of Cuba was manifest and valid. It ought to be redeemed, if necessary, even at some expense to American business.

His point of view in relation to all these questions of public policy was national. Each one of them involved an obligation on the part of the general government either to redeem a promise or to promote a genuine national interest; and it is not accidental that Senator Hanna was always found speaking and voting on this one side. He felt himself responsible for the promotion of the national welfare — in so far as it was involved in any proposed legislative action. He was not simply a Senator from Ohio. He was the leader of the party in complete control of the general government; and as the leader of the party and an influential member of the Senate, he became the representative in Congress of the responsible administration of the country. The President found it useful to consult with him about legislative affairs more than any other single Senator and Congressman. Senator Hanna was in a position to get things done. He could actually influence votes. A President who wanted to have things done was obliged to lean upon him.

Any attempt to describe Senator Hanna's position in the Senate during this session incurs dangers of exaggeration. His power was extraordinary, but it was very delicately balanced. As long as the balance was held, he could accomplish great things, but even a slight disturbance of the balance might have left him relatively uninfluential. Officially he was merely junior Senator from Ohio. All the rest was a matter of personal prerogative, depending on the confidence which the President, certain fellow-Senators, certain Republican leaders, and a certain part of the public had in him. If his power had been in any way strained or abused, the confidence on which it rested would have been shattered. If it had been even proclaimed or admitted, it would have encountered far more opposition. Nevertheless it was very real, and in attempting to find an analogy for it, one has to go outside American political experience. It was compounded of wholly different elements from the power exercised by any "Boss." It was compounded of somewhat different elements from the power exercised by any President or Governor. The analogy which most nearly fits Mr. Hanna's position is that of a Prime Minister, who is responsible to an Executive Chief, while at the same time dependent for the success of his administration upon the confidence and support of a majority in the Legislature. The power exercised by Mr. Hanna was coming to resemble in a rough, tentative, wholly unofficial way, that of a German Imperial Chancellor.

I have reserved until the last the most conspicuous illustration of his effective participation in the legislative action of the session of 1901–1902. All of Senator Hanna's minor speeches and achievements are overshadowed by the speech he made on June 5 and 6, 1902, upon the Panama Canal, and by the influence which that speech exerted upon the final action of the Senate and eventually of the House of Representatives. The intrinsic advantages of the Panama over the Nicaragua route were such that possibly the former would eventually have been selected in any event; but unquestionably the actual adoption of the Panama route by the fifty-seventh Congress was due to Mark Hanna far more than to any other one man.

Owing to a series of historical accidents the Nicaraguan route had come to be traditionally considered as the American route. Partly because American diplomats and promoters had been more successful in securing concessions from Nicaragua and Costa Rica and partly because American engineers had evinced a partiality for the northern route, the majority of American citizens accepted as a matter of course the idea that any canal built by the government of the United States or its citizens would be situated in Nicaragua. The first Interoceanic Canal Commission which made an exhaustive investigation, had reported in 1876 unanimously in favor of a Nicaraguan canal; and in all probability had it not been for the Clayton-Bulwer Treaty the construction of such a canal would have been undertaken at a much earlier date either by the government of the United States or by an American corporation under government assistance.

The beginning in 1881 of the construction of a canal across the Isthmus of Panama by a French company put an end temporarily to the agitation for a canal built and operated under American influence. Nothing could be done until the French experiment had been tried and its results known. Not until the French company went into bankruptcy in 1888 was any alternative enterprise considered; but when the French experiment did fail, it was inevitable that the Nicaraguan project should be revived and pushed with unprecedented vigor. Thoughtful Americans became more than ever convinced that any interoceanic canal should be controlled by this country. And apparently a canal controlled by this country would have to be built in Nicaragua. The ruins of the French enterprise blocked the path across Panama — even if the government of the United States or any group of its citizens had desired to take it. In February, 1889, Congress passed a bill incorporating the Maritime Canal Co., of the United States, which was organized a few months later and which raised some $6,000,000 with which to begin construction. During the next three years a good deal of work was accomplished with this money; but the panic of 1893 dried up the springs of capital and in that year the American company also went into the hands of a receiver. It could not resume work without the aid of the government, and although a considerable party in Congress was in favor of guaranteeing the company's bonds for a large sum, a bill providing for such a guarantee never did more than pass the Senate. Congress frequently discussed the matter during the next few years, and many bills providing for the construction of the canal by the nation were considered, but no action was taken. All that Congress did during these years was to constitute in 1897 another Isthmian Canal Commission, headed by Rear Admiral John G. Walker, and to appropriate $300,000 for the expenses of further investigation. In the meantime the concession of the Maritime Canal Co. expired and was extended for a short period only with difficulty.

Manifestly, however, the actual construction of the canal

could not be much longer delayed. The Spanish-American War had given a convincing object lesson of the embarrassments to American naval strategy and defence which resulted from the possession of two coast lines so remote one from the other. The growing commerce of the country with China and South America demanded an isthmian waterway. Public opinion was almost unanimous that some action be taken; but the more cautious among the Republican leaders, including President McKinley, did not want to act without full information and indubitable legal guarantees against future embarrassments. The appointment of the final Canal Commission was the result of this determination. The Commission of 1897 had presented a report which unanimously and emphatically decided in favor of the practicability and desirability of the Nicaraguan route. The Senate passed a bill providing for the construction of a Nicaraguan Canal by the national government; but Speaker Reed prevented it from being adopted by the House. The Panama route had a few able advocates, the result being that on the last day of the short session of 1898-1899, the President was authorized to send still another Commission to investigate both routes, and an appropriation of $1,000,000 was made to pay the expense of the investigation.

Apparently President McKinley had by this time become doubtful whether the country should commit itself irrevocably to a Nicaraguan canal. He had listened to the arguments in favor of Panama presented by William Nelson Cromwell, the legal representative in the United States of the new Panama Canal Co., and he had also asked Mr. Hanna to listen to Mr. Cromwell's pleading. It was owing to his advice that the Republican platform of 1900 pledged the party to the construction of an isthmian canal rather than a canal specifically situated in Nicaragua. In the meanwhile, he was seeking in good faith to remove the obstacles preventing the construction of a national canal by negotiating with Great Britain for the amendment of the Clayton-Bulwer Treaty. An agreement was reached with the English government, but the new treaty was rejected by the Senate, and not until late in 1901 was an acceptable arrangement consummated with Great Britain—one which enabled the United States to construct an isthmian canal on fair terms. A large proportion of the members of both Houses had wished to go ahead and build a canal without waiting for the signature of a new treaty, but fortunately the policy of the country was controlled by the wiser half of Congress. The final removal of all legal obstacles made it inevitable that some decisive action would be taken during the long session of 1901–1902.

Early in January, 1902, a decision by Congress in favor of a Nicaraguan canal looked inevitable. The third Canal Commission, after an exhaustive investigation, had submitted its report in December, 1900. It recommended the construction of a canal along the northern route, because, but only because, of the apparent impossibility of buying from the French company its property and franchises in Panama at anything like a fair price. A canal at Panama would cost about $60,000,000 less than one farther north, and it would be shorter, have fewer locks and slighter curvature. It was to be preferred for engineering reasons; but even though more expensive, the Nicaraguan canal was entirely practicable, and, considering the attitude of the French company, was the better selection. The practical effect of this report was to strengthen the hands of the friends of a Nicaraguan canal, while it made the directors of the French company understand that they must either offer reasonable terms or else lose practically the whole French investment in Panama.

The consequence was that after protracted negotiations and much backing and filling the French company offered on Jan. 4, 1902, to sell its property to the United States for $40,000,000, which brought the total estimated cost of the Panama Canal to a smaller figure than the total estimated cost of the Nicaraguan canal. In view of this offer the Commission reversed its former decision and reported on January 18 in favor of the adoption of the Panama route. Before this final report was submitted, however, the House of Representatives had passed a bill, introduced by Mr. Hepburn, authorizing the President to proceed with the construction of a canal at Nicaragua, at a cost of $180,000,000 and appropriating $10,000,000 on account for immediate use. An amendment had been proposed, leaving the choice of routes to the discretion of the President, but it had been rejected by a vote of 120 to 170. The House was almost unanimously in favor of this Hepburn Bill. As finally passed, there had been 308 votes in its favor against only 2 in opposition.

I have been obliged to tell at some length the foregoing story in order to explain the situation which confronted the Senate when in January, 1902, it began the consideration of the canal problem. With its usual deliberation the Senate decided to postpone action until a thorough investigation had been made by the Interoceanic Canal Committee. The House had acted hastily, and the final recommendation of the Canal Commission in favor of Panama placed the matter in an entirely different light. For two months the Committee on Interoceanic Canals took testimony, and about the middle of March decided by a vote of 7 to 4 to report in favor of the passage of the Hepburn Bill unamended. The minority, however, submitted a report of its own, in which a strong argument was made in favor of the Panama route. Senator Hanna was the instigator of this minority report, and thereafter he became the leader in the Senate of the pro-Panama party.

The subject was one which would have naturally aroused a lively interest in his mind. The United States was confronted with the necessity of deciding what was substantially a great business question — the greatest, perhaps, in its history. The question ought to be decided one way or the other chiefly on business grounds, although the business was chiefly technical in its nature. He was familiar from his own experience with many of the technical problems which were raised by the comparative advantages and disadvantages of the two routes. As he himself said in the Senate: "I have felt an interest in this question because it was a practical one. The operation of canals was one of the few subjects with which in my business life I had become acquainted from experience in all directions. When the Panama route was called to my attention by President McKinley himself, I was asked by him to give it my personal attention. He made the further request that I should go on the Committee on Interoceanic Canals, that he might have the benefit of my experience and advice." Everything conspired, consequently, to fasten his interest on the problem and to make him very competent to deal with it. He had instituted an independent and very careful investigation of his own, and some time in 1901 reached a conclusion in favor of the Panama route.

Just when Senator Hanna became convinced that the government would be making a grave mistake, in case the Nicaraguan route was adopted, I am not sure; but a visit, which M. Philippe Bunau-Varilla made to the United States early in 1901 had something to do with it. M. Bunau-Varilla had been chief engineer in charge of the work undertaken by the new French company and was peculiarly qualified both by his standing in his profession and by his practical experience in the work of construction at Panama to pass an authoritative opinion upon the comparative advantages of the two routes. He had been induced to come to the United States by a group of Cincinnati business men, whom he met by accident in Paris during the Exposition of 1900, and whom he had convinced of the superiority of Panama. The visit was made for the purpose of addressing various commercial associations in the United States on behalf of Panama, and wherever he spoke he left behind him a trail of converts. Among them was Colonel Myron T. Herrick, whose interest was so much aroused that he made a point of introducing M. Bunau-Varilla to Senator Hanna. A series of interviews followed, which had much to do with Mr. Hanna's decision to make a fight on behalf of Panama. This decision had been reached by the Senator before the Canal Commission finally reported in favor of Panama.

However much Mr. Hanna may have been influenced by the arguments of other men, he did not allow himself to be convinced without making an exhaustive investigation of his own — the same sort of an investigation which a responsible Minister would have made before submitting to a legislative body some important plan of legislation. He read all the available books on the subject and studied the surveys and plans. He sent for a number of men who had been over the ground, and listened to what they had to say. He consulted not merely engineers, but practical navigators — the captains in charge of large ocean-going vessels; and in this aspect of the inquiry he was helped by his personal association with the large American maritime interests. The further he pushed the investigation, the more convinced he became. He was dealing for the most part with a group of technical facts, the bearing and weight of which his practical experience had fully equipped him to estimate; and although he was not an engineer his final decision was in every essential respect that of an expert. No better example could be given of his ability to qualify himself for an important job by careful preparation. In order to make his own decision prevail he needed to be an authority, and an authority he became.

The fight was begun in the Committee. Throughout the hearings, during which several volumes of testimony was taken, Mr. Hanna was constantly putting questions to the witnesses,— particularly the members of the Canal Commission, — in order to bring out their emphatic preference on engineering grounds for the Panama route — his object being to prepare the mind of the Senators, who might read the testimony, for more light. The Committee itself he did not expect to convince. Its Chairman was Senator Morgan, long the most determined advocate of a Nicaraguan canal, and the majority of its members were already publicly committed in its favor. The real fight was made on the floor of the Senate, where Mr. Hanna as well as other able Senators were using all their personal influence to convert their colleagues to Panama. After a while they felt strong enough to take the aggressive. Senator Spooner offered an amendment to the Hepburn Bill which left nothing of the House measure except its enacting clause. It authorized the President to purchase the franchises and property of the French company for not more than $40,000,000, to secure by treaty with Colombia a canal zone and then to proceed with the construction of the canal. But he was also authorized to fall back on the Nicaraguan route — in case he could not make a satisfactory bargain with the French company or Colombia. This amendment was the idea and work of Senator Spooner, and its submission to the Senate was good tactics. It placed the advocates of the Nicaraguan canal where, considering the weight of expert testimony, they ought to be placed — that is, on the defensive.

The most important speech in favor of the Spooner amendment was made by Senator Hanna on June 5 and 6. He had carefully prepared the material for this utterance, but not a word of its actual text. He had before him two sheets of paper, containing twelve or fifteen lines of writing on each; and the majority of these memoranda were not even subject headings. They were merely references to the page numbers of reports and the like. His secretary sat behind, ready with some fifteen books and pamphlets, quotations from which the speaker intended to use. Backed up by this material he talked to the whole Senate just as he had already talked to many Senators in person — explaining in a conversational way the reasons which made the Panama route more desirable. He spoke on the first day for over two hours, until his knees gave out, and on the day following he concluded with a somewhat shorter additional argument. On June 18, the day before the vote was taken, he supplemented his first speech with a brief but very cogent plea for the Panama route.

A reading of Senator Hanna's Panama speech is sufficient to account for its remarkable effect. It is at once unmistakably sincere and really authoritative. With one exception he did not and could not advance any novel arguments in favor of Panama — although that exception is very important. It consisted of a large number of letters from the sailing masters of ocean-going ships, which he had solicited and obtained, and which testified unanimously and emphatically to the superiority of the shorter and straighter Panama Canal from the point of view of a practical navigator. But for the most part he could only repeat arguments which had already been advanced by engineers. What he did do was to present these arguments skilfully, to bring out and emphasize the substantially unanimous consensus of engineering authority on one side, and to discuss lucidly those phases of the subject with which his own experience had made him familiar. Senator Hanna's speech, as compared with the many long and dreary harangues which had been delivered in the Senate during the years of discussion of an interoceanic canal, produces a veritable sensation of candor, relevance, personal knowledge and reality.

The speech obtained an enormous success. His friends all

congratulated him, and hundreds of copies were demanded of him as soon as it was printed in the Record. Senator Orville Platt, a man of some experience, said that it was the most effective address which had been made in the Senate during his career. All observers testify that it actually changed votes. Up to the time of its delivery the outlook was very dubious. Thereafter the prospect of a favorable vote very much improved. Senator Frye states that after a lifelong public advocacy of the Nicaragua route, Mr. Hanna converted him to its rival. He told his friend that he was voting not for a Panama but for a Hannama canal. He asserted emphatically that Mr. Hanna, far more than any other single man, was responsible for the conversion of Congress and the country to Panama. It is almost unnecessary to add that the public speech was supplemented by vigorous private canvassing. The opinion of every Senator was learned, and wherever any chance of conversion existed, the argument was pushed home either by Senator Hanna himself or by some assistant, such as Senator Kittridge. The campaign for a successful vote was planned as carefully as was the campaign preceding an important popular election.

In his "Four Centuries of the Panama Canal" Mr. Willis Fletcher Johnson says (p. 128): "The result was generally regarded as doubtful until the vote was actually taken. That incident occurred on June 19, 1902, when the measure [the Spooner amendment] was adopted by the overwhelming vote of sixty-seven to six." This is misleading. The final vote did stand sixty-seven to six; but the comparative strength of the two parties had in the meantime been tested by a series of preliminary votes on various attempts to emasculate or modify the Spooner amendment. When these votes involved a decisive question, Panama usually won by about forty-two to thirty-four. The minority was composed for the most part of Democrats, but included such Republican Senators as Clapp, Hawley, Nelson, Penrose, Thomas Platt and Quay. On the other hand some half a dozen Democrats voted with the majority. The overwhelming final vote merely meant that, after being beaten, the Senators in favor of Nicaragua did not want to go on record against some kind of a canal. But a change of four votes would a few minutes earlier have at least temporarily defeated the Spooner amendment. The House of Representatives cheerfully agreed to the action of the Senate, and public opinion, which a few months before had not seriously considered Panama, accepted the decision without question. Neither has any doubt since been raised that the selection of the southern route saved the government from committing a grave error and sustaining a severe loss.

The incident constituted the most conspicuous single illustration of Senator Hanna's personal prestige. In this as in so many other cases he succeeded in decisively influencing the course of public policy because he deserved to succeed. Like other Americans he himself had first been predisposed in favor of Nicaragua; but his mind was open and his predisposition did not prevent him from making a thorough study of the question and reaching a proper conclusion. Once having done so, he carefully and deliberately qualified himself to convert Congress to his own decision. That was what he intended to do and that was what he did. He succeeded in doing it, not merely because he had mastered the subject and could speak with authority, but because his personality itself inspired confidence. On no other occasion did he exhibit so clearly and effectively in public the quality and the power, which account for his influence in private over his friends and associates. His Senatorial colleagues had come to trust in his personal good faith; and this trust permitted him to exert a decisive influence on a question which, momentous as it was, had not become seriously entangled in party politics and did not arouse sectional or class interests. The comparatively open mind which Senators and Congressmen brought to the consideration of the question offered an opportunity for an earnest and competent and trustworthy man to impose his selection on a sufficient number of his colleagues. Mark Hanna had made himself the man to seize the opportunity, and his country may well thank him, not only for what he did, but for being the kind of man who could do it.

CHAPTER XXV

THE CIVIC FEDERATION AND THE LABOR PROBLEM

IN the foregoing chapter we have seen that Senator Hanna's increasing personal power in and outside of Congress had brought with it a higher and broader sense of responsibility. The limitations which he had imposed upon his early behavior in the Senate were abandoned. He began to interfere in the discussion of a far larger range of public questions; and whenever he interfered he advocated not a sectional or a class, but what he believed to be a national, policy. He was no longer the representative to the same extent of merely a business interest in politics. He proposed to represent the whole country, and his power could not have increased as it did unless an increasing number of people had been convinced of the good faith of his intentions and his peculiar ability to make them good.

It is by no means accidental, consequently, that just when his personal political power was becoming nationalized in its expression, he became vitally interested in the better solution of the most critical national economic problem — the problem, that is, of the relation between capital and labor. This problem was fundamental from Senator Hanna's point of view, because all his economic ideas were based upon his personal experience as a productive agent and his political experience as the representative of certain productive agencies in American society. The equitable distribution and the abundant consumption of the economic product were supposed to take care of themselves — provided the productive agencies could be made to work efficiently, actively and harmoniously. He had in his own opinion contributed effectively to their active and efficient operation by helping to protect them against injurious political agitation; but the plain fact was that they did not work harmoniously. Capital and labor were in a condition of more or less constant warfare; and this warfare diminished the efficiency of the productive organization and constituted a threat to political security and social integrity. The temporary subsidence of the agitation against business only brought into sharper relief this fundamental discrepancy in his whole scheme of American economic salvation.

He had, moreover, other and more personal reasons to be interested in the warfare between capital and labor. The one serious dispute in which he had been engaged with his own employees had made an indelible impression on him. The bloodshed, the violence and the resulting spirit of suspicion and hatred seemed to him as unnecessary as it was deplorable and repellent to the American tradition of fair dealing among individuals and classes. The experience had profoundly influenced his subsequent attitude towards his own employees. It was at the root of his determination to keep personally in touch with them, so that he could know and understand their grievances and so that they could actually see his good faith in his eyes and in his manner as well as in his deeds. In spite, however, of his fair and generous treatment of his employees and of their loyalty towards him, he had been denounced as a labor-crusher; and this had been done apparently for no better reason than that, as a successful business man, he *must* have oppressed his men. He answered the attack vigorously and convincingly; but the ominous cloud which had descended upon his political career merely because he had been a large employer of labor forced upon his attention the very practical question: Why should he have been charged with being a labor-crusher when there was not the slightest evidence that he had been anything but very fair and generous in his treatment of his employees?

He sincerely believed that the policy which he advocated of unrestrained business stimulation and expansion was as beneficial to the wage-earner as it was to the employer. Prosperity meant as much as anything else the full dinner-pail. Without business activity and the confident investment by capitalists in business enterprises, laborers' wages could not increase. Unless labor was efficient and steady, the economic value of capital was very much impaired. All sorts of arguments could be used to prove the identity of the interests of employer and employee "in the long run"; but the fact remained that the two always had quarrelled about the division of the product and were still quarelling. As a severely practical political economist Mr. Hanna could not be satisfied with results "in the long run." Big strikes, particularly about wages, were very embarrassing to a political leader who was trying to convince the mass of the people that they were bound to get their full share of the fruits of prosperity. If his political system was to prevail, the ultimate identity of interests must somehow be made more immediate; and it became in a sense his duty to make it immediately effective. As a joint result, consequently, of his politico-economic system and his increasing personal prominence and responsibility, he was being driven to take an active interest in the settlement of labor disputes; and during 1901 it so happened that an instrument was placed in his hand which enabled him to give systematic practical expression to this interest.

In 1893 there had been organized in Chicago a Civic Federation, the purpose of which was to gather together people of all classes and interests for the purpose of investigating and discussing various questions of public policy. One of its chief objects was to bring to the investigation and discussion of these questions contributions from men who were dealing with them in a very practical way and from radically different points of view. The idea met with success, and as the conferences increased in size the Federation found imperceptibly its work and its membership becoming more than local. It had engineered conferences on combinations and trusts and on the reform of primaries, to which people from all over the country were invited; and finally in June, 1900, it changed its name to the National Civic Federation. Senator Hanna's attention had been called to the organization before and during the campaign of 1900. The Secretary of the Treasury, Mr. Lyman G. Gage, was an honorary President of the Federation and took a lively interest in its work and welfare. He introduced its Secretary, Mr. Ralph M. Easley, to President McKinley and Senator Hanna with the express object of having the purposes of the Federation explained to them. Mr. Hanna was not, however, at that juncture likely to be interested in a discussion club — no matter how intelligently conducted. The campaign was ahead of him. His attention was fastened on a little voting club — called the Electoral College. So the Secretary failed to arouse his interest, and the Federation probably looked to him merely like a body of conversational reformers.

During the following summer the strike among the anthracite coal miners raised the labor question in an acute form, and that question became the subject of first conference of the Federation as a national body. An Industrial Arbitration Department was formed, which subsequently assumed the better name of the Department of Conciliation and Arbitration. Little by little this department waxed in importance. Its work and the classes of men interested in it broadened. Besides many prominent business men, a number of even more prominent labor leaders joined the Federation and became active in the Conciliation Department. Mr. Samuel Gompers, President of the American Federation of Labor, was a member of the Executive Council. John Mitchell, President of the United Mine Workers of America, and Dan J. Keefe, President of the International Longshoremen, Marine and Transport Workers' Association, were closely associated with the work. The department had quickly grown to be a really efficient agency for the better association of business men with union leaders and economic experts.

In December, 1900, an increase of the arbitration committee was considered desirable. Mr. Easley asked Dan J. Keefe what employers on the Lakes his union dealt with largely, and found fair in their general attitude and behavior. He mentioned several, but added that Daniel R. Hanna, Senator Hanna's son and a member of the firm of M. A. Hanna & Co., was the fairest of them all. The Secretary shied away from the suggestion. He feared that any prominent association of the name of Hanna with the Federation would arouse political prejudices and hurt its proper work. The next day the Arbitration Committee met, with Mr. A. C. Bartlett in the chair. When the question of increasing the membership of the committee came up, Mr. Easley stated with reluctance that the name of Daniel R. Hanna, Chairman of the Dock Managers' Association, had been suggested, and awaited an explosion. But no explosion followed. George Shelling, a labor union man, a cooper by trade and a Commissioner of Labor under former Governor Altgeld of Illinois, rose and said: "There is no more radical Democrat on this committee than I am. I move that Daniel R. Hanna be made a member of it. I know from what Keefe said he is all right." The invitation to join the Committee was issued and accepted. The firm of M. A. Hanna & Co. had remained true to its traditional policy of dealing fairly and generously with its employees, and for that reason one of the partners was naturally suggested as a member of a general committee on conciliation and arbitration.

Early in 1901 the Industrial Department found itself very much in need of Senator Hanna's help in order to deal with a difficult dispute in the anthracite coal trade. We have already remarked that during the campaign of 1900 Mr. Hanna used his influence with the coal operators to settle a strike which was hurting the chances of Republican success. An agreement had been made which expired on March 31, 1901, but this agreement was a temporary compromise which satisfied neither side. The Union had voted to strike on April 1, unless a more satisfactory arrangement could be made with its employers. The Conciliation Committee could not get in touch with the operators in order to make an attempt at adjustment; and remembering Senator Hanna's contribution to the former agreement, they decided to ask his assistance. They were warned that the Senator's interest in the matter might not be as keen as it was during the campaign, but they decided to take the chance. Mr. D. R. Hanna arranged a meeting with his father. Senator Hanna responded immediately. He went to New York, had a conference with Messrs. Mitchell and Keefe and decided to place the matter before Mr. J. P. Morgan. The latter turned it over to President Thomas of the Erie Railroad. Senator Hanna arranged a meeting between Mr. Thomas and Mitchell, and as a result of this conference, an agreement was reached which was to run until April 1, 1902.

During his visit to New York on this business, the plans and purposes of the Conciliation Committee of the Civic Federation were explained to Senator Hanna and immediately aroused his interest. Its program was based upon the idea that the great majority of strikes might be averted, provided conferences could be arranged, grievances and demands fully discussed and a fair compromise embodied in some kind of a trade agreement. Such a program could not but appeal to the Senator. They were proposing to adapt to a larger field the methods of personal intercourse, which he had used in his own business and which had proved to be thoroughly practicable. Moreover, he could see an opportunity for effective work on his own part. The basis of his power was personal confidence and influence. Could not his own influence be effectively used in order to bring about these necessary and fruitful conferences between employer and employee? Later, after he had gone to Cleveland, Messrs. Mitchell and Keefe followed him thither, and spent some little time in explaining more in detail the ideas and hopes of the Committee. If there had been any hesitation left in the Senator's mind, it vanished. He not only approved, but would actively and cordially coöperate. "Boys," he said, "this looks right to me. I'll do anything you want."

During the summer of 1901 a strike occurred in some of the plants of the newly organized United States Steel Corporation. The dispute was serious, and involved both fundamental issues and a large number of men. The Conciliation Committee of the Civic Federation made several attempts to secure conferences and bring about an agreement. Mr. Hanna was intensely interested. Throughout the summer the strike and the means taken to end it bulked larger than any single subject in his correspondence. After many failures a conference was finally arranged between President Schwab and his associates and a labor committee, consisting of Gompers, Mitchell, Sargeant and others, which reached an agreement. Mr. Hanna had much to do with the arrangements for this decisive consultation, and its successful result convinced him, finally, that the Committee of the Federation was working with immediately fruitful methods. During the fall he publicly associated himself with the work.

As soon as Senator Hanna publicly identified himself with the Federation and its work, certain influential members of it, particularly Messrs. Mitchell and Keefe, proposed to make him Chairman of the Industrial Department. The suggestion provoked lively opposition. Many members of the association were by way of being reformers, and did not approve of Mr. Hanna's political purposes or methods. They and others who personally liked the Senator were afraid that the Federation would be injured by the political prominence of the proposed Chairman, and would begin to look like an annex to the Republican National Committee. The late Bishop Potter, who had recently joined the Federation, was particularly vigorous in his opposition. Nevertheless, Mr. Hanna was chosen, and no injurious results to the Federation followed. Public opinion was coming to place a fairer estimate on Mr. Hanna's motives. The tendency of editorial comment was to consider the Senator sincere and disinterested in assuming responsibility for the most important branch of the Federation's work. In the end opponents, such as the late Bishop Potter, admitted their error. He said: "Mr. Hanna has grown up to the size of the job."

On Dec. 16 and 17, 1901, the second National Conference of the Federation was held in the rooms of the Board of Trade and Transportation in New York. It was addressed by a number of the most prominent and representative union officials in the country, and by the heads of a number of large corporations and employers' associations. In all of these speeches the program of the Federation was explicitly and cordially approved. Mr. Hanna himself made a short speech, proclaiming his confidence in organized labor, his complete approval of the methods of the Federation, and his readiness to place his own services at the disposal of the Industrial Department. The meeting was a great success, and increased the prestige of the Federation. Public comment was widespread, and approved almost without a dissenting voice. Senator Hanna was made Chairman of the Executive Committee, Samuel Gompers, first Vice-Chairman, Oscar Straus, second Vice-Chairman, Charles A. Moore, Treasurer, and Ralph M. Easley, Secretary. The membership of the general committee was enlarged to forty, one-third of whom represented the unions, another third the employers and their associations and a final third the "general public." Out of this general committee were to be selected special committees to help in the adjustment of disputes in particular trades.

From the moment this committee was organized under its

new leadership, it was involved in an effort to avoid the most serious and dangerous American industrial dispute since the Pullman strike of 1894 — viz. a disagreement between the anthracite coal operators and the union of their employees, the United Mine Workers of America. As we have seen, Senator Hanna had already been personally interested in this quarrel. He had temporarily settled the strike of 1900, and had helped to prevent a strike from taking place in the spring of 1901. But the arrangement was limited to a year, and it was not to be made permanent, unless the Union proved to the operators that it could control its members. In October, 1901, Mr. Mitchell and his district presidents had gone to New York in order to have an interview with President Thomas of the Erie Road. They wanted to discuss mutual grievances, and pave the way for a general conference at a later date. After waiting for several weeks, the committee was finally denied even a hearing by Mr. Thomas and were made indignant by being most effectually snubbed. Consequently, Mr. Hanna was called up in Cleveland and after learning the facts suggested an interview between Secretary Easley of the Industrial Committee and Mr. Thomas, which developed nothing but the expression of a determination on the part of Mr. Thomas and the other operators not to have anything to do with the Union. It was a question, they declared, whether they or the Union should control their business. Such was the situation at the time of the National Conference of the Federation.

While in New York Senator Hanna investigated the difficulty and found the operators unanimous and determined in their resolution to have nothing to do with the Union and fully prepared, if necessary, to accept the consequences of a fight to the finish. Two months later, although he could not secure a conference between the Union leaders and the operators, he did arrange a meeting between Mr. Mitchell and Mr. J. P. Morgan. The interview was inconclusive. Mr. Morgan was friendly and courteous. He promised, in case the matter ever reached him, to do "what was right," but he had not the power and he evidently had not the disposition to interfere at that stage of the controversy. Hence up to the time of the convention of the miners at Shamokin on March 18, every attempt at conciliation made by Mr. Hanna and his association was thwarted by the attitude of the operators — which was dictated by a settled intention of ignoring the Union and breaking it. They did not want a strike. Apparently they believed that the miners would not carry hostilities that far. But the terms on which a strike was to be avoided were practically unconditional surrender on the part of the Union.

At the miner's convention Mr. Mitchell with difficulty prevented his followers from voting unequivocally for a strike. Finally it did declare for a suspension of work but upon a date to be decided by the district officers. On March 24, Mr. Mitchell telegraphed to Senator Hanna asking him, as Chairman of the Industrial Department of the Federation, to intervene on behalf of some settlement. A meeting was finally arranged between the miners, a committee of the operators, consisting of Presidents Baer, Truesdale, Thomas and Olyphant and the conciliation committee. At this conference the discussion was extremely bitter and the only result was a postponement of the threatened strike for thirty days from April 1, the operators promising in the meantime not to mine any more than the normal amount of coal.

Late in April another conference was held, the general tone of which was much more promising than that of the first interview. Both sides were still uncompromising, but an agreement was reached to continue the conference a few days later — the conferees being a committee of three operators and three representatives of the miners. This was the kind of a meeting which the operators had refused in the beginning. They even allowed Mr. Mitchell to attend the final conference, a proceeding to which they had formerly objected, because he was not one of their employees, but was a bituminous coal miner. They were beginning to understand that the national officers of a union may well be more experienced and reasonable men than the local officers.

The Committee of the Federation expected that a settlement would be reached at the new conference, and the disappointment was great when, on Wednesday afternoon, April 30, Mr. Mitchell in Reading telephoned to Mr. Hanna in Washington and reported a disagreement. The Senator refused to call the

Committee to receive such a report and during the next few days he exerted all his personal influence to prevent the strike. Says Mr. Easley in an article in the *Independent*, March 3, 1904: "He went back of the presidents of the roads and undertook to bring pressure on the stockholders, getting a committee of them together in one of the large banks and talking with them over the telephone for two hours. He cabled to important interests in Europe. On the labor side he urged Mr. Mitchell to name the lowest possible figure he would recommend his followers to accept, which was a five per cent increase (they were asking for twenty per cent), and this information was conveyed to the presidents of the roads; but they spurned the suggestion — so certain were they that the men would not actually strike. Senator Hanna, when informed of the results of this suggestion, said disgustedly, 'Well! they will not only strike, but they will get ten per cent increase before they settle.'" They were finally awarded ten per cent and in addition a sliding scale, which amounted in some instances to seventeen per cent.

On May 17, the miners again met in convention, this time at Hazleton; and Mr. Mitchell made a great effort to secure the acceptance of an appeal which had been telegraphed to the convention by the Conciliation Committee of the Federation. This appeal proposed that a strike be postponed, until an impartial committee be selected to make a full investigation of the condition of the laborers in the mines, their wages, hours of employment, and all other matters which form the subject of their complaints. But the effort failed. The delegates had been instructed to vote for a strike, and it was ordered by a vote of 461 to 439. Thus all attempts at conciliation or delay proved abortive, chiefly because the operators did not believe that a strike would actually take place. When it did take place they were inclined to blame the Civic Federation for the result and to accuse it of meddling mischievously in other people's business.

As soon as he heard that some of the operators had been criticising the Federation, Senator Hanna sent the following message to them: "You tell them that if I hear any more of that kind of talk I will go to New York, hire Carnegie Hall, and give them something to talk about." At another time when he was informed that certain operators had attributed his interest in the matter to the beneficial effect of his interference on a supposed Presidential boom, he replied: "Go and tell the operators that if they will arbitrate their differences with the miners, I will make an affidavit that I will not only refuse to accept the nomination for the Presidency if tendered to me, but, if elected, I will refuse to qualify."

For many weeks after the strike was called, Mr. Hanna and his associates on the Committee were obliged to concentrate their forces upon beating off an attack from another quarter rather than upon the settlement of the strike itself. Some of the unionists were seriously advocating the idea of calling out the bituminous coal miners on a sympathetic strike, in spite of the fact that these miners were working under a satisfactory unexpired agreement with their own employers. Such a war measure would have been almost fatal to the whole program of the Federation, which proposed to bring about trade agreements by means of collective bargaining. If such bargains were not kept, there could be slight hope of comparative industrial peace along these lines. No effort was spared, consequently, to prevent the calling of the sympathetic strike. For six weeks hard and systematic missionary work was carried on throughout the coal regions, both bituminous and anthracite, to prevent what was regarded by all friends of the Federation as a suicidal act; and in this work they were assisted by every labor leader on the Committee. They were successful. The convention of the bituminous miners held at Indianapolis on July 17 voted against a sympathetic strike, and their fidelity to their contract under such a severe pressure made, as well it might, a deep and lasting impression on Senator Hanna.

In his speech of Aug. 9, 1902, delivered at Chatauqua, he said: —

"If there ever was a situation which would tempt men of any class to violate an agreement — on the one side one hundred and fifty thousand idle men with hundreds of thousands of women and children depending upon them for their daily bread, approaching the verge of starvation, seeing, or believing they saw, the only remedy which would force their employers to a consideration of what they thought their rightful claim would be through a strike; and on the other hand their solemn promise, given only by word of mouth to their employers, that they would mine coal for the year 1902 at a fixed price — if there ever was a test that could possibly solve that question, there it was. It is one of the proudest moments of my life, that I can state from this rostrum to such an audience as this, that the men stood by their word. [Great applause.] Ay, unanimously, when the matter came before the convention, they declined to sign for the strike. I say it is a proud moment of my life, because it is a ray of light that comes to us who are working honestly in this field of labor — an encouragement which, had it been prophesied six months ago, would have been said to be impossible."

After the threat of a sympathetic strike had been averted, attempts were made to find some acceptable basis of settlement. I cannot trace the course of these negotiations in detail; but the plan, which was gaining ground, looked in the direction of submitting the whole dispute to the arbitration of a representative expert commission with full power and opportunity to make a careful investigation of the facts. In the meantime the summer had passed, and winter was near at hand. The coal-bins were empty. Public opinion was beginning to be alarmed at the prospect of the suffering which would result from an indefinite prolongation of the strike. The idea began to be expressed that industrial disputes should not be allowed to place the public welfare in such jeopardy. On September 27, President Roosevelt wrote to Mr. Hanna: "What gives me greatest concern at the moment is the coal famine. Of course we have nothing whatever to do with this coal strike and no earthly responsibility for it. But the public at large will tend to visit on our heads responsibility for the shortage in coal, precisely as Kansas and Nebraska visited upon our heads their failure to raise good crops in the arid belt eight, ten or a dozen years ago. I do not see what I can do, and I know the coal operators are especially distrustful of anything which they regard as in the nature of political interference. But I do most earnestly feel that from every consideration of public policy and good morals, they should make some slight concession."

Two days later Senator Hanna replied from Cleveland, as follows: —

"My dear Mr. President: —

"I am in receipt of yours of the 27th inst. and reply that I share with you the anxiety in regard to the coal situation. After leaving Oyster Bay, I spent the balance of the week in New York raising money for the Congressional Committee and trying to see what more could be done with the strike. Confidentially, I saw Mr. Morgan and I also saw Mr. Mitchell (the public knows nothing about that). I got from Mr. Morgan a proposition as to what he would do in the matter and I got Mitchell to agree to accept it — if the operators would abide by the decision. I really felt encouraged to think that I was about to accomplish a settlement. I went to Philadelphia and saw Mr. Baer and to my surprise he absolutely refused to entertain it. You can see how determined they are. It looks as if it was only to be settled when the miners are starved to it, and that may be weeks ahead as they are getting abundant supplies from their fellow-workmen all over the country. I am not unmindful of the importance of this coal situation and will not miss an opportunity to help if I can, but the position of the operators from the beginning has put all efforts of mine in a false light before the public, so I am only able to hold the confidence of the men and serve them if I can."

The foregoing letter of Senator Hanna's was received in Washington on September 30, and it may have had something to do with the action immediately taken by the President — asking the operators to meet Mr. Mitchell in a conference at the White House. On October 2, Mr. Hanna telegraphed to the President wishing him every success in his undertaking; but success did not follow. The obstinacy of the operators only increased with every effort to break it down. On October 3 the President wrote the following letter: —

"My dear Senator Hanna: —

"Well! I have tried and failed. I feel downhearted over the result, both because of the great misery ensuing for the mass of our people, and because the attitude of the operators will beyond a doubt double the burden on us, who stand between them and socialistic action. But I am glad I tried anyhow. I should have hated to feel that I had failed to make any effort. What my next move will be I cannot yet say. I feel most strongly that the attitude of the operators is one which accentuates the need of the government having some power to supervision and regulation over such corporations. I would like to make a fairly radical experiment on the anthracite coal business to start with.

"At the meeting to-day the operators assumed a fairly hopeless attitude. None of them appeared to such advantage as Mitchell, whom most of them denounced with such violence and rancor that I felt he did very well to keep his temper. Between times they insulted me for not preserving order (evidently ignoring such a trifling detail as the United States Constitution) and attacked Knox for not having brought suit against the miners' union, as violating the Sherman Anti-Trust Law. You have probably seen my statement and Mitchell's proposition. I regarded the latter as imminently fair and reasonable. Now it is over I may mention that if the operators had acceded to it, I intended to put you on the commission or board of arbitration. But the operators declined to accede to the proposition or to make any proposition that amounted to anything in return; and as I say I must now think very seriously of what the next move shall be. A coal famine in the winter is an ugly thing, and I fear we shall see terrible suffering and grave disaster."

The idea of a coal arbitration commission, once having been launched, found such support from public opinion that even the operators had to yield. During the negotiations which ensued, looking towards the appointment of the Commission and the return of the miners to work pending its report, President Roosevelt constantly consulted Mr. Hanna and the part which the latter played towards the end is indicated by the following letter: —

"CLEVELAND, OHIO, Oct. 15, 1902.
"MY DEAR MR. PRESIDENT: —
"I talked with Mitchell on the 'phone' yesterday, after my conversation with you, and I think he feels satisfied with the assurances given him, although, of course, he appreciates the unfairness in the proposition of the operators in not naming an *experienced miner* as a member of the Commission. At his request I sent him a telegram urging the acceptance of the proposition and giving him the assurance that the men could depend on *absolute fairness* at your hands. This, of course, was to show to influential men among the miners, for whatever effect my influence would have among them. I sincerely hope it will end the strike, and your interest in the matter will be appreciated."

It did end the strike, and the correspondence between the President and Senator over this critical matter may be closed with the following letter from the President: —

"WHITE HOUSE, WASHINGTON, Oct. 16, 1902.

"MY DEAR SENATOR:—

"Late last night when it became evident that we were going to get a Commission which would be accepted by both sides, I remarked, 'Well, Uncle Mark's work has borne fruit,' and everybody said, 'Yes.' The solution came because so many of us have for so long hammered at the matter until at last things got into shape which made the present outcome possible. I hardly suppose the miners will go back on Mitchell. If they do, they put themselves wholly in the wrong. I earnestly hope you are now in good shape physically."

While not attempting to tell the whole story of the anthracite coal strike, I have for several reasons dwelt in detail upon Senator Hanna's relation to it. The public scarcely realized at the time the amount of hard work which he devoted to the business, and the extent to which, as President Roosevelt's last letter indicates, he contributed to the settlement. The incident also provides an excellent illustration of the methods and policy pursued by the Conciliation Committee of the Civic Federation — an illustration which loses nothing because of the failure of Mr. Hanna's own efforts to effect a settlement. The experience convinced him that the Federation was working along the right lines, and that its unaided exertions in the present instance had proved abortive, chiefly because the operators had wofully misjudged the situation. They had underestimated the will and the ability of the Union to fight and to resist; and they had failed to anticipate that, if the Union did resist, their own position on the approach of winter and in the face of public opinion would become untenable.

The anthracite coal strike is one of the very few industrial disputes in which Senator Hanna personally participated and in which he failed to effect a settlement. Up to November, 1903, about a hundred disagreements were amicably adjusted by the Conciliation Committee; and their good offices failed in only eighteen cases. Mr. Hanna's services were constantly at the call of the Committee. He took part in many important negotiations and he contributed liberally to expenses. All his associates testify that he was absorbed heart and soul in the work, and that it was coming to occupy as much of his time and attention as was his political career.

A couple of instances of his successful interference in these disputes must suffice. For instance, there was a disagreement between the New York, New Haven & Hartford Railroad and its employees, which had been carried so far that the men were about to strike. The officers of the road would not consent to an interview with the officers of the Brotherhood, because the latter were not their own employees. The men appealed to the Committee of the Federation, and Senator Hanna was called up at Washington by the Secretary of the Committee. He inquired as to the real merits of the dispute and asked particularly whether "the boys were right." The next day E. E. Clark, Grand Chief Conductor of the Order of Railway Conductors, went over to Washington to state their case, and after hearing it Senator Hanna telephoned to Mr. J. P. Morgan and arranged an interview between the banker and the union leader. As a result of the meeting the strike was averted, and the incident is said to have resulted in a change in the management of the road.

In the heat of his last campaign in Ohio, when he was a candidate for reëlection to the Senate, and when he was overworked and in bad health, he responded with similar celerity and success to another demand made upon him. Mr. William D. Mahon, President of the Amalgamated Association of Street Railway Employees, came to the Committee and reported a disagreement between the Public Service Corporation of New Jersey and its employees. The officials of the Corporation refused to see him, and unless he could meet them a strike was bound to follow, because hard feeling had been aroused and the men could no longer be restrained. Senator Hanna was notified of the situation by telegraph. The President of the Public Service Corporation was a fellow-Senator — Mr. Dryden; and Mr. Hanna contrived a conference between him and Mr. Mahon, whereby the strike was prevented. In both of these instances the success of the Committee was due chiefly to the personal influence of the Chairman. The men responsible for the direction of large corporations could not afford to disregard the suggestions of a man to whom they owed so much. Even in those cases which were managed by the Committee without Mr. Hanna's help, his prestige was behind it and often enabled it to obtain a hearing and carry on its work of conciliation.

The accusation of the operators that Mr. Hanna's interest in the settlement of labor disputes was due to an ambitious politician's desire for personal popularity was frequently repeated; but as soon as a man had once heard Mr. Hanna talk about his plans and expectations they became convinced of his disinterestedness and sincerity. Mr. Ralph M. Easley states that an interview with Mr. Hanna was usually sufficient to convert not merely lukewarm and mildly antagonistic people, but radical and suspicious unionists and strong personal opponents. When an attempt was made to organize a local conciliation committee in Chicago, Judge Murray F. Tully, an able and influential Democrat, was invited to coöperate. Although he believed in the arbitration of labor disputes, he refused, because the Civic Federation looked to him merely as an annex to Mr. Hanna's Republican organization. He was, however, persuaded to attend a public meeting and hear Mr. Hanna and Mr. Mitchell talk. After the end of the Senator's speech, Judge Tully arose and said: "Mr. Chairman, I came to this meeting deeply prejudiced against the whole idea. I will be frank. I was against it because I deemed Senator Hanna to be nothing but a politician, and I did not think it was a good thing to have him at the head of the local federation. But I have heard him and I am with you."

From the foregoing account the Industrial Department of the Civic Federation may appear to have been merely a vessel wherein Senator Hanna's personal prestige was converted into a soothing industrial balm. But such a sneer would be very unjust both to Mr. Hanna and to the Federation. Undoubtedly the temporary success of the Committee was largely due to Mr. Hanna's personal influence with the heads of corporations, and the importance of this branch of the work of the Federation has since his death very much diminished. The program of the association was nevertheless based upon a sound analysis of the immediate cause of the majority of strikes, and it specified a practicable method of averting them. Strikes can usually be avoided, in case some means exists of bringing the two disputants together for the purpose of a full discussion of grievances, demands and differences of opinion. But conferences of this kind implied in practice the existence of some form of association among the employees and their representation by influential leaders. It implied as the result of a successful conference some sort of an agreement defining the terms of employment for a specified period; and it implied also the recognition of a set of rules which would help to determine the justice of the conflicting demands of the economic litigants. It implied, in short, the organization of both employers and employees, a definite theory of the economic relations between them and of the social and economic issues involved in their disputes. Like every serviceable piece of practical machinery its successful working embodied a creed, and it could not make any very permanent conquests, until that creed was defined and somewhat generally accepted.

Senator Hanna did not seem to be the man to give an explicit and persuasive expression to such a creed. He was not a student of economics. He had no knowledge of the history of industrial conflicts in other countries and other times. His general economic point of view was that of an extreme individualist who wanted public interference in business confined to the encouragement of private and class interests. Nevertheless, the desirable creed obtained a rough but very effective popular expression at his hands, and it did so because in his own life he had always lived up to the creed which he explained and advocated. The wholesome aspect of all his thinking was the close, the inseparable relation between it and his own personal experience. In so far as his business and political life had restricted his personal experience, his theories were correspondingly partial and inadequate. But in all the human aspects of business his personal experience had been large and edifying; and the thought in which it was reflected became luminous as well as sincere.

The ideas contained in his capital and labor speeches of 1902 and 1903 had for years been lurking in his mind. They had received occasional and very partial expression in his conversation and letters. But no immediate practical exigency had arisen which compelled them to overflow, and the only references to the labor question in his earlier speeches had been prompted by the vindication of his own personal relation with his employees. But between the spring of 1901 and the summer of 1902 he was, as we have seen, actively interested in several attempts to settle labor disputes by the use of certain methods. These experiences fermented in his mind, and stimulated his thought. Even then his ideas might have gone unexpressed, had he not consented, as usual without premeditation, to address in August, 1902, two Chautauqua meetings. The speeches delivered at that time, an article in the *National Magazine* on "Socialism and Labor Unions" and a final speech made before a labor union in Columbus, Ohio, in April, 1903, constitute his longest and most important utterances on the labor question. They deserve careful consideration, not merely for the light which they shed upon their subject-matter, but because they enable us to understand Mr. Hanna himself very much better. For the first time in his public career, some of those essentially social values, embodied in his personal life, received explicit expression.

He almost always began with an account of his own practical experiences with a prolonged and embittered strike — that of the Massillon coal miners in 1876. This one terrible instance, nearly thirty years before, had taught him to see the waste, the futility and the criminal danger of allowing such conflicts to settle themselves without any recognition of the endangered public interest. He had believed ever since that some effective machinery should be provided for the settlement of industrial disputes, and he welcomed the program of the Civic Federation, because it recognized a public responsibility in the matter and attempted seriously and intelligently to grapple with it. In his own words the Civic Federation was merely trying to apply the "Golden Rule" to the adjustment of such a quarrel — which meant that each of the two contestants should not oppose the legitimate demands of the other and that each should abandon any practices of their own, inimical to the best interests of society.

The employers, on their side, should recognize that unions were an indispensable and useful agency, not merely to protect labor against capitalistic selfishness, but for the gradual creation of a better understanding between the wage-earner and the wage-payer. Mr. Hanna never went so far as to advocate a thoroughgoing policy of recognizing and favoring union labor, but the tendency of his doctrine looks in that direction. If the laborer can obtain his fair share of the industrial product only by organization, his attempts to organize should be approved rather than opposed. "The natural tendency," he said in his Chautauqua speech, "in this country, ay, and in the world over, has been the selfish appropriation of the larger share by capital. As long as labor was in a situation which forced it to submit, that condition would to a very large degree continue. If labor had some grievance and each laborer in his individual capacity went to his employer and asked for consideration, how much would be shown to him? Not much. Therefore, when they banded together in an organization for their own benefit which would give them the power, if necessary, to demand a remedy, I say organized labor was justified." It is essential, he adds, that employers should admit the existence of such a justification, and establish a foundation for joint action and mutual good-will by conferring with the unionized laborers and their representatives and entering into agreements with them.

He had the utmost confidence in the practical value of such conferences. Frequently misunderstandings would be avoided, unreasonable demands mitigated, and comparative good-will restored merely by a frank discussion and ventilation of mutual grievances. "It is truly astonishing," he says in his article on "Socialism and Labor Unions," "to consider what trivial disagreements have occasioned some of the most serious strikes. I have seen two parties stand apart, each with a chip on his shoulder, defying his opponent to knock it off and moved by emotions and considerations that were very far from promoting the welfare of either party. There is more to overcome in the way of feeling on the part of capital than on the part of labor. Capital has been for many generations intrenched behind its power to dictate conditions, whether right or wrong; and the abrogation of this power is not going to weaken in the least degree the strength of the hitherto dominant party, for a manufacturing corporation can make no better investment than in the hearty coöperation and good feeling of its employees."

While he justified the organization of labor in the interest both of the wage-earners and their employers, he feared certain of its tendencies. He regarded it "as an imported article" which had aroused a natural prejudice against itself in this country, because its policy was that of aggressive warfare against capital — a warfare which was to be relentless and which was "at variance with American institutions," because it introduced a spirit of mutual suspicion and antagonism instead of a spirit of mutual confidence into the heart of American industrial life. But he believed that the program of the Civic Federation would "fit the unions to their surroundings and conditions in the country." The Federation would not countenance sympathetic strikes, the boycott, or any restriction of production in order to enhance prices. If the unions insisted on these policies, they would be converting themselves into industrial and social outlaws. As a condition of recognition they must make themselves worthy of approval by abandoning all practices based on an essential antagonism between their own interests and the demands of industrial efficiency and social well-being. He hoped to make the Civic Federation a constructive educational agency, which would gradually teach the two contending parties how far they could properly go without destroying a fair basis of conciliation and fruitful coöperation.

His purpose was fundamentally to re-create good feeling between employers and their employees by means of a personal intercourse and the mutual application of the "Golden Rule." "My theory is," he said in the Chautauqua speech, "that when you bring the men to you, every employee will feel that you are treating him as a man. Appeal to his heart and to his mind and you will succeed in establishing a bond of confidence." In all his utterances on the question he reiterates this fundamental idea. "Every man is vulnerable in some part," he says in his article on "Socialism and Labor Unions," "and it is a rare thing to find any man proof against methods of kindness and justice. If every man is treated as a *Man*, and an appeal is made to his heart as well as to his reason, it will establish a bond of confidence as a sure foundation to build upon. This is the condition aimed at by the Civic Federation — absolute confidence on both sides. Many of the ills that have crept into labor organizations are importations from older countries and will not live here because thay are not fitted to our conditions. While labor unions may have proved a curse to England, I believe that they will prove to be a boon to our own country when a proper basis of confidence and respect is established. We have, perhaps, been too busy and too engrossed in our rapid expansion to look upon the ethical side of this question, and have forgotten that two factors contributed to the prosperity of our nation, — the man who works with his hands and the man who works with his head — partners in toil who ought to be partners in the profits of that toil."

It will be admitted, I think, that the foregoing program is based upon a sound analysis of the immediate causes of ordinary strikes and that it prescribes a remedy which offers in the present emergency a fair chance of being useful. Of course the machinery whereby Mr. Hanna proposed to bring organized capital and organized labor together broke down. The Industrial Department of the Civic Federation did not continue to be an effective agency either for the settlement of labor disputes or for the establishment of better relations between American wage-earners and wage-payers. The employers came in the end to resent its unofficial interference. The unions no longer allow their leaders to coöperate with the Federation. The ill-feeling and the mutual suspicion between the two contestants have increased during the past ten years. But it is not fair to dismiss the whole program because the Federation itself did not prove to be as permanently useful a conciliating agency as it was during Mr. Hanna's leadership. The results which Mr. Hanna hoped to accomplish informally by the agency of a private organization backed by public opinion evidently demand a more powerful and authoritative engine of the social will — one which he himself might have been loathe to call into action.

Nevertheless it would not be fair to attribute the temporary success of the Industrial Department of the Federation merely to Mr. Hanna's personal and political influence. This factor counted, but it would not have counted much, unless Mr. Hanna had been disinterestedly engaged on behalf of what he believed to be a practicable plan of conciliation. His success was due, that is, not merely to his personal hold on business men and union leaders or his personal skill as a negotiator, but to his enthusiastic interest in the question and his increasing mastery of it. When he said to his audience at Urbana: "Oh! my friends, you have got to be with these men, among them and a part of them to understand this labor question thoroughly," he was describing his own actual position. He had remained, if not a part of them, at least close to them. They mutually understood and trusted one another. His friends in the unions had that very confidence in his good faith, which in a generalized form he postulates as the essential condition of any permanent improvement in the relations between capital and labor. They recognized his genuine sympathy with the wage-earner's ambition for a higher standard of living. He earnestly endeavored to instil the same feeling into his audiences and into his business friends; and whenever it is shared by a larger number of people of all classes, the labor question will lose much of its present critical character.

Many people who did not know him questioned the sincerity of his sympathy with organized labor and the validity of his ultimate purposes. He advocated labor unions, they said and still say, because he found it much more easy and convenient to get what he wanted out of a few labor leaders than out of a mob of unorganized workmen. Be it admitted that some such motive may have partly determined his preference for the unions. But the sincerity of his attitude was not thereby affected. Economic radicals, who believe in the inevitability and righteousness of class warfare, like to read into the mind of every representative of wealth a "class consciousness" similar to their own, and they insist upon interpreting every action of such a man as the result of a more or less conscious purpose of exploitation. But "class consciousness" of any kind was precisely the kind of consciousness which an American like Mark Hanna did not have. There welled up in him a spring of the old instinctive homogeneity of feeling characteristic of the pioneer American. His whole attitude towards labor and his program of conciliation are, indeed, the product of an innocent faith that his country was radically different economically and socially from Europe, and that no fundamental antagonism of economic interest existed among different classes of Americans.

All they had to do was to deal fairly and feel kindly one towards another.

He was, of course, too shrewd a political leader not to understand the added strength which advocacy of the labor unions gave to his advocacy of big business. His labor policy was undoubtedly framed partly as a supplement to his corporation policy. "I believe," he said in his speech to the Ohio State Convention in May, 1903, "I believe in organized labor, and I believe in organized capital as an auxiliary." But here again the labor program did not engage his support merely because it might sweeten the corporation pill for the palate of the American people. He was one of the first of our public men to understand that the organization of capital necessarily implied some corresponding kind of labor organization. He saw clearly that the large corporations could not survive in case their behavior towards their employees was oppressive, and that they would in the end strengthen themselves by recognizing union labor. Derived as the two forms of organization were from analogous sources, the future of both depended partly upon their ability to find some basis of mutual accommodation and coöperation, not incompatible with the public interest. In grasping this connection, and in insisting upon it, Mr. Hanna travelled far ahead of prevailing business and political opinion. The large corporations have at best been paternal in their policy towards their employees; and whether paternal or not they have usually been inimical to the unions. If their directors had understood the political and business interests at stake as clearly as Mr. Hanna did and had conciliated union labor, their situation at the present time in the face of American public opinion would have been very much better.

At bottom, however, and most of all, Mr. Hanna's labor policy was the expression of personal kindliness and good-will. As an embodiment and advocate of pioneer economics, he had always been sincere in his belief that business expansion and prosperity would be of as much benefit to the wage-earners as to the capitalist. But he was obliged to recognize that the former were not satisfied with the share of the product which they received under competitive conditions; and he came to realize that they were right in not being satisfied. His evident sincerity in introducing this exception into his general system of a state-aided process of economic production, but a socially irresponsible distribution of its fruits, proves his sincerity in claiming, as he always had, that he wanted to represent not one class but the American people as a whole. By emphasizing this exception, by proclaiming that capitalists had systematically exploited their employees and that in their dealing with labor a humane motive should be substituted for the ordinary economic motive — in assuming such an attitude he was showing once again how clearly he could read and profit by the lessons of his experience. His whole plane of political and economic thought was raised to a higher level. He had liberated and made articulate the underlying humanity of his own personal feeling towards the mass of his fellow-countrymen.

But in this instance, as in the other more important developments of his public personality, the revelation had been in a way imposed upon him. He had simply responded to a stimulus. In 1900 he had not the slightest expectation of attempting to alleviate the conflict between capital and labor. If it had depended on his own conscious will, he might have remained inarticulate until his death, and his friends would have been deprived of the most lucid and unalloyed public expression of his honest interest in the welfare of the laboring class. But the Civic Federation happened to be organized. His practical interest in the labor problem had left a trail behind it. The officials of the Federation found him out and went to him for help, not he to them for an opportunity. He responded to the call, divined the opportunity, seized it, and in seizing it, not only made it bigger, but made himself big enough to put it to good use. For the first time in his public career he became a reformer, dedicated consciously to the task of converting other people to a better way of dealing with a fundamental problem; and the best of it was that his public appearance as a labor reformer was the natural, although fortuitous, expression of his lifelong personal feelings and behavior.

CHAPTER XXVI

THE CAMPAIGN OF 1903 AND THE PRESIDENTIAL NOMINATION

A CONTEMPORARY observer of Mr. Hanna's career might well have surmised in the fall of 1901 that the Senator had climbed as high in public estimation as was possible for a man of his economic opinions and political methods. He was the undisputed leader of his party, and he was much more popular throughout the country than ever before; but how could a man as definitely committed as Mr. Hanna was to special business interests and to "machine" politics broaden any farther the basis of his public prestige? We have seen how he succeeded in doing so. The increased scope of his legislative interests, his willingness to consider all legislative projects from a responsible national standpoint, his decisive participation in the action of the Senate respecting an interoceanic canal, and finally his work on behalf of a better understanding between capital and labor, — his actions in all these matters had enhanced his stature still further in the eyes of the American people. There was no anticlimax in Mark Hanna's career. His public personality continued until the day of his death to gather size and distinction.

What he had gained was an increasing amount of confidence in him on the part of the public. He had always possessed the trust of the men, no matter of what class, with whom he came into practical association. After he went upon the stump he won the support of the Republican voters of his own state. But from the beginning his close association with "machine" politics and with merely business interests had made a large element in public opinion question his influence on public affairs. Many men who liked what they knew of his personality did not trust his methods or share his ideas. The tour in the Northwest during the campaign of 1900 had done a good deal to diminish this distrust, yet it continued to prevail, not merely among radicals, but among men of reforming tendencies all over the country. Much of it was bound to remain in any event, because it was partly due to divergent views of public policy. But during 1902 he came to be regarded with increasing respect even by his irreconcilable opponents, while at the same time the number of these opponents was substantially diminished. Many more people than formerly tended to accept his political leadership. Confidence in his personal good faith unquestionably attached thousands of the smaller business men of the country to the support of the existing system — the very class which, during the year or two after his death, went over to the cause of reform. He was a great power not merely in public and party business, but in his influence on public opinion.

A fair indication of the nature and extent of Mr. Hanna's influence is afforded by the merely external aspects of his life in Washington. The employees of the Senate all agree that no other Senator, when he was at the Capitol, had as many callers as did Mark Hanna; and certainly the office of no other Senator was over-run with so many and such different people. In his anteroom would be found politicians of high degree from all over the Union, an equally large assortment of "big" and little business men, state governors, Congressmen, labor leaders, fellow-Senators and even Cabinet officers. Rarely did Mr. Hanna at this time call on either a colleague in the Senate or a member of the Cabinet. He would usually telephone to the latter's office, say that he wanted to see the secretary and inquire when it would be convenient for him to call. Nine times out of ten the secretary would make an appointment to go and see Mr. Hanna. Towards the end the unusual consideration with which he was treated was partly due to his known physical enfeeblement; but his peculiar prestige in the world of affairs and politics was no less responsible. The one man in Washington on whom he invariably called was, of course, the President.

Another superficial fact of some significance is that he never used his committee room as an office. His mail, which at one time amounted to about half as much as all the rest of the Senate, was sent to his private office. When he wanted to receive callers at the Capitol, he used the room of the Vice-President, which was situated just across the hall from the entrance to the Senate Chamber. The Vice-President, Mr. Hobart, loaned him the use of this room whenever he needed it, and after Mr. Hobart's death, the new presiding officer of the Senate, Mr. Frye, was equally accommodating. This is a trivial fact, but it is an illustration of the privileged position to which he had obtained by virtue of personal ties and his public importance.

No man who had succeeded in placing so much private and public credit to his personal account could escape being hailed as a candidate for the Presidency. Nomination and election to the highest office in the land were about the only American political distinction which might have still further enhanced Mr. Hanna's prestige and power. It would, indeed, have been the only fitting culmination to a career which had gathered such unexpected and unprecedented momentum. Had Mr. McKinley and Mr. Hanna both lived until the fall of 1904, the latter's nomination and election would have been extremely probable. Mr. Roosevelt might have been a stiff competitor, but he could hardly have overcome the power of the administration, assisted by that of Mr. Hanna, his friends and followers. Mr. McKinley himself would have been the only man who could have prevented Mr. Hanna's nomination.

Mr. Hanna never deliberately intended and planned to make himself President — as he had planned and fought to make Mr. McKinley President and himself Senator. Had he retained his health, as well as his life, he would scarcely have refused a nomination offered to him by a substantial majority of his party; but at no time did he himself begin to contrive his own nomination or encourage his friends to do so. That was not his way, and if it had been his way, he would never have climbed as high as he did. He could not have used his peculiar personal and political advantages for the benefit of his own ambition without injuring the foundations of his power. His associates had confidence in him, because, as his career proved, he was working primarily for what he believed to be the interest of the party or the country. Whenever he felt himself entitled to a particular position, such as Senator, he fought for it; but he never attempted to manufacture a title which did not in a very real sense already exist.

There were, however, powerful individuals in the community, who both from friendship and interest, wanted to see Mr. Hanna in the Presidential chair. Immediately after McKinley's election in 1900 the newspapers began to publish articles, naming Mr. Hanna as the "logical" nominee of the Republican party in 1904 — as, indeed, at that time he unquestionably was. During the fall of 1901, just before Mr. McKinley's assassination, some followers of Mr. Hanna in Cleveland organized a Mark Hanna Club, and proposed to assemble at a public dinner and launch a Hanna "boom." They were immediately and effectually suppressed. Mr. Hanna publicly announced that he was not a candidate for the nomination; and at his bidding the Mark Hanna Club, with a glorious outlook towards the future, was dedicated to the memory of a dead statesman of Ohio — James A. Garfield. Even if Mr. Hanna was to be nominated, he obviously could not afford to have the agitation in favor of his candidacy originate so near his own doorstep.

The supersession of Mr. McKinley by Mr. Roosevelt completely changed the situation. The new President had been considered as possible nominee — even when he was no more than Vice-President. His promotion made him more than ever a candidate. A President who has served only one term and wants a renomination has a presumption in his favor as a matter both of personal justice and partisan expediency. The one effective way in which his party can approve his administration is to make him its candidate. To refuse him the distinction constitutes the gravest possible criticism of the man and weakens the strength of the party in the prospective campaign. It can be justified only in case the President has done nothing to deserve a nomination, or what he has done has lost him the support of his party. In Mr. Roosevelt's case he frankly wanted a nomination, and he wanted it all the more because he had never been elected to the Presidency. Whether his administration was a success or a failure, he could make a strong bid for the honor, as Chester A. Arthur had done in 1884, by virtue of his control over patronage. Any attempt to nominate Mr. Hanna would, consequently, meet at best with a powerful resistance from the friends of a President who had been popular enough to have the nomination for Vice-President thrust upon him against the will of Mr. Hanna and the administration. The advocates of Mr. Hanna's candidacy could only wait and hope for some mistake or accident which would injure Mr. Roosevelt's prospects.

Nothing, however, happened to make the President any less available as a candidate. He made some enemies, but he conquered or attracted more friends. His administration was approved, and he himself was increasingly liked and admired. The advocates of Mr. Hanna's nomination would necessarily have been very much discouraged, had not the corresponding increase in the Senator's personal prestige tempted them to believe that not even the President's power and popularity or Mr. Hanna's own indifference could block the road. Sentiment in favor of their favorite's nomination welled up spontaneously on any and every favorable opportunity.

The first occasion on which it obtained noticeable expression was at the meeting of the Ohio State Convention, held in Cleveland late in May, 1902. The Convention itself was not of any great importance. It assembled only for the purpose of nominating some minor state officials. Senator Hanna was present and controlled its action and its official deliberations. The platform contained a cordial indorsement of President Roosevelt's administration — one so cordial that the President wrote to Mr. Hanna and thanked him for it. But the aspect of the Convention which attracted and deserved most attention was the practically unanimous outburst among the delegates of Hanna Presidential sentiment. The feeling never obtained any official expression, but the manifest attitude of the delegates might be fairly construed as a pledge of support for a movement in favor of his nomination. It was so construed by the newspapers all over the country and a great deal of discussion followed as to the respective claims and chances of the President and the Senator.

In the meantime the relations between the two were cordial and even intimate. Both of them were loyal to the understanding they had reached on the day of Mr. Roosevelt's succession. The President consulted the Senator about the distribution of patronage, and usually took his advice. There were very few disagreements between them on that score. They coöperated in all legislative matters during the session of 1902, and Mr. Hanna's success in securing the favorable consideration of the Panama route made a deep impression on the President. Thereafter their joint interest in the canal constituted another bond between them — Mr. Hanna being the first man outside the Cabinet to be confidentially notified by the President that a good title could be secured to the French property. We have already indicated how closely they were associated during the critical days of the coal strike in October, 1902.

The following incident illustrates the candor of their relations and Mr. Hanna's attitude towards Mr. Roosevelt. In April, 1902, Mr. Charles Emory Smith, formerly Postmaster-General, published in the *Saturday Evening Post* an article in which he said: "But the only man who knows that Mr. Hanna has no aspirations towards the Presidency is President Roosevelt. The two men fully understand each other. There are questions of policy on which they do and will differ, but they differ in a frank and manly way, like two self-centred men accustomed each to think for himself, and it does not affect their good understanding." Mr. Hanna sent to Mr. Roosevelt the article with the foregoing passage marked and accompanied by the following note: —

4/8/1902.

"MY DEAR MR. PRESIDENT: —

"The enclosed article may not come under your eye. Therefore I send it to you, because I think it good, and because a man like Smith can see things outside the area of *smoke*.

"Sincerely yours,
"M. A. HANNA."

And the President returned a reply saying that he was delighted with the article, and thought Smith a very fine fellow.

But the smoke and the fire from which it came were not to be dissipated. During the summer very little fuel was provided for its consumption, and there were no flare-ups; but during the campaign in the fall, while Mr. Hanna was stumping the state, he was continually being hailed as the next Republican candidate for the Presidency. The campaign was opened on September 27 at Akron, which was the home town of Chairman Charles Dick of the State Committee, Mr. Hanna's political aide. The speakers, who consisted of Secretary Root and Senator Foraker, as well as Mr. Hanna, were continually being interrupted by cries from the audience: "Hanna in 1904," "Hanna in 1904." The newspapers remarked that the crowd was apparently interested in another candidacy besides that of Mr. Hanna. It was plentifully supplied with Dick as well as with Hanna buttons — Dick for Governor in 1903, Hanna for President in 1904.

In the speech made at the Akron meeting Mr. Hanna first introduced the phrase "stand-pat" into American politics. He began with the following words: "About a year ago it was my privilege to attend the opening meeting of the Republican campaign, and after thinking over the situation I concluded to give you a piece of good advice — 'Let well enough alone.' That was all there was in the campaign of interest to you. Now, I say, 'Stand-pat!' [Great applause.] You are not on the defensive to-day in Ohio, or anywhere in the United States, or in the Philippines." He continued to hold this note during his exhortations throughout the campaign; but after a little practice he improved upon the form of the introductory sentence, until it finally became a peculiarly effective example of his colloquial vigorous way of demanding the attention of his audience. Some days later at Steubenville he began as follows: "Two years ago I suggested to the people in view of the prosperous time that they knew their business. They replied that they did. One year ago I suggested that they 'leave well enough alone.' They replied that they would. This year I suggested that they 'stand-pat,' and they will reply, 'You bet.'" The "You Bet" coming after the "Stand-pat" brought down the house — as well it might. This man of action was becoming a maker of phrases.

The phrase "stand-pat," thus auspiciously launched on a long voyage in American politics, has since been adopted as the most popular description of stubborn political and economic conservatism. It is a strong phrase, and its implications have undoubtedly done the conservative cause some little harm. Conservative politicians dodge the word, and resent the idea that they are standing pat or standing still. As originally used by Mr. Hanna it did not necessarily mean any such immovability of purpose or ideas. He intended it to be merely an effective figurative description of the proper attitude of public opinion under the prevailing economic conditions. The sun of Republican prosperity continued to shine. Why not sit tight and enjoy its warmth? Any poker player knows that except on rare occasions a man who has a "pat" hand and does not "stand-pat" is a fool. He has not only nothing to gain by drawing cards, but usually he has everything to lose. That was precisely Mr. Hanna's point. A man who "stands-pat" in poker is in so strong a position that he can play an aggressive game without taking any of the usual chances. No happier characterization could be invented of a policy which was neither defensive nor experimental. To "stand-pat" on a complete hand is the only course to follow. Let your opponents risk the long chance.

Senator Hanna used the phrase in order to meet the demand already being heard among the Republicans of the Northwest for tariff revision. The tariff was the question above all others which he was afraid to reopen. He knew that as a matter of practical politics the tariff was the keystone of the whole Republican system. He knew that any revision upward would not be tolerated by public opinion, and any revision downward would tear the party to pieces. The result of a subsequent attempt at revision proved the soundness of his apprehensions. It both split the party and lost it the confidence of the country. The policy of protection upon which the Republican party was nourished for so many years may prove to be its undoing — unless it can gather strength to convert protectionism into a system which makes for national economic efficiency.

Shrewd, however, as was Mr. Hanna's attitude towards tariff revision as a matter of practical politics, no party could continue to follow his advice. At any particular moment it might be justified by the nature of its hand in "standing-pat," but a party which continued year after year to hold a "pat" hand and refused to take the chance of trying for something better, would inevitably be suspected either of bluffing or rigging the cards. "Stand-pattism," which under peculiar circumstances might be the most available practical policy, is impossible as a permanent course of action. A typical American will never admit that he is a "stand-patter" on anything but a particular question under a particular group of circumstances; and a political party or economic class which consistently held "pat" hands and proclaimed a policy of "standing-pat" would inevitably provoke among their opponents the cry that the deal was not square. How Mr. Hanna would have readjusted his policy to the demand for a square deal, it would be useless to predict. He himself was not a "stand-patter" in respect to the labor question, and the germs of reform, when once implanted in a man's system, have a tendency to ferment and spread. But in 1902 and 1903 he was undoubtedly in danger of being gradually forced, by his fear of raising difficult and dangerous questions, into the position of being a consistent "stand-patter."

Apart from conspicuous symptoms of Mr. Hanna's popularity as a Presidential candidate and his new enunciation of "stand-pattism," the only other novelty in the campaign of 1902 was the vigorous campaigning of Mr. Tom L. Johnson. Mr. Johnson had been elected Mayor of Cleveland in the spring of 1901 and was beginning his fight against the local traction monoply. His decisive success in the city tempted him to venture out into the state, and during the fall of 1902 he made speeches all over Ohio, carrying a circus tent with him, and enunciating unusually radical doctrines for a Democrat — including absolute free trade, the single tax and a relentless warfare against the trusts. Mr. Johnson's fierce onslaught in 1902 was generally understood to be merely a preliminary skirmish to the more serious battle of the following fall — when the question of Mr. Hanna's own reëlection to the Senate would be contested. For that reason the speeches assumed a personal character. The facts that the two men were both old residents of Cleveland, that they had been rivals in building and operating street railways, and that they stood for diametrically opposite views of public policy, — all these circumstances gave the campaign the appearance of a personal fight between the two men.

On election day Mr. Hanna was completely victorious. The Republican ticket carried the state by the enormous majority of 100,000. So sweeping a victory was unprecedented, particularly in an off year, and it showed conclusively that Mr. Hanna was more than ever popular in Ohio. His political leadership of the state was the issue on which the vote had been cast, and the result indicated a substantial increase of popular confidence in him. On the other hand, Mr. Hanna with all his prestige could not shake Mr. Johnson's hold on the people of Cleveland. The Mayor had the voters with him on the street railway issue. Tom Johnson won in the spring of 1903 relatively as decisive a victory in the municipal election as did the Republicans in the state election of the preceding fall.

The overwhelming character of his victory in the state and Senator Hanna's addition of a labor plank to his own personal political platform served inevitably to increase the conviction of Mr. Hanna's friends and supporters in his availability as a Presidential candidate. They were unable to take any overt action, in view of Mr. Hanna's steady refusal to encourage the enterprise; but beneath the surface the ferment was the more active because it had no regular public outlet. From December, 1902, until the end of January, 1903, Senator Hanna received about 700 letters, urging him to withdraw his refusal, or promising support in case his candidacy became serious. These letters indicate very clearly the strength of the sentiment in favor of Mr. Hanna, the sources of that strength and the varying motives of his supporters.

In the first place those large business interests with which Mr. Hanna had always been closely associated were strongly in favor of his nomination and were as strongly opposed to Mr. Roosevelt. In spite of the latter's caution in urging radical policies during his first administration, they regarded him as "unsafe." His action in the coal strike, the suit against the Northern Securities Co., and above all the general tone of his public and private utterances confirmed them in this opinion. Their natural preference for Mr. Hanna was intensified by their dread of the only alternative candidate. Indeed, to judge by their letters, they were as much interested in beating the man of their fears as in nominating the man of their choice. But the reason upon which they most insisted for their opposition to the President was that he could not possibly be elected. One correspondent wrote late in 1903: "I was astounded to see in that club [the Union League Club of New York]—presumably as representative a body of Republicans as there is in the country—conservative thoughtful men,—that there was not one out of that whole membership whom I met—not one—who believed that Theodore Roosevelt should be nominated, or if he were nominated, that he could be elected. The reasons given were not idle or prompted by personal feeling, but were based on the calm sober judgment of thinking men." Again and again this prediction is confidentially made. It came not merely from business men, but from politicians of experience. Both the business men and politicians always claimed to base it not merely on personal opinion, but on the result of careful inquiries among their customers, employees and associates. Confidence in its truth was apparently so universal among the supporters of Mr. Hanna that their solicitations assumed in their own eyes a holy war on behalf of party success.

Another large group of letters came from Republican politicians and office-holders in the South. Mr. Hanna had always been popular among them, because he had placed the distribution of patronage in the South on a regular basis and one which left it largely in the hands of the local organizations. Mr. Roosevelt, on the other hand, was less popular, because he had interfered with the smooth working of the established system and because he was appointing some negroes to office. Personal grievances lay behind many of these letters, as well as personal loyalty to a man who had done a great deal for them. They made it apparent that, in case a fight had occurred, the administration candidate would not have had his usual walkover in the South.

Besides letters belonging to the two classes mentioned above there were a large number of appeals from small business men and lawyers all over the country who were ardent admirers of Mr. Hanna and wanted him to be a candidate—not to save the country or the party, but merely because they approved of his policies and liked him as a man. Most of the correspondents belonging to this class had neither grievances against

Mr. Roosevelt nor fear of his political influence. Many of them professed a lively admiration of the President. But they admired Mr. Hanna still more, and urged that the accident of Mr. McKinley's death should not deprive him of a nomination to which his services to the party and the country entitled him.

Towards the end of 1902 the situation and the resulting gossip and discussion began to have an effect on the relations between President Roosevelt and Mr. Hanna. There was, indeed, no change in the latter, nor any reason for change. He was, as always, playing fair. In his promise to support Mr. Roosevelt he had expressly reserved the question of the next Presidential nomination. In spite of his increasing friendship for Mr. Roosevelt, he so far shared the opinion of his own supporters that he would have preferred another candidate. But he was not working for any other candidate, and he always expressly and emphatically discouraged his own supporters. He sympathized in a way with the President's ambition, and never believed that the latter's nomination would be or could be prevented. Nevertheless, honest and loyal as he was about the matter, the ambiguity and complications of the general situation invited misinterpretation. The opinions and preparations of Mr. Hanna's friends were known to Mr. Roosevelt. The President was fighting an opposition which was as vague and impalpable as it was powerful, but which derived its power chiefly from the possibility of Mr. Hanna's acquiescence or support. The latter held the key to the situation. He might not be able absolutely to lock the door against Mr. Roosevelt's nomination, but he could certainly at any moment throw the door wide open. Eventually he must do either one thing or the other. A man who holds a key but refuses to use it exposes himself to misunderstanding. Mr. Hanna as well as Mr. Roosevelt had his enemies. They soon began to use the equivocal aspects of the situation to make trouble between the President and the Senator.

The first and only occasion on which the trouble received public expression was in May, 1903, just before the meeting of the Ohio State Convention, and not long after a notable expression of the President's wish to please Mr. Hanna. The former was planning a long tour throughout the West after the adjournment of Congress. Before he departed he surprised and delighted the Senator by saying that he would like to attend the wedding of Mr. Hanna's daughter Ruth, which was scheduled for early in June — an unusual request, which made the wedding look like an affair of state. At the same time the President also consulted the Senator about the substance of his speeches while on tour; and their misunderstanding had not gone so far that they could not joke about its cause. On March 20 Mr. Hanna wrote to the President the following note, apropos of a published interview with General Charles H. Grosvenor, in which the Congressman stated at some length and with great emphasis that Mr. Roosevelt had the nomination for 1904 in his pocket, that the talk of opposition to him was nonsense, and that any man who opposed him would be committing political suicide. Mr. Hanna enclosed a copy of the interview and added: —

"My dear Mr. President: —

"This settles me. Does it also settle my candidate for the Pension Agency of Ohio? He 'bows too low.'
"Hastily yours,
"M. A. Hanna."

Of course the political enemies of Mr. Hanna in Ohio were among Mr. Roosevelt's most aggressive supporters. It was these gentlemen who caused the disagreeable incident that occurred just before the meeting of the Ohio State Convention. On May 23, 1903, a despatch from Washington was published in the newspapers containing an interview with Senator Foraker, in which the Senator alleged that "the talk about having our Convention declare in favor of President Roosevelt as our candidate next year was started by his [Mr. Hanna's] own friends," that Mr. Elmer Dover, Senator Hanna's secretary, and others had denied in the papers that such action would and should be taken, and that these anti-Roosevelt declarations had forced the issue. If no such announcement had been made, the Convention, according to Mr. Foraker, might very well have contented itself with a mere indorsement of President Roosevelt's administration, but now that the issue had been precipitated, it would have to be met. The Convention would either have to make such a declaration or refuse to make it.

The next day the following statement from Senator Hanna appeared in the press: —

"I have seen the reported interview with Senator Foraker with reference to the proposed indorsement of the nomination of President Roosevelt by the next Republican State Convention. At the outset I want to deny that Mr. Dover, my private secretary, or, so far as I know, any of my friends, had anything to do with raising this question. The first I knew of it was when I read in the papers a previous interview with Senator Foraker, which I construed as an expression of his own personal views. This was followed by an interview with General Grosvenor along the same line. These made it apparent that there was a disposition on the part of some people to suggest such action by the Convention.

"I have no criticism to make of any individual as to his right to entertain or to express such views, but I certainly do criticise the propriety of action along that line by the delegates to the State Convention who are chosen for the purpose of nominating a state ticket. It does not appear to me to be entirely proper for this Convention to assume the prerogative of the one to be chosen in 1904, and upon which will rest the responsibility of representing and expressing the sentiment in our state for any candidate.

"It would seem unnecessary for me to say that these conclusions are in no way influenced by any personal desires or ambitions of my own. I have often stated both privately and publicly that I am not, and will not be, a candidate for the Presidential nomination. On account of my position as Chairman of the Republican National Committee, and the further fact that this year I am supposed to have a vital interest in the results in Ohio as bearing upon my reëlection to the United States Senate, it would be presumed that I might have some influence as to the policy or action of the State Convention this year in national affairs. In that connection it would seem apparent that whatever that influence might be it had been exerted in a direction which would cause just criticism on the part of any other person who might aspire to be a candidate for the Republican nomination for President in 1904. For these reasons I am opposed to the adoption of such a resolution."

The issue thus raised was ugly and placed Mr. Hanna in an embarrassing situation. He was opposed to a Roosevelt indorsement for reasons soon to be stated in detail, but he had not wanted to show his opposition. If he indorsed the President, he was apparently shutting the door on any other candidate. If he opposed the indorsement, he would incur the opposition of Mr. Roosevelt's friends during his own campaign for reëlection. Mr. Foraker had cleverly contrived to force the issue into the limelight, while at the same time placing the responsibility for so doing on Mr. Hanna. Under such circumstances either alternative presented increasing difficulties. Mr. Hanna still hoped, however, to refuse the indorsement without alienating Mr. Roosevelt. On the day that he gave out the interview, he sent the following telegram to President Roosevelt: —

"SEATTLE, WASHINGTON.

"THE PRESIDENT: —

"The issue that has been forced upon me in the matter of our State Convention this year indorsing you for the Republican nomination next year has come in a way which makes it necessary for me to oppose such a resolution. When you know all the facts, I am sure that you will approve my course.

"M. A. HANNA."

President Roosevelt replied the same day and gave his telegram to the Associated Press.

"CLEVELAND, OHIO.

"HON. M. A. HANNA: —

"Your telegram received. I have not asked any man for his support. I have nothing whatever to do with raising this issue. Inasmuch as it has been raised, of course, those who favor my administration and my nomination will favor indorsing both, and those who do not will oppose.

"THEODORE ROOSEVELT."

This telegram and its immediate publication made it impossible for Mr. Hanna to escape the sharp edge of one of the two alternatives. He had confidently expected Mr. Roosevelt to accept his assurance that opposition to the indorsement did not mean enmity to the President. It simply meant that he did not want to shut the door on other candidates and that he did not want *his* campaign for reëlection in 1903 embarrassed by the personal issues of 1904. After the answering telegram, however, further opposition to the indorsement would be interpreted as a declaration of war against the President and might have split the party in his state. He was forced, consequently, to take his medicine; but it was a nasty dose and he resented the action which compelled him to back down in the face of his personal opponents. On May 26 he telegraphed to the President: —

"Your telegram of the 23d received. In view of the sentiment expressed I shall not oppose the indorsement of your administration and candidacy by our State Convention. I have given the substance of this to the Associated Press."

In the meantime he had written to Mr. Roosevelt explaining why he had opposed the indorsement. I have no copy of the letter, but probably it did not differ in substance from a letter which he had written on May 23 to George B. Cox of Cincinnati, and which is a perfectly candid statement of his actual grounds of opposition.

"My dear Cox: —

"You have seen the row which has been kicked up about the proposed indorsement of President Roosevelt at the next State Convention. This proposition was a surprise to me — not because I have the faintest idea of being a candidate — but because it is not a proper thing to do under present conditions for the following reasons. First the State Convention this year has no right to assume the responsibilities of the next year's Convention as to any expression of the choice of candidates. Second my objections on personal grounds are as follows: I am Chairman of the National Committee. This is my year in Ohio politics. I am supposed to have influence to control the Convention as to its policy. Therefore if President Roosevelt is indorsed at this time it would be charged that I was responsible for shutting the door in the face of any other candidate who might aspire for the place. Such action would be criticised and justly so. I do not believe that the President himself would favor it, and I know well he would appreciate the embarrassment under which I would be placed. I had hoped and expected that nothing would occur to give me trouble this year. But as I cannot favor this action for reasons given above, I shall certainly oppose the resolution of indorsement at this time and hope my friends will approve and support my action.

"Truly yours,
"M. A. Hanna."

On May 29 the President returned the following somewhat apologetic explanation of his belligerent telegram to Mr. Hanna.

"My dear Senator: —

"I thank you for your letter which gave me the first gleam of light on the situation. I do not think you appreciated the exact effect that your interview and announced position had on the country at large. It was everywhere accepted as the first open attack on me, and it gave heart, curiously enough, not only to my opponents but to all the men who lump you and me together as improperly friendly to organized labor and to the working men generally. The mischievous effect was instantly visible. The general belief was that this was not your move, save indirectly; but that it was really an attack by the so-called Wall Street forces on me, to which you had been led to give a reluctant acquiescence. I might not have said anything for publication at all, had it not been for the statement that I approved your course. In the way the movement was interpreted this looked as if I was approving having my throat slit. My view was that you, of course, had an absolute right to be a candidate yourself, but that if you were not one, you would be doing me and the Republican party serious harm by fighting and very probably beating the proposition to indorse me by the Ohio Convention.

"After thinking the matter carefully over I became sure that I had to take a definite stand myself. I hated to do it, because you have shown such generosity and straightforwardness in all your dealings with me that it was peculiarly painful to me to be put, even temporarily, in a position of seeming antagonism to you. No one but a really big man — a man above all petty considerations — could have treated me as you have done during the year and a half since President McKinley's death. I have consulted you and relied on your judgment more than I have done with any other man. Allow me to say that your magnanimous speech at the Cuyahoga County Convention is but another illustration of your course towards me and I appreciate it to the full.

"Faithfully yours,
"THEODORE ROOSEVELT."

Therewith the incident closed, and not many days after, the President was for twenty-four hours Mr. Hanna's guest in Cleveland. But the effects of the little bout were different from what appeared on the surface. Mr. Roosevelt had wanted Mr. Hanna either to open the door or to slam it, so that his suspense would be over and he would have a fight on his hands or a clear field. Apparently he had gained a clear field, but in reality he had only increased the Senator's indisposition unequivocally to indorse his candidacy. Mr. Hanna had been placed in a humiliating position at the very moment when he particularly wished to appear to the public as the conquering hero; and during the following fall, when the question of the Presidential nomination was finally becoming acute, his behavior was influenced by his recollection of the incident of the previous spring.

If Mr. Roosevelt wanted above all things to receive the personal tribute of a nomination and election to the Presidency, so Mr. Hanna wanted above all things a triumphant return to the Senate. The circumstances of his first election as Senator, the vicious personal opposition which had greeted his candidacy within and without the party, the narrow margin whereby he had secured the seat, and the way in which his title to the seat had been attacked in the Senate, — all these facts made him desire, not merely the public vindication of another term, but the reward and satisfaction of an overwhelming victory. As he wrote to "Boss" Cox, this was his year in Ohio politics, and he could not afford to have his probable victory either threatened, diminished or marred.

His good judgment and self-control in avoiding the issue which had been forced upon him, even at the cost of a retreat in the face of his enemies, were rewarded by success. There was no further hint of discord either in the Convention or in the campaign. It really became his year in Ohio politics. When the people cast their ballots on the following November, their verdict was not complicated by the intrusion of any irrelevant issues. The Convention nominated as the Republican candidate for Governor, not General Charles Dick, but Myron T. Herrick. Colonel Herrick had been closely associated with Mr. Hanna in politics since the Convention of 1888. As a friend of Mr. McKinley as well as of Mr. Hanna he had been constantly consulted by both men before and during the Convention of 1896; and probably no other political leader in Ohio, General Dick excepted, had been closer to Mr. Hanna. His candidacy had been announced in January, 1903, and it had been publicly accepted in April both by Mr. Hanna and "Boss" Cox of Cincinnati. The Foraker wing of the party had to be satisfied with the candidate for Lieutenant-Governor, which represented its usual share of desirable public offices. The fact, however, that the Lieutenant-Governor was associated with Mr. Foraker made some difference later, because when Colonel Herrick was mentioned as a possible running mate for Mr. Roosevelt, he was embarrassed by the fact that if he resigned, the state administration would be turned over to a follower of Mr. Foraker. Besides indorsing President Roosevelt and nominating Colonel Herrick the Convention also indorsed Mr. Hanna for another term; and his personality could not be intruded into the campaign without becoming its dominant point of attraction and repulsion.

The Convention with its stormy prologue and its harmonious ending was no sooner over than the eyes of the country were again turned towards Cleveland and the personal affairs of Mr. Hanna. On June 10 his daughter Ruth was married to Mr. Joseph Medill McCormick, the son of Mr. Robert S. McCormick of Chicago. Under the circumstances the marriage festivity could scarcely avoid becoming a tribute to Senator Hanna's prestige in public life and to his personal popularity — not merely among his neighbors but among his colleagues and political associates.

In making plans for the wedding Mr. and Mrs. Hanna had been somewhat embarrassed. They hoped that the President and all the Senator's Washington friends would attend; but they did not want them to feel obliged to do so. Much to their satisfaction the President and certain prominent public men indicated so plainly a desire for an invitation that the matter settled itself. Besides Mr. Roosevelt and Miss Alice Roosevelt there were present Senator and Mrs. Nelson Aldrich, Senator Hale, Senator and Miss Kean, Senator Beveridge, Senator and Mrs. Wetmore, Mr. and Mrs. Clement Griscom, General Corbin, Postmaster-General Henry C. Payne and his wife and many others. Not merely Senator Hanna's own house on the lake front was filled with guests, but also the house of his brother, Leonard C. Hanna, and that of his son, D. R. Hanna. On an occasion of this kind Mr. Hanna was in his element and at his best. He enjoyed nothing so much as having a crowd of friends and relatives gather in his house to celebrate some happy occasion or event. It brought out the abounding store of good-fellowship in his nature and the warmth of his feeling for his friends. He managed to be omnipresent, chatted with everybody, and made all feel how much pleasure their presence gave to him. As usual his good humor overflowed in jokes. On the evening of the wedding day he caused consternation in two of his guests, who never dined without champagne, by telling them that the supply had fallen short. They looked extremely unhappy, until they reached the dinner-table, and found that it was a false alarm. Mrs. Hanna states that she had never seen him in higher spirits and happier than he was on this occasion.

The summer was spent chiefly in preparations for the fall election. Not even the national campaign of 1896 was planned more elaborately and carefully. In view of the huge Republican majority in the fall of 1902, the prospects of a Republican victory looked brilliant, but it was always Mr. Hanna's practice to make assurance doubly sure. To judge from his correspondence he really believed that there was some danger of defeat. He is constantly repeating that he has the fight of his life on his hands. Assuredly he spared no effort which might contribute to success, and brought into play all his arts and resources as a campaign manager. His exertions during this canvass were a terrible strain upon his already enfeebled physical condition and aroused the anxiety of his friends and family.

In all probability he was not so much anxious about the result as very much excited. His reëlection was the dominant issue of the campaign. The Democrats had nominated Tom Johnson for Governor, and an excellent man, although not a particularly strong candidate, named John H. Clarke for Senator. Their platform advocated municipal street railways and the equalization of taxation, and made virulent attack on the privileges and powers of incorporated wealth. Tom Johnson was responsible for the platform and was leading the anti-Hanna fight. He aroused a good deal of enthusiasm on the stump, and put so much energy into his attack that there may have been some superficial cause for anxiety. Mr. Johnson had won a decisive victory in Cleveland in the spring of 1903. An industrial shadow had appeared which was depriving much of the business of the country of the warmth radiating from the sun of Republican prosperity. Mr. Hanna feared also that votes for Democratic legislators would be bought with votes for a Republican Governor. In any event he wished to be reëlected by a majority so overwhelming that the memory of his first election would be wiped out, and he would appear before the world as the undisputed possessor of the confidence of the people of Ohio.

Whatever the motive, plans were laid for an exhaustive canvass of the state. Mr. Hanna himself was to put in six weeks on the stump, and he was to be accompanied at times, not merely by Senator Foraker and Colonel Herrick, but by many prominent speakers from other states, including several cabinet officers. Mr. Dick wrote on behalf of Mr. Hanna to all Congressmen both in the Senate and the House whose services might be useful. Those who offered to help, and who testified in word and action to the extreme importance of a decisive victory for Senator Hanna, were not confined to Mr. Hanna's personal friends and followers. They included men like Senator Dolliver, Senator Beveridge and Senator Clapp, who at a later date repudiated "stand-pat" politics. But the most interesting letter which was received in answer to requests of assistance came from the veteran Senator George F. Hoar — the man who represented better than any other man the best traditions of the Senate and of the Republican party.

Mr. Hoar had not been asked to speak, but the Cleveland *Leader* had requested him to contribute a letter in support of Mr. Hanna's candidacy. Mr. Hoar upon receipt of the request sent the following private letter to Mr. Hanna, explaining the reasons for refusing a public testimonial: —

"WORCESTER, MASS., Aug. 31, 1903."

"DEAR MR. HANNA: —

"I have received the enclosed document from Mr. Starek. There is nobody living who feels more strongly the value of your public service to the country than I do. I am afraid you, with your modest appreciation of yourself, would think I was inclined to flattery if I were to state it to you as strongly as I have been in the habit of stating it to other people when some fit occasion has arisen. It is very seldom that men who bring to the public service the wisdom gained by long practice and most successful experience in business affairs combine with it the capacity for clear and powerful statement in debate or that they are wise counsellors in political matters outside of their own calling in life. You have no superior among your associates in the Senate in these things." Then Mr. Hoar goes on to explain that he had always felt obliged to refuse such requests and stated his reasons — which do not concern us here. Another private testimonial, which was never published, came from Senator Spooner. "I am extremely anxious," he writes, "that you should be reëlected. Your business experience, your desire for the prosperity and well-being of the country, your excellent judgment and aptitude for national legislation, your sense of responsibility as a Senator which leads you to give, without stint or regard for your own comfort, active study and work to the discharge of the duties of the Senatorship, your personal popularity in the Senate, and your ability as a debater,— all combine in my judgment to make you a powerful, patriotic and therefore valuable factor in national legislation and in determining our public policy. A failure to reëlect you to the Senate I should esteem a public misfortune."

Among his embarrassments at this critical moment was the state of his health. He passed the greater part of July on a friend's yacht, in order to gather strength for the coming campaign. Nevertheless he was laid up in bed for some days, just before he opened his speaking tour; and throughout the fall he was far from well. A few weeks on the stump were no longer an exciting and refreshing episode in his life. His increasing infirmities made the discomforts and the constant pressure of a long campaign irksome and even distressing. His state of mind is indicated by the following incident. One evening after a peculiarly hard day's work in cold autumn weather, and when he had returned to his private car and was finally warm and comfortable enough to regain something like his ordinary spirits, he told his companions (according to Colonel Herrick) the following story. During one of the battles of the Civil War a soldier was seen walking away from the front in an utterly dishevelled condition. He had been wounded before he left the firing line. He had been accidently run down and trampled on by a squadron of cavalry. His face was bloody. An arm hung limp from his side. He could scarcely drag one leg after another. There seemed to be no part of his body which was not the worse for war and wear. As he hobbled dejectedly along, he was heard to mutter: "I love my country. I would fight for her. I would bleed for her. Yes, I would even die for her. But I'm damned if I ever love another country."

In the speeches made during the fall of 1903, Senator Hanna added nothing essential to the past statements of his political and economic ideas, but he placed them before his public in an unusually effective manner. Always an easy speaker and impressive because of his powerful personality, he had gained by virtue of long practice an increasing mastery over his own methods of utterance. While his speeches were still improvised and they still rambled along a little incoherently, his individual sentences became more consecutive and precise, and certain phrases usually appear at the beginning or in the body of his speeches, which indicate an increasing tendency to prepare in advance effective methods of expression. But above all they benefited from the fact that his mind had become gradually stored with weightier matter. When he was very much stirred, he no longer expressed his feelings merely with a kind of explosive energy. He could rise, not quite to eloquence, but to some dignity of utterance, which made his evident sincerity still more impressive. His own public life was becoming identified with higher issues, and was reaching a higher plane of verbal expression.

On November 3 the people of Ohio gave to Mr. Hanna the overwhelming victory and the complete vindication which he so ardently desired. Colonel Herrick was elected by a majority of over 100,000. In 1901 Senator Foraker had obtained thirty-five more legislative votes than had his Democratic opponent, which was considered extraordinary. The Legislature elected in the fall of 1903 contained a Republican majority of 91 on joint ballot; and Mr. Hanna was afterwards elected by an actual majority of 90 — receiving 115 votes to his opponent's 25. One of the most gratifying aspects of the returns was the triumph in Mr. Hanna's own county of Cuyahoga. Mr. Herrick's plurality over Johnson was no

2 F

less than 8520, and every candidate on the Republican ticket was elected by a comfortable margin — and this in spite of Mr. Johnson's equally emphatic success only a few months before. Evidently many thousand votes which had been cast for Mr. Johnson on local issues were cast for Mr. Hanna on state and national issues. So far as any political leader's career can be justified by the approval of his own people, that justification was Senator Hanna's. The issue was as sharply drawn for and against him as it had been in 1897. His future career and his political leadership of the state were at stake. He could no longer be denounced as a labor-crusher; but the voters were asked to reject him as plutocrat and a friend of privilege in American politics and business. If the campaign had taken place in 1910 instead of 1903, he could not have been any more sharply attacked for his friendliness to the "Interests." But the people of Ohio refused to believe that the public interest was not among the interests he served. They declared at the polls their enthusiastic and overwhelming confidence in the integrity and good faith of his political leadership.

Early in November, when the results of his election were known, Mr. Hanna received hundreds of letters congratulating him on his success. These letters came from every state in the Union and were written by all classes of people — bankers, merchants, manufacturers, union leaders, professional men, "drummers," clergymen, college presidents and railroad employees. Half a dozen notes of congratulation were even received from Roman Catholic convents. One of the most interesting and instructive incidental phases of Mr. Hanna's political career was the support he obtained from prominent Catholics. Archbishop Ireland was in frequent correspondence with him and used his influence on Mr. Hanna's behalf. But this alliance did not prevent Mr. Hanna from getting along equally well with the Salvation Army, several of whose leaders congratulated him on his reëlection. There seems to have been an instinctive gravitation towards Mr. Hanna on the part of men who represented powerful organizations and believed in the principle and method of organization — no matter whether the purpose of the organization was religious, social, political, industrial or labor.

A large proportion of the letters congratulating Mr. Hanna on his election urged him to become a candidate for the Presidency. The decisive and overwhelming character of his personal victory strengthened enormously the hands of those of his friends who wished to make him President — whether he would or not. They had been discouraged by the Roosevelt indorsement, which had been extorted from the Ohio Convention in the spring, but they were merely biding their time. Throughout the campaign he had been repeatedly hailed at public meetings and dinners as the next President of the United States — although this fact was usually suppressed in the newspaper reports. It was part of his policy never to call public attention to these compliments either by encouraging or discouraging public comment. But they were a matter of general gossip, and his silence when actually under this kind of fire puzzled his friends and alarmed the supporters of Mr. Roosevelt.

The business men in New York, who were determined to push Mr. Hanna's candidacy, began immediately after the election seriously to organize. A committee was appointed. One hundred thousand dollars were raised and two hundred and fifty thousand dollars pledged for preliminary expenses. Promises were given of a much larger campaign fund to be subscribed whenever necessary. A comprehensive survey of the whole field was made and a careful calculation of the number of delegates which they could reasonably count upon getting. The outlook was considered to be very encouraging. They expected in the first place to secure a united delegation from Ohio. In spite of the fact that Mr. Roosevelt was a New Yorker, they counted on a united delegation from that state. The local machinery was controlled by Governor Odell, who was favorable to Mr. Hanna and had promised to use his influence on behalf of their candidate. In Pennsylvania Senator Quay was for Roosevelt, but they believed that they had a good chance of dividing the state. They were assured also that the delegation from Indiana could be secured. After an investigation of conditions in the South, they were hopeful of obtaining two-thirds of the delegates from that region. In case all these calculations were sound, it looked like a sure thing.

Preparations as elaborate as these were sure to reach the

ears of the President and his friends; and among Mr. Roosevelt's ostensible friends at this time were certain of Mr. Hanna's enemies — such as Senators Foraker and Quay. They were not slow to use the situation to embroil the relations between the two men. It was easy to suggest that the spontaneous expressions of opinion favorable to Mr. Hanna's candidacy which were constantly breaking out, were secretly inspired and encouraged by Mr. Hanna or his immediate lieutenants; and the ambiguity of Mr. Hanna's public attitude gave color to these suspicions. Mr. Roosevelt was naturally infected by them. If Mr. Hanna did not, as he had frequently stated, intend to be a candidate, why did he not suppress the dubious preparations of his friends by declaring unequivocally and publicly that he was in favor of the only alternative candidate?

There was danger for a while of an open break between the two men. Mr. Hanna's enemies tried to precipitate a fight by advising the President to ignore Mr. Hanna in certain matters connected with patronage in Ohio. Senator Foraker had in his own opinion always been deprived of his fair share of these Federal offices. As long as McKinley lived, he had, of course, no means of putting up an effective fight. He had to take what he could get, and he attributed to Mr. Hanna's influence some of Mr. McKinley's personal appointments. Being both a proud and ambitious man, he chafed at a situation which was making his political career end in a *cul-de-sac*. He had skilfuly managed in the spring of 1903 to use the question of Mr. Roosevelt's indorsement as a weapon with which to attack Mr. Hanna; and although winning a technical victory, he failed in his deeper purpose, which was to bring about an open breach between his colleague and the administration. While the President was in a suspicious state of mind about Mr. Hanna, Senator Foraker very nearly persuaded him to make certain appointments to the Postmasterships of Napoleon and Lima which would have been offensive to the junior Senator. Mr. Hanna was well aware of these machinations. There is evidence that, had he lived, he would at the next favorable opportunity have done his utmost to make Mr. Foraker thereafter a negligible factor in the politics of Ohio.

While the gentlemen mentioned and others were trying to convince the President that Mr. Hanna was acting in bad faith, certain friends of both Mr. Roosevelt and Mr. Hanna were working hard to prevent the breach from widening. Among them was Mr. George B. Cortelyou, who, as Mr. McKinley's private secretary, had been close to Mr. Hanna, and who was now secretary of the new Department of Commerce and Labor in President Roosevelt's Cabinet. Being disgusted at an absurd tale which had been carried to him, concerning some remarks which Mr. Hanna had been reported to make about the President, he decided to get at the root of the matter. With this intention he went to see the Senator at the Arlington Hotel, and the two had a long interview. Mr. Hanna declared without qualification that he was not a candidate, that he never had been and never would be a candidate. He had assured the President of that fact, and he was offended because his word was doubted. He was tired, he said, of going to the White House every day, of putting his hand on his heart and being sworn in. It was not a dignified thing for him to do. He had played fair with the President, and he thought that Mr. Roosevelt ought to accept his word at its face value.

Some days later Mr. Cortelyou went to see the President and found him in conference with three friends, one of whom was a member of the Cabinet and another a Senator. The burden of the conversation was that Mr. Hanna's conduct was suspicious and ambiguous. The President sprang from his chair, walked nervously to the open fire and then back to his desk, saying in his emphatic way, "Yes, Mr. Hanna ought to make an unequivocal public statement of his position." At this point Mr. Cortelyou broke in, and said: "You gentlemen do not know what you are talking about. I know that Mr. Hanna has no intention of being a candidate for President." Mr. Roosevelt accepted this assurance as authentic, because he had heard of Mr. Cortelyou's recent interview with Mr. Hanna. That an open breach was avoided was due chiefly to the good offices of such men as Mr. Cortelyou and Mr. James R. Garfield, then Commissioner of Corporations. The latter was in close communication both with Mr. Hanna and the President. While he thought the Senator should make a public statement which would clear up the ambiguities of the situation, he always credited Mr. Hanna with acting in perfect good faith, and he always advised Mr. Roosevelt to that effect. Mr. Theodore E. Burton also contributed effectively to the maintenance of good relations by advising Mr. Roosevelt about Ohio appointments in a sense which may have prevented the President from offending Mr. Hanna.

It is, of course, easy to understand the President's predicament. He wanted the nomination and had good grounds for wanting it. Mr. Hanna was the only man who could have prevented him from getting it. What Mr. Roosevelt desired, consequently, above all things was that Mr. Hanna should declare himself explicitly, not merely about his own personal candidacy, but in reference to other candidates for the office. A man of the President's disposition, to whom suspense which cannot be exorcised by vigorous and decisive action is intolerable, almost preferred an open fight to a prolonged condition of tantalizing doubt. He tried in every way to induce Mr. Hanna either to indorse his candidacy or explicitly to disapprove of it. His telegram on the occasion of the Ohio Convention of 1903 was his first attempt to force the issue. Later in the fall of the year with the same end in view he repeatedly urged Mr. Hanna to accept a reappointment as Chairman of the National Committee. But all to no purpose. For reasons which will be discussed later, Mr. Hanna would not commit himself in public either in favor of the President or against him.

Yet without the shadow of a doubt, Mr. Hanna neither intended to be a candidate himself nor did he intend to oppose Mr. Roosevelt's nomination. There are a number of letters in existence, written to correspondents with whom he was on terms of the utmost intimacy. Not one of them wavers a hair's-breadth from the assertion that he was not and would not be a candidate. Not one affords the slightest intimation that he intended to oppose Mr. Roosevelt's selection. Statements about Mr. Hanna's attitude have been taken from all of his confidential friends. None of them ever heard him suggest anything favorable to his own or necessarily inimical to Mr. Roosevelt's candidacy. Mr. Cornelius N. Bliss, than whom no friend was more affectionately intimate with the Senator, asserts that the burden of all of Mr. Hanna's conversation with him about the matter was: "Roosevelt is to be nominated. There is no question about it. I have never had any desire or ambition for the nomination, and under no circumstances would I accept." One day when the two were sitting together in the Waldorf, a "very influential man" turned to Mr. Bliss and said, "You know, we are going to nominate Mr. Hanna for President." "You are not," replied Mr. Hanna. "I am not going to have anything to do with it." Mr. Charles F. Dick's testimony absolutely coincides with that of Mr. Bliss.

One of the closest friends of Mr. Hanna in the Senate was N. B. Scott of West Virginia. His public attitude in respect to the nomination gave the joint friends of Mr. Roosevelt and Mr. Hanna a good deal of trouble, because of statements which in their opinion might mean that Mr. Hanna was a candidate under cover. On Dec. 23, 1903, he wrote to Mr. Hanna a letter, of which the following are the essential sentences:—

(Personal and Confidential)

"MY DEAR MR. HANNA:—

"No man on earth has any better opinion of your good judgment and hard sense than I have, but I do believe you are making a mistake. To my mind it is a foregone conclusion that if we renominate Roosevelt it means defeat. Are you going to accept the responsibility of allowing the Republican party to go to defeat? . . . Or if this man is reëlected, what kind of an administration shall we have? Shall we not have the Republican party, at the end of four years, in the same condition that President Cleveland had the Democratic party?

"I want you to sit down and pray with yourself for an hour and a half, as we used to do in the Quaker meetings, and then ask yourself whether you are doing your duty to the country and to your party by refusing either to allow yourself to be a candidate or to name some other man. I believe that if you will suggest the name of Cornelius N. Bliss, Senator Fairbanks or a number of other good men, one of them can be nominated and elected. . . . Let me hear from you in confidence. You have no idea of the amount of pressure that is brought to bear on me to have you say something.

"Your old friend, as ever,
"N. B. SCOTT."

To this letter Mr. Hanna replied on December 30:—

"My dear Senator: —

"I have just received your personal and confidential letter of the 23d inst., and it is needless for me to say to you how much I appreciate this latest expression of your personal regard. My recent illness has merely been one more admonition and warning to take care of myself and emphasizes the fact that my own interest forbids the course you advise. I do not see how I can be held responsible for the situation you describe. Neither can I see my way clear to being the instrument to create dissension, discord and confusion in the party. I have decided that the best thing for me to do is to say nothing more whatever on the subject. I believe that you will agree with me that this is the wisest course.

"Truly yours,
"M. A. Hanna."

Two days after the letter to Mr. Scott was written, Colonel Oliver H. Payne arrived in Cleveland on a secret mission to Mr. Hanna. He was a member of the committee which had been formed in New York to promote Mr. Hanna's nomination. He wanted an interview, in order to place before their candidate the results of their work up to date. He had a long conference with Mr. Hanna, who, after hearing what he had to say, repeated that he could not and would not be a candidate. He said that he wanted to remain in the Senate and that many questions in which he was deeply interested required his personal attention in that body. His whole life and all his interest were wrapped up in the work of the Civic Federation. He would rather succeed in bringing capital and labor into cordial relations with each other and open the way to permanent industrial peace and consequently to indefinite future prosperity than to be President of the United States. He feared that in case he became a candidate he would be misrepresented and that he would be accused of using the Civic Federation to promote his political fortunes. He would not put himself in a position which might cause any reasonable man to misconstrue his work on behalf of labor. He wound up by declaring that the state of his health would not permit him to enter the contest and that the work of the campaign would kill him. When Colonel Payne urged in response that he would not be compelled to make a campaign, that his name would sweep the Convention, that his friends would relieve him of all labor, and that all they wanted was an assurance that they could go ahead without his disapproval, he refused to budge an inch from his former assertions. Colonel Payne returned to New York very much disappointed, but not discouraged to the point of abandoning the fight.

Only one more item need be added to the foregoing exhibit. Mr. Elmer Dover, Mr. Hanna's private secretary, states that probably Mr. Hanna's closest associate in the Senate was Orville Platt of Connecticut. Now Mr. Platt, unlike some other friends of Mr. Hanna, believed not only that the President should be nominated, but that he was the only man who could be elected. Late in November, 1903, after Mr. Hanna had returned to Washington, Senator Platt wrote to a friend in Connecticut, who did not like the talk about Mr. Hanna's candidacy : —

"If I understand the situation, Mr. Hanna is not a candidate for the Presidency, will not be, and deplores all this talk ; but how can he stop it? That there is an opposition to the nomination of President Roosevelt is undoubtedly true. It is not very extensive or very influential, but it is noisy, and in my judgment will utterly fail when the Convention is held — indeed, I doubt if it manifests itself then. It comes from both ends of the party — from the moneyed influences in Wall Street and the agitators in the labor movement — one as much as the other. Each of these elements wishes to force the President to make terms with them, but he will not do it. I think I know that Senator Hanna does not sympathize with this in the least. I have a higher regard and more genuine respect for him than you seem to have. He is a straightforward, earnest, truthful man, who acts from conviction, fears no one, and makes no effort improperly to conciliate people who disagree with him. He is very much like President Roosevelt in this respect." (P. 515, "An Old-fashioned Senator.")

Towards the end the relation between the President and Senator Hanna improved, but they never again became entirely satisfactory. They could not become so until the question of the nomination was settled. The enemies of both men persisted in trying to create ill-feeling. The New York *Sun*, for instance, printed a story about some reported utterance of the President that he would soon make the Senator either fish or cut bait; and the story was told so circumstantially that Mr. Roosevelt wrote to Mr. Hanna a denial of its truth. In case the Senator had not been taken seriously ill, there is no telling how the business would have ended.

Inasmuch as Senator Hanna had decided absolutely never to accept the nomination — except, perhaps, in the impossible contingency of its being offered to him by acclamation — what is the explanation of his refusal to publish his private opinion that the President was bound to be nominated? The reasons he usually gives are not quite convincing. In the spring of 1903 they had a good deal of force. His position and influence in the party were unique. He was still its leader. As its leader and as Chairman of the National Committee, a declaration in favor of any one candidate a year in advance of the National Convention might have been unfair to other possible candidates. It was his business to represent the whole party. But in November, 1903, the only candidates in sight were the President and Mr. Hanna himself. An indorsement of Mr. Roosevelt could injure no candidacy but his own, and he did not want and would not take the nomination. Why not accept the situation and come out frankly in favor of the man whom he believed would have to be nominated? Prudence and a regard for the interests of the party might have counselled such a course, because the crisis was creating a dangerous tension of private and public feeling which might almost any day cause something to snap.

Just what Mr. Hanna's several motives were and what was their comparative force must always be doubtful; but statements made to close friends seem to justify the following general description of their effect. In the first place, his supporters in New York may have induced him to promise that, even if he would not consent to be a candidate, he would not, by declaring in favor of Mr. Roosevelt's nomination, extinguish all hope of preventing it. He might have made this promise, not only as a concession to a group of friends who were working hard in what they believed to be his interest, but because of his own personal attitude towards the President. While he liked Mr. Roosevelt much more than formerly, and while there was respect and admiration mixed with his liking, he shared to some extent the feelings of his supporters. He realized that the President represented a theory of the public interest different from his own,— a theory to which he was loath to give even by implication his public approval. For the present Mr. Roosevelt was bound by his promise not to depart from the McKinley policies; but if he were reëlected, particularly by a decisive majority, he would be justified in cutting loose. Mr. Hanna feared the effect of such an emancipation upon the leadership of the Republican party and the policy of the country.

Inasmuch, however, as he regarded Mr. Roosevelt's nomination as inevitable and had no intention of opposing it, what did he expect to gain by holding back? The question is difficult to answer, because Mr. Hanna in all probability did not clearly define to himself his own motives and intentions. It looks, however, as if he wanted to make the President feel and respect his power — not with the purpose of driving any bargain, but with the general idea of keeping his personal independence and so far as possible his leadership of the party. Whatever the future had in store for the President, for the organization and for himself, it was essential from his point of view that conservative Republicanism should under the new régime be kept somewhat separate and be strengthened in its independence. He knew that President Roosevelt would do much to avoid splitting the party; and he may have thought that he would be able to make better terms after the election, in case he continued for the present a demonstration of his personal power. He understood much better than did many of his own supporters Mr. Roosevelt's strength with public opinion, and he knew how much of an increase of prestige would follow from a triumphant election. He did not want the victory — if and when it came — to be merely Mr. Roosevelt's.

Finally personal feelings and motives were involved. He had never forgiven the way in which an indorsement had been extorted by the President from the Ohio Convention of 1903. He had been crowded into a corner, and obliged to choose between a breach in the party and a personal humiliation. He resented it. He resented also the efforts which were being made to force him prematurely on board the triumphal car of another candidate. He felt that his independence ought to be respected and recognized without exposing him to suspicions of bad faith. He may even have enjoyed the ferment of gossip, expectations, hopes and fears which his own much discouraged candidacy had created. If he was not to be President, he could hardly avoid some satisfaction and amusement in watching the ghost of his chance to be President haunt the corridors of the White House and at times hover ominously over the whole political landscape.

The question remains, whether, even if his health had not forbidden him to be a candidate, he would have considered any more favorably the solicitations of his New York friends. All who are most familiar with Mr. Hanna's attitude agree that it would not. No doubt many of the reasons which he gave for not wanting to be President could have been overcome. His assertion, for instance, that he preferred his peculiarly influential position in the Senate to the work of President was sincere; but his unquestionable satisfaction with his work and power as Senator would scarcely have prevented him from assuming the more irksome office, but the one which offered the greater opportunities of personal effectiveness and renown. He was also sincere in stating that he would not abandon his work on the Civic Federation even to be President. He was wrapped up heart and soul in that work. He had in his own mind a definite program of gradual development, which was to last over many years, and which was to culminate in nothing less than a permanent peace between capital and labor. He really hoped and expected to accomplish some such result, and had he succeeded, his fame would certainly have been more permanent and glorious than any which could result from a few years as President. But even so, he might have been persuaded that a President could accomplish more to carry on the work of industrial conciliation than a Senator — no matter how powerful.

The fundamental consideration, apart from his health, which probably determined his refusal, was a clear anticipation of the consequences to his own career and to the Republican party of an official candidacy. As I have said, his sense of the currents of public opinion enabled him to understand better than did his supporters and friends the strength of Mr. Roosevelt and the basis of that strength. He knew that instead of embarking on a safe voyage, he would really be facing many chances of shipwreck and the certainty of a hard and perhaps a bitter fight. He realized, as he wrote to Senator Scott, that the fight might drive a wedge into the party whose strength he had done so much to consolidate. Notwithstanding his close alliance with big business interests, he had always wanted to represent the whole people; and he may well have shrunk, as a result of a division in the party, from being forced to represent, even in appearance, only a class or factional interest. Apparently he had made up his mind, after Mr. McKinley's assassination, that the Presidency was not for him — that, even though he could get it, the game, as it had been played, was not worth the candle.

His political career, theretofore, had been a practically uninterrupted series of successes. Little by little he had disarmed much of the opposition and prejudice which had greeted his first appearance in politics. With no more official power than a dozen others had possessed, he had won for himself, as a matter of personal prerogative, a unique position in the party and with the people. In proportion as his power and its responsibilities increased, he had sought to represent something more than a business or a partisan interest. He had sought to represent a general popular interest, which embraced all classes and all sections. He was persuading people to believe in his good faith as a national leader. Why should he risk the most valued aspect of his leadership by engaging in a necessarily bitter and precarious fight — one in which the advantage of position would be on one side of his opponent, which would revive all the old animosities, and which, whether he won or lost, would leave him with a divided following and possibly a diminished prestige. Even from the point of view of personal ambition, would he not bulk larger in the history of the country by remaining the indispensable Prime Minister to any Republican President and by broadening still farther the scope and deepening the foundations of his unique personal political edifice?

I do not wish to imply that Mr. Hanna scorned the Presidency, and that in renouncing any attempt to get it he was not making a sacrifice. He had an almost superstitious respect for the office and probably would have liked to fill it more than he ever admitted to anybody. But he was not willing to pay the price, and in refusing to pay the price, he should have the credit, not merely of a shrewd calculation of comparative costs, but of a genuine disposition towards personally disinterested action. No man would fight harder for an honor or a prize to which he believed himself fairly entitled. No man was more modest and hesitating in claiming an honor to which his title was dubious. He renounced a contest, not only because it might cost him too much, but also because the party and perhaps the country might have to pay too high a price. And there can be little doubt that, with his usual insight into the complexities of a particular human situation, he had made the decision which, had he lived, would have best contributed to his cherished patriotic and personal interests.

CHAPTER XXVII

THE DEATH OF MARK HANNA

As has been frequently intimated in the foregoing pages, Mr. Hanna had not been for years a thoroughly well man. Particularly since his entrance into politics the handicap of certain physical infirmities had been constantly increasing, and had been the cause of grave alarm to his family and friends. The strain of his very active and wearing political life had manifestly been telling on his strength. He had been often advised and implored to go away and take a long rest, but he always refused. He was a man who did not know how to rest, and who became unhappy whenever he was deprived of his regular occupations and his familiar surroundings.

He was born with an exceptionally strong physique, and throughout his active life could under ordinary circumstances stand an enormous amount of work and strain. He was what used to be called a sanguine man — that is, a man of active disposition, red blood, high spirits and unflagging energy. This gift of abundant energy was never diminished by physical excesses. He was a total abstainer until past forty, and thereafter his consumption of alcohol was confined to an occasional glass of claret with his meals. He was not even a very large eater. His usual breakfast, for instance, consisted of a couple of soft-boiled eggs. He was not particularly addicted to tea or coffee, and ate fresh meat in moderation. His favorite dish of meat was corned-beef hash, which was made for him according to a very delectable recipe by a cook named Maggie, who had lived with the family for many years. One of Mr. Hanna's peculiar ways of entertaining was to invite guests to partake of Maggie's corned-beef hash for breakfast on Sunday morning. He also liked chipped beef, bacon and small deer-foot sausages. He was a great bread eater, but had no particular relish for cakes or sweets. The dessert which he preferred was a plain rice pudding as prepared by his excellent cook. Altogether his appetite seemed to run in the direction of starchy foods, — such as green corn, among vegetables, — and whatever he liked he liked very much. Perhaps he came nearer to excess in smoking than in any other physical habit. He had his own special brand of somewhat strong cigars, which had been carefully selected, and of which he consumed about a dozen a day.

Energetic, however, as he was by disposition, he was not physically an active man. He belonged to the generation of Americans who took no exercise. One could not by the utmost effort of the imagination associate Mr. McKinley and Mr. Hanna with a game of tennis; and when a tennis player was actually installed in the White House, a political revolution was evidently impending. Mark Hanna did not even enjoy open air and the country. He was essentially an indoor and a city man. The one kind of outdoor life which amused him was yachting or boating — particularly on the Lakes. He would occasionally take a drive, but late in life even this mild form of physical activity ceased to attract. The only stirring up which his body received came as the incidental result of the mental stimulus and excitement resulting from a keenly interesting occupation. Public speaking, for instance, was physically refreshing to him, because it afforded wholesome exertion both to body and mind.

There was nothing, however, in Mr. Hanna's physical habits which need have handicapped his work or shortened his life. His fundamental trouble seems to have been a legacy from the attack of typhoid fever from which he suffered in 1867. He was subject to attacks of congestion, which would send the blood to his head and cause him to faint. Sometimes they would last for several hours, throughout which his hands would be clenched and his body would become rigid. If he passed a year without a spell of this kind, he was lucky. They might be caused by indigestion, by a cold, or even by anxiety or emotion. If he ate a hearty meal and immediately after plunged into severe mental exertion, he was apt to suffer. The attacks were not, however, regarded seriously by the family. They usually yielded to simple remedies, and as soon as they were over Mr. Hanna immediately recovered his strength and was up again and doing business the same day. They indicated, however, an imperfection in the circulation of the blood, which, as he grew older, might well have other effects.

In 1899 his knees began to give him some trouble. The difficulty was diagnosed as rheumatism, but it proved eventually to be an increasing chalky deposit on the knee joints, which gradually affected his finger joints as well. After this ailment fastened on him, he was always suffering more or less pain, and when he made speeches and was compelled to be long on his feet his suffering was acute. It was to get rid of this discomfort that he went abroad in the summer of 1899. Baths at Aix-les-Bains were prescribed, and Mr. Hanna took them conscientiously for three weeks. But he refused to submit to an after-cure in Switzerland, and during the three following weeks hurried rapidly over a large part of Europe. He was always a bad patient, just as he was always a man who scorned to take precautions against sources of contagion and infection. He would not submit to hygienic dictation — even when he was threatened with illness.

The cure at Aix did him no permanent good, and thereafter he suffered from minor ailments — none of which prevented him from continuing his work, but all of which taken together indicated that his body was yielding under the strain imposed by his way of living. But he was not an apprehensive man, and he was too much interested in what he was doing to listen to any prudential advice. His wife soon began to realize that he was wound up too tight and was running too fast. She tells of warning him. "I don't know how you feel about it," she said, "but to me you behave like a person who is under some strong excitement, who is rushing onward and cannot stop." He admitted that she was right, but he refused even to discuss the matter of drawing back. "I am going on," was his final word. He continued his unremitting and almost feverish activity, and for a while stood it fairly well. But in 1903 there were premonitions of a breakdown. Before beginning his long and strenuous stumping tour in the fall, he went off on a yachting trip for a month. The rest did him little good, because the boat was too much in port, where there were people to see and big dinners to be eaten. After his return to Cleveland he was confined to his bed for a while, but he pulled himself together, and to his own intense discomfort, went through the most arduous and exciting stumping tour of his career. The way in which he sometimes felt and suffered during that tour is indicated by the story which he told one cold autumn evening to Colonel Herrick, and which is related in the last chapter.

After the election his immediate presence in Washington was required. An extra session of Congress had been called to deal with Cuban reciprocity. At the time he left Cleveland he looked extremely worn and debilitated. All his friends urged him to quit. Mrs. Hanna, too, was not well, and wanted to remain at home. But he insisted that both of them should go. He asserted that he had plenty of strength for his work and that they could save themselves by declining invitations to dinner. Such was their understanding, and they acted up to it. Between the beginning of November and Christmas they went out very rarely. On Tuesday, December 15, Mr. Hanna had a severe attack of the grip. He had planned to go to New York on Thursday for a meeting of the Civic Federation, and then to join Mrs. Hanna in Cleveland for the Christmas holidays. But on Thursday morning he was so miserable that it did not look safe to let him go alone. As Mrs. Hanna was in poor health, it was decided that Miss Mary Phelps, for many years the companion and friend of Mrs. Hanna, should accompany him. Mr. Hanna slept during the journey and that night had a little fever. Nevertheless he spent the whole of Friday at the meeting of the Civic Federation and in the evening attended a dinner of the McKinley Memorial Association. His fever still hung on, but it did not prevent him from continuing the next day his attendance of the sessions of the Federation. The dinner of that organization was scheduled for the same night. During the afternoon Mr. Hanna felt so ill that he decided to give up the dinner, but to drop in about nine o'clock and make a short speech. After dinner, however, he was taken with a severe chill, and was put to bed. His local physician, Dr. George E. Brewer, dosed him with the strongest stimulants. The chill was succeeded by a raging fever. At midnight his temperature was 103½, and he did not sleep until towards morning.

The next day, however, his temperature returned to normal, and he insisted upon going home to Cleveland for Christmas. Miss Phelps protested, but he would have his way. They left on Wednesday, the twenty-third, in the private car of the president of the New York Central Railroad, and reached home safely the next day. On Christmas there was a large party for dinner, and on Sunday Mr. Hanna drove across Cleveland to see his son, D. R. Hanna. The day after he was at his office in the Perry-Payne building and put in an immense amount of work during the following week. But on one occasion he called for Scotch whiskey to keep him going, which was unprecedented with him. On January 4 he went to Chicago for a visit to the dentist and to engage his accommodations for the approaching National Convention. Miss Phelps accompanied him and states that after a short session with the dentist in the morning the rest of the day until after midnight was spent in political conferences.

A few days later, January 12, found the indefatigable invalid in Columbus, Ohio, for the purpose of being present at his reelection to the Senate. After the result was announced, he made the following brief address to the Legislature — the last public utterance of his career: —

"Mr. President and Gentlemen of the Seventy-sixth General Assembly of Ohio: For the great honor that your action has conferred upon me to-day, I offer my most profound gratitude, appreciating the compliment, and may I not say the vindication. I also appreciate the responsibilities which come to me at your hands by conferring upon me this great office.

" I am not vain enough to assume that the result of the great victory in Ohio in the last campaign was a personal matter, great as has been my pleasure in the interests of the party at such a result. It is more tribute to the intelligence of the people of Ohio, when they were confronted by the propositions, such as were made the issue in that campaign. I say I attribute it to their intelligence, because the arguments and pleadings made upon every issue were well defined. There could be no misunderstanding as to what they meant. The time had come in the history of our state when the people were called upon to register their verdict upon great questions so all-important to our social conditions; the principles upon which the government itself had been founded were on trial.

"Proud I am, my fellow-citizens, and speaking through you members of this General Assembly to the people of the whole state whom I am to represent in the higher branch of Congress, that I go there not as a partisan, where the interests of my state are the issue, but as a representative of all the people, as a representative of all interests which are material to all the people, as a man to stand for you, for what are your interests socially, politically, industrially and commercially."

The day, happy as it was for Mr. Hanna, was clouded by the sudden illness or death of two old associates, both of whom were on their way to Columbus. One of these men was Charles Foster, a friend and ally of Mr. Hanna, who had been a Representative in Congress, Governor of Ohio from 1880 to 1884, and Secretary of the Treasury during President Harrison's administration. He had started for Columbus, stopped *en route* to see a friend, and died at the friend's house of cerebral hemorrhage. The other was ex-Governor Asa Bushnell, the man who had appointed Mr. Hanna to the Senate and then ruined his own career by joining in the cabal which sought to prevent Mr. Hanna's first election. Mr. Bushnell was visited by an apoplectic stroke while on the way to the train. A friend, who returned to Cleveland in Mr. Hanna's car, states that he was both distressed and depressed by the coincidence of these two deaths. Only those who knew him well could perceive any change in his manner; but far from well as he was at the time, he may have felt the uncertainty of his own life. As a matter of fact, there was an epidemic of typhoid at the time of his visit to Columbus, and he was there infected with the germ which caused his death.

Saturday, January 16, found him back in Washington. He went to the Senate on Monday and Tuesday and Wednesday mornings. On Wednesday afternoon, when Mrs. Hanna and Miss Phelps returned from a drive, they found Mr. Hanna lying down in his room at the Arlington Hotel. He assured them he was all right, but none the less went to bed and stayed there on Thursday and Friday and on Saturday until noon. On Sunday he was up all day until midnight. On Monday, January 25, he complained of a severe toothache, which during

FACSIMILE OF THE LETTER WRITTEN BY MR. HANNA DURING HIS
FINAL ILLNESS TO PRESIDENT ROOSEVELT

the evening became so bad that his physician, Dr. Rixie, was called, and morphine was administered. Nevertheless he was up the next day, and enjoyed very much a visit from his friend Mr. Bliss. Throughout the week he was very nervous and was constantly taking soothing or stimulating medicine, but he continued active, and on Saturday night attended a dinner given by the Gridiron Club. On Sunday, January 31, he had Mr. James Rhodes, Mr. Bliss and Mr. Grant B. Schley for breakfast, and in the afternoon conferred with Mr. James J. Hill. He was continually protesting that he was all right, but his hands were like ice. He hardly slept at all that night and complained that every nerve in his body ached. He was sick Monday and Tuesday, and on Wednesday, February 3, two weeks after he was first taken down, Dr. George Brewer came on from New York and diagnosed his complaint as typhoid fever.

In the beginning it did not look as if the attack would necessarily be fatal; and probably it would not have been fatal, in case Mr. Hanna's general condition had not been so enfeebled. He continued for a day or two to transact some business in bed. On the afternoon of February 5 Mr. Dover went to Mr. Hanna's room and consulted him about some matters which demanded the Senator's attention. When they had been disposed of, Mr. Dover told him that President Roosevelt had called during the morning in order to inquire after his health. This bit of attention touched him deeply, and an hour after Mr. Dover's departure he called for pencil and paper and scrawled the following note, which perhaps as much as any single utterance of his life, reveals the quality of Mr. Hanna's personal feelings:

"MY DEAR MR. PRESIDENT:—

"You touched a tender spot, old man, when you called personally to inquire after [me] this A.M. I may be worse, before I can be better, but all the same such "drops of kindness" are good for a fellow.

"Sincerely yours,
"Friday P.M.   "M. A. HANNA."

The next day a reply was received from the President accompanied by a note stating that it was to be shown to the Senator when Mrs. Hanna thought best. Mr. Hanna never saw the reply — which ran as follows: —

"Feb. 6, 1904.

"Dear Senator: —
"Indeed it is *your* letter from your sick bed which is touching, not my visit. May you soon be with us again, old fellow, as strong in body and as vigorous in your leadership as ever.
"Faithfully yours,
"Theodore Roosevelt."

About the middle of the preceding week, during which Mr. Hanna had been both in and out of bed, he had been carefully examined by Dr. William Osler; and as soon as his illness was known to be typhoid, Mrs. Hanna wanted particularly to obtain the best counsel and assistance. On Saturday Dr. Brewer saw Dr. Osler, who agreed to take the case, but inasmuch as neither he nor Dr. Brewer could be in constant attendance, he advised sending for still another physician, whom Mr. Hanna liked, and who could be present all the time. They telegraphed to Cleveland, consequently, for Dr. Edward Perkins Carter, who arrived on Monday, February 8, and who with Dr. Rixie and Dr. Osler constituted the physicians in charge. In the meantime Howard Melville Hanna had also been summoned, and came at once. The physicians continued to hope that they could save him, until Thursday of the same week. Dr. Osler had been with him the whole of the previous night, and in the morning was disturbed by his apathetic condition. The patient himself began to lose courage and wanted to have them telegraph for his lawyers. During the afternoon, while Mrs. Hanna was sitting by his bedside, he seized her hand after a long period of immobility, and said, "Old lady, you and I are on the home-stretch." She answered reassuringly, but he persisted in saying that he, at least, was on the home-stretch. The next day, Friday, he was even more discouraged, and complained that nothing did him any good. His brother Melville was called in to assure him that he could do more for himself than any one else and that he must fight on and win.

On Saturday he had his first bad sinking spell, but rallied well in the evening, and excited the admiration of the doctors by the stiff fight which he was making. On Sunday, while Mrs. Hanna was in the room, he seemed to be hunting for something in his pocket. She asked if he wanted a handkerchief. "Yes," he answered, "I would like one, but I suppose I cannot have it. My wife takes them all." Mrs. Hanna frequently used his handkerchiefs, and it was one of his jokes to accuse her of it and ask her why she did not buy some of her own. He distinguished all that day the people who were with him, but on Monday he was almost unconscious. He died on Monday evening, February 15, at forty minutes past six.

I have given in detail an account of Mr. Hanna's last few weeks partly because the story itself reveals more vividly than could any attempt at characterization his personal attitude towards his own way of living. Had he been willing to take ordinary precautions, he might have survived many years; but (be it added) if he had been willing to take ordinary precautions, he would not have been Mark Hanna. He could not allow scruples to interfere between himself and anything which he wanted to do and considered worth the doing. His interest and will were absolutely possessed by his various external occupations. He was incapable of pausing and inquiring how far prudence would forbid him to continue his exhausting career. His career was himself, and if he had hesitated or checked his pace, he would have, to his own mind, been playing the "quitter." The quality of his will, which was responsible for his peculiar achievements, which impelled and enabled him to nominate men for the Presidency, and to rise to one opportunity after another of useful service — that same quality kept him going until his death. The body of the man and the accidents of his life were carried along on a flood of a powerful impulse, which did originate within the field of consciousness, and which could not be checked or guided by conscious motives. He was bound to run until he dropped.

Mr. Hanna's family wished to keep his funeral as quiet and unostentatious as they could, but the sense of public loss was so acute and widespread that the ceremonies necessarily became a state affair. His associates in the Senate and his friends and neighbors in Cleveland both demanded and had a right to give public and formal expression to their affection for Mr.

Hanna and their grief at his death. The body was not, however, allowed to lie in state in Washington. On Wednesday, Feb. 17th, a memorial service was held in the Senate Chamber, which was attended by the President, the Cabinet, Congress and the whole official life of Washington, and which consisted chiefly of an eloquent and impressive address of the Chaplain, the Rev. Edward Everett Hale. At six o'clock on the same day the funeral party left for Cleveland. At noon on Thursday the body was carried into the auditorium of the Chamber of Commerce in that city by Governor Herrick, Samuel Mather, W. B. Sanders, J. B. Zerbe, Andrew Squire, C. A. Grasselli, A. B. Hough and W. J. McKinnie, and the same group of friends served as pall-bearers at the funeral on the following day. The body lay in state for twenty-four hours, during which more than 30,000 people visited the bier. Friday was a cold, bleak, windy and snowy day. The funeral services were held at one o'clock, at St. Paul's Episcopal Church, and were attended not merely by his close connections, but by an extraordinary number of distinguished men from all over the East and Middle West. Bishop Leonard delivered the eulogy. Mark Hanna's sepulchre is admirably situated on the brow of a high hill in Lakeview Cemetery in Cleveland, and consists of a severely simple Greek temple, designed by Mr. Henry Bacon, which makes an impression on its visitor both of beauty and solemnity.

There was nothing perfunctory in the grief inspired by Mark Hanna's death. Every one who knew him felt his loss as a deep personal sorrow. No man in the country had so many friends, whom he had attached to himself by services and kindnesses small and great; and even those who felt no grief themselves could not fail to be affected by the sincerity with which his associates mourned his death. "The most sorrowful scene," says Senator Spooner, "which I ever saw was in the Senate when we sat and waited for the news of Mr. Hanna's death. There was a feeling in every heart of personal bereavement, and this feeling was, if possible, more pronounced on the Democratic side than on the Republican. But it was personal everywhere and made the moments we waited for the sad news, which we knew would come, the most impressive in my life." In his eulogy of Mr. Hanna, delivered in the Senate, Mr. Platt of Connecticut said: "When Marcus A. Hanna died all the people mourned him with a grief that was deep and unfeigned. Something in his life and character endeared him to all classes. To but few men in this world is it given to inspire such respect and affection as did our deceased comrade and brother. His death saddened all. The sun of life was clouded and the whole air chill and dreary. It seemed as if the tie which bound his heart to every heart had been rudely sundered. While all shared the common grief, nowhere outside the circle of his domestic life was the mourning so deep as among his Senatorial associates. We had learned to admire him for his ability, to respect him for his strength, to wonder at his great influence, but more than that, each had come to love him as a friend."

The foregoing tribute to Mr. Hanna was delivered by Mr. Platt in the Senate Chamber on April 7, 1904. Some sixteen Senators spoke on that occasion, including Foraker, Scott, Platt, Dolliver, Beveridge, Blackburn and Daniel. Several of the speakers, particularly the Democrats, frankly admitted that in their attitude towards Mr. Hanna they had passed through much the same different phases of opinion as had the general public. They had begun by suspecting him. Little by little respect took the place of suspicion. Confidence was added to respect, and affection to confidence. The very men who could watch his public behavior most closely were most completely convinced of his good faith and loyalty, and they were most completely captivated by his warmth of feeling and his essential humanity. Thus it came to pass that they watched his growing personal influence with wonder, but without envy and without protest. The Senate is notoriously jealous of its independence, but never was there a suggestion that his power was being dictatorially used or was anything but the natural and desirable fruit of his personal worth and actual services.

In spite of all that Mr. Hanna's friends could say in his praise on that day in April, it remained for a man who was no longer his friend to pronounce the most discriminating appreciation of his career and personality. Beginning in 1884, the whole of Mr. Hanna's public life had been profoundly influenced, first by his intimacy with Senator Foraker and then by their mutual alienation. In every crisis of Mr. Hanna's career the threatening figure of Mr. Foraker can be distinguished in the foreground or the background, ready, wherever possible, to make trouble. On the other hand, if any single man, Mr. Foraker himself excepted, was responsible for the abortive ending of what promised in the middle eighties to be an exceptionally brilliant political career, that man was Mark Hanna. It is the more to Mr. Foraker's credit when, as senior Senator from Ohio, he was called upon to pronounce in the Senate the first of a series of tributes to Mr. Hanna's memory, that he could without any pretence of kindly feeling, sum up so honestly and fairly certain salient aspects of Mr. Hanna's achievements and disposition. The men who did injustice to Mr. Hanna after his death were not his personal opponents. They were, rather, certain political opponents whose formulas were so narrow and whose prejudices were so dense that their vision of the essential value of the man was obscured by their disapproval of certain aspects of his work and doctrine. His personality inspired sympathy and respect among all who became acquainted with him; and under favorable conditions the sympathy usually became affection and the respect admiration. His devotion to his friends aroused a corresponding warmth of feeling in them. In a very real sense he lived for and among other people.

He was not merely fond of companionship; he was quite dependent on it — particularly the companionship of men. Throughout his life he always liked to live, play and eat in the midst of company. Mrs. Hanna never knew how many guests he would bring home to dinner; but there would almost always be somebody — even when he was an obscure Cleveland business man. After his public career began, this tireless sociability increased rather than diminished. Just as during his early life he did his best to bring to his house all the interesting visitors to Cleveland, particularly the actors, so after he went to Washington, he remained as curious about people as ever, and as much interested in them.

During most of his career as Senator he and Mrs. Hanna

lived at the Arlington Hotel; but he occupied a large suite and practically kept house. His cook, Maggie, was provided with a special kitchen, which had formerly been a bathroom, and in which she provided for almost all the meals of the family. He was constantly entertaining. His Sunday morning breakfast parties had a special reputation; but his dinners were scarcely less popular. Whenever prominent men, strangers or not, registered at the hotel, Mr. Hanna always managed to meet them; and they usually received an invitation to dinner. He was not only expansive but inquisitive. He learned, not from the printed, but from the spoken, word. He acquired what Mr. Foraker describes as his "almost unnatural knowledge of human nature" from the zest with which he seized on every opportunity of getting in touch with other men, and from the powerful and candid intelligence which he brought to the digestion of this social experience.

Of course, he did not seek companionship consciously for the purpose of looking into the minds of other men. He sought it either to transact business, to exchange ideas or merely to have a good time. His insight into human nature was the unconscious by-product of his sociability. But in any event, he craved some external occupation which was shared with other people. If nothing better offered, he would play cards. During the evening, in the absence of male guests, his family would have to play with him, and wherever he lived he collected a group of friends, upon whom he could usually depend for a game of whist, and later of bridge. In Washington, Senators Aldrich, Spooner, Allison and others were frequently found at his card table. In Cleveland there were a coterie of old friends, including W. J. McKinnie, A. B. Hough, J. B. Zerbe, "Jack" Yates, E. P. Williams, Frederick E. Rittman and others with whom he habitually played. During the last years of his life, when in Cleveland, he spent a great deal of his time in the Union Club at the card table. He would lunch there and play all the afternoon, and on Saturday the whole evening up to midnight. He never seemed to tire of any occupation which he thoroughly enjoyed. A small stake was always waged on these games.

Interested as he was in his game of whist, he never allowed

it to degenerate into an unsocial sport. He was not one of your silent players, who are intent only on winning. He talked constantly and his friends say that he talked more than was good for the quality of his game. A stupid play would be pounced upon immediately and made the subject of emphatic comment. And it was not merely the incidents of the card table which he insisted on discussing. Any matter of local or general interest might come up for comment, and he was continually on the lookout for a chance to joke about the peccadilloes of his friends. There were few of them who escaped some kind of rigging.

Like most gregarious men, he liked to be socially conspicuous. He liked, that is, the idea of being prominent and popular among his own people, and of seeing himself reflected large in the eye of the world. An old friend states that he enjoyed going to the Opera House, sitting in his box, and being pointed out as the owner of the theatre. But this trait, in so far as it existed, was an amiable weakness. He was entirely without mere conceit, and he consistently under- rather than over-valued his own abilities. Flattery had little or no effect upon him. He was as little pleased with complimentary but exaggerated public tributes as he was with his abundant portion of unjust abuse. But his expansive disposition craved approval, and it was partly this desire for approval which always kept him so closely in touch with public opinion. He knew his own people so well that he divined instinctively what they would approve. Strong as was his individual will, it always sought an expression consistent with what he understood and felt to be the popular will.

Although he had hearty personal dislikes as well as likes, he was far from being vindictive. Just as his anger would quickly cool, so a personal repulsion might easily be worn down. His natural tendency was to like other men, and if he continued to dislike them, it was usually because he found them by experience personally untrustworthy. He required his associates to be, as he was himself, fair, frank, and honest. He forgave anything in a man quicker than a lie. When he said, "That man is a liar," he was going as far as he could in condemnation. He never deceived anybody himself, and he rarely got his own way with people by devious methods. He did not promise to do a thing unless he was sure he could do it; and if he promised anything, it was as good as done. In living up to such standards, he was, of course, helped by his quickness and soundness of judgment. When any demand was made upon him, he usually knew pretty well and pretty soon how far he could yield; and he escaped in that way entanglements in which other sympathetic but less sure-footed men are caught.

Mr. Elmer Dover, his private secretary for seven years, states that never during that interval did he pass an unpleasant word or an unkind criticism. He could be gruff and brusque with importunate callers, but he was never discourteous to people who had any claim on his time. He did not find fault with his immediate associates and assistants. Neither did he praise them. He showed his confidence merely by increasing their work, their responsibility, and, if necessary, their remuneration. All his associates testify that Mr. Dover was invaluable to him, that he imposed upon his secretary the most delicate and onerous personal missions and negotiations. But he never bestowed upon Mr. Dover any word of commendation, except on one occasion when a group of friends were entertaining Mr. Dover at dinner.

Mr. Hanna did not regularly belong to any church. When a young man he used to attend church on Sundays, but later in life Sunday became his day of social recreation, during which his house was even more full of people than usual, and he rarely heard a sermon. His disposition was obviously not religious or devout, and he was too sincere to pretend an interest merely for public purposes. On the other hand, he contributed freely, not merely to the building funds of churches, but to church work and charity. His gifts were not confined to any denomination or to any class of work. The Catholic Sisters received liberal assistance, but not less liberal were his gifts to various Protestant institutions of all denominations. Mr. Hanna was not known, except within a limited circumference in Cleveland, as a particularly charitable man. Yet throughout his life he was a sedulous contributor to all kinds of good causes. Mr. Lucius F. Mellen, who for twenty-five years was, as he himself says, perhaps the sturdiest beggar for charitable purposes in Cleveland, states that never once did Mr. Hanna turn him away empty-handed. When Mr. Hanna had confidence in a solicitor, as he had in Mr. Mellen, or in a Sister of Charity, he merely took out his cheque-book and asked them how much they wanted. He did not rub his hands and promise to have the matter investigated. He was not a scientific philanthropist. He was simply a kind-hearted, generous man, who wanted to help people in distress, and who in helping them wanted to avoid ostentation and publicity. When during a political campaign he made any considerable donation to a charitable cause or institution, he particularly requested that no public announcement of it should be made until after the election. He was utterly discomfited when on one occasion during his first stumping tour, Mr. Benjamin Butterworth related to the audience certain incidents which illustrated his generous warmth of feeling towards other people.

For the most part his gifts consisted of small sums contributed to needy causes or people. There were, indeed, one or two institutions to which he rendered systematic assistance. The Huron Street Hospital, for instance, in Cleveland received from him in all about $15,000. Late in life he became interested in Kenyon College and donated $75,000 as a fund with which to build a dormitory. But the acts of generosity, on which his friends liked to dwell, usually concerned individuals in whose need or distress he happened to be interested.

Some of these incidents deserve to be related. One rainy day some time in the early nineties, two Sisters of Charity called on him for a contribution with which to buy a horse. Their horse had died and they were seeking assistance toward the purchase of another. If Mr. Hanna had given them $10, they would have gone away well satisfied. But after he had heard their story, he pretended that he had exhausted his charity fund for that month, and brusquely asked them to return some other time. Upon leaving his office they were followed by his coachman, who insisted on putting them in a carriage and driving them home. As they were getting out, the coachman inquired: "Where shall I put the horse?

Mr. Hanna told me that he had given it to you." Another case was that of a woman who had inherited a small house from her father. Times were bad. There was a mortgage on the property which was being foreclosed. A real estate dealer went to Mr. Hanna, knowing him to be a shrewd business man, told him that the property could be bought for less than its value, and asked for authority to bid it in. Mr. Hanna did not know the woman, but he was disgusted at the man's heartlessness. He commissioned a lawyer to attend the sale and buy the property. The mortgage was transferred to Mr. Hanna and was not recorded. Mr. Hanna held the property until times improved, and then sold it for a good price. After paying the mortgage, the balance of the money was turned over to the woman, who never knew how near she came to losing her inheritance, or of Mr. Hanna's contribution to her welfare.

He was, of course, even more generous with needy friends. He would lend them money on what was often worthless security. Mr. James Dempsey was continually asked to investigate such security, but he was warned that in any event the loan was to stand. He recalls many instances of such loans which were never repaid, and which the lender never asked to have repaid. After Mr. Hanna's death his executors destroyed a basketful of acknowledgments of personal debts. They had been accumulating for years, and no attempt had ever been made to collect them. Neither was this negligence due to any mere looseness in money matters. While not, of course, an economical man, he was conscientious and systematic about his personal expenditures. He knew how much he was spending and upon what it was spent. He never submitted to extortion and he had a hatred of mere waste.

If he was sometimes lavish in his gifts and heedless about his personal loans, it was because such expenditures belonged to a different class. In neither case was he buying anything. He was giving something away, and he was always giving with it a part of himself. The weightiest tribute to this aspect of his nature comes from a man whom he knew only late in life, and who himself was, as Mr. Hanna said of Mr. McKinley, more Scotch than Irish in temperament — Senator Orville Platt: "His loyalty was something wonderful. With his friends, and no man had more friends, it carried him nearly to extremes. I often thought that he of all men would be willing to die for his friends. Friendship has its burdens as well as its joys, and he took upon himself all its burdens as easily and as heartily as he shared its joys."

CHAPTER XXVIII

CONCLUSION

A DISCRIMINATING estimate of Mark Hanna's public career must account, first of all, for the apparent disproportion between what he achieved and what he proposed or was equipped to achieve. He had no more training for public life than hundreds of other business men who dabbled in politics. His own will, strong as it was, and his abilities, exceptional as they were, account for only a certain portion of his success. To be sure, he willed and contrived the nomination of McKinley, just as he willed and contrived many other deeds which were of decisive importance in his career. But he did not plan his own political self-aggrandizement. Dominant as was his instinct for leadership, he never sought to concentrate in his own hands the various strings of his personal power. Throughout his career his effective influence gathered momentum from forces independent of its original source and of his own conscious purposes. Like a tropical bamboo, it derived much of its new growth from shoots which were rooted in fresh soil. Both he and his friends were amazed at his own triumphal progress; and they may well have been amazed, because his career was without precedent and is not likely to have any imitators.

Inasmuch as Mark Hanna was not a usurper and his career was not a *tour de force*, only one explanation will account for his peculiar success. He must have embodied in his own life and purposes some vital American social and economic tradition, which gave his personality, individual as it was, something more than an individual meaning and impulse; and he must have embodied this tradition all the more effectively because he was not more than half conscious of it. Mark Hanna could not represent anything unless he himself was what he represented. In truth, Mr. Hanna did embody the most vital social and economic tradition in American history — the tradition, that is, of the pioneer. He was an incarnation of the spirit and methods of the men who seized and cleared the public domain, developed its natural resources, started and organized an industrial and commercial system and determined most of our political and social habits and forms. All the salient characteristics of the pioneer are writ clear and large in Mr. Hanna's disposition and achievements. Indeed, they are, I believe, writ larger and clearer therein than in any other one accessible book. If Mark Hanna had not lived and tried and succeeded, something might have been permanently lacking in our understanding of the spirit and methods of the pioneer.

The foregoing assertions may well strike the average reader as doubtful. How can a man whose successful business career began after the Civil War and who did not become prominent in politics until 1896 — how can the life of such a man embody with particular success the spirit and methods of the men who conquered the American wilderness? During the culminating period of his life pioneering in its primitive sense had practically ceased. The wilderness had disappeared. The United States had become more like a European country than like the United States of 1830. The gulf which had been created between the America of 1830 and the America of 1900 would be fairly well measured by the gulf between the manner of life of the lean, hardy frontiersman and that of the affluent Cleveland merchant.

The difficulty is obvious, but it is not conclusive. The men who originate an economic and social impulse and start it off on a career of conquest do not bestow upon it a complete expression. They exhibit its fresh vigor, and they overcome the most serious obstacles in its path; but their expression of it is necessarily crude and partial. The completer revelation must wait on history and experience. Generations must pass before a national social and economic movement develops fully its own latent tendencies and capabilities. The primitive pioneers imposed their social, political and economic ideas upon the country, but by the time their ideas had become part of the national tradition, the conditions in which they originated had changed. After the Civil War the pioneer system had to meet the shock of new economic and social forces. Under the stimulus of these new opportunities and new responsibilities it became in certain respects a new system. The vitality of the movement was depleted by the effort to adapt itself to more complicated social and economic surroundings, but this effort and its results proved to be peculiarly illuminating. Its strength and its weakness became more clearly distinguishable and more fully revealed than ever before, and the hand-writing of its history became far more legible. Inasmuch as only within the past fifteen years has the pioneer been granted his proper place in American economic and social development, it is not unnatural that during the same years there flourished and died the most complete single embodiment of pioneer purposes and methods.

The primary economic task of the pioneer was that of appropriating and developing the land and natural resources of a continent, — a task which combined and confused individual and social profits. The combination and confusion was reflected in the human nature of the period. The early pioneer was an aggressive, energetic, hopeful, grasping individual. He worked and fought primarily for his own advantage, but his individualism did not prevent him from being the maker of a society. In an economic environment which provided opportunities for all, men could fight for themselves without cherishing ill-will or incurring it. As a matter of fact, the pioneer overflowed with good-will and good-fellowship. He and his neighbors were all striving for the same port. Their contests were merely a good-natured race for the quickest voyage and the biggest market.

From the beginning they recognized and acted on the theory that the individual and social profits were indistinguishable. They conceived it to be the business of their government, as the agent of social betterment, to assist them in attaining their personal ends. The public interest, which government was supposed to promote, was conceived chiefly as a collection of individual interests; and the way to promote it was to stimulate individual economic activity. Hence the passion for "public improvements" which possessed the pioneer states and their frequent inability, in making those improvements, to distinguish between the really private and the really public interests involved. It was during these years, long before corporate enterprise had assumed economic importance, that "special interests" established their control over state legislatures. It was during these years that the practice of making American business depend on American politics had its beginning.

In the meantime American business was ceasing to be local and was becoming increasingly national in its operations. As it became national, the successors of the pioneers began to lose their suspicion of the Central Government. They began to understand that the nation could contribute more effectually to the stimulation of economic activity than could the states. Stephen Douglas, rather than a Whig, was the politician who first proposed to make land grants out of the Public Domain to a railroad. The Civil War accelerated the change. It split the Democratic party and converted the best of the pioneer Democrats into Republicans, who were ready to use the powers of the Central Government to redeem a national responsibility. Washington became the headquarters from which was directed a comprehensive scheme of state-aided business. The agricultural states obtained the gift of free land to homesteaders. The industrial states secured and kept, as their share of the bargain, among the several localities, a high protective tariff. Other interests were satisfied by free mines, timber and pasture. The railroads claimed land grants as their share of the spoil. Business of all kinds was encouraged by loose corporation laws. In return for all these privileges the various special interests were required only to make use of them. They named their own liquor and drank it when and where and how they pleased. Public and private interests were still conceived to be substantially identical, and the national economic interest a comprehensive collection of special interests.

This Republican economic policy, to the perpetuation of which the public career of Mark Hanna was devoted, is plainly the adaptation to new conditions of the earlier purposes and methods of the pioneer Democrats. The continuity of the tradition is unmistakable. It consisted fundamentally of an attempt to convert the spirit and methods of the pioneer from an agency of local economic development into an agency of national economic development. The pioneer spirit and method, transformed in order to meet larger opportunities and responsibilities, was incorporated into the heart of the national economic system. In one way or another every kind of business was obtaining state aid, and was dependent upon state policy for its prosperity. At the very moment when both business and politics were being modified by specialization and organization, business itself was being fastened irretrievably to politics. And the association, dangerous as it is both for business and politics, lies deep and ineradicable in the American democratic tradition. Democracy has always meant to Americans a political system which contributed, by whatever means, to their individual economic well-being. The pioneer economy, both in its local and national phases, was merely the first attempt to realize this purpose.

To the generation of business men who came to the front after the Civil War and grew up in the midst of this system, it seemed like the order of nature. It assuredly accomplished the purpose for which it was intended, and its success was so considerable that it was accepted as a matter of course by the dominant mass of opinion. Mr. Hanna himself and many others like him was as much of a pioneer in his own region of work as had been the men who with axe and gun pushed their way into the wilderness. He developed mines, discovered or created markets, built furnaces, improved mechanical processes, organized industries and started commercial currents on their course. He watched among his own people the gradual accumulation of social benefits which resulted from the stimulation of individual enterprise, and these benefits seemed to him, not the result of temporary conditions, but the normal and permanent effect of stimulating individual business energy. Neither he nor the men of his generation could understand why the system should not continue of equal benefit to the individual and to society.

Nevertheless, certain parts of this economic system were passing out of the pioneer stage, in which there was a rough approximation of individual and social benefits. The essential character of pioneer economics consisted of an abundance of opportunities due chiefly to a superfluity of accessible natural resources. But even in a country as richly endowed as the United States, natural resources had a limit. As soon as the process of their appropriation had reached a certain stage and had given their proprietors a certain advantage over their future competitors, the machinery began to creak. Under such conditions the state encouragement of private enterprise assumed a different appearance and began to look less like a system of social and more like a system of individual benefits. Society might profit, but not in the same proportion to the profits which the state was showering on the individual. In fact, the balance of the whole system was upset as soon as natural resources became even a little scarce and as soon as the corresponding artificial opportunities, created by state law, became even comparatively inaccessible. Not long after the war public opinion, in those parts of the country which were suffering from local business depression, began to blame the system for their privations, and began to criticise the way in which the appropriated economic power was being exercised. The discontent increased, and thereafter the national policy of state-stimulated enterprise had to bear the burden of hostile political agitation.

The foregoing situation affords the clew to the political contests of the last twenty years. Just in proportion as natural resources and artificial economic opportunities were appropriated and developed, public and private interests did not coincide to the same extent as formerly. The private interests which had received public assistance were driven by the necessities of their position to seek the continuance of this assistance on other than public grounds. Business prosperity was entangled in a system whose assumptions no longer corresponded with the facts of American economic life. Every agitation for economic reform forced voters to choose between alternative evils. They could not withdraw the various privileges which business had been enjoying without disturbing confidence and checking expansion, yet they could not perpetuate the advantages enjoyed by certain kinds of business without making the state increasingly responsible for flagrant economic inequalities. The man who remained true to the traditional system was obliged to countenance and overlook many grave political and economic abuses. The man who attacked the traditional system was obliged to injure many innocent people, disappoint the immediate expectations of many more for a higher standard of living, and launch his fellow-countrymen on a career of dangerous economic and political reorganization.

Mark Hanna proved to be the ablest and most successful supporter of the traditional system developed by the crisis. He supported it, because he had become accustomed to its beneficial effects, without being aware that these benefits might be diminished by the gradual intrusion of scarcity values into the national economy. In his speeches he always assumed that economic opportunit es were as abundant and as accessible as ever, and he always refers to the country's natural resources as inexhaustible. He was quite sincere in failing to recognize the change and its consequences, the proof of his sincerity being the harmony between the old tradition and his own business and social habits and practices. Many of his associates reaped their profits from the pioneer system, and supported it by word and deed, but ceased to be the kind of men in which the system originated, and which gave to it its meaning. But Mark Hanna always remained a pioneer, both in his business practice and in his purposes, feelings and ideas. His own life embodied the mixture of individual and social purposes characteristic of the pioneer.

As we have seen, he always remained essentially local in his business enterprises and ambitions and always had the benefit of persistent and familiar social surroundings. While certain of his friends were becoming specialists in financial and business organization, he remained an all-round man, personally competent to manage every aspect of his extensive and complicated business. He was at once salesman, technician, financier, superintendent, organizer and personal chief; and he was all these things because he had not hardened down into a special kind of a man. He was every kind of a man demanded by his own pursuits and interests. Above all, he never became that special kind of a man known as a money-maker. As with the pioneer, business was to him the most interesting sort of life provided by his own society. It was an intensely human occupation in which human motives were ever present, and around which he himself gathered a group of essentially human values.

Being every kind of a man demanded by his occupations and interests, he inevitably became a politician as well as a business man. Personal participation in politics was an essential duty and joy of the pioneers. They associated in their own lives public and private motives just as they associated public and private interests in making state policies. His participation in politics was not determined by business motives any more than his participation in business was determined exclusively by business motives. He took it up because it was intrinsically so interesting, and he became more and more absorbed in it because a personal devotion to the careers of certain political friends made it finally much more interesting than business. Of course as a politician he could not help representing business, because business was a part of himself — because business was in his eyes not simply money-making, but the most necessary kind of social labor.

When the traditional system was attacked, his lifelong habits, associations and connections enabled him to defend it, not only with entire sincerity, but with abundant resources. He could keep personally in touch with every American interest which would be injured by the attack. He could personally exercise all the qualities most needed for the defence. He developed suddenly into an able campaign manager, who fought his troops and provided for their subsistence with unprecedented skill and energy. Yet, if he had been nothing but a campaign manager, he would have been far less efficient. The best work he performed for his cause was that of arousing and uniting in its favor an obviously hesitating public opinion. He brought many of the American people back temporarily to a sense of the value of their traditional economic system.

No American political leader ever appealed to the electorate so frankly as an advocate of pioneer economics. He asked his audiences to vote for the system under which they and their country had become prosperous and which could not be attacked or modified without a certain sacrifice of prosperity. He was accused of appealing to selfish and materialistic motives, but such derogatory epithets meant nothing to him or to his audiences. They knew that he was seeking to satisfy without equivocation their deepest and most active interest — the interest of individual economic amelioration. The American democratic state had promised its citizens prosperity and comfort and had recognized the responsibility by doing its best to stimulate economic activity. He asked them to continue the same policy with the expectation of reaching the same result, and his voice raised a responsive echo in their minds. They would not have listened to him merely as the spokesman of the New York financial district. They did listen to him as the spokesman of American business, irrespective of size or location, and of the individual and social ambitions with which American business had always been associated.

Political and economic conditions towards the close of the nineteenth century made it natural that the pioneer economic system should receive at that time its final and most candid expression. Prosperity had to be made an issue, because prosperity, with all the abuses which had become associated with it and with all the individual and social benefits traditionally attached to it, was being assaulted. Its frank and vigorous defence by Mark Hanna cleared the atmosphere of a great deal of confusing cant, and helped public opinion to choose between loyalty to the old system and the risk and danger of attempting to substitute for it a new system. As long as Mr. Hanna lived, the American people, partly because of his influence, remained true to the old system. He carried with him the small traders and proprietors. After his death this class of small traders and proprietors, largely because of Mr. Roosevelt's influence, switched to reform, and they have remained ever since on that same track. Whatever the outcome of the attempt now being made to devise and establish a new system, which will have the advantages, without the disadvantages, of the old, the traditional system has ceased, at least for the time being, to be one on which the American people can unite for the promotion of their joint economic interests. Mark Hanna's public career coincided with the culmination of an epoch, and he himself was unquestionably the hero of this culminating moment of a century of American development.

The assertion that Mr. Hanna constituted the most complete

embodiment of the pioneer spirit and method may now wear a more plausible aspect. He flourished at a time when a traditional system, which was losing its vitality but retained much of its authority, was under pressure. The peculiar mixture of transparency, candor and sincerity in his nature had enabled him to incorporate the system without distortion into his own life. Under the pressure of the attack and in the ardor of his defence, the meaning of the system, its merits and defects, were fully and clearly revealed. For the benefit of the cause, he turned himself and his own people inside out, and the exposure threw a great deal of light on the whole process, which was just then reaching its culminating stage. Many earlier aspects of American pioneerage can be better understood when considered in the light of Mr. Hanna's doctrines, methods and achievements, while Mr. Hanna himself, and what he achieved, remain wholly inexplicable when detached from their sources and surroundings. He added nothing to the traditional system, except some improvements in organization, and he took nothing away from it. He merely reflected it, and there is much to learn from the reflection.

Mark Hanna's political method and doctrine were no less characteristic of pioneer politics than his business doctrine and methods were characteristic of pioneer economics. The pioneer Democrats had organized party government in order to supply an irresponsible official political system with some machinery of responsible direction. The parties became the engines of government and received recognition at the hands of the state to an extent unprecedented in previous political history. The men of Mr. Hanna's generation knew only one kind of responsibility for political action. Party organizations dictated candidates and platforms, and were supposed to guarantee the acceptability of its nominees and the realization of its policies. The better party leaders, such as Mr. Hanna, took this responsibility very seriously. Under Mr. McKinley's leadership and his, the Republican party was more than usually successful in redeeming its promises; and its success was due to their ability in drawing and keeping the party together. They assumed power at a moment when the Republicans, like the Democrats, had been very much divided by the intrusion of sectional economic issues. They gradually converted it into probably the most efficient partisan machine for the transaction of political business that had been built up in this country.

The cause of partisan harmony and efficiency, like the cause of prosperity, demanded many sacrifices. Mr. Hanna himself was willing to make the needed sacrifices, and he required them of his partisan associates. He labored unceasingly in the attempt to persuade his fellow-Republicans to abandon local interests, and personal feelings and ideas for the benefit of a united and harmonious policy. He often required sacrifices which conscientious men could not make. Under his leadership good Republicans were asked to abandon protests against the corruption and tyranny of the machine in the interest of Republican success. But in order to understand this attitude, we must remember that from his point of view, the Republican party was the Government. Revolts against the partisan organization seemed to him the result merely of factious motives. They were no more worthy of respect than were the perverse class, sectional and personal quarrels which have always constituted the gravest obstacle to the realization of a really national policy. They indicated a lack of public spirit.

Here again Mark Hanna was faithfully representing an historical tradition. The party system, corrupt and tyrannical as it had become in many of its local manifestations, had been forged to meet a real need. It had constituted the most powerful of agencies for the nationalizing of public opinion in a country which was peculiarly liable to be distracted by local and class interests, and it had introduced some responsibility into an irresponsible official "machine." In Mark Hanna's time it contained and concealed many abuses; but it had not for that reason become any less necessary. Reforming legislation recognizes this necessity by incorporating the party systems in the organization of the state, and all effective reformers have been obliged, in order to accomplish their purposes, to become local or national partisan managers and leaders. If Mark Hanna acquiesced in and protected much that was evil in "machine" politics, he also brought out and developed the real responsibilities and capabilities of the system. Under his leadership the Republican party was an effective engine of government, conscious of its duties, responsive to public opinion and efficient in the exercise of its powers.

A careful analyst of American political institutions has said (Henry Jones Ford, "Rise and Growth of American Politics," p. 310): "Nowhere else in the world at any period has party organization had to cope with such enormous tasks as in this country, and its efficiency in dealing with them is the true glory of our political system. . . . The conclusion may be distasteful, since it is the habit of the times to pursue public men with calumny and detraction; but it follows that when history comes to reckon the achievements of our age, great party managers will receive an appreciation very different from what is now accorded them." If there is any truth in this prediction, Mr. Hanna will be better entitled to a revised judgment in his favor than any of the political leaders of his own day. He was the greatest and most successful of American party managers because he brought to the task of party management a peculiar combination of loyalty and adaptability. The power of a party leader is entirely a matter of personal authority. It is based on his ability to read correctly various phases of public and private opinion; to be always on the alert and ready for any emergency; and finally to understand other men, to convince them and obtain their confidence. His leadership has no definite term and no official sanction. It must be earned every day or it vanishes.

Mark Hanna's personal authority was the direct result, not merely of his competence, not merely of his reliability, but above all of his adaptability. He introduced the phrase "stand-pat" into American politics, and "stand-pattism" is usually considered equivalent to a blind and rigid conservatism. Reformers like to talk about a "stand-pat intellect," meaning thereby a mind inaccessible to the impact of fresh experiences and ideas. That is precisely the kind of mind which Mark Hanna did not possess. He was, of course, deeply attached to certain traditional ideas, but his advocacy of a traditional system should not obscure the essentially progressive nature and meaning of his personal life. His salient quality as a business man had been his flexibility, his enterprise, his power of being every kind of a man demanded by success in his business. His salient quality as a political leader remained his flexibility, —

his power of being every kind of a man demanded by success in politics. Few have been the leaders who escaped so completely from the limitations of their own past. His career was a series of surprises and accumulated achievements, because he proved adequate to one opportunity and responsibility after another. In the sphere of his own proper personal work his disposition was essentially adventurous. He was always undertaking new enterprises and assuming new duties. The limitations of his ideas were the result, not of the rigidity of his mind, but of the limitations of his experience. That experience was exclusively practical and was restricted by the desire for immediate results. But within the limits of a purely practical point of view he was the most flexible of men; and his flexibility was the personal reflection of that social fluidity so characteristic of pioneer Americanism.

The conclusion is that Mr. Hanna's personality and career had an essentially social value, which the opponents of his political and economic opinions should be the last to ignore. He gave a highly individual expression both to the practical aspect of pioneer Americanism and to its really underlying tendency. The aggressive and sometimes unscrupulous individualism of the pioneer was redeemed by the conviction that in doing well for himself he was also doing well for society. The pioneer honestly identified and confused individual and social interests, and he was honestly concerned as much for the one as for the other. The society in which he was interested was not an abstract, remote entity. It was a living group of men and women, whom one liked or disliked, helped or hindered, and who aroused in one another an essentially neighborly interest. His hopes and aspirations of a better social state was an extension of the actual good-will which he felt towards his associates individually and as a body.

In this region, also, Mark Hanna helps us to understand the pioneer American, and the pioneer helps us to understand Mark Hanna. Personal ties and associations composed the substance of his life. During each successive phase of his career he made a few enemies and many friends. He made enemies because he had to fight his way to his goal. He made friends because he could make his own the interests of other men. He was building up a better society in his own vicinity by treating his associates as he would like to be treated by them. According to his own lights, he always played fair — not merely towards his friends, not merely towards his business associates and employees, not merely towards his political associates, but towards his personal constituents and towards public opinion. This spirit of fair play is characteristic of pioneer Americanism and constitutes its best legacy to a future American society. But characteristic as it was, it received only occasional expression in the lives of the pioneers. While their good-fellowship and good-will are indisputable, their actual expression of the Golden Rule was not zealous or persistent. They were so eager to make their private fortunes that they were inclined to take the fortune of society for granted. They could not rise to the level of personal disinterestedness which the spirit of their social edifice demanded. Mark Hanna's distinction is that he did rise to the necessary level of personal disinterestedness. He was throughout all his business and political relations what the average good American is only in his better moments. His ability to give an exceptionally high expression to a spirit which Americans traditionally revere constitutes the secret of his extraordinary success. It was by virtue of this that his personality inspired confidence as soon as it became known. He awakened echoes among his followers, not merely of their traditional interest in economic self-betterment, but of their traditional spirit of social fair play.

The economic and political system advocated by Mr. Hanna may not make for social fair play; but any one who rejects the system should be the more willing to recognize the good faith of the man. His personal behavior towards other men was directed towards the realization of those social values, the promotion of which is declared to be the object of a better system. If he was lacking, as his critics have declared, in idealism, the deficiency was at least partly due to the very reality of a certain ideal element in his own life. An impulse toward a better quality of human association was instinctive with him. When, if ever, Mark Hanna's way of behavior towards his fellows becomes common instead of rare, we shall not need so much reform or so many reformers. That so typical an American should have realized in his own life such an edifying social standard encourages the belief that reformers who aspire to create a better society are fighting on behalf of an essential American national instinct.

In any event, the value inherent in Mark Hanna's example and life are durable — although they are not likely to be prized at their actual worth until greater harmony is restored between national traditions and individual ideals. Since Mr. Hanna's death, the trend of American politics has been diverging, not merely from his economic and political system, but from his peculiar emphasis upon the personal aspect of political relations. Politicians are coming to group themselves around principles and to behave as if devotion to principle was a sufficient excuse for a shabby treatment of political friends and for flagrant injustice to political opponents. No doubt some such tendency is natural during a period of changing conditions and fermenting ideas — in which the call of new convictions persuades men to break long-established ties and to repudiate time-honored traditions. But reformers should not accept the change too complacently. Human beings are more real than ideas or principles. Principles divide as well as unite. They inspire doubt as well as faith. If they are destined to conquer, they must have their militant and aggressive phase, yet while they are militant, they are in part untrustworthy. They do not become essentially trustworthy, until they have conquered and are embodied in men to whom candor, fair-play and loyalty in their personal relationships are of as much importance as devotion to principle. They do not become essentially trustworthy, that is, until they have become humanized. Once they have become humanized, their interpreters will place a fairer estimate upon the representatives of an earlier system, like Mark Hanna, whose life realized so much that was characteristic and good in the tradition of his own day and generation.

INDEX

Abolitionism, sympathies of Hanna family with, 12.
Actor acquaintances and friends of Mr. Hanna, 75.
Adams, Charles Francis, praises Mr. Hanna's services as director of Union Pacific R. R., 131 n.
Aix-les-Bains, Mr. Hanna takes the cure at, 449.
Akron meeting (1903), speech of Mr. Hanna at, 417.
Aldrich, Senator Nelson, 429, 459.
Alger, Russell A., 130–131, 180, 194.
Allison, Senator, 179, 180, 191, 459; President McKinley's choice for Vice-President in 1900, 308.
Anderson, A. T., candidate for Cleveland postmastership, 154.
Anderson, David, school-teacher in New Lisbon, 20–22.
Andrews, Sherlock J., 38, 91.
Andrews, W. W., 38.
Anthracite coal strike, of 1900, 389; of 1902, 393–400.
Aristotle, "Politics" of, quoted on intemperate conduct of demagogues and resulting dangers, 225.
Arlington Hotel, Washington, the Hannas' home at, 458–459.
Armor-plate question, the, 285–288.
Army service of Mr. Hanna, 44–46.
Ashtabula, Ohio, ore-handling business of Rhodes & Co. at, 60–61; attacks on Mr. Hanna based on lease of docks at, 69.
Assessment of campaign contributions, system of, organized by Mr. Hanna, 219–220, 325–326.

Bacon, Henry, designer of Mr. Hanna's sepulchre, 456.
Baird, S. H., 43.
Baldwin, Judge George E., quoted, 94.
Baldwin, Mrs. S. Prentiss, 34.
Bank (Union National) in Cleveland organized by Mr. Hanna, 70–72.
Banks, assessment of, by Mr. Hanna for campaign funds (1896), 220.

Barrett, Lawrence, friendship between Mr. Hanna and, 75.
Bartlett, A. C., 389.
Bayne, William M., 127, 128, 154.
Beveridge, Senator, 287, 429, 431, 457.
Blaine, James G., defeats Sherman for nomination for the Presidency, 122–124; dark horse at Convention of 1888, 135; mentioned, 151.
Bliss, Cornelius N., Treasurer of Republican National Committee in campaign of 1896, 213; refuses to run for Vice-President in 1900, 308–309; quoted on Mr. Hanna's view of the Presidential nomination for 1904, 438–439.
Bone, J. H. A., 69.
Bosses, early opposition of Mr. Hanna to and subsequent coöperation with, 114–115; contest waged with, by McKinley and Hanna, in 1895–96, 177–180; while making use of, Mr. Hanna never joined the ranks of, 188–189; victory in his first Senatorial election due to Mr. Hanna's differing from the, 265.
Bourne, E. H., 71; reminiscence of Mr. Hanna by, 98.
Bradbury, "Billy," New Lisbon innkeeper, 34–35.
Brainard, O. D., quoted, 86.
Branley, Assemblyman, 253.
Brewer, Dr. George E., 450, 453, 454.
Bribery, charge of, in connection with Mr. Hanna's Senatorial campaign, 259–264.
Brown, Bennett, 93.
Brush, Charles, 170.
Bryan, William J., McKinley contrasted with, as a speaker, 167; nomination of, in 1896, 204, 209; an earlier election date would have meant the success of, 209; class and sectional feelings aroused by, in campaign of 1896, 210–211; reasons for especial appeal of, to public opinion, 210–211; personal stumping tour by, 214–215; defeat of, by

McKinley by a large majority, 216–217; speaks in Ohio against Mr. Hanna in the Senatorial campaign, 247, 249; the Democratic candidate in 1900, 304; Mr. Hanna's speech against, at Lincoln, Nebraska, 338–339; decisive defeat of, by McKinley (1900), 341.
Buffalo, assassination of President McKinley at, 358–360.
Bunau-Varilla, Philippe, French Panama Canal Co.'s engineer, 381.
Burke, Vernon H., 253, 254, 260, 288–289.
Burton, Theodore E., "Life of Sherman" by, quoted, 136, 233; controversy between Mr. Hanna and, over Cleveland postmastership, 154; works in Mr. Hanna's interests in Senatorial campaign, 254; advises President Roosevelt on Ohio appointments, 438.
Bushnell, Governor Asa, 176; reluctant appointment by, of Mr. Hanna to Sherman's former seat in Senate, 239–241; a leader in conspiracy against Mr. Hanna for Senator, 251; injures his own political career in attacking Mr. Hanna, 256; death of, 452.
Butterworth, Benjamin, 132, 138, 151, 462; warm friendship of, for Mr. Hanna, and letters by, 154–156.

Campaign contributions, systematizing of, by Mr. Hanna, 219–223, 324–326.
Campaign literature, volume of, in McKinley's first election (1896), 217–218.
Campbell, James E., and patent ballot-box episode, 153.
Campbell, Thomas C., 259, 262.
Canals, development of, in Ohio, for transportation purposes, 28–29.
Capital and Labor problem, Mr. Hanna's interest in, 386–410.
Card, Jonathan F., 50.
Card-playing, recreation found in, by Mr. Hanna, 459.
Carnegie, Andrew, 170.
Carter, Dr. E. P., 454.
Carter, Thomas H., 167, 288, 293.
Cartoons of Mr. Hanna, 224, 339, 340, 365, 370.
Catholics, political support of, given to Mr. Hanna, 434.
Chadwick, Admiral F. E., quoted, 237.
Chandler, Frank M., letter of Mr. Hanna to, 299; advice given to, by Mr. Hanna, on selection of assistants, 300.
Chandler, Senator, 287.
Chapin, George W., 46, 51.
Charities, extent of Mr. Hanna's, 461–463.
Chautauqua speeches on the labor question by Mr. Hanna, 396–397, 404.
Chinese exclusion legislation, 373, 374.
Chisholm, Henry, 66.
Chisholm, William, 170.
Church, Mr. Hanna's attitude toward the, 461.
City of Superior steamboat, 40.
Civic Federation. *See* National Civic Federation.
Civil Service law, indifference shown by Mr. Hanna to, 299.
Clark, M. B., 43.
Clarke, John H., Democratic nominee for Senator in 1903, 430.
Clarkson, Ohio, founding of, 3.
Clarkson, James S., 178, 180.
Class feeling aroused by Democrats in election of 1896, 210–211.
Clay, Senator, tribute paid by, to Mr. Hanna's power, 343.
Clayton, Powell, 123, 214.
Cleveland, Ohio, removal of Leonard and Robert Hanna to, 32; early years of the Hanna family in, 36–46; advantages of situation of, 40, 54–56.
Cleveland, Grover, anti-protectionist campaign of (1888), 143 ff.; effect on McKinley's prospects of defeat of Harrison by, 167; business depression and panic during administration of, 168–169; weakening of administrations of, by mistakes in selections for office, 297.
Cleveland City Ry. Co., Mr. Hanna and the, 77–83.
Cleveland Iron Mining Company, 59.
Cleveland Rolling Mills Company, 59.
Cleveland Transportation Company, 59, 61.
Coal miners, labor troubles with, and part taken by Mr. Hanna in, 89–95, 389, 393–400.
Coal mining business of Mr. Hanna's firm, 56–57, 62.
Columbiana County, Ohio, 1, 8.
Commerce and Labor, establishment of Department of, 373, 374.
Conciliation and Arbitration, Department of, of Civic Federation, 389;

INDEX

D. R. Hanna chosen a member of, 389–390; interest of M. A. Hanna aroused in, 390–391; work of, in connection with anthracite coal strike of 1902, 393–400.
Conger, A. L., 176.
Conkling, Roscoe, 116, 117.
Connell, Charles C., historian of New Lisbon, 22.
Converse ancestry of M. A. Hanna, 5–7.
Converse, George O., 3 n.
Converse, Hattie, school-teacher, 17, 19–20.
Converse, Helen, 34.
Converse, Samantha (Mrs. Leonard Hanna), 5–7, 17.
Corbett, Henry W., 277.
Corporate interests, development of, with Republican supremacy, 296–297; position of, as an issue, in McKinley campaign of 1900, 305–306, 323–327.
Corruption, political, Mr. Hanna's attitude toward, 80–83; emphasis laid on objections to use of campaign funds for, by Mr. Hanna, 184–185.
Cortelyou, George B., 359, 360; considers that McKinley was an abler politician than Mr. Hanna, 365; testifies to Mr. Hanna's influence with President Roosevelt, 372; good offices of, in preserving friendly relations between Hanna and Roosevelt, 437.
Cowles, Edwin, editor of Cleveland *Leader*, 66, 67, 68, 118, 119; defeats Mr. Hanna in election as delegate to National Convention of 1884, 120–121.
Cox, George B., 129, 176, 252; letters from Mr. Hanna to, 294–295, 426.
Cox, Peter, quoted, 86–87.
Crawford County system of direct primaries, 355–356.
Cromwell, William Nelson, 378.
Cuban reciprocity question, 375.
Cullom, Senator, 179, 183.
Currency issue, rise of the, 168–169; in Republican platform in 1896, 192–205; Democrats take a positive attitude toward, in Convention of 1896, 204–205; settlement of, by the 56th Congress, 282.

Daugherty, H. M., 292, 295.
Davenport, Homer, distorted impressions of Mr. Hanna promulgated by cartoons by, 224, 339, 340, 370.

Davis, Senator, 179.
Dawes, Charles G., 183, 214; work of, in persuading Mr. Hanna to acquiesce in nomination of Roosevelt for Vice-President, 316.
Debating club, New Lisbon, 23–24.
Dempsey, James H., quoted, 104–105; cited on Mr. Hanna's ambition to become Senator, 231–232; on Mr. Hanna as a public speaker, 244; mentioned, 463.
Depew, Chauncey, 283.
Dewstoe, Charles C., 300.
Dick, Charles, 166–167, 175, 177, 181; Secretary of Republican National Committee in 1896, 214; mentioned in connection with bribery charges brought against Mr. Hanna, 260, 289 n.
Dingley Law, the, 249; passage of, 275; Mr. Hanna's contributions to making of the, 276.
Dixon family, the, 3.
Dolliver, Jonathan, mentioned for Vice-Presidency in 1900, 309, 311.
Dolliver, Victor, companion of Mr. Hanna's on speaking tour of Northwest (1900), 334–335.
Donaldson, J. C., state committeeman, 161; political aide of Senator Sherman, 234; correspondence of, quoted, 235–236.
Dover, Elmer, 245, 322, 334, 346, 360, 423, 424, 441, 453; testimony of, to even disposition of Mr. Hanna, and remarks on value of Mr. Dover's services, 461.
Droste, Charles F., 253, 254, 256, 258.
Durbin, Winfield T., work of, in campaign of 1896, 214.

Easley, Ralph M., secretary of National Civic Federation, 388, 389, 392, 393; quoted on Mr. Hanna's work to settle anthracite coal strike, 395.
Eels, Dan P., 66.
Ellsler, John, 72–73.
Ellwood, William, 93.
Employees, Mr. Hanna's relations with his, 86–89, 95, 338, 339, 387–388.
Engineer, incident of the, and Mr. Hanna, in Nebraska tour, 337.
Eshelby, Edward O., 253.
Europe, trips to, by Mr. Hanna, 281, 449.
Everett, Sylvester T., 66, 71, 72, 121.

Fairbanks, Charles M., 190; mentioned for Vice-Presidency in 1900, 309.

484 INDEX

Filley, Chauncey I., 178.
Flagler, H. M., 66.
Fogg, William P., 66.
Foraker, James B., at Convention of 1884, 122–124; close relations resulting from Convention of 1884 between Mr. Hanna and, 124–126; election as Governor of Ohio, 125–126; break with Mr. Hanna, and causes, 128–137; effect on Ohio politics of enmity between Mr. Hanna and, 138–139; growing rivalry of McKinley and, 141–142; defeat of, for Governor in 1889, 152–153; the patent ballot-box incident, 153; defeat of, for Senator by Sherman in 1891, 158–162; obtains victory over Mr. Hanna and Governor McKinley in 1895, 176–177; supports McKinley's candidacy for the nomination for President in 1896, 182; places McKinley's name before Convention of 1896, 191; honor of inserting gold clause in Republican platform of 1896 claimed by, 193; on Committee on Resolutions at St. Louis, 195–196; pamphlet on "The Gold Plank" by, cited, 202–203; questionable attitude of, in Mr. Hanna's first Senatorial campaign, 254; as a debater in the Senate, 282; takes part in state election of 1901, 357; clever work of, in forcing Mr. Hanna into a corner on Roosevelt issue (1903), 423–425; tries to embroil relations between Roosevelt and Hanna in 1903, 436; on death of Mr. Hanna, pronounces the most discriminating appreciation of his career and personality, 457–458.
Ford, George H., quoted, 38.
Ford, Henry Jones, work by, quoted, 476.
Foster, Charles, 118, 132, 138, 165; death of, 452.
Frazee, John N., description of Lieutenant Hanna by, 46.
Frick, H. C., 170.
Frye, Senator, on Mr. Hanna as a stump speaker, 248; with Mr. Hanna during speaking tour in Northwest (1900), 334–335; converted to the Panama route for Isthmian canal by Mr. Hanna's speech in Senate, 384.

Gage, Lyman G., 388.
Gallinger, Senator, 284.

Gardner, George W., 118, 121, 126.
Garfield, James A., campaign of 1880, 110, 116–117; succeeded by McKinley on Ways and Means Committee, 142; helped financially by National Committee, 160.
Garfield, James R., mentioned in connection with Mr. Hanna's first Senatorial campaign and the charges of attempted bribery, 253, 258, 260, 290; testifies to Mr. Hanna's freedom from corrupt methods, 264; helps to maintain friendly relations between Hanna and Roosevelt, 437–438.
Garretson, Hiram, 32, 36, 43.
Gary, James A., appointed Postmaster-General by McKinley, 230.
Gathmann Torpedo, the 280–281.
Gerrard, Jephtha A., 258–259.
Gessner, Francis B., newspaper correspondent, 267.
Gleason, Major, description of Lieutenant Hanna by, 46.
Globe Ship Building Company, 61.
Goebel, Judge, 253.
Gold plank in St. Louis platform (1896), 192–199.
Gold standard, establishment of, by the 56th Congress, 282.
Gompers, Samuel, 389, 391, 392.
Gowdy, John K., 181.
Grant, President, and James A. Garfield, 116–117.
Grasselli, C. A., 456.
Gridiron Club dinner, and tribute paid to Mr. Hanna at, 369–371.
Griffith, John E., 257, 258.
Griscom, Clement, 429.
Grosvenor, Charles H., 254; interview with, on Roosevelt's chances in 1904, 423.

Hahn, William M., 160, 214.
Hale, Rev. Edward Everett, memorial address on Mr. Hanna delivered by, 456.
Hale, Senator, 284, 429.
Hanna, Benjamin, grandfather of M. A. Hanna, 2–5, 8–11, 15, 16; the eleven children of, 4–5; financial ruin and death of, 31–32.
Hanna, Daniel Rhodes, son of M. A. Hanna, 49, 429, 451; a member of M. A. Hanna & Co., 60; chosen a member of Conciliation and Arbitration Committee of Civic Federation, 389–390.

INDEX 485

Hanna, Elizabeth, ancestor of M. A. Hanna, 2.
Hanna, H. Melville, younger brother of M. A. Hanna, 13, 14, 15, 34, 43; service in navy during Civil War, 44; buys M. A. Hanna's refinery and sells out to Standard Oil Company, 51; introduction of steel vessels on the Great Lakes by, 61; quoted, 100; on McKinley's tact and attractive personality, 175–176; with M. A. Hanna in his last illness, 454.
Hanna, James B., nephew of M. A. Hanna, 88.
Hanna, Joshua, uncle of M. A. Hanna, 5, 10–11, 12, 32.
Hanna, Kersey, uncle of M. A. Hanna, 3 n., 4, 10, 14, 18.
Hanna, L. G., manager of Cleveland Opera House, 73.
Hanna, Leonard, father of M. A. Hanna, 5–6, 11, 17, 18; marriage to Samantha Converse, 6; takes prominent part in temperance and political movements in Ohio, 13–15; removal from New Lisbon to Cleveland, 32; illness and death of, 42.
Hanna, Leonard C., brother of M. A. Hanna, 41; a member of Rhodes & Co., 60 n.; quoted, 85, 101, 102; becomes head of M. A. Hanna & Co. on withdrawal of M. A. Hanna, 173–174.
Hanna, Levi, uncle of M. A. Hanna, 3 n., 11.
Hanna, Marcus Alonzo, birth of (Sept. 24, 1837), 1, 7; ancestry, 2–7; boyhood home and school life, 17 ff.; religious trend of father and mother, 18; personal appearance, 19; activities in debating club and in mimic warfare, 23–27; as a leader among boys, 27, 38–39; removal with parents to Cleveland, 32; engagement to Mary Ann McLain, 32–33; schooldays in Cleveland and at Western Reserve College, 36–39; attitude toward book education and education of real life, 39; entrance into business of Hanna, Garretson & Co. (1857), 39–41; roustabout, purser, and commercial traveller, 40–41; active social life led by, 41–42; effect on, of death of father in 1862, 42–43; a member of firm of Robert Hanna & Co., 43–44; in the Civil War, 44–46; descriptions of, as a soldier, 46; love affair with and marriage to Miss C. Augusta Rhodes, 47–48; vicissitudes of early married life, 48–50; becomes a member of firm of Rhodes & Co., 50; refinery previously owned by, sold to Standard Oil Company, 51; speculation on effects on career of, had he joined the Rockefellers, 51–52; energies put into Rhodes & Co. make him its leading member, 52–53; success of Rhodes & Co. and M. A Hanna & Co. due to nature of management initiated by, 63–64; business ventures outside of his special line, 65 ff.; experiences as proprietor of the Cleveland *Herald*, 66–70; false impression of personality of, resulting from contest with the *Leader*, 68; the answer to accusation of being a boss, 70; organization of Union National Bank by, 70–72; Cleveland Opera House purchased and managed under direction of, 72–75; acquaintance among actors, 75; street railway affiliations of, 76–83; attitude toward corruption in Cleveland politics, 80–83; relation between his employees and, 84 ff.; street railway men and, 86–89; experiences with labor difficulties, 89–95; generally broad and humane treatment of employees by, 95; characteristics of, in business, 96 ff.; his initiative, 96–97; capacity for hard work, 97–98; success as a salesman, 98; aptitude for mechanics, 98–99; control of business campaigns by, 99–101; mixture of balance and prudence in business policy of, 101–103; success as an organizer, 103; absolute integrity the keystone of his business structure, 103–104; a shrewd judge of people, 105–106; manner in dealing with business associates, 106–107; can be summed up as a business man who carried over into the period of industrial expansion the best characteristics of the pioneer, 107–108, 465 ff.; mistake of viewing him as essentially a money-maker, 108–109; beginnings as a politician, 110; interest in politics antedated street railway connection, 112–113; patriotic motives at the base of his interest in political matters, 113–114; early opposition to and subse-

486 INDEX

quent coöperation with the bosses, 114–115; essential features of creed of, regarding politics, 115; the Garfield campaign in 1880, 116–117; broadening of political interests after Garfield's election, 117–118; member of state Republican committee, 118; the experimental period of his political career, 118–119; plunge into national politics with election as delegate to National Convention of 1884, 120 ff.; close relations between James B. Foraker and, 124–126; activities in electing Foraker Governor and in Cleveland municipal politics, 126–127; backed by important business men rather than professional politicians, 127; rupture between Foraker and, and causes, 128–137; constant support of John Sherman for the Presidency, 129–137; appointed director of Union Pacific R. R., 131; at the National Convention of 1888, 133–136; permanent hostility of Foraker and, and effect on Mr. Hanna's career and on Ohio politics, 138–139; McKinley definitely replaces Sherman in mind of, as a Presidential possibility, 140–141; increased interest in national politics due to the tariff issue, 143; as a campaign fund contributor and successful solicitor of campaign contributions, 145–147; his assistance of McKinley and Kimberly in money ways, 146–147; visit to Washington in 1889 to help McKinley's fight for Speakership, 150; open hostility to Foraker in latter's candidacy for Governorship in 1889, 152–153; open dislike and lack of recognition of, by President Harrison, 153–154; controversy with Congressman Burton over the Cleveland postmastership 154; growing friendship with Sherman, McKinley, and Butterworth, 154; letters of Butterworth to, 154–156; McKinley's cautious letters to, 156–158; successful efforts by, to elect McKinley as Governor and Sherman as Senator (1891), 158–162; grateful letter from Sherman to, but total neglect of mention of in Sherman's "Reminiscences," 162–163; work for McKinley at Minneapolis in 1891, 165–166; offered Treasurership of National Committee by Benjamin Harrison but declines in order to leave hands free to work for McKinley (1891), 165; great help given to McKinley during latter's financial ruin, 170; importance of McKinley's brilliant reëlection in 1893 appreciated by and made full use of, 171; decision of, to withdraw from direction of M. A. Hanna & Co. to give time to politics, and reasons for decision, 172–174; rents house in Georgia to help McKinley's cause in the South, 175–176; management of McKinley's campaign for the nomination in 1896, 175 ff.; cost of McKinley's campaign for nomination in 1896 paid by, 183–184; strict objections of, to illegitimate use of money by his lieutenants, 184–185; reasons traced for success of his ambition for McKinley, 188–189; attitude of, favorable to a gold standard, 194; letter to A. K. McClure concerning St. Louis Convention, 198–199; recognition of services of, and speech by, on nomination of McKinley, 205; made Chairman of National Committee, 206; ovation to and speeches by, on return to Cleveland, 207–208; masterly generalship displayed by, in managing campaign of 1896, 209–227; amount of money raised by, for election expenses, 218–221; defence of his methods of meeting campaign expenses, 221–223; made the victim of malignant personal attacks, 223–225; popular approval of and interest in, after McKinley's triumph, 228; declines Cabinet position (Postmaster-Generalship) offered by McKinley, 229–230; reasons, 230–231; ambition to become Senator, 231–232; history of appointment of, to Sherman's seat in Senate, 232–241; reason for desirability of seeking election to Senate, to preserve personal prestige, 242; story of confirmation of his title to Senatorship by the people and Legislature, 242–271; first stump speaking by, 243–247; bribery charge against, 259–263; rejection of corrupt methods by, 263–264; speech to supporters in the Legislature, 266; letter to David K. Watson concerning attack on Standard Oil Co. by, discussed, 266–271; first three years of, in the Senate viewed as a transition period, 272 ff.; handicapped by prominence as a friend of the President and as Chairman of the National Committee, 273; work in connection with the Dingley Law, 275–276; committees on which he served, 276; attitude on public questions as indicated by his votes, 277; attitude on the Spanish War, 278–279; as an Imperialist, 279–280; his ship-subsidy bill, 280, 344 ff.; interest in the Gathmann Torpedo, 280–281; votes against seating M. S. Quay, 283; takes active part in armor-plate debate, 286–288; Senator Pettigrew's attack on, and Mr. Hanna's defence, 288–290; part taken by, in Ohio politics in 1898 and 1899, 291–296; skill displayed by, in distribution of patronage, 297–298; rules laid down by, on appointments, 299–301; preparations of, for Convention of 1900, 302 ff.; the trust issue, 305–307; opposes Roosevelt's nomination for Vice-President, 310; forced to acquiesce in the nomination of Roosevelt for Vice-President, 315–317; McKinley's hesitation in selecting Mr. Hanna to manage campaign of 1900, 320–321; eminent skill displayed by, in conducting the campaign, on receiving appointment to Chairmanship of National Committee, 321–322; irritation over certain attitudes taken by McKinley, 329–330; his stump-speaking tour in the Northwest, 331–340; resentment of, over McKinley's attempted interference, 333–334; overwhelming success of tour, 340; prestige of, after McKinley's reëlection, 342–344; ship-subsidy legislation urged by, 344–354; failure of, to control his party's politics in Cleveland, 355; at Buffalo at time of the President's assassination, 358–360; exchanges pledges as to mutual behavior with Roosevelt, on death of McKinley, 360–362; comparisons and contrasts drawn between McKinley and, 363–368; change in public sentiment toward, following McKinley's death, 369; the Gridiron Club dinner and address, 369–371;

continued influence of, at the White House and friendship with Roosevelt, 371–372; takes part in debates on Department of Commerce and Labor, Chinese Exclusion Act, Pennsylvania R. R. station in Washington, Cuban reciprocity, etc., 374–375; position in the government in 1901–1902 analogous to that of a German Imperial Chancellor, 375–376; great importance of work of, in behalf of Panama Canal, 376 ff.; becomes leader in the Senate of pro-Panama route party, 380; exhaustive investigation by, of advantages and disadvantages of different canal routes, 381–382; speech of, in behalf of Panama route (June 5 and 6, 1902), 382–384; interest aroused in capital and labor problem, 386 ff.; publicly identifies himself with work of National Civic Federation, 391–392; chairman of Industrial Department, Civic Federation, 391–392; work of, to settle anthracite coal miners' strike of 1902, 393–400; settlement of various labor disputes by, 401–402; description of official life of, at Washington, 412–413; probability of election to Presidency, in case McKinley had lived, 413; numerous advocates of Mr. Hanna's nomination in 1904, 414–415, 416–417, 420; effect on relations with Roosevelt of efforts of friends in behalf of nomination, 422–423; cornered on Roosevelt nomination question by the Foraker faction, 423–425; indorsement of, by Ohio state convention of 1903, 429; celebration by, of marriage of his daughter Ruth, 429–430; efforts put forth by, in state election of 1903, 430–433; reëlection by a large majority in 1903, 433; letters of congratulation to, from widespread sources, 434; renewed efforts by supporters to boom him for the Presidency, 435; supposed motives of, for not coming out decisively for Roosevelt's renomination, 442–444; question if he could have been persuaded to accept nomination had health permitted, 444–446; personal habits relative to eating, smoking, and exercise, 447–448; premonitions of physical breakdown in 1903, 449–450; visit to Europe, 450; last

488 INDEX

public utterance, his address to the Legislature on being reëlected to Senate, 451–452; depressed by death of Mr. Foster and ex-Governor Bushnell, 452; forced to take to his bed by attack of typhoid fever, 453; last exchange of notes with President Roosevelt, 453–454; death of (Feb. 15, 1904), 455; memorial and funeral services, 455–456; honest, fair, and discriminating appreciation of career and personality of, pronounced by Senator Foraker, 457–458; further description of personal life and characteristics of, 458–464; to be regarded in the final summing-up as the embodiment of the pioneer spirit, whose conception of the business of the government was to further the interests of individuals, 465–471; analysis in this light of his business and political career, 471–477; his crowning distinction his spirit of fair play, his constancy to a standard which the average American attains only in his better moments, 478; durability of the value inherent in his example and in his life, 479.

Hanna, Robert, great-grandfather of M. A. Hanna, 2–3, 4.

Hanna, Robert, uncle of M. A. Hanna, 3 n., 5, 11; removal from New Lisbon to Cleveland, 32; mentioned, 43, 50.

Hanna, Ruth, daughter of M. A. Hanna, 34; wedding of, 423, 429–430.

Hanna, Thomas, ancestor of M. A. Hanna, 2.

Hanna, Thomas B., uncle of M. A. Hanna, 3 n., 11.

Hanna & Co., M. A., succeeds Rhodes & Co., 60 n.

Hanna-Frye Subsidy Bill, 280, 345, 347; failure of, 353–354.

Hanna, Garretson & Co., firm of, 36, 39–40, 43.

Harbaugh, Porter, 6.

Harrison, Benjamin, election of, as President by small margin, 149–150; dislike and lack of recognition of Mr. Hanna by, 153–154; nomination and defeat of, in 1891–92, 164–166; a possible rival of McKinley's in 1896, 177–178, 179, 180; weakening of administration by mistakes in selections for office, 297.

Hartz, Augustus F., 73–74.
Hawley, Senator, 284.
Hay, John, 170; letter by, concerning Mr. Hanna, 228.
Hayes, Rutherford B., 93.
Hayward, W. H., 45.
Hearst, William R., malignant attacks on Mr. Hanna by yellow journals of, 224.
Heath, Perry, 214.
Hepburn Bill relating to proposed Nicaraguan Canal, 379–380.
Herald, the Cleveland, Mr. Hanna's experience as publisher of, 66–70; use of, by Mr. Hanna, in the Garfield campaign, 117.
Herrick, Myron T., 132, 192, 456; McKinley aided by, when financially ruined, 170; at St. Louis Convention, 196–198; with Mr Hanna in Buffalo at time of President McKinley's death, 360; interest of, in Panama Canal route, 381; nomination of, for Governor in 1903, 428–429; great majority by which elected Governor, 433–434.
Hill, James J., reminiscence of Mr. Hanna by, 105; introduces Mr. Hanna in Wall Street in campaign of 1896, 219.
Hitchcock, Henry V., 38.
Hitchcock, John F., 38.
Hitchcock, President of Western Reserve College, 37.
Hoar, George F., 284; letter to Mr. Hanna from, 431–432.
Hobart, Garret A., 180, 191–192.
Hollenbeck, H. H., 260.
Hord, A. C., 120.
Hough, A. B., 98, 207, 456, 459.
Hoyt, James H., 170, 176.
Hubbell, Mr. and Mrs. Henry S., 34.
Hughes, Gideon, 2.
Hunter, Frank, 88.
Huntington, John, 112.

Imperialism, acceptance of doctrine of, by McKinley and Hanna, 279–280.
Industrial Department, National Civic Federation, Mr. Hanna as chairman of, 391 ff.; work of, in anthracite coal strike and other labor disputes, 393–402; ultimate non-success of, as an agency for settling labor troubles, 407.
Initiative, Mr. Hanna's salient characteristic of, 96–97.

INDEX

Ireland, Archbishop, a friend of Mr. Hanna's, 434.
Iron-handling business of Mr. Hanna's firm, 57–62.

James, John, secretary of Miners' National Association, quoted, 94–95.
Johnson, Tom L., and Cleveland street railways, 82; first election as Mayor of Cleveland, 355; campaign of, throughout Ohio in 1902, 419; defeated in state but continues to hold city of Cleveland, 420; defeated by Myron T. Herrick for Governor in 1903, 430–434.
Johnson, Willis Fletcher, "Four Centuries of the Panama Canal" by, quoted, 384.
Jones, John P., 254.
Journal, New York, attacks on Mr. Hanna by, 224.

Kean, Senator, 429.
Keefe, Dan J., 389, 390, 391.
Kennedy, James H., quoted, 117.
Kenyon College, Mr. Hanna's address at, 247; donation to, 462.
Kimberly, David H., reminiscence by, 120–121; election to county treasurership, 126–127; Mr. Hanna's financial assistance of, 147–148.
King, Rufus, "Ohio" by, quoted, 29.
Kinney, Major Lewis, founder of New Lisbon, Ohio, 1.
Kittridge, Senator, 384.
Knox, Philander, 170.
Kohlsaat, H. H., 170, 192; claims responsibility for inserting gold clause in Republican platform of 1896, 192–193; at St. Louis Convention, 196–198.
Kurtz, Charles L., 176–177; enforced retirement of, as Chairman of State Committee arouses his animosity against Mr. Hanna, 243; a leader in the conspiracy against Mr. Hanna in his first Senatorial election, 251–252.

Labor problem, keen interest of Mr. Hanna in the, 386 ff.
Labor unions, speeches and articles by Mr. Hanna on, 404–406; analysis of motives underlying Mr. Hanna's treatment of, 408–410.
Lac la Belle steamboat, 49, 52.
Landis, C. B., 332.
Lauterbach, Edward, 203.
Leach, Charles F., quoted, 110; advice on appointments given to, by Mr. Hanna, 299–300.
Leader, the Cleveland, war waged on Mr. Hanna and the Cleveland *Herald* by, 66–68; responsibility of, for grossly false impressions of Mr. Hanna's character and personality, 68. *See also* Cowles, Edwin.
Leland, Cyrus, Jr., work of, in campaign of 1896, 214.
Leonard, Bishop, delivers eulogy on Mr. Hanna, 456.
Leonard Hanna, steamboat, 59.
Letter, the historic Hanna-Watson, concerning Standard Oil Co., 266–271.
Lewis, Alfred Henry, false and libellous attacks on Mr. Hanna by, 224–225.
Lodge, Henry Cabot, 190, 192.
Long, John D., mentioned for Vice-Presidency in 1900, 309, 311.
Lynchburg, Va., laid out by ancestor of Mr. Hanna's, 2–3.

McClure, A. K., letter from Mr. Hanna to, 198–199.
McClure's Magazine article on Mr. Hanna, 71–72.
McCook, Dr. Henry G., "Threnody" on M. A. Hanna by, 19, 24; description of Mark Hanna as a schoolboy, 22–23.
McCook, General Anson, G., description of New Lisbon debating club by, 23–24.
McCook, George, 26.
McCook, John, 26.
McCormick, Joseph M., marriage of Ruth Hanna to, 429–430.
McDougal, Thomas, 170.
McKinley, Abner, 359.
McKinley, James, 2.
McKinley, Mrs. William, Jr., devotion of her husband to, 363.
McKinley, William, father of the President, 2.
McKinley, William, Jr., 2; defence of striking coal miners by, 93–94; possible first meeting between Mr. Hanna and, 94; at National Convention of 1884, 122–123; mentioned, 132; voted for, at National Convention of 1888, 135–136; vital effect on relations between Mr. Hanna and, of latter's rupture with Foraker, 137–138; definite replacing of Sherman by, in Mr. Hanna's mind, as a Presidential possibility, 140–141; increasing political rivalry

of Foraker and, 141–142; popularity of, on account of attractive personality and high protection principles, 142–143; financial assistance rendered to, by Mr. Hanna, 147; defeat of, in fight for Speakership (1889) and beneficial effects of, on political career, 150; as Chairman of Ways and Means Committee becomes responsible for new tariff act, 150–151; unites with Mr. Hanna in opposition to Foraker for Governor in 1889, 152–153; wary nature of, as shown by correspondence, 156–158; successful campaign of, for Governorship in 1891, 158–162; effect on Presidential ambitions of election to Governorship, 164; immediate steps taken for nomination in 1896 after Convention of 1891, 166–167; effect of Democratic victory of 1892 on prospects of, 167; contrasted as a public speaker with W. J. Bryan, 167; effect of business depression under Cleveland on chances of, 168–169; unexpected bankruptcy of, and threatened political ruin, 169–170; ill-fortune of, works to his advantage in the end, 170–171; reëlected Governor by brilliant majority in 1893 and acclaimed as next Republican Presidential candidate, 170–171; effect on candidacy for President of passage of Wilson Bill and continued bad times under Cleveland, 172–173; history of campaign of 1896, 174 ff.; the contest with Platt, Quay and other bosses, 177–180; cost of campaign for nomination in 1896, 184; freedom of campaign from corruption and preëlection promises of political rewards, 184–187; success due not only to pleasing personality but because he represented a national group of ideas and interests, 187; vote cast for, in National Convention of 1896, 191; the currency issue forced upon, in Republican platform, 192–193; position of, on the gold and silver question, 193–195; the campaign of 1896 and election of, 209–227; receptions and speeches by, at Canton, to offset Bryan's personal stumping tour, 215–216; handsome majority finally won for, 227; offer of Cabinet position (Postmaster-Generalship) to Mr. Hanna by, 229; history of appointment of Sherman as Secretary of State, to make room for Mr. Hanna in the Senate, 232–239; advice to Mr. Hanna before first stump-speaking tour, 245; administration embarrassed by Cuban question, 273–274, 276–277, 278; credit due, for success of administration and united support of Republican party in 1900, 296–297; change in relations between Mr. Hanna and, in 1900, owing to the latter's increasing personal power and popularity, 320–321; correspondence with Mr. Hanna concerning discharge of government employees during the campaign, 329–330; his biographer kept a good deal in mind by, 331, 363–364; attempts to interfere in Mr. Hanna's conduct of the campaign by trying to prevent the latter's Northwestern tour, 332–334; effect on cause of, of Mr. Hanna's successful tour of Northwest, 340–341; overwhelming plurality received by, 341; second inauguration of, 355; assassination of, at Buffalo, 358–360; depth and strength of Mr. Hanna's attachment to, 362–363; a colder man in disposition than Mr. Hanna, 363–364; an abler politician than Mr. Hanna, 365; Mr. Hanna's remarks on, at unveiling of memorial statue at Toledo, 367.

McKinley Bill, tariff policy embodied in, 150–151.
McKinnie, W. J., 456, 459.
McKisson, Robert E., in the conspiracy against Mr. Hanna for Senator, 251; reasons for hostility to Mr. Hanna, 252; nominated as anti-Hanna candidate for the Senate, 255; defeat of, 259; fails of reëlection as Mayor of Cleveland, 294.
McLain, Mary Ann, 32–33.
McLean, John R., unsuccessful candidate for the Senate, 255; defeated in election for Governor by George K. Nash, 295–296.
McMillan, Reuben, school teacher, 23.
McMillan, Senator, 284.
"Maggie," the Hannas' family cook, 447, 459.
Maine, blowing up of the, 277, 278.
Manderson, General. 181.

INDEX

Manhattan steamboat, 40.
Manley, Joseph H., 178, 214.
Mason, Assemblyman, 253.
Massillon coal district strike, 89–90, 92–94.
Mather, Samuel, 170, 456.
Mechanics, M. A. Hanna's aptitude for, 98–99.
Mellen, Lucius F., quoted, 98; on Mr. Hanna's charities, 461–462.
Merriam, William R., 150, 180, 192, 194, 196, 197, 198; instrumentality of, in getting gold plank past the Committee on Resolutions, Convention of 1896, 202.
Milburn, John G., 359.
Minneapolis, Republican National Convention of 1892 at, 165–166.
Mitchell, John, 389, 391; mentioned in connection with anthracite strike of 1902, 393, 394, 395, 398, 399.
Moore, Charles A., 392.
Morgan, J. P., meeting of John Mitchell and, 393.
Morgan, Senator, 382.
Morrow, James B., 67, 235, 263, 269.
Morse, Jay C., 46.
Morse, Mrs. Jay C., 6.
Morton, Levi P., 179, 180, 189, 219.
Mulhern, George G., 77, 86, 87, 88.
Municipal corruption, Mr. Hanna and, 80–83.
Myers, Allen O., 250–251.
Myers, Daniel, 112.

Nash, George K., 46, 254; made Chairman of State Committee, 243; elected Governor of Ohio, 294–296; reëlected Governor (1901), 356–358.
Nash, Samuel K., 176.
National Civic Federation, 388 ff.; Mr. Hanna publicly identifies himself with, 391–392; failure of Industrial Department as an agency for settling labor troubles, 407; definite program of gradual development projected for, in Mr. Hanna's mind, 444.
National Convention, of 1884, 120–124; of 1888, 133–136; of 1892, 165–166; of 1896, 190–208; of 1900, 302–318.
National Magazine articles, on ship-subsidy question, 350; on "McKinley as I knew Him," 363; on "Socialism and Labor Unions," 404, 405, 406.

Nebraska, tour of, by Mr. Hanna in 1900, 336–340.
New Lisbon, Ohio, 1–2, 3, 4, 5, 6, 7, 8, 10, 19; ruined by mistaken transportation policy; Mr. Hanna's visit to, in 1890, 33–35.
Newspaper-owning experience of Mr. Hanna, 65–70.
Nicaragua route for isthmian canal, 376 ff., 384–385.
Northern Lights steamboat, 40.

Odell, B. B., 329, 435.
Office, skill in selections for, displayed by President McKinley and Mr. Hanna, 297–298.
Ohio, position of, in M. A. Hanna's young manhood, 1; stock from which early settlers sprang, 7; effects on, of introduction of canals and railroads, 29–31.
Ohio Canal, the, 29.
Ohio Patriot, The, 10.
Opera House, Cleveland, ownership of, by Mr. Hanna, 72–75, 460.
Orient Transportation Company, 59.
Osborne, General, 196.
Osler, Dr. William, attends Mr. Hanna, 454.
Otis, Charles A., 112.
Otis, John C., 253, 254; story of attempted bribery of, in Mr. Hanna's first Senatorial campaign, 259–264.

Panama Canal legislation, 373, 376 ff.; importance of Mr. Hanna's work in behalf of Panama route, 376–378, 380, 381–382; decisive speech delivered by Mr. Hanna (June 5 and 6, 1902), 382–384.
Pankhurst, J. F., 61, 98.
Parsons, Richard C., 66.
Patent ballot-box episode, 153.
Patronage, Mr. Hanna's skill in distribution of, 297–298.
Patterson, Raymond, address to Mr. Hanna by, 370–371.
Payne, Henry C., 180, 192, 196, 197, 198, 429; work of, in campaign of 1896, 214.
Payne, Oliver H., urges nomination for 1904 on Mr. Hanna, 440–441.
Pennsylvania R. R. Co., relations between Rhodes & Co. and M. A. Hanna & Co. and, 60–61.
Penrose, Senator, 286.
Perkins, Senator Harry B., 117, 287.
Pettigrew, Senator Richard F., per-

sonal attack on and quarrel with Mr. Hanna in Senate, 288–290; Mr. Hanna's efforts to defeat for reëlection, 332–333, 337–338; loses seat in election of 1900, 341.
Phelps, Mary, 450, 451, 452.
Philadelphia, National Convention at, in 1900, 302–318.
Pickands, James, 170.
Pioneer purposes and methods as embodied in Mr. Hanna, 107–108, 465 ff.
Plain-Dealer, the Cleveland, aggressive attitude of, toward Mr. Hanna, 68.
Platt, Orville, 277, 279, 284; on Mr. Hanna's Panama Canal speech, 384; letter by, on the talk of nominating Mr. Hanna for the Presidency in 1904, 441; eulogy of Mr. Hanna by, in the Senate, 457; quoted on Mr. Hanna's wonderful loyalty, 463–464.
Platt, Thomas C., 178, 179, 180, 189, 191, 265; "Autobiography" of, quoted on Mr. Hanna, 180; asserts that gold plank in St. Louis platform was inserted by him, 192; "Autobiography" of, quoted concerning the gold plank, 203; the nomination of Theodore Roosevelt for Vice-President in 1900, 309, 311–314; claim of, that he persuaded Mr. Hanna to acquiesce in nomination of Roosevelt for Vice-President, 316.
Politics, interest of all citizens in, before and immediately after the Civil War, 111; Mr. Hanna's interest in, shown to antedate his street railway connection, 112–113; patriotic motives for the pioneer type of man's interest in, 113–114; essential points of M. A. Hanna's creed regarding, 115, 465 ff.; Mr. Hanna's standard of behavior in, not as high as in business, 188–189; total lack of parallel to part played by Mr. Hanna in, 189.
Polydelphian Society of New Lisbon, 23–24.
Pope, A. A., 170.
Populism, speeches of Mr. Hanna's dealing with, 334–340; death of, in decisive victory of McKinley and Roosevelt in 1900, 341.
Potter, Bishop, on choice of Mr. Hanna for chairman of Industrial Department, Civic Federation, 392.
Proctor, Senator Redfield, at St. Louis Convention, 196, 197, 198; mentioned, 284.
Protection, Republican principle of, and McKinley's advocacy of, 142 ff.; superseded by the currency issue in the campaign of 1896, 192 ff.
Puerto Rico question, 281, 282.

Quaker strain in Mr. Hanna's ancestry, 2, 7, 12, 18.
Quay, Matthew S., plots against McKinley's candidacy in 1896, 178, 179; shares in work of campaign, 214; distinction between Mr. Hanna and politicians of type of, 265; disputed Senatorial seat of, 277, 283; Constitutional question involved in title of, to seat decided in the negative, 283–284; Mr. Hanna incurs hostility of, by voting against, 284–285; discontent with McKinley régime shown by, at Convention of 1900, 302; attempts to embarrass the administration by indorsing Roosevelt for Vice-President (1900), 314; favors Roosevelt's candidacy at time of projected Hanna boom (1903), 435.

Railroad alliances of M. A. Hanna's firm, 59–61, 62.
Rathbone, E. G., connection of, with bribery charge against Mr. Hanna, 260, 262, 263, 289 n.
Reed, T. B., letter from, to McKinley on latter's election as Governor, 161–162; candidacy of, for nomination for President in 1896, 177–178, 179, 180, 182, 190–191.
Rhodes, C. Augusta (Mrs. M. A. Hanna), 47.
Rhodes, Daniel P., 47–53, 56.
Rhodes, James Ford, a member of Rhodes & Co., 60 n.; mentioned, 92.
Rhodes, Robert R., member of Rhodes & Co., 50, 60 n.; quoted, 52, 54, 97.
Rhodes & Co., firm of, established, 50; energies of M. A. Hanna in building up, 53–54; business conditions favorable to, 54–56; description of business of, 56–64; becomes M. A. Hanna & Co., 60 n.
Richards, J. K., 177, 195.
Rittman, Frederick, 459.
Rockefeller, John D., 36, 41, 43, 66, 268.

Rockefeller, William, 36.
Rocky River R. R., 76.
Roosevelt, Alice, 429.
Roosevelt, Theodore, elected Governor of New York, 294; first proposal of, for Vice-Presidential candidate in 1900, 309; urged by Thomas C. Platt but objected to by McKinley and Hanna, 309–310; quoted on effort of New York delegation headed by Platt to force nomination on him, 311–314; forces outside of New York which compelled him to accept nomination, 314–317; unanimous vote for, on first ballot, 317; strength given to the Republican ticket by, 317–318; speaking tours of, in campaign of 1900, 327–328; on the death of President McKinley agrees to continue the latter's policies, 360; Mr. Hanna's promise to make his administration a success, 361; avails himself of Mr. Hanna's help, 371–372; quoted on phases of the anthracite coal strike of 1902, 397–400; aspirations of, for nomination in 1904, 414–415; continuation of cordial relations with Mr. Hanna in 1902, 415–416; interests opposed to nomination of, in 1904, 420–421; lack of popularity in the South, 421; Mr. Hanna's ugly dilemma over matter of indorsing, 423–426; attends wedding of Ruth Hanna, 429; efforts to nominate Mr. Hanna against, 435; Mr. Hanna's motives in not coming out openly for (1903), 442–444; last exchange of notes between Mr. Hanna and, before latter's death, 453–454.
Roy, Andrew, "History of Coal Mines of United States" by, 91.
Rutan, D. L., 254.

St. Louis, Republican National Convention of 1896 held at, 190–205.
Sanders, Judge W. B., quoted, 106–107; mentioned, 456.
Sandy and Beaver Canal, the, 29–31.
Saunders, A. C., 60 n., 112; quoted, 97, 102–103.
Schlesinger, Ferdinand, 100–101.
Schools and school-teachers at New Lisbon, 19–23.
Scott, N. B., 214; correspondence between Mr. Hanna and, 439–440.
Scott, William A., 254.
Senate, national, beginnings of Mr. Hanna's career in, 272 ff.; feeling in, at time of his death, 456–457.
Shayne, C. C., 262.
Shelling, George, 389.
Sherman, John, candidacy for nomination for President, 122–124; Mr. Hanna's support of, for Presidential nomination, 129–137; acquaintance between Mr. Hanna and, 131; Foraker's lukewarmness toward, at Convention of 1888, 132–136; defeat of, by Benjamin Harrison, 134–135; replacing of, in Mr. Hanna's mind by McKinley as a Presidential possibility, 140–141; indorses Mr. Hanna's recommendations for appointments which were later turned down by President Harrison, 153–154; characterization of, by Butterworth, as a fast and loose player, 155; desperate Senatorial fight successfully carried through by Mr. Hanna (1891), 158–162; letter of gratitude by, to Mr. Hanna but neglect to mention name of latter in his "Reminiscences," 162–163; appointed Secretary of State by McKinley and seat as Senator given to Mr. Hanna by appointment of Governor Bushnell, 233 ff.; attitude of, toward the President and Mr. Hanna when made Secretary of State, 233–236; appointment of, proves a mistake, 237–239.
Ship-building at Cleveland, 56.
Ship-subsidy legislation urged by Mr. Hanna, 280, 344–354.
Sims, Charles, 66.
Sims, Elias, 76, 79.
Siney, John, 91.
Slavery, opposition of Mr. Hanna's ancestors to, 12.
Smith, Charles Emory, 333; article on Roosevelt and Hanna by, quoted, 416.
Smith, Joseph P., 175, 177.
Smithnight, Captain, 128–129.
South, skilful political work of Mr. Hanna in the, in interests of McKinley, 175–176, 180; popularity of Mr. Hanna in, as compared with President Roosevelt, 421.
South Dakota, Mr. Hanna's speech-making tour of, 334–340; defeat of Pettigrew in, 341.
Spanish War, the, 274, 276–277; the President and Mr. Hanna's attitude on, 278–279; effect of, on the administration's fortunes, 279.

494 INDEX

Spear, J. C., 181.
Spoils system as administered by McKinley and Hanna, 299–301.
Spooner, Senator, 284, 287, 353; private testimonial to Mr. Hanna from (1903), 432; on effect of Mr. Hanna's death on the Senate, 456.
Spooner amendment to the Hepburn Bill, 382–385.
Squire, Andrew, 97, 98, 102, 104, 112, 254, 456.
Standard Oil Company, Mr. Hanna and the, 51–52; contribution of, to McKinley's campaign expenses (1896), 220; letter from Mr. Hanna to David K. Watson concerning, and results, 266–271; contribution to Republican campaign fund in 1900, 325.
"Stand-pattism," enunciation of policy of, by Mr. Hanna, 417–419; change in significance of, 419, 476.
Steamboats, effect of transportation by, on development of country, 29; line of, established by Hanna, Garretson & Co., 40; fleet owned by members of Rhodes & Co., 59; the first steel vessels on the Great Lakes, 61.
Stone, Amasa, 66.
Stone, Melville E., 196.
Straus, Oscar, 392.
Street railways, history of Mr. Hanna's business connection with, 76–83; employees of, and Mr. Hanna, 86–89; political capital for Tom Johnson furnished by Mr. Hanna's holdings in, 355, 419, 420.
Strikes, early experiences of Mr. Hanna with, 88–95; in plants of United States Steel Corporation (1901), 391; of anthracite coal miners in 1900 and in 1902, 389, 393–400.
Stump speaking, Mr. Hanna's start in, 243–247; tour of Northwest in campaign of 1900, 331–340.
Sun, New York, story concerning Roosevelt and Hanna, 441–442.
Surplus, question of reduction of the, in campaign of 1888, 143 ff.

Taft, Charles, helps in financial rescue of McKinley, 170.
Taft, President, administration of, weakened by mistakes in selections for office, 297.
Tarbell, Ida, "History of Standard Oil Company" by, 267.

Tariff, the main issue in campaign of 1888, 143 ff.; the McKinley Bill, 150–151; bungling of Democrats in revising (Wilson Bill), 171–172; the Dingley Law, 249, 275, 276.
Temperance movement, championship of, by Hanna family, 12–13.
Thomas, E. B., 45.
Thomas, President, and anthracite coal strikers, 390, 393.
Thomasville, Ga., lease of house at and visits of Mr. Hanna to, 175–176, 281.
Thurman, Allen G., 133.
Thurston, John M., 190.
Tillman, Senator, 286.
Todd, David, 14.
Transportation, problem of, in early 19th century, 9, 28; solution of, by steamboats and artificial waterways, 28–29; the coming of railroads, 31; revolutionizing of, on Great Lakes, by introduction of steel vessels, 61.
Trusts, identification of growth of, with Republican supremacy, 296; as a campaign issue in 1900 welcomed by Mr. Hanna, 305–306, 323–324.
Tully, Murray F., 402.

Underground railroad, 12.
Union National Bank, Cleveland, organization of, 70–72.
Union Pacific R. R., services of Mr. Hanna as director of, 131.
United States Steel Corporation strike (1901), 391.

Vermont, origin of Mr. Hanna's maternal ancestry in, 5–6.
Voight, Ohio State Senator, 253, 254, 258.

Wade, J. H., 66, 170.
Wade, Senator Benjamin, 14.
Walker Canal Commission, 377.
Wall Street and the election of McKinley in 1896, 219–220.
Warmington, George H., member of Rhodes & Co., 50, 60 n., 93.
Watson, David K., story of letter from Mr. Hanna to, 266–271.
Waymire, James A., 181.
Wellington, Senator, 180.
Western Reserve College, experiences of young Hanna at, 36–39.
West Side Street Ry. Co., Mr. Hanna's connection with, 76–83.

INDEX

Whist-player, Mr. Hanna as a, 459–460.
White, William Allen, quoted, 71.
Williams, E. P., 459.
Wilson Bill, the, 171–172.
Wolcott, Edward O., 46.
Woodland Avenue and West Side Street Ry. Co., 77.
Woodruff, Timothy, candidate for Vice-Presidential nomination in 1900, 309, 314; reported conversation between Mr. Hanna and, 310.

Yates, "Jack," 459.
Ydrad Boat Club, 41.
Yellow journalism, attacks of, on Mr. Hanna, 223–225.
Young, Lafayette, speech made by, nominating Mr. Roosevelt for Vice-President, 317.

Zanesville, State Convention at (1895), 176–177.
Zerbe, J. B., Cleveland associate and friend of Mr. Hanna's, 456, 459.

Printed in the United States of America.

THE following pages contain advertisements of Macmillan books by the same author.

Progressive Democracy

By HERBERT CROLY
Author of "The Promise of American Life"

Cloth, 8vo, $2.00

The object of the author in this book is threefold. He has in the first place analyzed the modern progressive democratic movement in this country in order to separate its essential from its non-essential ingredients to discover whether there is any real issue between American progressivism and American conservatism. In the second place he has tried to reconstruct the historical background of progressivism to see what roots or lack of roots it has in the American political and economic tradition. And finally he has attempted to trace what we may reasonably expect from the progressive movement, to show what tools it must use in order to carry out its program and what claims it has on the support of patriotic Americans. The work seeks, therefore, to express for the first time a consistently educational theory of democracy.

"Mr. Croly has been a pioneer in the reconstruction of American political opinion. His books show originality as well as keen analysis." — *Political Science Quarterly*.

"A work of first-rate importance . . . admirably written." — *The Dial*.

"Mr. Croly shows himself to be a master of interpretation of the trend of American democracy." — *Boston Herald*.

"His spirit is admirably candid . . . and his ultimate purpose is in the broadest sense constructive and humane." — *New York Times*.

THE MACMILLAN COMPANY
Publishers   64-66 Fifth Avenue   **New York**

One of the earliest and most suggestive expressions of the spirit of
"New Nationalism"

Mr. HERBERT CROLY'S Important Work

The Promise of American Life

Cloth, 8vo, $2.00

No worker on any period of United States political history should miss this disclosure of the bankruptcy of our political theorizing in the past, "conceived and executed with penetration and ability," according to the *New York Evening Post*, which opens a three-column review with the statement, "This is an eminently notable book."

Collier's Weekly classifies it as "dynamic in quality, a book in which a vital force resides which makes reading less a recreation or an ingestion of information than an impetus to one's own thought."

"In the long list of political books his stands out for breadth of vision, sanity of judgment and inspiration. . . . Few recent books have been so vital." — *Chicago Evening Post*.

"A contribution of marked value." — *World To-day*.

"A starting-point for a later and advanced school of American polemics; the beginnings of a new and broader philosophy of national life." — *Philadelphia North American*.

"So fairly does he state both sides of a question that those who are opposed to him will find many of his sentences worth quoting." — *San Francisco Chronicle*.

"A profound study, deep in thought and broad in suggestion." — *St. Louis Star*.

"For its keen analysis, its profound and original thought, and its fascinating interest, the book is assured of a wide hearing." — *Herald*.

"One of the truly notable books of the season, a book for thoughtful, progressive, and earnest thinkers on pressing and vital problems. Every page attracts keen interest in contemporary ideas and tendencies." — *Chicago Record-Herald*.

THE MACMILLAN COMPANY
Publishers   64–66 Fifth Avenue   **New York**

COLONEL ROOSEVELT'S OWN STORY OF HIS LIFE

Theodore Roosevelt : An Autobiography

Illustrated, 8vo, $2.50

"The vigor and directness for which he is justly admired show themselves in every sentence of his book. . . . Emphatically and unmistakably the author has stamped himself on every page of his book, and no reader desiring a better acquaintance with him will be disappointed in this ample autobiography." — *The Dial.*

"A book of extraordinary personal fascination. . . . A record of Theodore Roosevelt's internal and external life, a survey of his boyhood, his youth, and his manhood. A book of his ideas, his ideals, and his practical outlook on life, a book that reflects his temperaments."
— *Boston Evening Transcript.*

TWO NOTABLE BIOGRAPHIES OF THEODORE ROOSEVELT

Theodore Roosevelt : The Boy and the Man
By JAMES MORGAN

Illustrated, 12mo, $1.50

"My aim," says the author, "has been to present a life of action by portraying the varied dramatic scenes in the career of a man whose energy and faith have illustrated before the world the spirit of Young America."

"The ideal biography of President Roosevelt." — *New York Times.*

"It portrays vigorously and with enthusiasm the very dramatic scenes in a life of unusual originality." — *Philadelphia North American.*

Theodore Roosevelt : The Citizen
By JACOB RIIS

Cloth, 12mo, $.60

"It is written from the heart. It breathes sincerity and conviction in every line. It emphasizes not too much the forces and influences which lifted Theodore Roosevelt to the Presidency, as the qualities that make his personality and underlie his character. It is a refreshing and stimulating picture — one that will carry encouragement to every reader whose heart is enlisted in the struggle to exorcise corruption and oppression from our body politic." — *New York Tribune.*

THE MACMILLAN COMPANY
Publishers   64-66 Fifth Avenue   **New York**

THE WORKS OF H. H. POWERS, PH.D.

The Great Peace
Cloth, 12mo, $2.25

"What shall be the terms of the peoples' peace — the Great Peace? What are the principles of that better statecraft which has been slowly and half unconsciously taking shape in the minds of those who through the will to victory have slowly won the right to will the world's peace? And what do these principles require in the way of concrete adjustments and arrangements among the mountains and the rivers and the seas where men have chanced to be born and have snugly nested themselves in the traditions, the prejudices, the loves, and the hates of a hundred generations?" It is with such questions as these that Dr. Powers is concerned.

America and Britain
The Story of the Relations Between Two Peoples
Cloth, 16mo, $.40

"The reading of this little book of seventy-six pages makes it very plain that these two English-speaking countries, America and Great Britain, should be closer and better friends than ever before. We have had evidence on the part of Great Britain that she may be regarded as a sincere friend of the American Republic." — *The Milwaukee Sentinel*.

The Things Men Fight For
Cloth, 12mo, $1.50

"An able, unprejudiced, and illuminating treatment of a burning question." — *Philadelphia North American*.

"Probably no other book dealing with the war and its sources has made so dispassionate and unbiased a study of conditions and causes as does this volume." — *New York Times*.

America Among the Nations
Cloth, 12mo, $1.50

"All the great problems that here confront us are discussed from the standpoint of an international observer free from cant, and the result is refreshing. This is particularly true of his treatment of Pan-Americanism."
— *Argonaut*, San Francisco.

"Thoughtful, interesting, unsentimental, and stimulating."
— *New Republic*.

THE MACMILLAN COMPANY
Publishers   64-66 Fifth Avenue   New York